A Handbook
For Specific
Learning Disabilities

A Handbook
For Specific
Learning Disabilities

Edited by
WILLIAM C. ADAMSON, M.D.
and
KATHERINE K. ADAMSON, M.S.

With a Foreword by
JULES ABRAMS, Ph.D.

GARDNER PRESS, INC., NEW YORK

Distributed by Halsted Press
Division of John Wiley & Sons, Inc.

NEW YORK ● LONDON ● SYDNEY ● TORONTO

GARDNER PRESS, INC.
19 Union Square West
New York, New York 10003

Distributed solely by the Halsted Press
Division of John Wiley & Sons, Inc., New York

Library of Congress Cataloging in Publication Data
Main entry under title:

A Handbook for specific learning disabilities.

    Includes index.
    1. Learning disabilities. I. Adamson,
William C. II. Adamson, Katherine K.
LC4704.H36   371.9'26   73-43
ISBN 0-470-26308-3

Printed in the United States of America

DEDICATION

This Handbook is dedicated to all those persons . . . our own parents and children, as well as other parents, children and adolescents, teachers, supervisors, colleagues, and students who have led us to a greater understanding of the complexities and potentialities to be found in human relationships.

FOREWORD

There is no single etiology for learning disabilities, nor is there conclusive evidence to support the idea that there is only one method of intervention. Learning disorders are caused by any number of a multiplicity of factors, all of which may be highly interrelated. Unfortunately, all too often, the child who is experiencing a learning problem is approached with a unitary orientation, so that extremely important aspects of his unique learning disorder may be ignored completely. The tendency of each professional discipline to view the entire problem "through its own window of specialization" often obscures vital factors which may contribute to, or at least exacerbate, the basic difficulty.

In a field beset by emotional controversies and evangelical fervor, the Adamsons and their colleagues have brought forth a much needed and desirable book. In their own words, they have attempted to "bridge the gap" between frequently controversial and ostensibly conflicting approaches. Utilizing an essentially developmental-interaction approach, they give real meaning to the oft-abused concept of multidisciplinary approach. Even as each chapter stresses a particular slice of the pie, there is a kind of integration here which focuses consistently on the whole child as a physical organism operating in a social environment in a psychological manner.

With this type of global orientation, this book becomes required reading for educators, psychologists, psychiatrists, pediatricians—in fact, for anyone who must be concerned with learning disabilities. In the last analysis, it should be so for everyone. In the complex world in which we live today, it is important that we become aware that there are no simple solutions to the many personal and social problems that we must face. The task of dealing with our educational problems is no less intricate. It is always so tempting to look for "pat answers" to complex issues; happily, this is a temptation which the editors of this book have been able to resist. Lucidly and objectively, they point out the pitfalls of extremism; they are candid with their biases and just as ready to point to the alternatives. In the field of learning disabilities, this is most refreshing!

The editors have done a masterful job in selecting authors who are not only expert in their particular disciplines, but who have also had extensive experience in working with learning disabilities. This is demonstrated not only in the manner in which the theoretical concepts are advanced, but also by the inclusion in practically every chapter of a number of case histories which make the children come alive. Pervading the entire book is the basic premise that the multitude and variety of factors which affect the child's development and which may contribute to the learning disability can not be considered in isolation but, rather, as they relate to all aspects of his/her life. For example, in the chapter on psychological assessment, a developmental point of view is taken with real sensitivity for the affective domain as well as the child's problem-solving and cognitive processes.

Diagnosis and intervention are considered from the perspective of the psychologist, psychiatrist, educator, vision specialist, social worker, group therapist, family therapist, and creative arts therapist. Each author certainly stresses his/her own specific approach; nevertheless, at no time is the whole child ignored. Nowhere is this better exemplified than in the brilliant chapter on individual psychotherapy in which there is an excellent integration of the roles of the teacher, parent, and therapist. Dr. Adamson has also contributed a chapter on medical therapies which not only delineates the kind of medication frequently prescribed for children with learning disabilities, but also puts a number of "fads" into truer perspective. There is no intention here on the part of the author to be heavy-handed and destructive in his criticism, but simply to lend a sense of reality to what has frequently been a very confusing issue.

This book is a major contribution to the field of learning disabilities. It effectively accomplishes its major goal, to bridge the gap between and among the many professionals involved in this extremely important area. As such, it is a book that should be read by students, parents, professionals—anyone who is seriously interested in the child's learning processes. It will go a long way to prevent one from going down a road that leads to frustration, disillusionment, and apathy.

Jules C. Abrams, Ph.D.

PREFACE

This volume is a "How to" Handbook for all educators and clinicians, along with concerned parents who are interested in what can be done to help the thousands of children and adolescents whose self-concept and personal pride have been hurt by their inability to learn in the classroom. Because of their Specific Learning Disabilities, these children have not been able to read, write, spell, or count as have their brothers, sisters, or friends. Yet, it is clear they are not mentally retarded but have average or near-average intellectual potential. It is also clear that learning failures in these children have led to such intense feelings of self-failure and self-doubt that the problems in learning have become inextricably enmeshed with associated behavioral problems in their social and emotional development.

It is the thesis of this Handbook that the chronic learning and socialization problems in these children are so intertwined that it is impossible to assign one facet of the problem to the educator and another to the clinician.

As currently written, PL 94-142 of the Education for All Handicapped Children Act centers largely on educational assessment and remediation to the exclusion of clinical components designed to offset the poor self-concept and low sense of self-esteem universally associated with learning disabilities in these children and adolescents. This Handbook emphasizes a "both-and" approach in the conceptual framework of an Individualized Education Program plan (IEP) and a related Individualized Clinical Program (ICP).

It is significant that, as a result of the confusion over terminology, etiology, and methodology for remediation and intervention, there is no one predominant opinion about the nature and treatment of Specific Learning Disabilities (SLD), Minimal Brain Dysfunction (MBD), or Hyperkinetic Reaction Syndrome (HKS). Rather, it is clear that the soundest approach, with today's educational and technological knowledge, is a multidisciplinary one.

This has been the approach in writing this Handbook. Leading experts in each area of concern have written specific chapters related to their educational and clinical experiences. The Editors are gratified that colleagues at The Hahnemann Medical College and The Pathway School, along with specialists in the fields of early intervention, visual function, and behavior modification, have added to the richness and experiential contents of the book, both for their contribution and out of respect for the quality of their work in this field.

Finally, this Handbook has been completed through the dedicated interests of many people, including parents, children, educators and clinicians. Only a few can be recognized in this preface. Frank Jepson, President, and the Board of Directors of The Pathway School, have provided the climate for student, family, and staff growth and understanding of the issues related to MBD/ SLD/HKS over the decade-and-a-half of the school's existence. Dr. Champion would like to thank Marsha Wolfson and Domenic Colaiacomo for their Language and Educational assessments. Jules Abrams, recognized clinician and educational authority in the learning disability field, has added to the depth and breadth of the presentation through his critical reading of the manuscript and his constructive suggestions concerning chapter content. His incisive mind and compelling conceptualizations are apparent in his Foreword, setting the tone of a rapprochement between the educational and clinical thrusts so essential to the ongoing assessment, treatment, and remediation processes for these children and their concerned parents.

Not the least of those who made this edition possible were Israel Zwerling, Chairman of the Department of Mental Health Sciences, and Herman Belmont, Deputy Chairman and Head of the Division of Child and Adolescent Psychiatry, Hahnemann Medical College and Hospital. It has been their encouragement and support of the interface among clinical services supported by strong supervision, training programs for all mental health disciplines by an experienced and competent faculty, and an outstanding research and evaluation program and staff which motivated the co-editors to assemble this Handbook.

The Editors would also like to acknowledge the able and competent services of Helene Perry and Linda Lindblom whose patient retyping of sections of the manuscript several times over has allowed for the achievement of a better product.

William C. Adamson, M.D.
Katherine K. Adamson, M.S.

Rydal, Pennsylvania

CONTRIBUTORS

JULES C. ABRAMS, Ph.D.,
Professor and Director of
Graduate Education in Psychology
Hahnemann Medical College and Hospital, Philadelphia, Pennsylvania

WILLIAM C. ADAMSON, M.D.,
Clinical Professor of Child Psychiatry and
Chief, Education and Training in Child/Adolescent Psychiatry
Department of Mental Health Sciences, Hahnemann Medical College and Hospital
Philadelphia, Pennsylvania
and Medical/Psychiatric Services Director, The Pathway School
Audubon, Pennsylvania.

LISA BILLOCK,
Clinical Instructor and Movement Therapist
Department of Mental Health Sciences, Hahnemann Medical College and Hospital
Philadelphia, Pennsylvania

AGNES BORNEMANN, B.A.,
Master Teacher
Center for Preschool Services, Franklin Institute Research Laboratories
Philadelphia, Pennsylvania

CYNTHIA A. BRIGGS, M.M., RMT,
Senior Instructor and Director
Music Therapy Education, Department of Mental Health Sciences
Hahnemann Medical College and Hospital
Philadelphia, Pennsylvania

BENJAMIN W. CHAMPION, Ed.D.,
Educational Director
The Pathway School, Audubon, Pennsylvania

DIANNE DULICAI, M.A., DTR,
Assistant Professor and Director
Movement Therapy Education, Department of Mental Health Sciences
Hahnemann Medical College and Hospital
Philadelphia, Pennsylvania

ROBERT F. GAMACHE, Ph.D.,
Clinical Psychologist
The Pathway School, Audubon, Pennsylvania.

FLORENCE KASLOW, Ph.D.,
Associate Professor
Department of Mental Health Sciences, Hahnemann Medical College and Hospital
Philadelphia, Pennsylvania

MYRA LEVICK, M.Ed., ATR,
Associate Professor and Director
Creative Arts in Therapy Program, Department of Mental Health Sciences
Hahnemann Medical College and Hospital
Philadelphia, Pennsylvania

DOROTHY FISHER OHRENSTEIN, M.S.W., ACSW,
Chief Social Worker
Handicapped Children's Unit, St. Christopher's Hospital for Children
Philadelphia, Pennsylvania

DONALD H. PAINTING, Ph.D.,
Clinical Director
The Pathway School, Audubon, Pennsylvania

LOUISE SANDLER, Ph.D.,
Professor
Department of Mental Health Sciences
Hahnemann Medical College and Hospital and Director
Center for Early Childhood Services, 1823 Callowhill Street
Philadelphia, Pennsylvania

ARTHUR SEIDERMAN, O.D., M.A.,
Optometrist and Lecturer
Pennsylvania State University, Ogontz Center
Abington, Pennsylvania

CONTENTS

Foreword, by Jules C. Abrams, Ph.D.

Preface, by William C. Adamson, M.D. and
Katherine K. Adamson, M.S.

PART I.   **BUILDING BRIDGES FROM
PAST TO PRESENT**

Chapter   1.   **Questions, Definitions, and Perspectives** **3**
by William C. Adamson, M.D.

PART II.   **THE CORNERSTONES:
THE ASSESSMENT PROCESS**

Chapter   2.   **Psychosocial, Medical, and Neurological
Assessments** **23**
by William C. Adamson, M.D.

Chapter   3.   **Cognitive Assessment** **63**
by Donald H. Painting, Ph.D.

Chapter   4.   **Educational Assessment, Diagnosis, and
Evaluation** **107**
by Benjamin W. Champion, Ed.D.

Chapter   5.   **Visual Function Assessment** **145**
by Arthur S. Seiderman, O.D., M.A.

**PART III.   MANY PILLARS OF SUPPORT:
              INTERPRETATION AND PRESCRIPTIONS**

Chapter 6.   **Individual Psychotherapy: An Illustrative
               Case Study** 193
               by William C. Adamson, M.D.

Chapter 7.   **Parent Counseling** 237
               by Dorothy Fisher Ohrenstein, M.S.W., ACSW

Chapter 8.   **Group Psychotherapy with SLD Children** 255
               by William C. Adamson, M.D.

Chapter 9.   **The Time Out and Life Space Interview
               Processes** 287
               by William C. Adamson, M.D.

Chapter 10.   **Therapy Within the Family Constellation** 313
               by Florence W. Kaslow, Ph.D.

Chapter 11.   **Behavior Therapy: Applications within the
               Home and School** 333
               by Robert Gamache, Ph.D.

Chapter 12.   **The Creative Art Therapies** 361
               by Myra Levick, M.Ed., Dianne Dulicai, M.A.,
                   Cynthia A. Briggs, M.M., and Lisa Billock

Chapter 13.   **Medical Therapies** 389
               by William C. Adamson, M.D.

**PART IV.   THE CENTRAL SPAN: PLANNING
              EDUCATIONAL REMEDIATION**

Chapter 14.   **Intervention in Early Childhood Education** 449
               by Louise Sandler, Ph.D., and
               Agnes Bornemann, B.A.

Chapter 15.   **Educational Remediation: From Planning to
               Implementation** 487
               by Benjamin W. Champion, Ed.D.

THE COMPLETED BRIDGE: EPILOGUE 501

Subject Index 503

Author Index 509

PART I

BUILDING BRIDGES
FROM PAST TO PRESENT

CHAPTER 1

QUESTIONS, DEFINITIONS, AND PERSPECTIVES

WILLIAM C. ADAMSON, M.D.

I walked down an echoing corridor through the long silent tiers of stacks that contained all the madness, all the wisdom, all the loneliness of centuries. Here imperishable thought lay waiting in the great social brain, waiting to strike fire in the minds of similar affinities.

—Loren Eiseley, *All the Strange Hours*

Today's parents are becoming very sophisticated in the many issues related to specific learning disabilities from all they read, see, and hear in the different media. Recently, for example, a concerned parent asked these twelve questions of the child psychiatry resident who was evaluating her three-year-old son.

(1) Can you suggest some specific daily activities for my son at home?

(2) What will be done or what can we do to correct dysmaturation?

(3) Will he always have to go to a special school? How do you go about deciding what school or combination of school programs is best for him?

(4) What specific psychiatric help does he need now, or does he need any?

(5) How can we toilet train him using the best method?

(6) How can we help him establish a healthy degree of independence from me at his age? As he grows older?

(7) How can we correct flapping of the arms?

(8) How can we increase his attention span?

(9) How can we help to expand his knowledge and encourage him in following directions?

(10) How can we improve his language development?

(11) How can we improve his motor and fine motor coordination? (The mother may have also asked about his eye-hand coordination.)

(12) Also, how can we cope with and handle obstinacy and the necessary explanations of situations in which he cannot receive immediate gratification?

One rule of thumb to be established early for this child psychiatry resident and for parents, teachers, clinicians, and others reading this book is that none of these questions should be answered in a single, simplistic, "this is the answer for all time" way. Rather, we would emphasize the frame of reference that would focus on growth and development of the child in the home, school, and community setting, over a period of time. This process might be referred to as a combination of an analytic evaluation and a series of Individualized Education Program plans/Clinical Prescriptions (IEP/CP) over a span of time. This principle will be restated again and again throughout this handbook. However, it is of such importance and is so often distorted or handled improperly that a brief case illustration is presented here to underline the basic principle.

CASE STUDY 1.1

An Illustration of the Diagnostic Evaluation over Time
(An analytic evaluation and prescription synthesis)

Presenting Problems

This two-year-old was referred by the family pediatrician for late onset of talking and suspected "autism." After beginning to talk in single words and word approximations at 15 months, he stopped talking at 19 months, 1 month before a brother was born. He began "blood-curdling screams" at 24 months when he was left with grandparents for 3 days while his parents were away for a weekend. At that time, his behavior changed. He could not be reached by his parents' efforts to communicate, became more distractible, restless, and withdrawn, seemed agitated and preoccupied with self-centered interests, and was noncommunicative and momentarily out of contact with his environment.

Initial Impressions as to Nature of Problem

(1) Consider *regressive behavior* related to mother's pregnancy and impending confinement, separation from parents for a weekend, and the mother's emotional separation from first offspring as she contemplated birth of the second.

(2) Consider regressive behavior as a derivative of a *depressive reaction* in response to emotional loss felt in the mother-infant dyad from factors described in (1). Infants and young children often show agitation and anger (e.g. excessive screaming) as expressions of hurt, anger, feelings of abandonment or loss, or the handling of feelings which, in older children, would be viewed as a depressive reaction.

(3) Consider the possibility of a severe emotional problem, such as severe ego disturbance of the early infantile autism or mother-child symbiotic psychosis type.

(4) Rule out by appropriate studies a central nervous system impairment or dysfunction, suggested by the apparent delay in language and history of distractibility, restlessness, and narcissistic vulnerability (self-centeredness) which could account for the regressive pattern suggested in (1).

(5) Recognize that, with a moderate degree of language deficiency

in a child with apparent normal intelligence, one would explore the possibility of a specific learning disability.

Brief Case History

The mother had signs of mild toxemia of pregnancy during the last trimester (swelling of ring finger, ankles, elevated blood pressure). The baby was born 5 weeks premature, in eighth month of gestation, and weighed 5 pounds, 13 ounces. He had a light case of chicken pox at 3 to 4 months and a virus at 12 months and became listless and dehydrated with elevated temperature for one week at home as a result of the virus. He was slow in turning from back to front, never crawled, and walked without support at 12 months. Word approximations began at 15 to 18 months; he then stopped talking at about the time his brother was born. He was active in temperament, had been in constant motion from birth, and seldom slowed down. He had uncontrolled temper tantrums, which began after his parents left him for the first time (age 24 months) for a 3-day weekend, with loud, frequent screams.

His parents were older than average (late thirties). They were frightened, troubled, confused, and "heartsick because he is so distressed."

Observation of Child

In the two visits, the child showed (1) adequate uniformity in integration of motor development, social development, and cognitive development; (2) an appropriate sense of identity as a two-year-old; (3) no impaired sense of reality as to time, place, and person in relation to his chronological age; (4) an age-appropriate pattern of relating in the one-to-one situation, responding to questions, directions, and verbal requests with appropriate motor activity, although with little or no spoken language; (5) use of such distal receptors as eyes and ears (while exploring playroom), rather than proximal receptors of taste, touch, and smell in a manner often characteristic of children with severe ego disturbances; (6) no persistent pattern of withdrawal or inability to risk and to trust the adult in these two visits; and (7) attempt at maximum degree of nonverbal communication and relatedness.

These seven observations ruled out any consideration of a severe emotional disturbance. However, he did show dysinhibition, hyperactivity, low frustration tolerance, some emotional lability, perseverative behavior, only fair gross and fine motor coordination for his age, and complete avoidance of any tasks requiring him to sit at a table or desk, such as a Play School puzzle. These observations suggested the presence of a central nervous system dysfunction (MBD), with the associated behavior pattern often seen in children with this symptom complex.

Supportive Evaluation

The parents were helped, over a period of 6 months, to prepare their child for a neurological and an electroencephalogram (EEG) study. The neurologist's report was as follows: the child showed hyperkinetic behavior, immature speech of a nonspecific nature, coordination more that of a 2-year-old than a 2½-year-old, occasionally a palmer rather than a pincer grasp, awkward manipulation of objects, and a wobbly gait. The deep tendon reflexes were hypoactive, if anything, and tone seemed normal throughout, except that the adductors were somewhat tight.

An electroencephalogram was obtained with the patient awake and spontaneously asleep. Quite surprisingly, the technician's comment on this child was that he was a real doll-baby. There was no difficulty at all with the tracing, and this was felt to be due largely to the careful preparation which he received from his parents. We had spoken with them over the 6-month period about the nature of the study, which they had explained to the little boy in appropriate language and in a low-key presentation.

The EEG tracing was quite abnormal, showing a general background dysrhythmia of considerable degree, with irregularity of wave forms both in frequency and amplitude. It achieved its abnormality chiefly because of a focus in the left posterior temporal area of runs of almost triangular appearing waves, often notched. In some ways, these were repetitive and abnormal enough to be thought of as subclinical temporal seizure activity, although he did not appear to have an overt seizure during the tracing. The wave was described as a psychomotor variant.

It was the impression of the consulting pediatric neurologist that this child was showing an abnormal EEG based on organic brain dysfunction, cause unknown, possibly related to factors revolving around the maternal toxemia and the premature delivery. The child was placed on a 2-month trial of Dilantin, 50 mg. per day for a month with an increase to 50 mg. twice a day in case of no improvement on the smaller dose and no side effects.

Initial Parent Interpretation Conference

As these parents asked their twenty questions, the clinician constructed a developmental graph focused on the frame of reference of an evaluation over time (see Figure 1.1).

In constructing the figures shown, a line was drawn horizontally (abscissa) to represent chronological age (CA) and vertically (ordinate) to represent mental age (MA). The dotted line was drawn as an average point for each age showing the MA/CA as 12/12; 24/24; etc. The child's initial evaluation results were then plotted as shown, at 26 months along the chronological age coordinate, where the estimated motor (M) development, adaptive (A) behavior and personal/social (P/S) developmental levels were placed at 20 to 21 months along the mental age coordinate.

The parents were helped to see that language development, on the other hand, was nearer a mental age of 13 months at a chronological age of 26 months. This constituted a baseline for the first study and they were advised that it would take at least three points, over time, to draw a growth curve. One cannot draw a curve with a single point but can draw many lines through a single point. It is possible to draw a straight line through two points, but a curve requires at least three points spaced apart, which would represent an evaluation every year or two. In Figure 1.1, the child was reevaluated at 38 months and again at 62 months. These evaluations show dramatically how the child's development can change, over time, following appropriate clinical intervention and prescription.

The 38 months evaluation indicated that language had progressed from 12 months to 38 months in less than a year. The motor development remained below an average level, at approximately a 24-month level at 38 months of age. By 5 years of age, the language had progressed to an 8-year level, adaptive and personal/social development were at a 6-year level, and motor and perceptual-motor development were 6 months to a year behind the chronological age.

It is important to recognize that if the clinician had used the single evaluation at 26 months as a predictor of the future, such erroneous statements as "mentally subnormal," "language disabled," "mentally retarded," or "aphasic-like syndrome" might have been branded on the child. Instead, it was suggested that this baseline

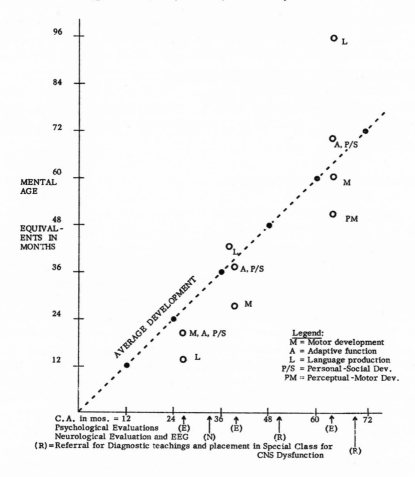

Figure 1.1   Evaluation over Time

evaluation did accomplish the following: (1) it had ruled out a severe emotional disturbance of childhood; (2) it did point in the direction of a dysfunction problem, probably related to some neurologic involvement which was influencing both language development and social and emotional growth; (3) it did suggest a need for parental guidance in helping them talk to the child and put some structure and limits into his life, along with counseling for the child to help him adjust to and cope with the setting of limits; and (4) it suggested the need for a diagnostic educational workup in approximately one year. The parents' response to this type of presentation and interpretation represented an immediate relief and release of a great deal of stored tension.

Much more will be said about the nature of parent counseling for children with specific learning disabilities in Chapter 7. However, it is important to recognize that concerned parents need to be helped to reduce their own anxiety; to begin to see their child in a time frame which allows for both natural growth as well as skillful intervention through several disciplines, such as special education, psychology, speech and language therapy, and when necessary, individual or family psychotherapy.

Definitions and Terminology

There has been much confusion in the various definitions used for this SLD/MBD population of children and adolescents. Historically, the term "learning disability" was first used by Kirk and Bateman (1962), and it has gained acceptance because it focuses on the educational needs of the child and not on issues of etiology and brain function which are more strongly related to the field of medicine.

The most recent definition of Specific Learning Disability (SLD) was made by the National Advisory Committee to the Bureau of Education for the Handicapped, Office of Education, in 1968. It was this definition which Congress included in Public Law 94-142, The Education for All Handicapped Children Act of 1975, as follows:

> Those children who have a disorder in one or more of the basic psychological processes involved in understanding or in using language, spoken or written, which disorder may manifest itself in imperfect ability to listen, think, speak, read, write, spell, or do mathematical calculations. Such disorders include such conditions as perceptual handicaps, brain injury, minimal brain dysfunction, dyslexia, and developmental aphasia. Such terms do not include children who have learning problems which are primarily the result of visual, of emotional disturbance, or environmental, cultural, or economic disadvantage.
> PL 94–142 §5(b)

This is the definition most uniformly used today to identify pupils eligible for special educational SLD services. It is also used to request financial support for research and teacher training in this important area of special education.

There are three operational requirements which must be met for the child to qualify under the above definitions. They are:

(1) Normal intelligence. The child should be able to perform at or above the normal range on nonverbal measures which involve language concepts.

(2) Academic achievement deficit. The child should exhibit an academic achievement deficit in at least one subject area, such as oral expression, listening comprehension, written expression, basic reading skill, reading comprehension, mathematics calculation, mathematics reasoning, and spelling, with deficit defined as the inability to score above a given percentile on standardized achievement tests measuring proficiency in that subject area. Although it is not presently possible to specify exactly all components of each specific learning disability, there must be a major discrepancy between expected achievement and ability which is not the result of other known and generally accepted handicapping conditions or circumstances.

(3) The absence of other primary handicapping conditions. The child should show no evidence of visual or hearing impairment, mental retardation, severe cultural neglect, or a severe emotional disturbance.

Within the American Psychiatric Association's Diagnostic Statistical Manual (DSM II), the classification for a child with such a specific learning disability diagnosis would be category 306.1. See Table 1.1 for comparative definitions.

Some clinicians and educators have argued that the operational definition from the Office of Education is impractical for school use, not specific enough for a well defined research sample, and too broad to allow for specific prescriptions for educational and clinical program planning for a particular child (Ross, 1976).

Unfortunately, with the emphasis of this definition on the educational components of disability, the major medical insurance companies which serve as third party payors may not approve reimbursement for educational and special educational programs for children who have been placed diagnostically in this category of specific learning disabilities. This kind of bias may be overcome in time as justification for programs and for the needs of these children can be presented in an organized way. On the other hand, these insurance carriers often require for approved funding a designation of minimal brain dysfunction or, more specifically, organic brain syndrome, in one of the DSM II 309.0 categories.

The third classification, Hyperkinetic Reaction of Childhood or Adolescence, DSM II 308.0, is a disorder characterized by overactivity, restlessness, distractibility, and short attention span, especially

Table 1.1
Comparative Definitions

		DSM II*	
SLD	Specific Learning Disturbance	301.6	one or more processes
			understanding or using spoken or written language
			disorders of:
			listening reading
			thinking writing
			talking arithmetic
			spelling
MBD	Organic Brain Syndrome	309.0	developmental learning imbalance from perinatal distress
			biochemical system
			associated behavioral reaction
HKS	Hyperkinetic Reaction of Childhood	308.0	not caused by organic brain damage
			suspect genetic factor characterized by overactivity, distractibility, restlessness, short attention
			usually diminishes in adolescence
		Proposed DSM III	
	Attention Deficit Disorder without Hyperactivity	314.00	
	Attention Deficit Disorder with Hyperactivity	314.01	
	Specific Developmental Disorders	315.00	Reading disorder
		315.10	Arithmetic disorder
		315.31	Language disorder
		315.32	Articulation disorder
		315.40	Coordination disorder

*DSM II refers to the Diagnostic and Statistical Manual of Mental Disorders, Second Edition, American Psychiatric Association, 1700 18th Street, N.W., Washington, D.C. 20009, 1968.

established pattern of denial of the existence of any problem within one's self, with a frequent projection on sources outside the self as the cause of the problem.

Finally, pediatric neurologists have been able to identify a group of signs, referred to as "neurological soft signs," which are helpful in establishing the diagnosis of minimal brain dysfunction. These will be discussed more fully in Chapter 2. Classification of the minimal brain dysfunction diagnosis as a subcategory under specific learning disabilities would be achieved by a careful medical history, identifying some of the eight areas of dysfunction of the higher cortical processes, and identifying two or more of the neurological soft signs felt to be associated with this symptom complex. A detailed description of the characteristics of minimal brain dysfunction which allow for its identification will also be presented in Chapter 2.

Ross (1976) has suggested that the use of the terms "minimal brain dysfunction" or "psychoneurological learning disability" are residuals of historical origins of the field and that there is little evidence to support the notion of brain dysfunction other than difficulty in learning or poor performance on a psychological test. He favors limiting the term "learning disability" to those children whose learning problem is associated with difficulties in sustaining selective attention, which probably is a derivative of a delay in the child's development. Wender (1971), on the other hand, has made a strong case for the existence of the minimal brain dysfunction syndrome, arising from several distinct and separate etiologies, including: (1) an insult to the central nervous system which may be structural or chemical, (2) a polygenetic abnormality which has been genetically transmitted, (3) an intra-uterine pattern of variation in biologic development, resulting in what has been referred to as developmental delay or dysmaturation, and (4) fetal maldevelopment or perinatal distress which has a specific effect on the central nervous system, either in a gross morphological way or by altering the spontaneous action of the neurochemical relationships within the neurons of the brain, which would then result in the minimal brain dysfunction symptoms complex.

It would appear that the proposed DSM III, as shown in Table 1.1, may be more explicit in its focus on attentional deficits, with or without hyperactivity, as well as a classification for specific developmental disorders. An additional advantage of the DSM III will be the multi-axial classification system in which each individual will be diagnosed according to:

Axis I —Clinical psychiatric syndromes
Axis II —Personality disorders (children and adolescents)
Axis III—Nonmental medical disorder
Axis IV—Severity of psychosocial stressors
Axis V —Highest level of adaptive functioning past year

In summary, two separate diagnostic categories exist for the educator and the clinician in attempting to arrive at a definition and diagnosis of the population about which we are concerned. The educational bias has pointed in the direction of a specific learning disability syndrome which appears to cover most of the cases where there is normal or near normal intelligence with associated perceptual problems in the auditory and visual functioning area, a resulting academic achievement deficit of a year or more in at least one of the major subject areas, and the absence of a primary handicapping condition such as mental retardation, severe cultural neglect, or severe emotional disturbance. This is the diagnostic category favored by the Bureau of Education for the Handicapped. The medical bias favors the diagnostic classification of minimal brain dysfunction or organic brain syndrome, which would appear to be a subcategory of the more all-inclusive specific learning disability. While many educational and clinical authorities strongly favor one or the other classification according to their own professional biases and expertise, it would appear that both classifications do have a place within the system, and the clinician should be able to recognize the predominating problem and determine whether there is sufficient neurologic impairment to warrant the medical classification vis-à-vis a strictly educational one. Unfortunately, because of the nature of the current funding practice through third party payments, the educator and clinician may be forced to bend the diagnosis to fit the practical funding realities.

Perspectives

In developing an historical backdrop for the many issues related to specific learning disabilities, it should be recognized that the work of Strauss and Werner at the Wayne County Training School in Michigan, and later at the Cove School in Racine, Wisconsin, in the early 1940s, represented a pioneering effort in the field. This group, along with Lehtinen, undertook to separate from a mentally retarded population those children who had evidence of a neurologic impairment as a basis for their learning problems. They referred to this group as "brain damaged or brain injured children" (Strauss and Werner, 1942; Strauss and Lehtinen, 1947).

During the 1940s and 1950s, this population was largely viewed as a problem for the neurologist. A. Silver and Perlstein were central figures in the identification process. During the same period, Bender, in collaboration wth Schilder (1950), made a significant contribution with insights into the psychopathology of children with organic brain syndrome and observations on the impact of psychopathology on the child's body image. She is also known for the development of the Bender-Gestalt Visual Motor Test, which has become a standardized tool today in the evaluation and assessment of these children.

In the 1950s, the Institute for Neurological Diseases and Blindness began a nationwide collaborative study on the influence of perinatal factors on subsequent development, and, in 1966, Clements summarized the findings of the Joint Study Committee of the National Institute of Neurological Disease and Blindness and the National Society for Crippled Children's Committee. He indicated that no fewer than 38 terms were used in the professional literature to identify and label these children, and this joint committee chose as the most appropriate designation "children with minimal brain dysfunction."

In the 1960s, the psychologists and educators began to make significant contributions to the remediation of these children, particularly Kirk (1963), Kephardt (1960), and Cruikshank (1961).

In 1971, Wender wrote one of the more authoritative books on the subject. Then, beginning with a monograph published as one of the Annals of the New York Academy of Science (1973), there emerged a plethora of books directed toward the concerned parents of learning disabled children, as well as books focused on specific aspects of the multiple disabilities in these children.

It is interesting to note that the classification of learning disabled children presented by Pearson (1952) has stood up well over time. Pearson's observations in relationship to genetic dynamic formulation have also had a significant impact on clinical assessment and program planning for the treatment and remediation of these children. Briefly, Pearson's classification was as follows:

I. Diminished capacity to learn due to organic disorders
   A. Differences in intelligence
   B. Diminished capacity to learn due to physical defects or illness

II.   Diminished capacity to learn due to improper or unpleasant conditioning experiences (updated, this would be related to behavioral modification and negative conditioning)

III.   Diminished capacity to learn due to disturbed current object relations

IV.   Diminished capacity to learn due to deflection of attention (currently the area of major interest in research and educational studies)

    A.   Engrossing conscious apprehensions of dangers to the child's security

    B.   Engrossing conscious feelings of guilt, shame, and embarrassment as the sign of fear of real detection and punishment or of superego disapproval

    C.   Engrossing conscious feelings of horror and fear

    D.   Engrossing conscious involvement with instinctual drives

    E.   Focusing of attention on daydreams

V.   Diminished capacity to learn because the learning process itself is involved in a neurotic conflict

    A.   Disorders of the use of learning

       1.   Disorders in the use of learned knowledge as an expression of sibling rivalry

       2.   Disorders in the use of learned knowledge because of feelings of guilt or dread of castration

          a.   Examination anxiety

          b.   Difficulties in the use of learning due to repudiation of learning because it is associated with masculinity or femininity

          c.   Inhibition of the use of learning to avoid feelings of guilt or fear of castration

    B.   Diminished capacity to learn due to disturbances in the assimilation and digestion of knowledge

VI.   Diminished capacity to learn because of a disturbance in the relation to reality

VII.   Diminished capacity to learn because the child has never learned to tolerate the anxiety produced by the lack of gratification of instinctual drives

To summarize briefly the overall perspectives, as a surveyor might do in sizing up the location for a bridge to be built, one can say that medicine and psychology had an early involvement in looking at the deviations they saw in children whom we now recognize as either SLD or MBD children. Increasing efforts were made to determine causality and to prescribe some medication which might alter an arrhythmic brain wave pattern or reduce the child's hyperactivity and help increase the attention span.

Meanwhile, education was making significant contributions through a diagnostic educational process which refined the observations about higher cortical functions far beyond an EEG tracing or the clinical subtests of the Wechsler Intelligence Test for Children. Special Education has always had its important place in remediation, and it needs to be included in the initial evaluation to assay the strengths and weaknesses of the child's learning process.

Psychiatry and, to a lesser extent, psychology initially avoided involvement in the concerns for the mentally retarded child and, only gradually, saw the emotional problems of the SLD/MBD child and family as an arena for clinical intervention and therapeutic management. More recently, learning theorists and behaviorally oriented psychologists have added their important input into prescriptions for remediation. The result has been an interdigitation of medicine, psychology, education, and sociology which creatively helps the individual child cope with and master, when possible, the areas of deficit and inadequacy. At the same time, this integration of services supports the family in its role as provider of a climate of acceptance, firmness, life-relationship structure, and realistic expression of the hurt pride, anger, and self-doubt so often associated with these conditions.

The strength of the bridge we shall build in the succeeding chapters of this handbook will be contingent on the skill of the individual builders of each chapter to plumb the depths of knowledge in his or her field, to articulate it clearly, and to integrate those separate paths of knowledge into a firm roadway upon which all of us can travel, in practice, in performance, and in perfecting our respective skills and professional competencies.

REFERENCES

Annals of the New York Academy of Science, 1973, 205.

Cantwell, D. Psychiatric illness in the families of hyperactive children. *Archives of General Psychiatry,* 1972, *27,* 414–417.

Cantwell, D. *The hyperactive child: Diagnosis, management, current research.* New York: Spectrum Publications, Inc., 1975.

Clements, S. *Minimal brain dysfunction in children.* NINDB Monograph #3 (USPHS Publication #1415). Washington, D.C.: U.S. Department of Health, Education & Welfare, 1966.

Cruickshank, W. *A training method for hyperactive children.* Syracuse: Syracuse University Press, 1961.

Diagnostic & statistical manual of mental disorders, Second Edition (DSM II), Washington, D.C.: American Psychiatric Association, 1968.

Eiseley, L. *All the strange hours.* New York: Charles Scribner's Sons, 1975.

Gallagher, J. Children with developmental imbalances: A psychoeducational definition. In W. Cruickshank (Ed.), *The teacher of brain-injured children.* Syracuse: Syracuse University Press, 1966.

Hartman, H. *Ego psychology and the problem of adaptation.* New York: International Universities Press, 1958.

Kephardt, N. *The slow learner in the classroom.* Columbus: Charles E. Merrill, 1960.

Kirk, S. A behavioral approach to learning disabilities. In *Conference on Children with Minimal Brain Impairment.* Chicago: Easter Seal Foundation Research, 1963, 40–51.

Kirk, S. & Bateman, B. Diagnosis and remediation of learning disabilities. *Exceptional Children,* 1962, *29,* 73–78.

Morrison, J. & Stewart, M. Evidence for polygenetic inheritance in the hyperactive child syndrome. *American Journal of Psychiatry,* 1973, *130,* 791–92.

Pearson, G. A survey of learning difficulties in children. *Psychoanalytic Study of the Child,* 1952, *7,* 375–386.

Public Law 94–142: The Education for all Handicapped Children Act of 1975, Part B as amended November 29, 1975. *Federal Register,* December 30, 1976, 41, (252), 56966–56998, Washington, D.C.: Office of Education, Department of Health, Education & Welfare.

Ross, A. *Psychological aspects of learning disabilities & reading disorders.* New York: McGraw-Hill, 1976.

Satterfield, J., Saul, R., Cantwell, D., Lesser, L., & Podosin, R. Central nervous system arousal in hyperactive children. *Journal of the American Academy of Child Psychiatry,* in press.

Schilder, P. *Image and appearance of the human body.* New York: International Universities Press, 1950.

Strauss, A. & Lehtinen, L. *Psychopathology and education of the brain-injured child.* New York: Grune & Stratton, 1947.

Strauss, A. & Werner, H. Experimental analysis of the clinical symptom perseveration in mentally retarded children. *American Journal of Mental Deficiency,* 1942, *27,* 185–187.

Wender, P. *Minimal brain dysfunction in children.* New York: Wiley-Interscience, 1971.

Werry, J. Organic factors in childhood psychopathology. In H. Quay & J. Werry (Eds.), *Psychopathological disorders of childhood.* New York: John Wiley & Sons, 1972.

PART II

THE CORNERSTONES:
THE ASSESSMENT PROCESS

CHAPTER 2

PSYCHOSOCIAL, MEDICAL, AND NEUROLOGICAL ASSESSMENTS

WILLIAM C. ADAMSON, M.D.

As diagnosis is inferred from multiform observations, so treatment is inferred from diagnosis, and prognosis from treatment ... Thus, despite the disparate definitions ..., when taken outside the covers of the dictionary (or the Diagnostic Statistical Manual), diagnosis, prognosis, and treatment cannot be divorced.

—Sheldon R. Rappaport, *Childhood Aphasia and Brain Damage, Volume II*

INTRODUCTION

No bridge is stronger than its basic design and the foundations upon which it is built. This handbook will have as its basic design the concept, so succinctly stated by Rappaport (1965), that diagnosis, prognosis, and (habilitative) treatment cannot be divorced from one another.

This is clearly the intent of Public Law 94-142, derived from the Education of the Handicapped Act of 1975, whose proposed rules will be used to establish the "count" of SLD children in local educational systems throughout the nation, which, in turn, will determine allocation of federal funds, beginning October 1, 1977. These rules, proposed by the Office of Health, Education, and Welfare:

(1) Require establishment of an evaluation team consisting of the child's regular classroom teacher and at least one other diagnostic

person, such as the school psychologist, speech teacher, or remedial reading teacher. The team must use individual standardized diagnostic techniques, and at least one team member must observe the child's academic performance in class. If a medical problem appears to be involved, the team must request a complete medical examination for the child.

(2) Require that the evaluation team not identify a child as having a specific learning disability if the severe academic discrepancy is primarily the result of a visual, hearing, or motor handicap, mental retardation, emotional disturbance, or environmental, cultural, or economic disadvantage.

(3) Provide that the team may determine a child has a specific learning disability if there is a severe discrepancy between academic achievement and intellectual ability in one or more of the following areas: oral expression, listening comprehension, written expression, basic reading skill, reading comprehension, mathematics calculation, mathematics reasoning, and/or spelling.

(4) State that a "severe discrepancy" is defined to exist when achievement in one or more of the areas falls to or below fifty percent of the child's expected achievement level, when age and previous educational experiences are taken into consideration.

As of October 1976, some hard data on the first "counts" of handicapped children began to filter into the Bureau of the Emotionally Handicapped and were later published in *Insight* (1977). Table 2.1 shows the beginning trend in five of the most populous states.

In addition to the mandatory count and proposed rules, PL 94-142 calls for the development of an Individualized Education Program (IEP) for each handicapped child needing special education and/or related services. The documentation of such a program (or process) will be referred to as the Individualized Education Program (IEP) plan. In general, the components of an IEP plan (as stated by the National Learning Resource Center, 1977) are to include the following:

(1) A written statement of the child's present levels of educational performance.

(2) A statement of annual goals, identifying how much and what one can reasonably expect the child to learn by the end of the year and specifying the behavior to be achieved through the implementation of the child's IEP.

(3) A list of short-term instructional objectives which serve as the steps in achieving each annual goal.

(4) A statement of appropriate objective criteria and means to

Table 2.1 *

Counts of Handicapped Children by States

State	Total K-12 Enrollment	No. of Handicapped	Percent of Enrollment
California	4,419,571	315,862	7.15
New York	3,401,214	230,010	6.76
Texas	2,812,888	211,475	7.52
Illinois	2,269,892	204,509	9.01
Pennsylvania	2,246,218	193,871	8.63

*Reprinted from *Insight, 5,* June, 1977.

measure (or evaluate) the child's progress, on at least an annual basis, to determine whether the instructional objectives are being achieved.

(5) A statement of the extent to which the child will be able to participate in a regular education program.

(6) A description of all the education programs and related services required to meet the child's needs, including any special instructional media or materials to be provided, and the type of physical education program in which the child will participate.

(7) The projected date for the initiation and anticipated duration of these services.

As defined in the Definition Section of PL 94-142, "related services" means transportation and such developmental, corrective, and other supportive services as audiology, psychological services, medical services (for diagnostic and evaluation purposes only), and physical education (regular or adaptive). In some states, speech and/or language correction or remediation is not considered a related service to be included.

The nature of the IEP plan directs its focus initially on the psychoeducational assessment or evaluation, the content of which will be discussed later in this chapter. Once the request for a psychoeducational evaluation has been approved in writing by the parents/-guardian/surrogate(s) and has been completed, the parents/-guardian/surrogate(s) of the child are to be informed of the results. If, through psychoeducational evaluation, it appears that the child is handicapped (exceptional), a due process notice is sent (see letters 2.1 and 2.2).

Although the authors of this handbook endorse and support the underlying philosophy and intent of PL 94-142, they feel that it fails to allow for and to allocate to the states noncategorical funding to set up programs for early diagnostic/intervention classrooms within the basic educational system for preschool children between 3 and 7 years who present the broader and less well defined syndrome of developmental disability which defies labeling in one of the specific categories of SLD or SED (severe emotional disturbance) now included in the Educational Act for the Handicapped. For this developmental disabilities group, as well as for SLD/MBD/HKS children with associated emotional problems, the basic design should be augmented to include an Individualized Education Program/Clinical Prescription plan (IEP/CP plan). In any event, when developing an IEP or an IEP/CP plan, it is essential that educators, clinicians, and parents join hands in the best interest of all SLD/MBD/HKS children and adolescents.

GUIDELINES FOR ASSESSMENT AND EVALUATION

One of the ways in which hands can be joined is to advocate the guidelines in Table 2.2 which are essential for a constructive psycho-educational evaluation and assessment prescription process.

Indices of Suspicion which Suggest Referral

Teachers, parents, and practicing clinicians should be suspicious of the presence of SLD in children or teenagers who may show some difficulty in one or more of the following areas:

(1) *Perception.* Visual function, visual-motor or eye-hand coordination difficulties as seen in the Rutgers Drawings, Bender-Gestalt Visual Motor Test, or the Frostig Test of Visual Perception; auditory discrimination with the Wepman Auditory Discrimination Test; and position-in-space and body image with the Purdue Perceptual Motor Survey.

(2) *Conceptualization.* Problems in· abstract reasoning, reading comprehension, and inferential thinking.

(3) *Language.* Delay in language development and problems in sequencing, perseveration, syntax, and written expression reflected in the Illinois Test of Psycholinguistic Abilities (ITPA).

Table 2.2
Guidelines for Psychoeducational Evaluation
and Assessment/Prescription Process

Have a high index of suspicion about which children to refer for psychoeducational evaluations.

Consider multiple rather than single handicaps as a frame of reference.

Work toward an interdisciplinary "team" evaluation.

Do not pin a static label on a child.

Develop individual and team member sensitivity to the many issues involved in working with SLD/MBD/HKS children and their families.

One person should organize and integrate the findings of the interdisciplinary workup and sit in with the parents and teacher/supervisor when recommendations for the IEP or IEP/CP are made.

Help parents avoid the "one-shot, dreary rounds" approach. Plan for annual or more frequent follow-up and reevaluation of the child's using of and response to the IEP or IEP/CP.

---

(4) *Memory.* Variations in immediate and remote auditory, visual, and associated recall.

(5) *Attention.* Distractibility, figure-ground variability, and generally short attention span.

(6) *Impulse control.* Dysinhibition, hyperactivity, hyperkinesis, and low frustration tolerance with labile or explosive emotionality.

(7) *Feelings of inadequacy (hurt pride).* Poor self-concept, low self-esteem, negative body image, with compensatory efforts at manipulation and control of persons in the environment.

(8) *Task or failure avoidant behavior.* Avoidance of learning tasks which are difficult and subject to exposure of failure, often manifested by changing the subject, leaving the desk or learning area on the pretext of sharpening a pencil, going to the bathroom, or "clowning around," and frequently the source of "testing-out" or "limit-seeking behavior."

(9) *Two or more neurological soft signs* (see subsequent discussion on this topic). These might include the following observations at home, in the office, or in the classrooms:

(a) *Coordination problems*: poor gross motor functions in walking, jumping, riding tricycle/bicycle; poor fine motor manipulation skills in buttoning, typing, and drawing, and in rapid alternating movements of the hands, fingers, and tongue (dysdiadochokinesis). (b) *Choreiform movements*: abrupt, short muscle jerks when outstretching hand. (c) *Mirror movements*: movements of the opposite hand in response to volitional movements of the index hand. (d) *Difficulty crossing the midline*. (e) *Difficulty drawing figures in space*. (f) *Tandem Rhomberg*. Difficulty in heel-toe walking with eyes open and closed (prepare to support child during this procedure to prevent falling to either side). (g) *Crawling pattern*. Note whether the pattern is in the immature homolateral (simultaneous right arm/right leg) or in the mature contralateral (right arm/left leg) movement pattern. (h) *Sensory modality problems*. Tactile agnosia (inability to name common objects when blindfolded); poor position sense in identifying direction of passive movement of toes or fingers; poor two-point discrimination; and inability to recognize letters or numbers written on the palm of the hands. (i) *Occasional momentary* (*seconds*) *loss of consciousness*: petit mal symptoms. (j) *Strabismus*. The turning in or out of the eyes, especially when fatigued. There is evidence to suggest that children with strabismus have an associated history of SLD/MBD.

(10) *Isolated academic deficits*. Poor word recognition, math difficulties, and difficulties in written expression, punctuation, spelling, grammar, and syntax.

Consider Multiple Rather than Single Handicaps

Children with SLD/MBD/HKS seem to have multiple problems, including the emotional concomitants of their underlying problems. In planning an IEP or IEP/CP, it is important to assess and evaluate for combinations of problems in the neuromuscular system, the visual function system (see Chapter 5), the auditory discrimination, language arts, and mathematics processing systems (see Chapter 4), and the cognitive function systems (see Chapter 3). Often, such an assessment process and psychoeducational evaluation can be accomplished best by an interdisciplinary "team."

Do Not Pin a Static Label on a Child

The assessment and labeling of children with SLD/MBD/HKS syndromes is like the three Major League umpires discussing how they call balls and strikes. "I call them as I see them," says the first. "I call them as they are," says the second. "They aren't anything until I call them," cracks the third. (Taken from the "repertoire" of Jane Kessler, Professor of Psychology, Case Western Reserve University.)

Careful, dynamic labeling is of positive value because it directs the IEP plan and clinical intervention to possible sources for the dysfunction in the primary atypicality or impairment in the central nervous system.

On the other hand, we must remember that cumulative school records, insurance company files, and other medical-educational data banks may carry for a lifetime the labels, often pejorative in nature, with which we brand these SLD/MBD/HKS children and adolescents. Such well-intentioned labeling may also increase existing negative family and community attitudes towards SLD, and thus, it is important to include in the psychoeducational evaluation process not only the parents, but also other significant persons concerned with the child's eventual education, treatment, and habilitation outcome.

Hobbs (1976) noted that classification of exceptional children is essential to get services for them, to plan and organize helping programs, and to determine the outcomes of intervention efforts. He cautioned, however, that classification is not a simple, scientific, and value-free process with predictable and certain benign consequences. It may be derived from and perpetuate the value of the cultural majority, while infringing upon the freedom and rights of individual children or classes of children. In its negative thrust, classification identifies children who do not fit the norms and who, by virtue of their differences or deviancies, pose a threat to the equilibrium of the system. Efforts are then mobilized to change or to isolate those who pose the greatest threat. In a more positive frame of reference, classification can be seen as part of the larger scientific methodology seeking greater clarity as to the laws and principles of human behavior. As part of this scientific thrust, national and international bodies work to achieve the codification and uniformity of variables necessary to facilitate communication and to accumulate cross-cultural comparisons of data from different conditions, periods, or populations.

Finally, a diagnostic label from an assessment outside the classroom, or one which does not include the type of diagnostic teaching (and assessment) described in Chapter 4, often does not tell the responsible teacher what needs to be done to help the SLD/MBD/HKS child.

When Cohen (1973) suggested that all these children should be included in the EBD (Etiology Be Damned) category, he was speaking only a half-truth. He was correct in insisting that, regardless of the presence of a central nervous system impairment and its origin, these children needed to be taught by special education methods determined and prescribed by diagnostic-educational teaching rather than by strictly clinical methods of assessment.

What Cohen omitted from his EBD formulation was the recognition that children with learning problems are feeling persons, living with and learning from other feeling persons. The feeling and relational transactions between SLD/MBD/HKS children and their familial, social, emotional, cultural, and educational environments determine to a great extent the rate, the quality, and the quantity of total learning, both affective and cognitive, which takes place in these children. Chapers 7 and 10 will enlarge on the significant transactional issues.

Develop Sensitivity to Issues in Working with SLD Children and their Families

Parents of SLD/MBD/HKS children carry an important key to helping their children achieve social, emotional and educational mastery of their disabilities. No one approach to helping parents is a panacea. However, a growing body of knowledge and counseling skill is being developed for the process of affecting growth and change in parents' attitudes and effectiveness in helping their children achieve a greater sense of self-mastery (see Chapters 7 and 10).

One Person Should Organize the Findings

The interdisciplinary team should have a leader to organize and integrate the findings, to sit in with parents and teacher/supervisor when the recommendations for the IEP or IEP/CP are made, and to integrate the total efforts of school, family, physicians, parent counselors, and supporting community agencies. The designated leader could come from any of the professions which made up the diagnostic "team," and usually is an educator, school psychologist, or school guidance counselor. In any case, it should be someone who works closely and well with the school personnel and who can successfully build a bridge of trust between the teacher/school and the child/family.

Help Parents Avoid the "One-Shot-Dreary-Rounds"

When parents are told about the psychoeducational evaluation completed by school personnel or nonschool clinicians, they will often react with denial, anger, or projection of blame onto the school system, and will vigorously seek out another person to observe and evaluate their child who may be more positive and optimistic. Hersh (1961) noted that, once a problem surfaces in a child, the parents often want a quick, comfortable solution to the problem. Few parents can fully accept the idea of a disability or handicap in their child and need counseling and planned follow-ups over time, as suggested in the annual IEP review process, to work through the feelings and implications aroused by the first indication that something is wrong. The educator or clinician designated to work with these parents needs to make him/herself available, and, with patient understanding, sensitive forthrightness, and honesty about not having a "crystal ball," work to help parents take steps with their child little by little, year by year, in order to obtain a realistic appraisal over time. Then these parents will be less likely to wear out themselves, their child, and their family in making the "dreary rounds" for another point of view.

KNOWLEDGE OF NORMAL PERSONALITY DEVELOPMENT

Knowledge of the phases and stages of personality development is important in any assessment process of psychoeducational evaluation, whether it is completed by an individual or by an interdisciplinary "team." Table 2.3 highlights these stages from the point of view of four developmental theorists: Mahler, Freud, Piaget, and Erikson.

By comparing the developmental levels of the child under study with the normal chronological-age-appropriate ego functions, it is possible to determine the level and degree of social and emotional problems associated with the SLD/MBD/HKS Syndrome. A significant variation between the expected age-appropriate ego functions and the profile of actual ego function level in the child being studied would indicate the need for adding an Interventive Clinical Prescription (ICP) to the Individualized Education Program plan (IEP). A description of the various modalities of treatment suitable for SLD/MBD/HKS children and adolescents has been included in Chapters 6, 8, 9, 10, 11, 12, 13, and 14 below.

Table 2.3
Normal Stages of Personality Development*

Months	Characteristics	Mahler	Freud	Erikson	Piaget
1-2	Differentiated crying. Responds to speech.	Normal autism			
3-4	Vocalizes, laughs, follows moving objects, carries hand to mouth.	Normal symbiosis	Oral stage		
4-5	Sits with support, holds head steady. Recognizes familiar objects.		Oral passive	Trust vs. Basic Mistrust	Stage I Sensory-Motor Intelligence
5-6	Reaches for objects out of reach. Teething begins.				
6-7	Expresses anger. Grasps and manipulates objects. Makes some vowel sounds.	Ego Differentiation (Hatching)	Oral aggressive		
7-8	Sits alone. Stranger anxiety; emotional response to known objects and people.				
10	Peek-a-boo game. Creeps. Says one word, responds to name. Pulls self up.				
12	Plays with others. Walks with support. Two or more words. Finger feeds self, scribbles.	Practicing period			
18	Walks alone. 10 words. Follows directions, names pictures. Temper tantrums.	Rapprochement			
Years 2	Runs well. Plays alone. Verbalizes toilet needs, sphincter muscle developed. Uses phrases.	Libidinal Object Constancy	Anal stage / Urethral stage	Autonomy vs. Shame and Doubt	Stage II Preoperational stage
3	Rides tricycle. Copies circle and cross. Resents new sibs. Takes turns. More verbal.	Gender identity	Phallic stage		

*After Borrero et al., 1974)

Table 2.3 *(Continued)*

Years	Characteristics	Mahler	Freud	Erikson	Piaget
4	Concepts of numbers and shapes. Uses conjunctions Aggressive and cooperative. Can draw a man. "I"	Increasing Internalization	Oedipal/ Electra Stage	Initiative vs. Guilt	
5	Counts to 10, names primary colors, dresses self. Articulation good. Ready for kindergarten.				
6-8	Concerned with rules. Early anxiety in separating for school, later adventuresome. Poor frustration tolerance.	Differentiated Self and object representation.	Latency Early Latency	Industry vs. Inferiority	Stage III Concrete Operation
8-11	Better self control. Plans ahead. Hero worship. Beginning intellectualization.		Late Latency		
12-14	Early adolescence			Identity vs. Role Confusion	Stage IV Stage of Formal Operation
14-18	Late Adolescence				

*After Borrero *et al.*, 1974.

PSYCHOSOCIAL ASSESSMENT: A COMMON DENOMINATOR FOR ALL EVALUATION/ASSESSMENT STUDIES

Just as a knowledge of normal personality development is important in psychoeducational evaluation/assessment studies, so, too, is the psychosocial assessment a common denominator in *all* evaluation studies. This section will outline four principal parts of such a psychosocial assessment process, including: (1) preliminary case study information, (2) taking a medical, social, and educational history, (3) recognizing the emotional concomitants of SLD/MBD/HKS, and (4) working with parents, parental surrogates, or guardians.

Preliminary Case Study Information

Responding to a request to evaluate a child can often be greatly facilitated by arranging for the parent(s), guardian(s), or parental surrogate(s) to complete a Preliminary Case Study Information form similar to the one outlined here.

Other clinicians and investigators have worked up similar and, in some cases, more complete medical and social history forms (Satterfield, 1976). CIBA Medical Horizons (1973) compiled a well-organized and well-edited *Physician's Handbook: Screening for MBD* which contained much valuable information and usable forms for the collection of data including history, neurological examination, psychological screening, language screening, preschool and educational screening. This material was prepared by S. Clements *et al.* of the Child Study Center of the University of Arkansas Medical Center and T. Hicks of the State of Arkansas Department of Education.

In completing such a form, parents or parent surrogates are helped to focus on significant aspects of the child's longitudinal development, to supply basic and often vital information related to the developmental history, and to recall earlier evaluations, including dates, places, studies, and the names of the consultants/evaluators/therapists. Parents appreciate the opportunity of being included from the outset in this aspect of the evaluation, and it prepares them more adequately for the second step, which includes taking a medical, social, and educational history from the parents or the responsible informants.

Taking a Medical, Social, and Educational History

Essentially, there are at least four key issues in taking a history from the parents of children suspected of functioning within one of the SLD/MBD/HKS Syndromes:

(1) *Establish a basic trust between the parents and the historian and/or evaluators.*

(2) *Enhance the credibility of the parents as informants,* by helping them feel comfortable, supported, unthreatened, and appreciated as the providers of life-long ongoing care and support to their developing LD child and to other children in the family.

(3) *Establish a flow* in the interview which allows for a longitudinal developmental orientation, as well as for the parents' expressed concern

Address block for parents'
name and address

Dear (Parents'/Guardians'/Surrogates' Complete Name):

As part of the _____(School District)_____ response to the new Public
Law 94-142 we would like to provide a psychoeducational evaluation for
__(child's complete name)__ to assure that he/she has been appropriately placed in our educational system.

Our teaching faculty has referred your child for this evaluation in
relation to the following areas of learning: _____
_____
_____

Our plan for the evaluation includes:

Type of Test Procedure   Suggested Date of Evaluation

_____   _____

_____   _____

_____   _____

We have encouraged our teaching faculty to share with you all the information which went into our consideration of your child for this evaluation. In
addition, you have the right to see, to study, and to discuss with our staff all
the information in your child's school record. If you would like to review
your child's records and/or arrange a school conference, you may call
__(Staff member, phone number, and hours during day when (s)he can__
__ be reached)__ .

If this evaluation shows that your child could benefit from and is eligible
for the program and its related services, we will ask for your assistance in preparing an Individualized Education Program for him/her.

If you feel you have enough information without reviewing your child's
records and without requesting a conference, please indicate your approval
by signing below:

_____

Signature of parent/guardian/surrogate   If you do not wish the
                                               evaluation done, please sign
Date: _____   here and we will call you
                                               about a conference time

_____   _____

Signature of parent/guardian/surrogate
Date: _____   Date: _____

Sample Letter 2.2
Due Process Notice for IEP Plan

Address block for parents'
name and address

Dear   (Parents'/Guardians'/Surrogates' complete name):

We are happy to share with you this official notice that your child
___(name of student)___ has been recommended for the following
educational assignment as a result of our psychoeducational evaluation
completed on ___(date)___ .

We would like to encourage you to participate with our school personnel
in a program planning conference to discuss this assignment and the recommended program content. You may agree or disagree with the outcome of
this conference and request a hearing with the local school district if you
have questions or reservations about the Individualized Education Program
as it is developed.

If you wish to participate in a program conference to assist in planning
your child's educational program, please sign below and return within 10
days if this was sent to you by certified mail or within 5 days if you received
this notice at a school conference.

If you do not plan to return this notice within the time period specified,
you should know that you waive the right to a program planning conference
and your right to a hearing for one year.

_____

_____

_____

Local School District and
Responsible Official

( )   I wish to sit in on a program planning conference to discuss the
educational assignment and program proposed for my child.

( )   I do not wish to participate in the program planning conference
and understand that I waive my right to a conference and a hearing
for one year.

Date: _____   _____
                             Signature of parent/guardian/surrogate

Date: _____   _____
                             Signature of parent/guardian/surrogate

PRELIMINARY CASE STUDY INFORMATION
(Please print or type all information)

Child's Name _____ Birthdate __/__/__ Age___
      (last)   (first)   mo. day yr.

Address _____ Phone _____
    (street)   (city)   (state)

Father's Occupation_____ Bus. Phone _____

Father's Business Address _____

Marital Status of Parents: Married ____ Separated ____ Divorced____ Widowed_____

Member of Family (Name)	Age	Birthdate	Address	Education
Father:				
Mother:(inc. maiden name)				
Siblings				
(1)				
(2)				
(3)				
(4)				
(5)				
(6)				

Other in Household	Age	Relationship to Child		

Problems presented by your child:_____
_____
_____
_____
_____
_____
_____
_____

Preliminary Case Study Information

Check the appropriate colums for any of the following:

ILLNESSES	Age	Hospitalized Yes	No	Dates	One parent remained with child at hospital (overnight also) Yes	No
Asthma						
Bronchitis						
Chicken Pox						
Diabetes						
Diphtheria						
Ear Infections						
Eczema						
Encephalitis						
Epileptic Seizures						
Food Allergies						
Gastro-Intestinal Disorder						
Hay Fever						
Kidney Disease						
Measles						
Meningitis						
Mumps						
Pneumonia						
Rheumatic Fever						
Scarlet Fever						
Thyroid Disease						
Tonsillitis						
Tuberculosis						
Whooping Cough						
Other						

OPERATIONS

	Age	Yes	No	Dates	Yes	No
Appendix						
Circumcision						
Hernia						
Teeth						
Tonsils, adenoids						
Other						

INJURIES (specify type) _____

_____

_____

Preliminary Case Study Information

If your child has had any accidents, describe. Include age at that time   whether stitches or surgery were necessary, and whether hospitalization resulted.

_____

_____

_____

_____

_____

If your child has any difficulties in vision, speech, or hearing, describe:_____

_____

Describe any other physical handicaps your child may have _____

_____

If your child needs any help at the toilet, describe:_____

_____

If your child is subject to constipation or bedwetting, describe:_____

_____

If your child is subject to fainting spells, monentary lapse of consciousness, or seizures, describe:_____

_____

If your child is allergic to insect bites, to penicillin or other drugs, or to anything else, describe:_____

Has your child reached puberty? If so, when, and any emotional reactions to it?_____

_____

Does your child receive any medication ?_____ Name of medication_____

Medication prescribed by _____ Date prescribed _____

Name of child's physician_____ Phone _____

Address _____ Date of last Physical_____

List other doctors, hospitals, clinics, etc. where you child has been examined.
Name and Address _____ Purpose _____ Date_____

_____

_____

_____

_____

_____

Preliminary Case Study Information

Has your child had a psychological examination? (Check)   Yes _____   No _____

If yes, Where ? _____ Date _____

Has your child had psychotherapy? (check)   Yes_____   No_____   If yes,

with whom ? _____ Inclusive Dates _____

Have you received professional counselling about your child? (Check) Yes _____ No _____

If yes, by whom ?_____

Inclusive Dates_____

Has either parent received any type of psychological help other than in connection with your

child? _____   Mother _____   Father _____

With whom ? _____

Inclusive Dates _____

Has your child attended school?   Yes _____   No _____

If yes,   WHERE   WHEN

_____

_____

_____

Who referred you to Dr._____? _____

_____

The completed case study with recommendations can be sent to any professional person or
agency responsible for your child's welfare or progress.

To whom do you want the report sent? (Indicate below - full name and address)

      Name   Address

_____

_____

_____

_____

This information was supplied by _____

Date _____

about the emerging problems of the present (cross-sectional developmental issues).

(4) *Set in motion* (*mobilize*) *a process* with parents or parent surrogates which may include: (a) collecting historical data; (b) assaying the transactional quality of mothering, the mother-infant dyad, and the larger family system; (c) preparing the child for inclusion in all aspects of the evaluation which will take place over a period of time and, perhaps, with different consultants or evaluators in different offices or laboratories; (d) organizing and integrating the data; and (e) interpreting, or being part of the team which will interpret to parents the inferences and the IEP plan to be drawn up from the data collected.

In regard to the educational/clinical inferences and their relevance to the design of an IEP plan, Rappaport (1965) succinctly stated:

> Diagnosis classically is defined as the art of identifying a disease (or syndrome) from its symptoms. Prognosis is defined as the art of foretelling the course of a disease (or syndrome) and the prospect of recovering from it . . . The greater the information, the more astute the inferences we can draw. (p. 53)

An outline of significant topical areas and a possible order for taking the history might include the following:

Chief concern or presenting problems. It is good to begin where parents are in their concerns and to note whether these concerns parallel those expressed by the schools as the basis of their request for a psychoeducational evaluation.

Elaboration of the problem. Encourage parents to discuss the problem more fully as it affects the family, siblings, peers, and the impact on the child and his/her parents.

Family constellation. Inquire about all the siblings and near relatives living in and out of the home, including a description of their school achievements and personality characteristics.

Family history. Inquire about the assets and liabilities in the mother's and father's experiences while growing up in their own individual families, and obtain a brief medical and social history of mother's and father's families and nature of the extended family support in the past and present.

Gestational history. Should include questions related to reproductive cycle, marital and financial situation at time of pregnancy, mother's sense of support in new role of motherhood, and questions pertaining to the following:

(a) mild toxemia (edema, increased BP, scotomata);

(b) diabetic symptoms;

(c) spotting, hemorrhage, or threatened miscarriage;

(d) certain drugs, such as diethylstilbestrol, tobacco, coffee;

(e) virus infections (German measles and other viruses); and

(f) prematurity.

Perinatal history. Questions pertaining to the following:

(a) labor and delivery (length, nature, instruments);

(b) anesthetic;

(c) resuscitation;

(d) APGAR scores at one and five minutes (may be requested from the hospital where child was delivered); and

(e) infant's response at birth: cry, color, sucking reflex, feeding patterns, activity patterns, and sleep patterns.

Developmental history (may be taken from Preliminary Case Information Form). Questions by ages from newborn period up to current time, including:

(a) developmental landmarks (social smile, rolling over, sitting alone, anxiety with strangers, crawling, walking, babbling, speech, toilet training—wetting, soiling);

(b) significant medical/surgical problems and hospitalizations;

(c) psychosocial adjustment within and outside the family.

(The Vineland Social Maturity Scale [Doll, 1936] is sometimes useful in helping parents pinpoint how their child has developed in relation to self-help/care skills and in social relationships.)

Educational and recreational history. Careful review of the cumulative educational record, by grades, for areas of strengths and weaknesses, including also sports interests and skills and extracurricular social activities.

Current attitudes and feelings toward both parents. Inquire how child/adolescent shows positive, caring, loving feelings toward mother and father, and how negative feelings of disagreement, difference, irritation, and anger are expressed toward each parent.

Summarize factors influencing the parent-child-family relational patterns. Such as:

(a) degree of visibility of the disability or handicap;

(b) anticipated prognosis of disability;

(c) parental fantasies about what child ought to be;

(d) realistic or excessive levels of parental over- or under-expectations;

(e) child's capacity to satisfy or frustrate parental expectations, ego needs, and parental role strivings;

(f) relationship to other adequate or handicapped siblings; and

(g) cultural factors, such as rural or urban living, religion, and economic status.

Recognizing the Emotional Concomitants to SLD/MBD/HKS

An important part of the psychosocial assessment of SLD/MBD/HKS children is the recognition of the emotional concomitants associated with these syndromes. Rappaport (1964) was among the first investigators to offer a useful grouping of the cardinal behavioral symptoms of MBD.

His grouping is included here with some elaborations (*) by the author:

I. Inadequate Impulse Control or Regulation
    A. Hyperactivity-hyperkinesis
    B. Hyperdistractibility
    C. Disinhibition (constant motion)
    D. Impulsivity
    E. Perseveration
    F. Lability of affect
    G. Motor dysfunctions (poor motility control)
    *H. Inability to delay or "transform" impulses into trial-action functions, such as:
        (1) thought processes
        (2) verbalizations which carry both feeling and motor action
    *I. Attentional problems, such as:
        (1) coming to attention
        (2) delaying impulse/gratification response
        (3) sustaining task over time
        (4) motivation and intention factors

II. Inadequate Integrative Functions
    A. Perceptual difficulties
    B. Conceptual difficulties

III. Defective Self-Concept and Narcissistic Hypersensitivity
    A. Low frustration tolerance
    B. Failure-avoidant behavior (flight from challenge)
    C. Overcompensation

D.   Control and manipulation of others
E.   Negativism or power struggle
*F. Feeling of body mutilation and poor body image
*G. Low self-esteem: being different equated with being bad
*H. Internalization of anger, may lead to:
      (1) passive-resistant personality
      (2) agitated-depression
*I. Persistent quest for identity and adequacy
*J. Fear reactions:
      (1) fear of new experiences
      (2) fear of failure
      (3) fear of separation
      (4) fear of own aggression
      (5) fear of being unloved

Several case studies are presented in Chapter 3 to illustrate how these behavioral symptoms may be present in SLD/MBD/HKS children during a psychological evaluation to assess cognitive function. In Chapter 6, a case study is presented which illustrates how these emotional concomitants, along with the predominant ego coping mechanisms outlined below, can be manifested in an emotionally crippling way, and the part individual psychotherapy may play in undoing and resolving many of these symptoms.

Abrams (1968) added the observation that the ego defense mechanisms were the most significant of the emotional factors affecting learning and that all studies of learning disabilities and psychoeducational evaluations of SLD/MBD/HKS children should be oriented toward the concept of ego defense. This brief outline of some of the ego coping mechanisms has been added to the Rappaport (1964) grouping described above:

IV. Predominant Ego Coping Mechanisms
    A.   Denial (most prominent)
    B.   Withdrawal reaction into:
        (1) isolation
        (2) fantasies
        (3) illness and dependency
    C.   Regressive reaction to earlier, safer levels
    D.   Use of the symptom as a defense: "I am injured, damaged so I can't do it." There is generalization of one or two deficiencies into a total defense or a more self-limiting, constricted personality pattern.

E. Use of a "clowning reaction" to cover deficiencies: "I am silly and a dunce because I have chosen to be, not because I have deficits which make me that way."

F. Reaction formation leading to ego constriction

Abrams (1968) recognized that the concept of ego defense referred to any psychological operation that is intended to block the discharge of threatening, rejected impulses and, thereby, the painful emotional consequences of such a discharge. When the ego defenses are threatened, the student's ability to function in a learning situation may be impaired by the breakthrough of drive derivatives, the return to primary process functioning in regression, or the intensification of the defensive efforts.

Pearson (1972) noted that primary process functioning served to distort the student's ability to catalogue, associate, and make logical the knowledge which is learned. In adolescence particularly, increased sexual and aggressive drives reactivate elements of the Oedipal/Electra conflicts which also intensify the utilization of defense mechanisms.

Abrams (1968) also postulated the effects these various coping mechanisms of defense might have on learning. *Repression and inhibition* of ego function could limit the accumulation of knowledge by restricting the amount of material available for assimilation. The *withdrawal reaction* with *isolation of affect* could mean stifling both feelings and fantasies, critical elements in the learning process. *Reaction formation* would put SLD/MBD/HKS children and adolescents in the bind of being unable to differentiate between activity which is constructively aggressive and that which is destructively aggressive. An ego constriction could result in which expression of any aggressive impulses are muted and become passive, compliant, and inadequate. To maintain these various ego-coping mechanisms of defense often requires such a large expenditure of energy that very little mental energy is available for the more complex, higher cortical learning functions (Blanchard, 1964).

Working with Parents, Parental Surrogates, or Guardians

An effort has been made throughout this chapter to illustrate the basic philosophy of working with parents, parental surrogates, or guardians. Chapter 7 will describe in greater detail the process of counseling parents. Chapter 10 will elaborate on the relational dynamics within the family constellation and describe the various methods of effective intervention in working with families.

SCREENING METHODS

Two general methods might be used for screening the large numbers of children suspected of functioning with SLD/MBD/HKS. These could be referred to as the gross screening methods ("lumping") and the fine screening methods ("splintering"). The essential differences in the two methods center around manpower and economic realities, as well as basic philosophic polarities.

It seems doubtful that either the public educational system or private agencies will have the trained personnel and economic resources to complete an extensive (fine screening) evaluation on all the preschool and school-age children who should be evaluated for possible SLD/MBD/HKS. Consequently, some of the well-designed gross screening methods which have been developed would be a good initial starting point for the population to be evaluated. This process would serve to identify and "lump together" all children with learning problems into several categories, such as Developmentally Disabled (DD), Learning Disabled (LD), Mentally Retarded (MR), or Emotionally Disturbed (ED), and to allow for an Individualized Education Program plan (IEP) to be set in motion from such an assessment and prescription. The designation "developmentally disabled" has the advantage of being close to a noncategorical funding designation which cuts across all developmental systems: educational, psychological, biological, neurological, and sociocultural.

At the other end of the continuum would be the more complete fine screening methods useful for subdividing the larger categories into smaller subgroups of homogeneous syndromes largely by etiology, results of refined laboratory procedures, or higher cortical functions assessed in carefully designed and standardized neuroeducational and cognitive studies.

It is important to note that these two methods should not be mutually exclusive. Rather, in any case in which gross screening methods indicate the need for more extensive and refined studies and/or the student has failed to progress academically and socially in response to the IEP, these fine screening methods should be completed as well.

Gross Screening Methods

BASIC PSYCHODIAGNOSTIC EVALUATION

This is the cornerstone for school-age children and would follow the outline of this handbook, including the following areas:

(1) Assessment of the past medical, social, and educational history, as described in Chapter 2.
(2) Assessment of physical health, psychosocial and intrafamily adjustment, as described in Chapter 2.
(3) Assessment of cognitive functions, as described in Chapter 3.
(4) Assessment of educational functions within a diagnostic teaching and task analysis frame of reference, as described in Chapter 4.
(5) Assessment of visual, hearing, and language functions, as described in Chapters 4 and 5.

PHYSICIANS' HANDBOOK: SCREENING FOR MBD

This handbook, described earlier under preliminary case study information, suggested that the most useful, all-inclusive screening test for reading, writing, spelling, and math is the Wide Range Achievement Test (Jastak, 1940). It was noted that, although scores from this test tend to be high, it gives a quick and fairly comprehensive evaluation of the student's major academic skill areas.

DENVER DEVELOPMENTAL SCREENING TEST

This is an excellent instrument for the primary physician to use in screening out developmental delays during infancy and the pre-school years. As an adaptation of the Gesell Developmental Schedules, it can be used for annual evaluations of the young child from ages 1 month to 6 years. This screening tool may serve to pinpoint developmental deviations which may need more complete investigation, as it focuses on gross and fine motor functions, speech and language development, adaptive functions related to cognitive, perceptual, and conceptual processes, and personal-social interactive development. Measurement of head circumference, height, and weight is also an important part of this screening process.

OTHER GROSS SCREENING TOOLS FOR SCHOOL AGE CHILDREN

For the primary physician evaluating a school-age child with suspected SLD/MBD/HKS, the following studies may be done to select those children who will need a more complete psychodiagnostic-educational-neurological workup.

(1) Peabody Picture Vocabulary Test (1965). Although this test should be interpreted with considerable caution because it gives spuri-

ously "high" results, it is easily administered and gives an estimation of the child's receptive vocabulary. The child is given a word signal which calls for the selection of the correct pictorial representation from a choice of four items. This test has been standardized for ages 1 year, 9 months to 10 years.

(2) The Draw-a-Person Test. The child is asked to draw a person. From the drawing, one can derive an approximation of the child's social/mental age scored by the Goodenough system (1926) or by the Bakwin *et al.* (1948) modified list of 28 criteria. Additionally, the drawing reflects the level of the child's perceptual-motor development and elements of the projections of himself/herself as a person: the body image (Schilder, 1935) and the self-concept (Wylie, 1961). Machover (1949, 1953) has become the most widely quoted in the field of personality projections in human figure drawings. However, she offers no scoring system or controlled research to support her hypotheses. Koppitz (1968) hypothesized that human figure drawings reflect primarily the child's current level of development, attitudes toward himself/herself as a person and toward significant others in the environment, and attitudes and concerns toward life's stresses, fears, and anxieties and ways of coping with them. She concluded that the particular value of human figure drawing could be seen in its sensitivity to change within the child: a portrait of the inner child in that moment or space of time.

(3) Visual-motor association processes tests. Any one or two of the following tests can be administered in the physician's office or in the office of a clinical psychologist or psychiatrist to evaluate the eye-hand coordination level of development.

(a) The Rutgers Drawing Test (Starr) is easily administered and reflects levels of visual-motor development from 3 to 6 years.

(b) The Slosson Drawing Coordination Test is a well structured visual-motor test also easily administered and scored.

(c) The Imitation of Gestures Test (Berges and Lezini is reported to be a fair test for culturally disadvantaged children ages 3 to 6 years and scored without difficulty.

(d) The Bender Visual-Motor Gestalt Test can be administered to children and adolescents age 5 to 21 years. It is described in Chapter 3.

(4) Academic achievement and auditory perception. These areas should be surveyed by specialists in diagnostic education as outlined in Chapter 4. However, for those physicians and clinicians unable to secure these services the following evaluation tools could be used:

(a) The Gray's Oral Reading Paragraph Test is graduated reading from grades 1-12.

(b) The Slosson Oral Reading Test is a graded word recognition test.

(c) The CIBA *Screening for MBD* handbook has sections for spelling and arithmetic skills.

(d) The Wepman Auditory Discrimination Test is widely used to determine auditory discrimination ability from ages 5 through 8 years.

Fine Screening Methods and Complete SLD/MBD/HKS Evaluation

A full and complete evaluation would consist of most, if not all, of the procedures outlined below:

(1) *Complete past medical, obstetric, perinatal, and developmental history,* as outlined earlier in this chapter. Since parents are not always reliable informants, it is helpful to ask for permission to write to hospitals for specific information and to look at baby books, pictures, and home movies, if they are available.

(2) *Complete family history,* including the financial, marital, and emotional conditions into which the child was born, as well as the current situation. Also, the educational and emotional history of the family constellation, including grandparents, parents and siblings.

(3) *Complete physical examination,* with special reference to minor physical anomalies of hands, feet, head, ears, face, and mouth. Quinn *et al.* (1977) have highlighted the positive correlations between the high frequency of anomalies at birth and hyperactivity at 1 year with a family history of hyperactivity, obstetrical complications, and/or behavior disorders. Goodman and Gorlin (1977) have written an excellent survey of genetic influences resulting in SLD/MBD/HKS symptomatology, especially those conditions which can be identified in infancy by facial anomalies.

(4) *Complete neurological examination,* including careful assessment of sight and hearing. There has been some controversy as to how helpful this procedure is in identifying problem and laying the groundwork for remedial education. An unbiased, scientific point of view would strongly point to the necessity for such an assessment as part of a full and fine screening evaluation. A more complete statement of the neurological evaluation of newborns and infants, as distinct

from the evaluation of school-age children, has been added to this chapter to underline the importance of this procedure in the total evaluation.

(5) *Complete assessment of cognitive functions,* as outlined in Chapter 3.

(6) *Complete assessment of educational achievement and learning skills,* as described in Chapter 4.

(7) *Complete assessment of neurophysiological status using the electroencephalogram,* basic waking and sleep records, hyperventilation and photic stimulation responses, and the evoked potential responses, if available. EEG studies in SLD/MBD/HKS populations have been highly variable. An apparent breakthrough in the electrophysiological measurements of brain function related to information processing has been reported by John *et al.* (1977). A computerized electrophysiological test battery for the quantitative assessment of brain function was developed and tested by John and his associates at the New York Medical College. The method has been called "neurometrics" and comprises EEG and average evoked response measurements under conditions which assess sensory, perceptual, and cognitive processes, as well as the structural integrity of the brain.

Studies completed on 533 children from a school for the educationally handicapped as compared to data on 85 children considered unequivocally normal revealed the following:

(a) 78.3% of the LD children had unusual EEG features, compared to 20% of the normal children.

(b) 77.3% of the LD children revealed EEG dysfunctions derived from more than one anatomical location of the brain, compared to 0% of the normal group showing similar multiple region dysfunction in the parietooccipital, central, or temporal areas.

(c) Certain abnormal EEG patterns were found more frequently in children under 12 years, while other pattern clusters were found mostly in teenagers.

(8) Assessment of chromosomal, endocrine, skull x-ray studies, and other biochemical laboratory studies as indicated by the seven areas above, and suggested in Table 2.4.

Neurological Evaluation of Newborns and Infants

Gold (1977) has stressed the importance of a neurodevelopmental approach in the pediatric neurologic examination. What is considered

Table 2.4
Laboratory Assessment Procedures

6-hour glucose tolerance test (evaluation of sugar metabolism)

17-keto steroid in urine (evaluation of male hormone function)

T_4 by column (for thyroid function)

PBI (for thyroid function)

Electroencephalogram

Skull X-rays

Blood serology

Chromosome studies (for cerebral metabolic disorders)

24-hour urine for chromatographic studies of amino acid and protein metabolism

normal for one chronologic age would be abnormal at an older age. He emphasized that many of the so-called "soft" neurological signs observed in the SLD/MBD population are related to deficient neurological development. In highlighting the essential features of a neurologic examination of infants and children, Gold stressed the following eight areas:

(1) *Brain growth,* as determined by measurement of head circumference, which correlates roughly with brain size and weight. For example, the head circumference of the normal neonate is approximately 35 cm (300 gms. in brain weight) and increases to 46 cm (900 gms. in brain weight) by 1 year.

(2) *Postural, oral, and ocular reflexes* in the newborn period. The symmetrical Moro reflex of the normal neonate disappears by 3 to 4 months. Relative spasticity with hyperactive reflexes, clonus, and an extensor Babinski reflex response are normal for the newborn infant. The Babinski response should become a normal flexor, toe-down response by 24 months of age. The rooting, lip, sucking, and swallowing reflexes should be strong and active at birth, with a gradual disappearance of all but the swallowing reflex by 12 months of age. It has been known for some time that a poor, weak, or inadequate sucking reflex in the newborn is strongly suggestive that the child is at risk for the subsequent development of language skills and, perhaps, other higher cortical skills associated with learning as well.

(3) *Developmental gross motor (locomotion) milestones* in the normally developing infant and preschool child have been outlined by

Gesell and Amatruda (1947), Gold (1977), and others, as follows:

Birth to 1 month: infant lifts head lying in prone position
5 months: turns over
6-8 months: sits without support
10 months: crawls and stands
12-15 months: walks alone with toddler gait
3½ years: rides tricycle
5 years: walks with narrower base gait
and can hop on one foot
6-7 years: rides bicycle without training wheels

(4) *Developmental language milestones* represent a central feature in the distorted development of many SLD/MBD/HKS children. Gold's (1977) discussion of this central factor influencing learning and personality development can be greatly expanded in regard to this population of children and adolescents.

The sequence of normal language development has been ably studied and described by many investigators, including Leopold (1939), Gesell and Amatruda (1947), McCarthy (1954), Piaget (1929), Mecham (1959, 1963), McCarthy and Kirk (1961), Brown (1975) and, most recently, K. Nelson (1977) and K.E. Nelson (1977). For purposes of evaluating developmental language milestones in SLD/MBD/HKS children, it is important to recognize several of the self-organizing individual experiences which take place concurrently but with different degrees of primacy, during the process of language development. Strauss and Kephart (1955) identified these experiences as the development of the sensorimotor perception of the environment, the mechanics of vocalization, including the neurophysiology of phonation and audition, and personality development, which includes the emerging nonverbal and verbal interactions and interpersonal relationships developing between the child and the significant others in his/her environment. As perceptual development continues in the child, different words are perceived to have different meanings, or symbols, and a process of language symbolization becomes established. By isolating certain similar elements from a number of perceptions, the beginning of concept formation can take place. This process of conceptualization is normally well under way by the seventh to eighth year, so that the child is less perceptual in both thinking and behavior and more and more conceptually oriented.

K. Nelson (1977) has added to this formulation by observing that language has its roots in both the social communication system of the child and in the child's cognitive organization of the world. She stressed, however, that neither of these serves as a sufficient language base without exposure to a language model (i.e., talking in a short and simple style, both in content and form, to avoid using language with children which is beyond their ability to process). Nelson emphasized that there is enormous variability among children in their ways of expressing meaning, ranging from a spontaneous creative gesture to vocalization of a precise language symbol. The best predictor of eventual language competence appeared to be early language comprehension, although Nelson noted enough variability in the pattern of the acquisition to suggest caution in making long-range predictions. She concluded that, with the present knowledge of the process of language acquisition, it would be a mistake to conclude that a child of 2 or 2½ who is slow in expressive language would continue to be slow later, or even that such slowness would reflect persistent underlying difficulties. On the other hand, it has been the observation of the author that, in later elementary and secondary school years, auditory receptive language skills, written expression, syntax, and occasionally spelling are often more significant areas of difficulty for the SLD/MBD/HKS children than are the verbal (oral) expression areas.

In addition to the above, Rutherford (1977) noted that little attention had been paid to the ability to retrieve from memory the significant words needed to represent thought content. He suggested that this type of language dysfunction, referred to as dysnomia or word-finding difficulty, was frequently found in children with SLD/MBD/HKS and in 35% to 50% of young children who stutter. The specific instrument used in these clinical studies was the Northwestern Word Latency Test.

Although different children have different rates and different patterns in the development of language, there is general agreement that most children in our western culture show the language landmarks outlined in Table 2.5.

(5) *Development of fine motor manipulation skills* is another significant area in the examination suggested by Gold (1977). He observed the following developmental pattern:

> at birth: neonate maintains a fisted hand and flexed elbow ("straphanger's position")
> 3 months: hand opens up
> 4 months: midline hand play
> 5 months: reaching for objects
> 6/7 months: transfers objects from one hand to another

Table 2.5
Normal Developmental Language Landmarks*

Age	Pattern and Process
1 month	Differential crying for discomfort, pain, and hunger.
2 months	Random vocalization: definite reaction to different voices.
2-6 months	Coos as response: coos or crows to express pleasure.
5-6 months	Babbling: experimenting with primitive sounds.
7-9 months	Reduplicated monosyllables: "ma-ma" and "da-da."
12 months	Imitation of words with circular reflex reaction pattern (by making sounds, stimulates self to make more sounds). Normal echolalia: imitation with blind repetitious parroting.
13-15 months	Expressive jargon: imitation of speech with inflection and fidelity.
11-17 months	Obeys simple commands and prohibitions.
15-17 months	Recognizes names of common objects and parts of his/her body.
17-24 months	Combines words: two-word sentences.
24-30 months	Expressive vocabulary of 50 to 275 words. Uses pronouns: I, me, and you. Understands two prepositions: up and down. Mainly egocentric speech, centered around self. Greater use of verb-like words, possessive forms, and prepositions to make comparisons, define boundaries, and express feelings of ownership.
36 months	Simple "kernel sentences" with subject, verb, and object. Up to 900 expressive words. Less egocentric communications.
42 months	Mastery of *b, m, p, h,* and *w* sounds.
48 months	Names all primary colors accurately. Beginning to understand number concepts (2) and to follow three individual commands using prepositions. Can apply transformational rules to produce more complex sentences. Vocabulary of 1,600 words. Has mastered all vowel sounds and nine consonants. Responds to who, what, where questions.
54 months	Mastery of *y, k, g, (f),* and *d* sounds.
60 months	Uses speech as a social tool and for social communication. Responds appropriately to question "how many?" Carries out three-part commands.
66 months	Mastery of *f* (*s* and *z* only temporarily) sounds. Understands number concept of 10. Has good right-left orientation. Has concepts of more and less, many and few, morning and afternoon.

Table 2.5 *(Continued)*

Age	Pattern and Process
78 months	Mastery of *v, zh, sh, th* and *l* sounds.
96 months	Mastery of *r, z,* and *s* sounds.
	Bulk of language learning is complete.
	An increase in abstract reasonsing and mastery of complex ideas.
	Conceptualization process underway.

*The above table is a summarization of observations from Stone and Church (1957), Mecham (1963), Blanchard (1964), and Striffler (1976).

> 12 months: pincer movement and apposition of thumb and index finger
>
> 5/6 years: tripod positioning of crayon and pencil between thumb and index finger with support from middle finger.
>
> 8 years: tripod positioning with flexion and extension of finger joint which allows for cursive writing.

Difficulty in buttoning and tying laces and palmar grasp of crayons and pencils beyond the age of 5/6 years would suggest delayed or impaired fine motor manipulation skills. In the area of normal and abnormal motor function, Johnston (1967) has written one of the more comprehensive descriptions, especially focused on aberrant development in cerebral palsy.

(6) *Development of perceptual-motor skills.* In his review of the essential features of a neurologic examination of infants and children, Gold (1977) mentioned but did not elaborate on the area of perceptual-motor skills. For many SLD/MBD/HKS children and adolescents, this is a central area of dysfunction. One of the reasons suggested is that the visual-motor pathway which runs from the visual center in the occipital cortex (the posterior part of the cerebral hemisphere) to the frontal motor cortex (the anterior part of the cerebral hemisphere) is one of the longest and, therefore, most vulnerable pathways in the brain to perinatal or viral insults.

Normative data have been obtained on geometric figures such as the Rutgers Drawing Test (Starr, 1969) and the Bender Gestalt Visual

Motor Test (1946) described in Chapter 3. The former has been standardized from ages 3 to 6 years, and the latter picks up neurological developments from age 6 and extends to ages 8 or 9 years (Koppitz, 1963).

(7) *Behavioral evaluation* is the final area which Gold (1977) suggested should be part of the developmental neurological examination. In this area, Tronick and Brazelton (1975), along with Greenberg (1971), made a strong and most significant observation when they noted that the problems of at-risk infants are compounded by maternal and familial environments which are not able to adjust to their neonate's special needs. The marital, environmental, and personal stresses on the quality of mothering (and parenting) available to the newborn serve as an additional force that may prevent the kind of integration of the central nervous system (CNS) that is necessary for recovery and plasticity in the biologic development and biosocial (ego) maturation of an already vulnerable central nervous system.

In addition, these authors suggested that the APGAR and pediatric neurological examinations, as presently designed, are successful in detecting growth abnormalities but have been less effective in detecting mild CNS dysfunction during the neonatal period. Brazelton (1973) developed a Neonatal Behavioral Assessment utilizing 26 behavioral responses to environmental stimuli which included the kind of interpersonal stimuli mothers use in their efforts to help their newborns adapt to new environments. In addition to an assessment of the 26 items of behavior on a 9-point scale, 20 reflexes can be assessed on a 3-point scale. This Brazelton assessment scale features the infant's response to repeated visual and auditory stimuli, to pinprick, to inanimate visual and auditory stimuli (a ball and rattle), and to the animate visual and auditory stimuli (examiner's face and voice). Brazelton also suggests noting the quality and duration of alert periods, general muscle tone, responses to being cuddled, reactions to a cloth over the infant's face, nature of the child's consolability, and such things as the degree of tremulousness, excitement, and capacity to control the self, the rapidity of the buildup of the crying state, the lability of skin color, and the self-quieting activity or the attempts of the infant to console himself or herself.

Beyond the neonatal period so carefully monitored by the Brazelton Scale, the developmental behavioral evaluation might follow the items suggested in Table 2.3 of this chapter, which outlines the normal stages of personality development within the framework of the developmental theorists Freud, Erikson, Piaget, and Mahler.

Neurological Evaluation of School Age Children

Schain (1973) observed that the neurological evaluation for the young school-age child was quite similar to the conventional neurological examination for adults. He stressed that no normative data or standards of reliability are available on the age of acquiring adequate performance for rapid pronation-supination of hands, tandem walking, the choreiform response of outstretched hands, and the occurrence of "mirror" or overflow movements from the voluntary hand to the hand on the opposite side of the body. All of these functions are evaluated as potential "soft" signs of neurologic impairment.

Schain cautioned the neurological consultant not to allow suspicion of the hazier "soft" neurological signs to justify a diagnosis of brain dysfunction, minimal or otherwise. Adams *et al.* (1974) also observed that 9- and 10-year-old learning-disabled children could not be reliably distinguished from normally achieving children by the use of "soft" neurological signs used in their study. In their opinion, classroom observation and selected psychoeducational testing appeared a more logical approach to the identification of learning disabilities in this population of older elementary school age children.

Establishment of laterality, on the other hand, does have normative data from Belmont and Birch (1963), who found wide variations in using their Body Awareness Test. For a population of bright, normal, middle-class children, they found that reliably preferential hand usage (in four handedness tasks) had been established by the age of 9 years. Ninety-five percent of these children above 7 years were able to respond to seven questions concerned with right-left awareness of their own body parts.

McCormick (1977) has written a description of a complete pediatric evaluation appropriate for the school-age child with learning problems. His statement goes beyond the routine pediatric examination and would supplement the guidelines discussed in this handbook.

Psychiatric Evaluation and Assessment of Psychopathology

In focusing so explicitly and extensively on the learning disabilities and possible neurologic impairments from which they may be derived, it is possible to overlook very significant emotional problems and borderline conditions in these children.

Lewis (1976) described such a case and cautioned that, if treatment of such borderline or ego-disturbed children was prescribed solely on the basis of presumed SLD/MBD/HKS which the child may or may not have, there was the risk of the child's acquiring "an added iatrogenic vulnerability" (p. 131). That is, the overzealous clinical team could miss or inadequately treat the severe emotional disturbances by being overly concerned about the SLD/MBD/HKS symptomatology.

Lewis suggested that the use of A. Freud's (1965) metapsychological profile would be one safeguard against this kind of clinical blind spot and oversight. This diagnostic profile was extended and elaborated upon for infants by W. Freud (1971), for latency age children by Meers (1966), and for adolescents by Laufer (1965).

Chapter 6 below highlights many of the central emotional conflicts with which SLD/MBD/HKS children struggle and ways in which individual psychotherapy may assist them in coping with these problems. Chapter 11 describes the current application of the principles of behavior modification to the emotional needs of these children at home and at school. Chapter 12 describes the ways in which the therapies of art, music, and dance (movement) may be helpful to the SLD/MBD/HKS population. Chapters 7 and 10 focus on some of the broader issues related to counseling the parents and families of these children.

SUMMARY

This chapter has outlined the gross and fine screening methods which might be used by general practicing physicians, pediatricians, family practitioners, psychiatrists, psychologists, social workers, and educators to screen populations of children following the mandate of Public Law 94-142.

Techniques range from general methods to scientific procedures, but a multidisciplinary approach is emphasized for the most complete fine screening method. An attempt has been made to present this material in an unbiased, scientific way while maintaining a clinical approach which is also deeply caring and humane in respect to the individual child/adolescent, his/her family system, and sociocultural environment into which he/she is born.

REFERENCES

Abrams, J. The role of personality defenses in reading. In G. Natchez (Ed.), *Children with reading problems.* New York: Basic Books, Inc., 1968.

Adams, R., Kocsis, J., & Estes, R. Soft neurological signs in learning disabled children and controls. *American Journal of Diseases of Children,* 1974, *125*(5), 614–618.

Bakwin, R., Weider, A., & Bakwin, H. Psychologic aspects of pediatrics. *Journal of Pediatrics,* 1948, *33,* 384.

Belmont, L. & Birch, H. Lateral dominance and right-left awareness in normal children. *Child Development,* 1963, *34,* 257–270.

Belmont, L. & Birch, H. Lateral dominance, lateral awareness, and reading disability. *Child Development,* 1965, *36*(1), 57–71.

Bender, L. *Bender motor gestalt test: Cards and manual of instructions.* American Orthopsychiatric Association, Inc., 1946.

Berges, J. & Lezini, I. The imitation of gestures. *Clinics in Developmental Medicine,* 1965, No. 19.

Blanchard, P. Psychoanalytic contributions to the problem of reading disabilities. *Psychoanalytic Study of the Child,* 1946, *2,* 163–170.

Borrero, Krynski, & Short, J. *Growth phases.* Table presented at Annual Meeting of Western Psychiatric Institute. Pittsburgh, Pa.: Western Psychiatric Institute and Clinic, 1974.

Brazelton, T. Neonatal behavioral assessment scale. *National Spastic Society Monograph.* London: William Heinemann and Son, 1973.

Brown, R. Development of the first language in the human species. In B. Friedlander, G. Sterritt, & G. Kirk (Eds.), *Exceptional infant: Assessment and intervention,* New York: Brunner/Mazel, 1975.

CIBA Medical Horizons, *Physician's handbook: Screening for MBD.* Summit, N.J.: CIBA Pharmaceutical Co., 1973.

Clawson, A. *The Bender visual motor gestalt test for children. A manual.* Los Angeles: Western Psychological Services, 1962.

Cohen, S. Minimal brain dysfunction and practical matters such as teaching kids to read. *Annals of New York Academy of Science,* 1973, *205,* 251–261.

Denver Developmental Screening Test. St. Louis, Missouri: C.V. Mosby Company, 1971.

Doll, E. *The Vineland Social Maturity Scale.* Vineland, N.J.: Vineland Training School, 1936.

Dunn, L. *Peabody picture vocabulary test.* Circle Pines, Minnesota: American Guidance Service, Inc., 1965.

Fineberg, H. Computerized tomography dilemma of health care technology. *Pediatrics,* 1977, *59*(2), 147–148.

Freud, A. *Normality and pathology in childhood.* New York: International Universities Press, 1965.

Freud, W. The baby profile. Part II. *The Psychoanalytic Study of the Child,* 1971, *26,* 172–194.

Gesell, A. *Gesell developmental schedules.* The Psychological Corporation, 304 E. 45th St., New York, New York.

Gesell, A. & Amatruda, C. *Developmental diagnosis: Normal and abnormal child development.* New York: Hoeber, 1947.

Gold, A. The neurological examination and MBD. In G. Millichap (Ed.), *Learning disabilities and related disorders: Facts and current issues.* Chicago: Year Book Medical Publishers, Inc., 1977.

Goodenough, F. *Measurement of intelligence by drawings.* New York: Harcourt, Brace and World, Inc., 1926.

Goodman, R. & Gorlin, R. *Atlas of the face in genetic disorders.* St. Louis, Mo.: The C. V. Mosby Co., 1977.

Greenberg, N. A comparison of infant-mother interactional behavior in infants with atypical behavior and normal infants. In J. Hellmuth (Ed.), *Exceptional infant, Vol. 2.* Studies in Abnormalities. New York: Brunner/Mazel, 1971.

Haslett, N. Treatment planning for children: A complete child psychiatry evaluation outline. *The Journal of Continuing Education in Psychiatry,* 1977, *16*(11), 21–34.

Hersh, A. Casework with parents of retarded children. *Social Work,* 1961, *6*(2), 61–66.

Hobbs, N. (Ed.). *The futures of children: Categories, labels, and their consequences.* San Francisco: Jossey Bass Publishers, 1976.

Jastak, J. *Wide range achievement test.* Wilmington, Del.: G. I. Story, 1940. (published by Guidance Associates, 1526 Gilpin Avenue, Wilmington, Delaware).

John, E., Karmel, B., Corning, W., Easton, P., Brown, D., Ahn, H., John, M., Harmony, T., Prichep L., Toro A., Gerson, I., Bartlett, F., Thatcher, R., Kaye, H., Valdes, P., & Schwartz, E. Neurometrics. Numerical taxonomy identifies different profiles of brain functions within groups of behaviorally similar people. *Science,* 1977, *196*(4297), 1393–1410.

Johnston, R. Motor function: Normal development and cerebral palsy. In R. Johnson & P. Magrab (Eds.), *Developmental disorders: Assessment, treatment, education.* Baltimore: University Park Press, 1976.

Koppitz, E. *The Bender gestalt test for young children.* New York: Grune & Stratton, 1963.

Koppitz, E. *Psychological evaluations of children's human figure drawings.* New York: Grune & Stratton, 1968.

Laufer, M. Assessment of adolescent disturbances. The application of Anna Freud's diagnostic profile. *Psychoanalytic Study of the Child,* 1965, *20,* 99–123.

Leopold, W. *Speech development of a bilingual child: A linguist's record.* (Studies in the Humanities). Evanston: Northwestern University Press, 1939.

Lewis, M. Transitory or pseudo-organicity and borderline personality in a 7-year-old child. *Journal American Academy of Child Psychiatry,* 1976, *15*(1), 131–138.

Machover, K. *Personality projection in the drawing of a human figure.*

Springfield, Ill.: C.C. Thomas, 1949.

Machover, K. Human figure drawings of children. *Journal of Projective Techniques,* 1953, *17,* 85–91.

Mahler, M., Pine, F., & Bergman, A. *The psychological birth of the human infant.* New York: Basic Books, Inc., 1975.

McCarthy, D. Language development in children. In L. Carmichael (Ed.), *Manual of child psychology.* New York: Wiley, 1954.

McCarthy, J. & Kirk, S. *Illinois test of psycholinguistic abilities* (Examiner's Manual). Urbana, Ill.: Institute for Research on Exceptional Children. University of Illinois, 1961.

McCormick, D. Pediatric evaluation of children with school problems. *American Journal of Diseases of Children,* 1977, *131,* 318–322.

Mecham, M. *Verbal language development scale.* Springfield, Ill.: Educational Test Bureau, 1959.

Mecham, M. Developmental schedules of oral-aural language as an aid to the teacher of the mentally retarded. *Mental Retardation,* 1963, *1,* 359–369.

Meers, D. A diagnostic profile of psychopathology in a latency child. *The Psychoanalytic Study of the Child,* 1966, *21,* 483–526.

Nelson, K. First steps in language acquisition. *Journal American Academy of Child Psychiatry,* 1977, *16*(4), 563–583.

Nelson, K.E. Aspects of language acquisition and use from age 2 to age 20. *Journal American Academy of Child Psychiatry,* 1977, *16*(4), 584–607.

Quinn, P., Renfield, M., Burg, C., & Rapoport, J. Minor physical anomalies. A newborn screening and 1-year follow-up. *Journal American Academy of Child Psychiatry,* 1977, *16*(4), 662–669.

Pearson, G. *Psychoanalysis and the education of the child.* Westport, Conn.: Greenwood Press, 1972.

Piaget, J. *The child's conception of the world* (Translated by J. & A. Tomlinson). New York: Harcourt, 1929.

Rappaport, S. (Ed.). *Child aphasia and brain damage: A definition.* Narberth, Pa.: Livingston Publishing Co., 1964.

Rappaport, S. (Ed.). *Childhood aphasia and brain damage: Volume II. Differential diagnosis.* Narberth, Pa.: Livingston Publishing Co., 1965.

Rutherford, D. Speech and language disorders and MBD. In J. Millichap (Ed.), *Learning disabilities and related disorders: Facts and current issues.* Chicago: Year Book Medical Publishers, Inc., 1977.

Satterfield, J. Medical and social history. In G. Leisman (Ed.), *Basic visual processes and learning disability.* Springfield: Charles C. Thomas, 1976.

Schain, R. The neurological evaluation of children with learning disorders. *California Medicine,* 1973, *118*(6), 24–32.

Schilder, P. Image and appearance of the human body. *Psychological*

Monographs, 1935, No. 4.

Slosson, R. *Slosson drawing and reading tests.* Slosson Educational Publications, 140 Pine Street, E. Aurora, N.Y. 14052.

Starr, A. *Rutgers drawing test.* 126 Montgomery St. Highland Park, N.J. 08904.

Stone, L. & Church, J. *Childhood and adolescence.* New York: Random House, 1957.

Strauss, A. & Kephart, N. *Psychopathology and education of the brain-injured child.* New York: Grune & Stratton, 1955.

Stiffler, N. Language function: Normal and abnormal development. In R. Johnston & P. Magrab (Eds.), *Developmental disorders: Assessment, treatment, education.* Baltimore: University Park Press, 1976.

Tronick, E. & Brazelton, T. Clinical uses of the Brazelton neonatal behavioral assessment. In B. Friedlander, G. Sterritt, & G. Kirk (Eds.), *Exceptional infant, Vol. 3, Assessment and intervention.* New York: Brunner/Mazel, 1975.

Wylie, R. *The self-concept: A critical survey of pertinent research literature.* Lincoln: University of Nebraska Press, 1961.

CHAPTER 3

COGNITIVE ASSESSMENT

DONALD H. PAINTING, Ph.D.

Especially at the beginning of life, but also throughout, cognitive functioning is only partially autonomous but is to some degree an aspect of the overall adaptation of the human organism. It goes on at a smoothly integrated or distorted and confused or disintegrated level, depending to a varying extent on the level of integration of the child as a whole, (on the intactness of the central nervous system), and on his (or her) interaction with environmental circumstances which may enhance or interfere with this development.

—Ilse Mattick and Lois B. Murphy, *Cognitive Studies, 2: Deficits in Cognition*

INTRODUCTION

As professionals become increasingly aware of children with specific learning disabilities, and as the demand intensifies to provide the indicated remedial programs for such children, the need to improve the quality of diagnostic resources becomes evident. Not only is it important to identify these children as early as possible, but also it is essential that identification/assessment procedures lead to appropriate recommendations for remediation. Too often, unfortunately, the psychological assessment leads to erroneous or insufficient diagnosis and/or a written report which provides little or no assistance in the development of a treatment plan. This chapter describes an approach which may enhance the diagnostic usefulness of the psychological assessment in the multidisciplinary evaluation of children with specific learning disabilities. Combining a developmental point of view with a sensitivity for a child's problem-solving and cognitive processes adds a valuable dimension to standardized testing procedures.

A DEVELOPMENTAL PROCESS APPROACH

Normal human development is an extremely complicated and not entirely understood process, whether one is concerned with physical growth, motor skills, social/emotional maturation, or cognitive and other processes. Similarly, the clinical assessment of deviant development in any of these areas can be an extremely complicated process which is not entirely understood by many professionals. This is particularly evident in the assessment of children with specific learning disabilities.

The following discussion will focus upon the cognitive assessment of such children, although many of the issues are equally applicable to other areas of psychological, psychiatric, educational, or similar types of assessment. Hopefully, the supplemental procedures and suggestions which are described will facilitate a more accurate and meaningful assessment of children with specific learning disabilities (SLD)/minimal brain dysfunction (MBD)/hyperkinetic syndrome (HKS). These procedures and suggestions appear to have empirical validity and have emerged from a developmental, prescriptive orientation.

Definition of Developmental Process Approach

The psychological assessment must include more than the sterile administration of a test battery with strict adherence to standardized procedures in which results are reported primarily in terms of quantitative scores. The importance of such standardized procedures is incontestable, but the evaluation process must not stop with these. Assessment is not an end in itself but is a preliminary step toward differential diagnosis, prescription, and remediation. Therefore, the psychological assessment must also include: (a) a systematic scanning of skill levels to establish patterns of assets and deficits (e.g., visual skills more intact than auditory skills), (b) a translation of skill levels into approximate developmental levels to ensure that an appropriate treatment plan is developed (e.g., a scaled score of 7 indicative of a dull-normal level of functioning may be roughly equivalent to a developmental age level of nine years or to a fourth grade level of functioning), (c) an analysis of the child's problem-solving processes to determine some of the possible reasons for "failure" on test items (e.g., perseverative interferences, auditory sequencing difficulties, conceptual problems), (d) an appraisal of the conditions under which the child may be expected to function/learn optimally (e.g., tight structure, firm limits, verbal explanations supplemented by visual cues), and (e) an estimate of the child's potential with a prognostic statement concerning the attainment of objectives and anticipated duration of remediation. It is true that prognostic statements can place the professional in a tenuous position, but carefully considered and conservative statements can provide the basis for longitudinal planning, especially when such prognostic statements are routinely reconsidered in the light of actual progress.

The developmental assessment process described above bears some similarity to the procedure described by Gesell and Amatruda (1967):

> Behavior grows. Behavior assumes characteristic patterns as it grows. The principles and practice of developmental diagnosis rest on these two simple but far-reaching propositions. Developmental diagnosis is nothing more or less than a discriminating observation of patterns of behavior and their appraisal by comparison with normative patterns.. . . . The order in which behavior patterns appear is significantly uniform (and thus) developmental diagnosis translates behavior values into age values. (p. 6)

Rationale

In the assessment of SLD/MBD/HKS children, the primary reason for endorsing such a developmental assessment process instead of a strictly standardized and quantified procedure, would appear to be related to (a) the nature of the symptomatology, (b) various pitfalls of quantitative scores, and (c) the need for prescriptive recommendations for remediation.

NATURE OF SYMPTOMATOLOGY

As discussed in Chapter 1, it is clear that there are numerous labels and sometimes conflicting definitions for this population. It is also recognized that SLD, MBD, and HKS are not specific disease entities, but represent clusters of symptoms and signs which make up nonspecific syndromes. Although there are many symptoms which characterize these children, not all symptoms are evident in every child with such a learning disability. Frequently, the symptoms are very subtle and are easily overlooked or explained away on some other basis, e.g., emotional factors. Sometimes the symptoms are erratic, appearing on some tasks, but not others; appearing on some days, but not others; appearing when the dysfunctioning system is placed under stress, but not in the absence of stress. These subtle, erratic, "soft" signs may often escape recognition by the examiner who is tuned in primarily to "standardized procedures" and who does not vary the procedure sufficiently to see whether such signs can be elicited.

PITFALLS OF QUANTITATIVE SCORES

The kinds of data which are represented by quantitative scores include: a summation of the number of right/wrong responses on a particular test (e.g., raw scores); a comparison of an individual's performance on a particular test with that of a normative group (e.g., scaled scores, IQ scores, percentile scores); a global indication of an individual's level of performance on one test as compared with another (e.g., a prorated WISC Vocabulary IQ versus Peabody Picture Vocabulary IQ); and a global comparison of an individual's test-retest performance (e.g., 1974 WISC Full Scale IQ versus 1976 WISC Full Scale IQ). Clearly, such data are essential in any meaningful assessment but should be acknowledged as only skeletal information in the full body of information which may be obtained.

Quantitative data do not, however, reveal such useful diagnostic information as a self-derogatory attitude and a fear of potential failure, a driven, restless behavior pattern, perseverative interferences with test performances, tangential associations or poorly established conceptual boundaries, or many other pieces of information which not only facilitate a differential diagnosis but also guide the development of a prescriptive treatment plan.

This need to go beyond quantitative scores has been emphasized by Sattler (1974):

> For the most part, quantitative test indices (e.g., pattern analysis, scatter, or scores on specific tests or subtests) . . . have not proven useful in differentiating brain-damaged children from children who are not brain-damaged. . . . Evaluation of the child's total performance on the examination is required. . . . (p. 290)

Hence, the appropriate and meaningful interpretation of quantitative scores in the assessment of children with specific learning disabilities becomes greatly facilitated when done in the context of the associated qualitative data.

PRESCRIPTIVE RECOMMENDATIONS FOR REMEDIATION

As noted earlier, the psychological assessment of children with SLD/MBD/HKS (as well as any type of suspected pathology) should lead not only to a differential diagnosis but also to remedial recommendations which are geared specifically to each child's areas of deficit. General remedial guidelines may be suggested by quantitative scores, but the finer details which are essential for the actual implementation of a remedial program are generally found in a careful analysis of qualitative data. According to Lerner (1971):

> A diagnosis that culminates in merely attaching a label such as dyslexia, or that names the presumed cause of the learning problem (such as a lesion in the angular gyrus, or perhaps an overindulgent mother) is not operational because it provides insufficient guidelines for devising strategies to help the child learn. (p. 44)

For example, it may be evident from quantitative scores that a particular child experiences more difficulty when stimuli are presented auditorily rather than visually. Global remedial recommendations may be made on the basis of this limited information, but they become far more accurate, specific, and potentially effective if the examiner interprets the quantitative data in the context of such qualitative information as: auditory skill difficulties were most evident when the tasks required abstract conceptual processing and sequencing skills rather than concrete conceptual processing and rote memory; distractibility and hyperactivity increased as stimuli became more abstract; a structured presentation of the task which involved conceptual processing and sequencing skills resulted in a significantly higher level of performance, and so on.

Unfortunately, valuable qualitative data may be lost or distorted unless the examiner is adequately sophisticated in the observation, recording, and interpretation of such information. As Small (1973) observes: "The very facts that the signs associated with MBD occur in other disorders as well and that such signs are exhibited by great numbers of children emphasize the necessity for the most meticulous diagnostic procedure" (p. 19).

PRELIMINARY CONSIDERATIONS

The assessment process can be significantly more productive (and a more pleasant experience for both the child and the examiner) if the examiner gives careful preliminary consideration to several important factors, remembering that the child with SLD often tends to be hypersensitive, task-avoidant, distractible, and so on.

Previously Obtained Information

Some examiners may prefer to test a child "cold," i.e., without the knowledge of background information which may bias the interpretation of the test data. This approach may have its place, such as in the training experiences of graduate students. However, one would expect that the professional objectivity which develops with experience would enable the practicing clinician to review previously obtained information in a manner which is sufficiently critical to provide some sense of what to anticipate in the assessment session. Furthermore, this objective review may provide the examiner with clues as to which presenting problems are primarily a function of the child's deficits and which may be a function of the child's response to significant adults (parents, teachers, examiners) whose limited understanding of the child's deficits may have contributed to his or her previous "failure" experiences.

Selection of the Assessment Battery

In selecting the battery of psychological tests for assessment of a child's cognitive skills, the examiner must be guided by background information relative to the presenting problems. For example, if a six-year-old child is suspected to have relatively wide gaps in skill development, it may be more productive to administer the Wechsler Primary and Preschool Scale of Intelligence (WPPSI) (1967) than the Wechsler Intelligence Scale for Children (WISC) (1949) or the Wechsler Intelligence Scale for Children, Revised (WISC-R) (1974). Similarly, if the child has significant expressive language difficulties, the Stanford-Binet Scale of Intelligence (1960), which is heavily loaded with verbal items, would hardly be the test of choice.

Because of the variety of verbal and nonverbal items, the Wechsler scales are very useful instruments in the cognitive assessment of children with SLD. The appropriate Wechsler scale in conjunction with the Peabody Picture Vocabulary Test (PPVT) (1959, 1965) and the Bender Visual-Motor Gestalt Test (BG) (1946) constitute the battery of tests which will be discussed in this chapter. Other examiners may prefer differing combinations of tests, but so long as the test instruments are selected from among the more valid and reliable instruments available for assessing a child's cognitive skills, it is less important which tests are selected than how they are used by the examiner. In essence, the assessment process is a type of interview both guided and structured by the nature of the test instruments which are selected. The examiner's understanding of the child's cognitive processes and deficit areas is greatly enhanced by perceiving test instruments in this individualized way rather than primarily as a means by which a quantitative score is obtained.

Preparing the Child for the Assessment Situation

Each child should be prepared for the evaluation. In general, the child's parents and/or teacher could provide the appropriate preparation, under the supervision of the psychologist who will be making the assessment.

Most children with SLD have some awareness of their problem areas and, consequently, experience varying degrees of anxiety when facing situations which may expose their deficits to others or result in failure. This anxiety may lead the child into various defensive maneuvers to protect his or her self-pride from further wounding. Usually it is reassuring to the child to realize that adults understand the problems which are producing the anxiety.

The preparation which is offered to the child should supportively (a) recognize specific problem areas which the child has demonstrated, (b) recognize the unhappy and even scary feelings which such problems have aroused in the child, (c) indicate the parents' and/or teacher's concern for the child and desire to help find a solution for the problems, and (d) explain that one of the first steps towards finding a solution is to obtain the psychological assessment. Preparation for psychological reevaluations should also refer to the importance of determining the child's progress—what kinds of things the child now finds to be easier than before and which things still require additional help.

By all means, the preparation should avoid deception! Telling the child he is going for a ride or that he is going to play games with the psychologist may lead to a negative reaction when stress is aroused by the various tasks required in the evaluation.

THE DEVELOPMENTAL ASSESSMENT PROCESS

In this section, the discussion will focus upon (a) the process of collecting the data, with suggestions for handling various kinds of behavioral management problems, and (b) the process of interpreting the quantitative and qualitative data which are obtained.

Data Collection

The procedures which are followed in the careful administration of a test battery may vary significantly from one child to the next, according to the child's chronological age, developmental skill levels, and emotional/social maturity. However, an important thread of similarity should be woven throughout the process of data collection regardless of these different sources of variance. The elements of this similarity follow.

Role of the Examiner

Aside from any previous knowledge of the child which the examiner may have, the collection of new data begins from the moment the examiner meets the child and lasts until the child leaves at the completion of the assessment. Information is obtained from perceptive observation of the child's behavioral response to each facet of the assessment. Some of the diagnostically more important pieces of behavioral data which may be obtained through careful observation include:

(1) How does the child entertain himself or herself while waiting for the examiner to arrive (cries; clings to parents; sits quietly; plays in a controlled manner; is disruptive)?

(2) How does the arrival of the examiner affect the child's behavior (ignores or seems unaware of the examiner; greets the examiner in an age-appropriate manner; appears frightened, embarrassed and/or shy; uses approriate language)?

(3) How does the child separate from his parents to accompany the examiner (separates immediately and comfortably; separates hesitantly; refuses to leave unless a parent also comes)?

(4) How does the child proceed with the examiner to the examination room (walks with the examiner in an age-appropriate manner; holds the examiner's hand; carries on an appropriate discussion; asks irrelevant questions; becomes excessively curious about things which are seen enroute to the examination room)?

(5) How does the child become involved with the testing procedures (becomes distracted by various objects in the examination room; seems eager to begin the examination; appears to be passively resistant)?

(6) How well developed are the child's motor skills (ascends or descends stairs age-appropriately; seems awkward for gross and fine motor movements; handedness seems established)?

(7) How well developed are the child's speech and language skills (appropriateness of articulation; syntax; sequence of sounds in words and words in sentences; relevance of language to the immediate situation?)

(8) How well developed are the child's social/emotional skills (attention span; appropriateness of affect; degree of behavioral control; typical defensive maneuvers; manner of relating to the examiner; response to stress, frustration, fatigue)?

(9) How does the child's behavior change as he is exposed to different kinds of tasks (auditory-vocal tasks; visual-motor tasks; concrete tasks; abstract tasks; easy tasks; difficult tasks)?

The value of being sensitive to such behavioral data is acknowledged by Small (1973):

> The "nose" of the astute diagnostician is a hallowed concept among clinicians, indeed some insist that the best test instrument of organicity is such an astute clinician. This emphasis stresses the process within the clinician, the rapid concatenation of observation, evaluation, and judgment, the on-the-spot selection of tests in response to observation, even the invention of tests to assess a specific function in an individual patient. It is not that standardized tests are not deployed, but that their deployment is not formalized, and that it is the clinician who is the primary test instrument via his observation of "how" the patient performs, not what he scores. (p. 250)

A warm, casual but firm attitude should be maintained throughout the examination in order to help the child feel as comfortable as possible, but without allowing him to control the situation and turn it into a play period. The examiner's movements, rate of speech, tone of voice and choice of words should communicate to the child an atmosphere which is friendly, unhurried, and yet sufficiently professional to accomplish the goals of the assessment. An unhurried rate of speech with emphasis placed upon key words may enable the child with auditory perception and processing difficulties to understand more readily, especially whenever instructions are being given. As needed, the examiner should be prepared to use a firm tone of voice and/or gentle physical restraint if the child's behavior becomes disruptive. The child needs to be told in a nonthreatening manner that there is work to be accomplished which, when completed or at appropriate intervals such as rest breaks, may be followed by some type of quiet play activity.

A supportive and encouraging attitude should also characterize the examiner. The anxious SLD/MBD/HKS child with negative self-concept and fear of failure may find part or all of the assessment session to be quite unpleasant. Consequently, he will usually respond best and attempt more difficult tasks when his effort is appropriately praised, regardless of the success or failure of his performance. He should be encouraged to try or even guess whenever he wants to give up quickly, or whenever he responds with "I don't know" on items which may be within his range of ability.

Flexibility is another important characteristic of the examiner's role. The child's levels of functioning and behavioral reactions may necessitate impromptu modifications of the examiner's customary procedures, unexpected changes in the sequence and/or selection of tasks, and adjustments in time schedules. The examiner may, at times, need to modify the situation, in order to abort the emergence of resistive behavior, or reassure the child by interjecting a relatively easy task after a difficult and frustrating one. If the examiner remains sensitive to the child's needs, it will usually be apparent when such flexibility must be exercised.

Use of Structure

The role of the examiner and the use of structure in the assessment of SLD/MBD/HKS children are inseparably interwoven. Structure may be broadly defined as the various amounts and kinds of emotional support, situational limits, and task simplification which can be given to enable a child to perform with optimal efficiency and success without providing cues to the expected response. Whenever possible, the examiner should initially administer each task or test according to the standardized procedures in order to obtain quantitative baselines which may be useful both for determining the apparent severity of current deficits relative to normative data and for longitudinal observations and reevaluations. However, once the standardized procedures have been completed, the examiner may feel free to determine the extent to which the child's performance could be improved by introducing additional amounts and kinds of structure. Such information becomes invaluable when the examiner must translate the test data into remedial recommendations.

Basically, there are three types of structure in the assessment situation: relationship structure, situational structure, and task structure.

Relationship structure, the most essential and pervasive form, has been characerized by Rappaport (1969) as the ability to understand a child sufficiently well at any given moment to aid in the development of his/her ego functions. This would include the sensitive and perceptive ways the examiner offers the child reassurance, supportive comments, recognition of feelings, encouragement, and appropriate limits or behavioral controls. For example, the child with poor inner control who is distracted by extraneous stimuli often offers impulsive, arbitrary responses. The examiner may respond in the assessment relationship by quietly encouraging the child to think before responding, and by refocusing his/her attention before presenting each task or question. Many SLD/MBD/HKS children will "test" the strength and fairness of the examiner and the limits of the relationship by teasing, leaving the immediate area of test involvement, or by attempting to turn the assessment into a play situation. The examiner may respond, according to the age of the child, (1) by gently restraining the child's efforts to leave the test area; (2) by stating firmly the importance of completing the task *first* and then enjoying a brief period of play; (3) by stating that the longer it takes to settle down, the longer the testing session will last; or (4) by offering some concrete reward which will be given *after* the testing session is completed.

The second type of structure is *situational.* It includes the various ways in which the physical setting, the presentation of the tasks, and time are planned and controlled. For the SLD child who may be hyper-alert to distracting or uncomfortable stimuli, the chair and work table should be properly sized, the room as quiet as possible, with minimal disturbance from outside noises, the temperature of the room comfortable, and the light adequate, with minimal glare on the work area.

The immediate work area should be well organized, with distracting objects placed out of sight or at least put out of the child's line of vision. If the child is overly hyperactive and inattentive, it may help to place the child's chair in the corner of the room with the table and the examiner in front of the child. In this position, the two walls simulate the boundaries of a carrel in which the child can focus attention on the task and the examiner.

Although selection of tasks may need to be determined by the child's behavioral responses and/or skill competency relative to the tasks at hand, the examiner should control the sequence of tasks and the time allotted to each. Unrestrained manipulation by the child may render the assessment meaningless.

The assessment procedures should not be rushed, but the child should not be permitted to work endlessly on any one task. If the child shows a fascination for a certain task or is determined to master it in spite of obvious skill problems, such persistence should be noted but a way should be found to proceed smoothly to the next task. Otherwise, excessive fatigue and/or frustration with one task may impair the child's subsequent functioning. In addition, time for other parts of the assessment may be curtailed and valuable information lost.

On the other hand, some children may rush through each task in an impulsive, arbitrary manner just to "get through." If the examiner does not attempt to modify this rapid pace, the resulting data will be of limited value. These children should be reminded to slow down, the effects of their rushing explained, and guessing encouraged for "I don't know" responses. Time limits should not be emphasized and the examiner's behavior should explicitly suggest a slower, more deliberate manner.

For additional suggestions concerning the examination room and situational considerations in the assessment of children, see Wechsler (1974), chapter 5 and Sattler (1974), chapters 5, 6, and 7.

The third type of structure is *task structure*. The specific manner in which a verbal or nonverbal task is presented may significantly influence the child's responses and/or reduce some of the extraneous situational/examiner variables which confound the test data. Most aspects of task structure are simply methods recommended as part of standardized testing procedures. Examiners may stray from them as instructions become rotely administered, schedules become pressured, or the child presents provocative behavior. Task structure may be illustrated by the manner in which instructions or questions are articulated at a slow conversational pace with appropriate emphasis placed upon key words or phrases. This is particularly important for the child with an auditory processing difficulty who may hear rapid instructions given without inflection or appropriate word emphasis as a foreign language not yet mastered. Also, the more conversational the atmosphere, the less the questions come across as "test items" on which the child may pass or fail.

Materials for all tasks should be prearranged to minimize the time a child must wait for the materials to be presented. Examples of task structure will be discussed in the following section concerning testing of limits.

Testing of Cognitive Function Limits

Most examiners must be reminded occasionally about the purpose of a cognitive assessment. The purpose is not only to determine a child's particular intelligence quotient in accordance with how well he/she performs on the various tests, but also to explore the processes by which problems are solved and to establish some estimate of potential ability. After initial administration of the test battery according to standardized procedures in order to retain the validity of the quantitative scores, the examiner must frequently go beyond these procedures to test limits of the child's skills. Any data obtained from such testing of limits may not be used in the formal scoring procedures but may be reflected in interpolated extensions of the scoring.

Methods of testing limits may include the following:

(1) testing on each task beyond the permitted number of consecutive errors (which may reveal fragments of higher level skills and the erratic nature of cognitive functioning which frequently characterizes children with SLD);

(2) testing beyond the permitted time limits on timed tasks (which may reveal that the associated problem-solving skill is intact or functional, but for various reasons the processing or response time may be slow);

(3) providing additional cues in small increments to determine the amount of information needed for correct response (e.g., on the Wechsler Block Design, first reconstruct the child's incorrect solution for a design and ask that the design be made to look more like the picture; if the child cannot, then construct

a correct model of the stimulus without revealing the steps involved to determine if the child can reproduce the design more accurately from the three-dimensional model than from the two-dimensional picture; and if this is still not possible, then separate the blocks in the design slightly to determine if the child's efforts are more accurately guided by the more evident contours of each block within the design);

(4) having the child explain the solution to a task to make the problem-solving more explicit for the examiner's benefit and to determine whether or not verbalizing the process has a self-correcting influence (e.g., on the Wechsler Picture Arrangement, the child may understand the situation portrayed in the pictures but, due to sequencing or directionality problems, the pictures may have been arranged in a right to left order; or, as the logic of the picture sequence is made verbally explicit, the child can perhaps better monitor appropriate visual-motor efforts to solve the task correctly);

(5) having the child close the eyes to eliminate distraction from visual stimuli when trying to improve attention and concentration efforts (e.g., when having to recall digits, compute arithmetic problems mentally, recall previously drawn Bender designs, or organize his/her thoughts in response to a verbal task).

In the cognitive assessment of the SLD/MBD/HKS child and in designing an Individual Educational Program for remedial purposes, it is less important to know that a child earned a particular subtest score or failed on a certain item than it is to know what kinds of errors were made. The child may fail an item for various reasons, and the validity of the prescriptive remedial recommendations will depend upon knowing those reasons.

Data Interpretation

As noted earlier, the test battery in this chapter includes the Wechsler Scales, the Peabody Picture Vocabulary Test (PPVT), and the Bender Visual-Motor Gestalt Test (BG). Many of the comments concerning the interpretation of these data may, however, be readily generalized or adapted to other tests which assess the cognitive functioning of children. This is possible because it is the child with his/her problem-solving efforts, and not the test *per se,* which forms the common demoninator.

For the sake of simplicity, quantitative and qualitative assessment data will be given separate consideration. However, the skillful examiner will find that these two kinds of data are essentially inseparable and that there is a need for constant interweaving throughout the interpretive process.

Background information and test data from a Case Study will serve to illustrate the interpretation process.

Case Study 3.1

Jeffrey enrolled at the age of 8 years in a private residential school for children and adolescents with learning disabilities and associated emotional/social adjustment problems. He was a physically attractive boy, somewhat small for his chronological age, with a history of being hyperactive, impulsive, and, at times, defiant. Because of his insufficiently developed basic skills and his behavioral problems, Jeffrey repeated kindergarten. Subsequently, he entered a special education program in first grade, but, due to continuing problems with learning and behavioral control, he was referred for residential placement.

Jeffrey presented himself as a very pleasant, sociable and verbal youngster who was quite adept at holding a relatively mature social conversation. However, his tenuous ego controls and limited frustration tolerance became evident whenever certain environmental limits were imposed or whenever educational tasks became difficult for him. At the time of his enrollment at age eight (chronologically appropriate for third grade), Jeffrey's reading skills were at a readiness/preprimer level and his math skills were at a first level. His psychological test data which were obtained at that time are shown below.

Psychological Evaluation

Name: Jeffrey
Age: 8-3

PURPOSE OF TESTING

At the time of the preenrollment assessment, psychological test data were available from an evaluation of Jeffrey made two years previous at his public school. Those data revealed IQ scores within the average range, but details of his scores and test performance were minimally explained in the report. However, this information, in conjunction with other testing which was done prior to his acceptance for enrollment in the residential program, indicated that this program would be appropriate for his needs.

The evaluation reported here was done to update the available information concerning Jeffrey's cognitive functioning so that his initial treatment plan could be elaborated.

BEHAVIORAL OBSERVATIONS

Jeffrey was generally well motivated and relatively attentive to each task initially. However, after approximately 30 minutes, he began to demonstrate signs of fatigue and restlessness. So that the test data might reflect his optimal level of functioning, testing was discontinued and rescheduled for the next day. Again, he was unable to sustain his efforts effectively beyond 30 minutes, so a third session had to be scheduled for the following day.

During each session, Jeffrey related to the examiner in a friendly, sociable manner. Physically small for his chronological age he appeared somewhat younger, and as a result, his verbalizations seemed overly mature. However, when one kept his chronological age in mind, most of his comments and social poise seemed to be essentially age-appropriate. There was evidence of generalized restlessness and impulsivity, but his controls were sufficient to allow him to remain focused upon each task in these one-to-one situations which were moderately structured and supportive.

It was felt that the resulting test data represented a relatively reliable estimate of his current levels of cognitive functioning at that time.

TESTS ADMINISTERED

Wechsler Intelligence Scale for Children (WISC)
Peabody Picture Vocabulary Test, Form A
Bender Visual-Motor Gestalt Test

COGNITIVE FUNCTIONING

Intelligence. On the WISC, Jeffrey earned a Verbal IQ of 97, a Performance IQ of 96, and a Full Scale IQ of 96, each of which

Table 3.1
Summary of Subtest Performance
at Chronological Age 8-3

WISC Subtest	Scaled Score	Test Age
Information	8	7-2
Comprehension	14	10-6
Arithmetic	6	5-10
Similarities	9	7-6
Vocabulary	13	9-10
(Digit Span)	7	6-6
Picture Completion	6	5-6
Picture Arrangement	11	8-10
Block Design	9	7-2
Object Assembly	9	7-6
Coding	13	9-10

falls within the average range of intelligence. These scores are somewhat deceptive, however, in view of the fact that his subtest performance varied from the borderline to the superior level of intelligence, reflecting uneven levels of skill development. It is estimated that Jeffrey's intellectual potential extends into the bright-normal to possibly the superior range.

A summary of Jeffrey's subtest performance is shown in Table 3.1.

In the verbal sphere, Jeffrey's best performance occurred on the subtests which measure expressive vocabulary (9-10 year level) and social judgment (10-6 year level). He appears to have very adequate understanding of the meaning of various verbal concepts and is able to explain or express the meaning of such concepts in ways which reflect very adequate oral language skills. Furthermore, he demonstrated an above average ability to understand appropriate behavior patterns in social situations, although his impulsive behavior patterns may frequently interfere with the application of his social sophistication. Somewhat related to these skills is Jeffrey's average ability to categorize verbal concepts and to understand relatively abstract relationships (7-6 year level).

On the other hand, there are notable deficits in the verbal sphere which contribute to a lowered level of cognitive efficiency. These deficits include difficulty in recalling factual information, which may also reflect an impairment in long-term auditory memory (7-2 year level). His

short-term auditory memory is essentially at the same level of development. These skill deficits, in conjunction with notable difficulty with
number concepts and basic units of measurement, contributed to a
borderline level of functioning (5-10 year level) in the area of mental
arithmetical computations.

In the nonverbal sphere, Jeffrey performed at an average level
on a task which measured visual-motor integration and spatial relationships, as well as on a task involving the sequential arrangement of
visual stimuli into socially meaningful patterns. However, even though
his skills in thinking logically and sequentially and his awareness of
socal interaction patterns were age-apropriate, it is significant to note
that his sequences were either arbitrarily arranged or in a right-to-left
arrangement. For example, on the first sequential arrangement, Jeffrey
placed the pictures in an arbitrary fashion, although he pointed to the
proper sequence of pictures as he told a logical and appropriate story.
When encouraged to arrange the pictures in subsequent items in the
order of the story, he arranged pictures in a right-to-left sequence and
pointed to them in that order as he told appropriate stories. A superior
level of functioning occurred on the associative learning subtest which
measures speed and accuracy of symbol transcription. To perform on
this task successfully, one must make the proper association between
a symbol and a number and then record the symbol in the appropriate
location. It was evident from Jeffrey's performance on this task that he
was learning the code as he worked, so that he did not always need to
refer to the sample of the code which he was transcribing. This seems
to have important implications prognostically concerning his potential
ability to learn to read and spell.

On the other hand, Jeffrey performed at only the borderline level
(kindergarten to first grade) on a task requiring him to be perceptually
aware of essential and nonessential visual details. His score was also
relatively low (second grade level) on the Block Design subtest which
measures analytic-synthetic conceptualization. On such a task, a child
must analyze a complex visual stimulus and synthesize its parts to make
a meaningful whole. Again, perhaps Jeffrey's difficulty in attending to
visual details would make such an analysis and synthesis difficult for
him.

According to a Bannatyne analysis of WISC subtest clusters, Jeffrey's conceptual skills are at the bright-normal level, his sequencing
skills are at an average level, while his spatial skills are at the dull-normal
level. It should be noted, however, that while Jeffrey's overall score
on sequencing tasks seems to be adequate for his age, it masks the

difficulty which he has with directionality and with auditory sequencing (and/or short-term auditory memory).

On the Peabody Picture Vocabulary Test, Jeffrey earned a mental age of 8-11 and a corresponding high-average IQ of 109. His performance on this test of receptive language is comparable to his performance on the WISC Vocabulary subtest which requires expressive language.

PERCEPTUAL-MOTOR DEVELOPMENT

Jeffrey's reproductions of the Bender designs reflected errors involving difficulty with angulation, integration, and rotation. According to the Koppitz scoring system, he earned a score which places his level of perceptual development at a 6- to 6½-year level, which represents essentially a two-year gap in this area of development.

Jeffrey's short-term visual memory, as measured by his immediate recall of these designs, is notably above average for his chronological age; he recalled seven out of nine designs. The same types of errors were evident in his designs drawn from memory as were present when he copied a visual stimulus, with an even more evident tendency toward reversals or rotations of designs.

CONCLUSIONS AND RECOMMENDATIONS

Jeffrey is an 8-year-old boy who is currently functioning within the average range of intelligence but whose skill levels extend from the borderline range to the superior range of intelligence. This is comparable to grade level equivalents which would range from kindergarten to fifth grade. Jeffrey's previous evaluation two years earlier showed an IQ of 102 on the Stanford-Binet Intelligence Scale. Those results are compatible with the current test results.

These findings would support the diagnostic impression of a minimal brain dysfunction with secondary behavioral adjustment difficulties. In view of Jeffrey's positive response to structure, his demonstrated ability to learn symbolic information (coding), and the level of intact skills, the prognosis for his being able to profit from a prescriptive remedial program appears favorable.

The following *assets* are suggested by the current data:

(1) Ability to handle verbal concepts and to deal with abstract relationships.
(2) Receptive and expressive language skills.

(3) Social judgment and social perception.
(4) Short-term visual memory.

On the other hand, notable *deficits* are suggested in the following areas:

(1) Short-term and long-term auditory memory.
(2) Number concepts and basic units of measurement.
(3) Directionality and the tendency to make perceptual rotations.
(4) Discriminant visual perception of essential and nonessential details.
(5) Spatial relationships.
(6) Age-appropriate impulse control.

On the basis of these findings, the following *recommendations* would seem appropriate for the purpose of helping Jeffrey to strengthen or develop his deficit skill areas which are interfering with his effective functioning in the classroom and in various social situations:

(1) To help Jeffrey recall information which he has previously learned, provide him with frequent review sessions and with practical applications of basic information or concepts,, e.g., days in a week, seasons, fractional concepts such as half. His auditory memory should be reinforced with his excellent visual memory by presenting visual cues whenever possible to support verbally presented information. It may also be necessary to involve tactile and kinesthetic cues. In general, a visual-auditory-kinesthetic-tactile approach would seem to be quite helpful in many of his learning activities.

(2) To help him with his understanding of arithmetical concepts and processes, continued use of concrete materials would seem advisable. Perhaps various activities such as a play store in which he would buy articles or make change would facilitate the reinforcement of these concepts as well as teach him some applications.

(3) To help Jeffrey develop a better sense of directionality and laterality, emphasize input from the adapted physical education program and developmental movement therapy.

(4) To help him with discriminant visual perception as well as with his tendency to think in rather concrete terms, the concepts of sameness and differences must be developed. Exercises in which he must categorize objects and pictures, or verbally describe objects and pictures, may enable him to become more aware of internal details and relationships.

(5) His difficulty with spatial relationships and with discriminant visual perception might be improved by activities involving puzzles, matching letters and shapes, and so on. Also, developing a better appreciation for spatial relationships at the gross motor level through adapted physical education may transfer to desk activities.

(6) To help Jeffrey with his impulse-control problems and behavioral difficulties, provide him with well-defined limits in a structured environment. Also, additional support should continue to be provided through behavior modification techniques and psychotherapy.

Follow-up

In spite of an intensive habilitative program (educational, residential, and clinical input), Jeffrey's progress was very slow. Two years after his enrollment, he had reached only the primer level for reading instruction and the second level for math. Behavioral controls had improved markedly, but he continued to have a definite need for a structured environment, firm limits, and psychotherapeutic support (therapy and crisis intervention). A psychological evaluation reflecting these observations is summarized and compared with initial findings in Table 3.2.

During the following year, however, Jeffrey's rate of educational progress began to accelerate. By that time, basic skills were more intact, behavioral controls were more age-appropriate, and motivation to learn was more positive. Educational gaps were beginning to narrow; instructional levels improved essentially two years prior to the end of the school year.

Analysis of Psychological Assessment

QUANTITATIVE ASSESSMENT DATA

The examiner must avoid looking at quantitative data with the preconceived notion that children with SLD/MBD/HKS may be identified on the basis of a characteristic test pattern, which is far from the truth! The pattern of test scores will be determined not by the generic syndrome but by the specific clusters of skill deficits.

Intelligence quotients. On the Wechsler scale, the verbal IQ may be significantly higher or lower than the performance IQ, or there may be no significant difference according to whether the sphere of primary

Donald H. Painting, Ph.D.

Table 3.2
Comparison of Psychological Test Data
of Chronological Ages 8-3 and 10-3

WISC Subtest	CA: 8-3		CA: 10-3	
	Scaled Score	Test Age	Scaled Score	Test Age
Information	8	7-2	8	8-10
Comprehension	14	10-6	15	15-6
Arithmetic	6	5-10	4	6-10
Similarities	9	7-6	11	11-6
Vocabulary	13	9-10	11	10-6
(Digit Span)	7	6-6	8	7-6
Picture Completion	6	5-6	7	7-6
Picture Arrangement	11	8-10	9	9-6
Block Design	8	7-2	12	12-2
Object Assembly	9	7-6	11	11-6
Coding	13	9-10	10	9-10

IQ Scores

WISC Scales	CA: 8-3	CA: 10-3
Verbal Scale	97	97
Performance Scale	96	99
Full Scale	96	98
PPVT	109 (Form A)	106 (Form B)
Bender Designs	Koppitz Perceptual Age Level	
	CA: 8-3	CA: 10-3
	6-6	8-6

deficits is performance, verbal, or scattered throughout both areas of functioning. Looking at Jeffrey's data obtained at age 8-3, it can be seen that there was no significant difference between the verbal and the performance IQ scores, both of which fell within the middle of the average range. Although verbal, performance, and overall IQ scores will provide an initial impression of the child's global mean level of functioning in each area, any of these may fall within the average range as a result of subtest scores which extend from the mental defective to the superior level of intelligence. Therefore, they can be extremely misleading and should never constitute the basis for determining the child's educational group assignment.

The IQ score obtained on the PPVT may be considered a gross indication of the child's functional receptive vocabulary skills. Since the child points to one of four pictures which best represents the stimulus word presented verbally by the examiner, the child's ability to respond appropriately to verbal concepts at the auditory-motor level is assessed. It is useful to compare this score with a prorated IQ based upon the Wechsler Vocabulary subtest, which depends essentially upon auditory-vocal functioning and reflects expressive vocabulary skills. Some preliminary cues may thus be provided concerning the relative effectiveness of these two systems (auditory-motor versus auditory-vocal) which, substantiated with additional data, may be important in formulating a remedial plan. At age 8-3, Jeffrey earned a PPVT IQ at the upper limits of the average range, which is comparable to his prorated WISC Vocabulary IQ within the bright-normal range. Hence, both receptive and expressive vocabulary skills appear to be adequately developed relative to his overall level of cognitive functioning.

Intertest and intratest variability. After determining the child's global or mean levels of cognitive functioning as reflected in the IQ scores (perhaps the least meaningful piece of data), the next step in the interpretation process might be to study the extent of test performance variation between and within subtests. The upper limits of this variability range may be indicative of the child's intellectual potential which might be realized were his/her functioning not impaired by various skill deficits. At the same time, however, performance expectations for the child in various situations (e.g., classroom or social performance) must never be established on the basis of either the estimated potential or the actual IQ scores, but rather on the kinds of skills required for successful performance in a particular situation and the child's current levels of functioning in those skill areas.

Seldom, if ever, should any assessment instrument be considered pure in the sense that it measures only the skills which it purports to measure. Indeed, there are usually several additional skills which support successful performance on the instrument; knowing and identifying these skills, the examiner can determine more accurately the level of the child's difficulty with a particular task and prescribe more meaningful remedial measures.

First, consider the surface skills which are measured by the Wechsler subtests:

Information—fund of factual data
Comprehension—social judgment

Arithmetic—concentration and mental computation
Similarities—analogical and inductive reasoning and
    verbal concept formation
Vocabulary—knowledge of word meanings
Digit Span—attention and short-term auditory memory
Picture Completion—discriminant visual perception of essential
    from nonessential details
Picture Arrangement—social perception
Block Design—analysis and synthesis of complex visual patterns
Object Assembly—visual perceptual organization
Coding—speed and accuracy of symbol transcription
Mazes—foresightful planning

For a more detailed discussion of these skills associated with the Wechsler subtests, see Sattler (1974).

Referring again to Jeffrey's data at age 8-3, it can be seen that his functioning is extremely erratic, varying from the borderline range (Arithmetic; Picture Completion) to the superior range (Comprehension; Coding) of intelligence. Similar erratic functioning is evident in his intratest performance on many of the subtests: partial credit or no credit was often earned on test items at the relatively easy end of the items of some subtests while, at the same time, credits which could not be included in the IQ computations were sometimes earned beyond the allowable number of consecutive errors. These findings would suggest that Jeffrey's potential ability may extend at least into the bright-normal range. Relative to his apparent potential ability, Jeffrey has notable to significant difficulty with tasks which involve recall of factual information, concentration and mental computation, attention and short-term auditory memory, discriminant visual perception of essential from nonessential details, and analysis and synthesis of complex visual patterns. Slight difficulty may be suspected on tasks involving inductive reasoning, verbal concept formation, and visual perceptual organization.

Bannatyne Analysis. Several years ago, Bannatyne (1968) suggested that the Wechsler subtests could be grouped into clusters to highlight relative functioning in basic skill areas. These areas included conceptual thinking (as measured by Comprehension, Similarities, and Vocabulary), sequencing abilities (Digit Span, Picture Arrangement, and Coding), and the ability to deal with spatial relationships (Picture Completion, Block Design, and Object Assembly).

As noted earlier, Jeffrey's mean performance in each of these basic skill areas indicates that his conceptual thinking skills fall within the bright-normal range, his sequencing abilities within the average range, and his ability to deal with spatial relationships within the dull-normal range.

However, upon examination, it can be seen that even within such clusters there is variability of performance, indicating various areas of deficit within a skill area which appears to be relatively intact. In Jeffrey's case, for example, his performance on the Similarities subtest appears significantly weaker than on either of the other subtests within the conceptual thinking cluster. Also, Digit Span and Picture Completion are notably lower than the other subtests within the sequencing and spatial relationships clusters, respectively. This is the point at which a cognizance of the additional underlying skills and an examination of the qualitative data become crucial as the examiner attempts to interpret the assessment data.

Test ages/developmental levels. Wechsler (1949, 1967, 1974) provides tables in the test manuals which enable the examiner to convert the scaled scores from each subtest to a test age. These test ages are essentially equivalent to mental ages which reflect the developmental levels at which the child is functioning on the various subtests. Such information may provide the examiner with a more meaningful basis upon which to establish remedial recommendations than do the scaled scores. Test interpretations which rely exclusively upon scaled scores to the exclusion of test ages not only communicate less usable information to the recipient of the psychological report (e.g., classroom teacher), but may also communicate a qualitatively different impression, perhaps to the child's disadvantage.

For example, suppose the psychological report which summarizes Jeffery's data stated that he earned a scaled score of six on theArithmetic subtest which falls within the borderline range of intelligence. The recipient of this report may have little understanding of what is meant by "scaled score" and may focus upon the statement that Jeffrey's mental computational skills are at the borderline level which may connote a degree of prognostic pessimism. Interpretive comments which are couched in terms of classifiable labels (i.e., borderline intelligence) often imply a static, unchangeable condition. However, were the examiner to qualify such a statement by adding that Jeffrey's performance on the Arithmetic subtest is essentially equivalent to that of a preschool child aged 5 years, 10 months, or that Jeffrey is functioning nearly three years below the expectations for his chronological age, the recipient of the report may be able to judge more accurately the approximate level at which remediation should begin in order to help Jeffrey narrow this developmental gap. As the examiner goes on to supplement the report with qualitative data which further explain the nature of Jeffrey's difficulties with the Arithmetic subtest, the reasons for his current level of functioning may be perceived from a more dynamic point of view as a process which needs assistance to develop rather than as a condition which may remain unchanged.

Scoring the Bender designs. The Bender Gestalt Test consists of nine geometric designs which are shown to the child one at a time to be reproduced on a blank piece of paper. In essence, it is one measure of visual-motor performance. Generally, the child's reproductions of the Bender designs are judged by the examiner as either impaired or accurate, though the degree and nature of impairment should not be left entirely to the subjective judgment of the examiner. A more accurate assessment may be obtained by comparing the child's drawings with normative expectations, e.g., Koppitz (1963) scoring system. Quantitative scoring of the child's designs provides the examiner with a perceptual age level which enables the examiner to determine which distortions in the child's reproductions are age-appropriate. Knowing when a particular type of distortion ceases to be age-appropriate and becomes indicative of a brain dysfunction is, of course, vital information. Also, such quantitative scores make test-retest comparisons more meaningful in assessing the child's rate of progress over a specific period of time.

A meaure of short-term memory may be obtained by having the child draw as many of the designs as he can remember immediately after administering the test and after removing his initial reproductions from view.

At age 8-3, Jeffrey's reproductions of the Bender designs resulted in a Koppitz perceptual age level of 6 years, 6 months. This score suggests nearly a two-year gap in his ability to handle such a visual-motor task and is perhaps comparable to his ability to handle spatial relationships as indicated by the Bannatyne analysis of the WISC subtest clusters. His errors included rotations, distortions of shape and problems with integration, each of which is considered by Koppitz to be either significant or highly significant as an indicator of brain injury. In the memory portion of the test, Jeffrey recalled seven of the nine designs which, even in the absence of established norms, would subjectively appear to be above average for a child of his chronological age. It would seem reasonably safe to consider, at least at this point, that Jeffrey's short-term visual memory is more efficient than his short-term auditory memory (as measured by the WISC Digit Span). Again, however, the examiner must be cautious in concluding that these results reflect differences in visual versus auditory memory *per se* before considering which additional skills are involved in the successful performance of each task. It is of diagnostic interest to note that a reversal occurred in Jeffrey's memory reproduction of design A which may reflect a difficulty in reproducing other symbols (e.g., alphabet or numbers) from memory (which, in fact, was true).

Interpretation of Qualitative Assessment Data

The efficacy of a child's functioning on any task is seldom, if ever, a function of the primary or surface requirements of the task *per se*. Whether it be a task which purports to measure auditory memory, visual discrimination, or concept formation, the child's response will reflect the extent to which those surface skill requirements are supported by and integrated with intact skills at other levels of development. For example, a seemingly discrete skill such as auditory memory will be dependent upon the existence and effective functioning of such skills as attention and concentration, auditory discrimination, auditory sequencing, visualization, and, perhaps, mnemonic techniques which rely upon certain higher level conceptual skills. The skills associated with one sensory modality may be affected significantly by skills at various levels within that modality, as well as by skills within other sensory modalities and by skills which are multisensory in nature. Rappaport (1969) has also discussed this interrelatedness of skills and the ways in which the intactness of skills at different levels affect learning.

Clearly, this is a complex state of affairs and it is often impossible, if not unnecessary, to tease out every skill which may be contributing to a child's performance in any specific situation. The point is, however, that there are multiple determinants of behavior and that cognizance of the essential determinants in any particular situation may prevent the examiner from misjudging the apparent source of difficulty and, in turn, from recommending a course of action which may not be completely relevant. The child's response to a particular task and/or to specific items within a task may suggest deficits in skills which are only incidentally associated with successful performance on the task, or skills which are absolutely essential for successful performance. In the discussion that follows, some of the skills which should be acknowledged by the examiner in the assessment of children with specific learning disabilities will be considered. Rappaport's (1964) outline of response patterns which characterize such children will, in part, serve as the focus for organizing the discussion. These response patterns have been described in Chapter 2 as emotional concomitants to SLD/MBD/ HKS. Keep in mind, however, that each child is different and that no child need necessarily display every symptom which will be discussed. The clinical behavior and test responses of two children may be quite different from each other, yet both may reflect a specific learning disability.

INADEQUATE IMPULSE CONTROL OR REGULATION

Hyperactivity. Clinical observation of the child throughout the examination is the primary source of data indicative of hyperactivity. The child's behavior may not necessarily be unacceptable *per se* but may appear to be driven and in double-time relative to age-appropriate behavior patterns; it may be exceptionally inquisitive and even intrusive. Interest in objects or topics of conversation may be fleeting, due to a short attention span. A quality of restlessness may be present, ranging from generalized mobility to remaining seated but being fidgety (e.g., moving legs, tapping fingers, balancing on the back legs of the chair, and reaching for test materials).

On the other hand, some children with specific learning disabilities may be hypoactive, relatively inactive even to the point of being phlegmatic. Conversation may be abbreviated and minimally spontaneous. Hence the activity level may range from being overactive to being underactive.

In Jeffrey's case, mild to moderate physical and verbal hyperactivity tended to characterize his behavior. He moved about the examination room to inspect various objects; he asked numerous questions about objects; he had a difficult time remaining seated and required intermittant "breaks;" he would frequently offer irrelevant comments stimulated by a test item; and he generated the feeling of being impatient even though on the surface he was cooperative and seemingly interested in performing well on each task. Jeffrey's roaming, inquisitive behavior could generally be controlled with verbal limits from the examiner and a refocusing upon the task at hand. The frequency of "breaks" had to be structured relative to the completion of various tasks rather than relative to time segments (e.g., "in ten minutes") because his concept of time was not adequately developed and he would frequently ask,

"Is it time yet?" The "breaks" were limited by the examiner to such activities as getting a drink of water, going to the bathroom, informal conversation with the examiner, or quiet and calm mutual involvement with some object in the room. Were such limits not imposed, Jeffrey's hyperactivity would have been escalated by the activities, and returning to a relatively controlled test-taking attitude would have been more difficult and time consuming. For some children, permitting unstructured "breaks" could sabotage the remainder of the assessment session.

Hyperdistractibility. Clinical observation is again the primary source of data on the extent to which a child's attention and concentration are interrupted by a shift toward extraneous, irrelevant stimuli. Selective attention is often difficult for the child to maintain; external background stimuli attract the child's attention away from the stimulus situation in the foreground.

Hyperdistractibility may also be elicited by internal stimuli. An irrelevant thought or question may spontaneously occur within the child and, rather than ignoring it and continuing with a task, he/she will express the thought or question and disrupt the assessment process. The examiner must decide whether, for the sake of a meaningful assessment, it would be better to ignore or turn off the irrelevant comments or to provide some type of response. If the comments seem to be associated with situational anxiety or other factors which could impair optimal test performance, a simple explanation or reassurance may be indicated. If, on the other hand, the comments seem to be essentially a function of distractibility *per se,* then structure and limits should be imposed to preserve the assessment process.

Such was the situation with Jeffrey. He would attempt to lure discussion away from test items (which might reveal his deficits) and toward social discourse with which he felt more comfortable. Occasional reassurance from the examiner, praise for Jeffrey's efforts, comments that it is all right to make mistakes when an item is too hard, and indication that certain comments would be discussed at the end of testing if time permitted sufficed to refocus Jeffrey's distracting behavior.

Disinhibition. Whenever the child has an insufficiently developed sense of social propriety, comments or behavior may occur which most people at a similar age or older would suppress because of social embarrassment or a sense of politeness and empathy. However, the inhibitory function of the cerebral cortex may not always develop in tandem with inner needs and social awareness, due to a minimal brain dysfunction, and as a result, the child may behave similarly to someone who is intoxicated.

Clinical observation would be the primary source of data for this characteristic. During the testing sessions with Jeffrey, none of this type of behavior was evident.

Impulsivity. The impulsive child is essentially unable to restrain the overt expression of various kinds of behavior, without conscious effort. An impulse to action sequence without an intermediate period of delay tends to characterize much of the child's daily experiences.

In the assessment situation, this is clearly evident from certain aspects of test behavior. For example, the child may respond quickly to test items, especially when the task is being timed, almost as though he/she is attempting to demonstrate adequacy in dealing with the test item. In so doing, however, the impulsivity may cause careless errors on items which are within the child's range of ability. Or, the impulsive child may attempt to anticipate the examiner's instructions and literally jump into the task before the instructions are completed.

Sometimes impulsivity is reflected on verbal items when initial comments are either erroneous or of poor quality but improve as the child continues to explain an answer. Of course, this type of situation could also result when the child needs to think out loud. The auditory feedback of the thought processes at times enables the child with SLD/MBD/HKS to organize these thoughts better and to approximate a response of higher quality (a type of zeroing in on a target when one does not have the marksmanship skills to hit a bull's eye on the first attempt).

On performance items, impulsivity may be evident from the child's hurried trial-and-error approach in the absence of deliberation. Again, trial-and-error behavior on performance items may serve a function similar to thinking out loud on verbal items. Alternatively, impulsivity may emerge at times when situational stress is increased even though impulsivity is not generally characteristic of the child (an important observation in prescribing a remedial program).

Impulsivity *per se* was not characteristic of Jeffrey's behavior during the assessment situation, even though it was evident in daily situations whenever he was expected to function independently and the task was subjectively too difficult. In the one-to-one assessment situation with periodic reassurance and support from the examiner, he was able to contain his frustrations with difficult tasks and persist until it became evident to both Jeffrey and the examiner that the task could not be completed successfully. Hence, one might predict at this point that impulsive behavior and/or emotional blow-ups could be minimized in Jeffrey's daily functioning through a noncritical, supportive atmosphere and/or one-to-one assistance in new situations until he develops sufficient skill to function more independently.

Perseveration. The continuation or persistence of a response beyond the point of its being appropriate or accurate is indicative of perseveration. Examples may be found both clinically and within the test data of some children with SLD/MBD/HKS. Clinically, the examiner may observe that the child repeatedly asks questions about a particular topic, draws the same type of picture again and again, or continues with some type of behavior or expression after the situation has changed. For example, in the process of establishing rapport the examiner may engage the child in an informal discussion to which the child attempts to return throughout the examination, even to the point of interrupting a task.

Numerous examples may be found within the test data. On the Information subtest, a child may indicate correctly that there are five pennies in a nickel, then proceed to indicate incorrectly that there are five days in a week and five items in a dozen. Comments or responses which may be at least partially correct for one item may be offered in response to subsequent items on the same task, such as the Comprehension, Similarities, or Vocabulary subtest. On the Digit Span subtest, perseverative interference with performance may be evident when some numbers from one series of digits are included erroneously in the next series of digits. Perseverative interference may also be present on the Coding subtest whenever the child begins to transcribe the symbols according to the sequence of the model, rather than according to the randomized sequence of the task. On the Bender designs, perseveration may be suggested if the child continues to make the series of loops or dots across the width of the paper rather than stopping when the correct number of loops or dots had been reproduced. Finally, on the Peabody Picture Vocabulary Test, a perseverated response set may be revealed whenever the child persistently points to the same response location (e.g., picture #4) for each subsequent stimulus word.

Perseveration may occur for a variety of reasons: e.g., the child has difficulty shifting from one response set to another; a response is so gratifying that it is repeated primarily for the associated pleasure; a response "worked" or was correct once, so perhaps it will "work" in another situation when the child is unsure of the correct response; the child's anxiety in a situation is partially controlled by repeating a response, as in repetitious play; and so forth. Although it is not always possible to determine the rationale for a particular child's perseverations, the examiner should go beyond applying the label of "perseveration" to the child's responses and attempt to explain why the perseveration (or any other characteristic) was elicited. Again, such information would have definite implications concerning the kinds of remedial recommendations which can be offered.

Jeffrey's data did not reveal any strong indication that perseveration interfered with his test performance, nor was perseveration particularly evident clinically.

Lability of affect. Children with SLD/MBD/HKS often display emotional instability and may tend to overreact to a situation and/or shift abruptly from one affect to another. Such characteristics are primarily evident in the child's clinical behavior.

Frustrations associated with various tasks may result in a sudden temper outburst or negativism, with possible refusal to complete additional tasks. The examiner needs to remain alert to behavioral cues that frustration is building up or that interest in the tasks is waning so that appropriate amounts and types of support may be offered. It is almost always easier to maintain a meaningful assessment session by aborting a build-up of negative affect than it is to reestablish rapport and motivation after an emotional outburst or after disinterest or negativism has decreased the child's productivity. Although the examiner's efforts to maintain optimal involvement often fail, it is diagnostically important to know how the skillful use of support and reassurance influences the child's response to frustrations or situational stress.

Motor dysfunction. In many cases, the child with SLD/MBD/HKS will experience degrees of difficulty in executing integrated and co-ordinated movements involving both large and small muscle systems. Gross motor skills (involving primarily large muscles) and fine motor skills (involving primarily small muscles) may be differently affected. It is often difficult to separate a motor dysfunction *per se* from a visual-motor dysfunction because most motor tasks are also highly dependent upon the visual system (as well as upon feedback from tactile and auditory cues). Hence, multidisciplinary assessment is indicated.

In the psychological assessment, some indications of gross motor difficulties may be gleaned from observing the manner in which the child walks or runs, ascends or descends stairs, puts on or takes off a coat, and so on. Skills associated with laterality and directionality may be assessed by observing: the extent to which both sides of the body function harmoniously and support each other on various tasks; the ability to cross the midline on paper-pencil tasks; the ability to discriminate directional concepts (e.g., right and left, up and down); and so on. Fine motor difficulties may be suggested by the way in which the child handles buttoning and unbuttoning a coat, tying shoes, holding a pencil or crayon, and so on. Poorly articulated speech may also suggest the presence of motor dysfunction.

Jeffrey's skills in this area were generally acceptable, with the exception of apparent difficulties with laterality and directionality. These difficulties were suggested by the following: on the Picture Arrangement subtest, the pictures were arranged in the proper sequence but in a right-to-left order; on the Block Design subtest, an occasional block in the reproduced pattern was rotated; in the recall portion of the Bender test, design A was reversed 180 degrees from the correct position; and in writing his name in cursive on the test paper, Jeffrey's movements were very segmented and there was notable indecisiveness each time the direction of his pencil had to change. The contributing influence of visual perceptual factors in each of these examples must not be overlooked.

INADEQUATE INTEGRATIVE FUNCTIONS

As the examiner looks beyond the surface skills which are assessed by the various tasks in the psychological test battery, supportive skills can be seen to influence the child's performance. Some of the more apparent skills are listed below. While this is not an exhaustive list of subsurface skills, it will highlight the kinds of additional data which may be cautiously teased out of surface data to provide a more comprehensive assessment of the child.

Perceptual difficulties.

(a) *Impaired spatial relationships and spatial organization.* These skills are necessary for successful performance on the Block Design subtest, the Object Assembly subtest, and the Bender designs. The child must be able to perceive the manner in which the blocks, puzzle pieces, or parts of each design relate to each other, and then to organize the pieces or parts according to those relationships. As the stimulus materials become less structured and offer fewer cues concerning the correct organization of each task, the intactness of these skills becomes increasingly important.

After successfully completing block designs A, B, and C which are highly structured and which offer cues from three dimensional models, Jeffrey was initially unable to reproduce designs #1 and #2. He worked beyond the time limit on design #2, then suddenly developed insight into the relationships between the two dimensional stimulus and the three dimensional blocks. He quickly assembled design #2, returned to design #1 and correctly assembled that within 18 seconds, then proceeded to assemble correctly designs #3 and #4. Although credit could not be given for designs #1 through #4 in computing the IQ scores according to standardized procedures, this situation illustrates the kind of valuable information which might be obtained by allowing the child to continue with tasks beyond the time limit and/or beyond the number of consecutive errors which standardized procedures specify. This additional information in Jeffrey's case gives quite a different impression about his potential ability as well as a better indication of the kind of remedial assistance he may require.

(b) *Impaired figure-ground relationships.* Difficulty with figure-ground relationships would seem to affect the child's performance on both the Picture Completion subtest and the Block Design subtest. In the former, the more subtle missing details may be masked to various degrees by the pictured details, similar to "hidden pictures" tasks. In the latter, the child may reverse the color of part or all of the stimulus design while retaining the shape, which suggests possible confusion or interference between the figure (shape) and ground (color).

(c) *Impaired sequencing skills.* The Digit Span subtest involves auditory sequencing skills, while visual sequencing skills support successful performance on the Picture Arrangement and Coding subtests. The proper use of number sequences is also essential on the Arithmetic subtest.

(d) *Impaired visual imagery.* Successful performance on some tasks is dependent upon the child's ability to visualize an object or a situation. This would seem to be particularly important on such subtests as Comprehension, Arithmetic, Similarities, Picture Completion, and Object Assembly, as well as on the recall portion of the Bender test.

(e) *Impaired gross and fine visual-motor functioning.* Observations of deficits in this area can be made throughout all performance tasks and clinical behavior. Productions on paper-pencil tasks (Coding, Bender designs) will perhaps be the most obvious. However, the examiner should also make notations concerning the smoothness with which performance task items were manipulated and the general coordination of behavior throughout the session.

(f) *Impaired memory.* The child with SLD/MBD/HKS may show evidence of difficulty with any or all combinations of short-term, long-term, auditory and visual memory. Short-term auditory memory skills may be revealed by the Digit Span subtest, as well as the child's ability to remember verbal instructions or questions. Short-term visual memory is, in part, measured by the recall of the Bender designs; however, the recall of these designs is also reinforced by the kinesthetic experience of having drawn them previously. Long-term visual and/or auditory memory may be associated with performance on the Information subtest, according to the manner in which the factual information had been learned or experienced.

(g) *Global perceptual functioning.* Frequently the child with SLD/MBD/HKS tends to retain a global perceptual orientation beyond the normal age when this occurs developmentally. A task or situation is perceived as an undifferentiated whole so that many of the details or nuances are ignored or missed. Not only could social judgment be impaired by this global orientation, but also the child's performance on various tasks could be affected, e.g., Picture Completion, Picture Arrangement, Block Design, Object Assembly.

(h) *Skip-counting.* On the first three items of the Arithmetic subtest, the child must count blocks. The child with SLD/MBD/HKS often has difficulty synchronizing his counting efforts with the motor act of pointing to each block. Consequently, the child's response may be incorrect, even though he/she has the required counting skill *per se.* On the verbal arithmetic items which require mental computation, such a child may offer answers which are one more or one less than the correct response. This "plus or minus one" error may represent an internalization of the skip-counting type of error.

(i) *Impotence.* It is not unusual for the child to recognize that an error has been made on a performance task but be unable to correct it. This type of difficulty most frequently occurs on the Block Design and Object Assembly subtests and on the Bender designs.

Conceptual difficulties.

(a) *Associative word finding problem.* The child with SLD/MBD/HKS may have difficulty responding to verbal tasks because of a problem with word retrieval, processing auditory stimuli, and organizing a verbal response. All spontaneous conversation and test-related verbalizations may provide evidence of this kind of deficit. However, responses which are elicited by the examiner or by test items are more likely to reveal this problem than spontaneous conversation because the child must make immediate associations to the stimulus rather than being able to rely upon automatic expressions or rehearsed comments. Word retrieval problems could be suggested by the following: delays or intermittant pauses when offering a verbal response; peripheral comments or "talking around" the topic (when the specific concept or word which is needed cannot be retrieved, as differentiated from the situation where the child had never learned the concept); frequent use of such comments as, "You know what I mean," following an incomplete response; responding to Picture Completion items with, "The thing that goes here," or by misnaming the missing part, such as calling the missing teeth to the comb "points."

(b) *Arbitrary and "clang" associations.* Sometimes the child may offer an arbitrary guess rather than admit that he does not know an answer, in an attempt to protect his pride and the hope that, like a shot in the dark, it will be accurate. To the Arithmetic subtest question which asks, "If I cut an apple in half, how many pieces will I have?" Jeffrey responded with, "About four or three."

At other times, the child assumes, through concrete logical reasoning, that if his answer rhymes with or sounds like the stimulus in some way, it must be similar or equivalent to the stimulus. On the Vocabulary subtest, Jeffrey responded to the word *nuisance* with, "Like a newspaper."

These responses may occur on any verbal task. Evidence of arbitrary associations (or arbitrary responses) may also occur on performance tasks and would be suggested by a haphazard assembling of pieces in the apparent hope that the solution will be correct (e.g., pushing all the blocks of a design together at the same time with both hands).

(c) *Conceptual generic spread and tangential associations.* Conceptual difficulties may impair the development of specific "boundaries" for individual concepts and thus contribute to a fuzziness in the child's thought processes which may decrease the accuracy of his responses to test items. Jeffrey, for example, defined *diamond* as, "Something like a ruby; it's valuable and it's gold." Also, when asked to name the four seasons of the year, he replied, "Fall, Easter (pause)." When told that Easter is a holiday and not a season, he then added, "Spring and summer." He could not name the fourth until he was asked, "In what season do we have snow?" "Winter" was his immediate reply.

Also, when asked how to make water boil, Jeffrey replied, "Put it on the stove and fry it." Here, the meaning of one concept seems to blend with that of a different, but related concept.

Similarly, the child's response may blend with related associations so that his comments become somewhat tangential. When asked to define *brave,* Jeffrey said, "Brave enough to do something like a tribe—an Indian tribe—a tribe can be called brave." Here, there was essentially a fusion of two meanings of the word *brave* (i.e., courageous and Indian brave); Jeffrey began to define the word to mean courageous, but tangentially ended up with a confused reference to Indian brave. Tangential associations may also be evident when part of one response stimulates an association for additional, irrelevant responses or comments.

Evidence for conceptual generic spread and tangential association may be found in spontaneous conversation and in responses to most verbal tasks.

(d) *Concrete, rigid thought processes.* The thought processes of the child with SLD/MBD/HKS may be notably concrete and rigid. Stimuli may be interpreted literally without recognition of the subtle nuances of meaning, and there may be an insufficient degree of flexibility in problem-solving efforts. The effects of such thought processes might permeate all test data from both verbal and performance tasks. Rather than thinking abstractly, the child will think in specific, functional and narrow channels. Or, perhaps the correct solution to a Block Design or Object Assembly item is ever so close, but the child's rigid, unchanging approach to the task seems to "blind" him from aware-ness of the solution.

(e) *Immature language patterns and transpositions.* The gram-matical structure of expressive language and the sequential order of words (or of sounds within words) often provide cues to the examiner that the child's conceptual development is immature or impaired. Again, all spontaneous conversation and test-related verbalizations may provide examples of this type of difficulty.

DEFECTIVE SELF-CONCEPT AND NARCISSISTIC HYPERSENSITIVITY

Emotional and social adjustment difficulties develop secondarily to the frustrations, failures, rejections, and conflicts which the child has experienced as the result of his various skill deficits. According to the intensity of such difficulties, the examiner may either recognize subtle interferences with test performance or take definite steps to deal with the more blatant interferences of emotional factors. The child may display some or all of the following: low frustration tolerance; labile affect; task-avoidant behavior; self-deprecatory behavior; an exceptionally strong preference for tasks related to skill assets as an overcompensation for skill deficits; behavioral patterns which are designed to control or manipulate others; and negativism and a proclivity for eliciting power struggles.

It would be important for the examiner to note not only whether these behavioral factors are task-related or generalized, but also the extent to which structure is effective in modifying and controlling the behavior.

TEST-RETEST COMPARISONS

Whenever longitudinal test data are available for a child, comparisons between the sets of data should focus not only upon the quantitative differences but also upon the qualitative differences. Sometimes a factor which was present previously (e.g., perseveration) is not evident in a subsequent reevaluation, but perhaps other factors have emerged. The examiner cannot, of course, separate the influence of maturational factors from remediation. However, reference to the remedial program which the child experienced during the time interval may suggest possible explanations for the changes.

If the retest data reveal lower quantitative scores in some areas, the examiner should not be too quick to explain the change on the basis of regression. Close examination of the data may reveal, for example, that the child actually answered more items correctly, but received a lower score because the amount of growth was not sufficient to keep pace with normative expectations relative to increased chronological age.

In looking at Jeffrey's retest data, it can be seen that he earned lower scaled scores on the Arithmetic, Vocabulary, Picture Arrangement, and Coding subtests; however, an inspection of raw scores and test ages of these subtests reveals that he performed at a higher level during the reevaluation than he did initially. Hence, there is evidence of cognitive growth in each area measured by the Wechsler subtests, even though some of the gains were less than normative expectations.

Differential Diagnosis of SLD/MBD/HKS Children

Inexperienced psychologists frequently attempt to rule out the presence of SLD/MBD/HKS primarily on the basis of signs which are characteristically associated with some types of brain damage, e.g., low scores on performance tasks and distortions in the reproduction of Bender designs. When such signs are not strikingly evident, some psychologists conclude that a brain dysfunction is not present and interpret the findings in terms of an emotionad disturbance. While secondary emotional factors are almost always present to some degree in children with SLD/MBD/HKS, it is essential to consider the various quantitative and qualitative data discussed earlier so that the primary diagnosis of MBD is not prematurely ruled out.

While there is no specific pattern of Wechsler subtest scores which characterizes all children with SLD/MBD/HKS, test performance can be used to differentiate such children from those with endogenous retardation. The test performance of children with SLD/MBD/HKS tends to be erratic, with relatively high and low scores scattered throughout the test protocol; the test performance of children with endogenous retardation tends to be more uniformly low. Also, the former would demonstrate some evidence of at least near average potential, whereas the latter would not. Data from other areas of assessment (e.g., developmental history and educational evaluation) would provide valuable additional information to facilitate the differential diagnosis.

Differentiating the child with SLD/MBD/HKS from the child with a characterological, neurotic, or psychotic disturbance is more difficult, and the importance of data from a multidisciplinary evaluation is great. Part of the difficulty in making such a differential diagnosis stems from the fact that the child with SLD/MBD/HKS may have a superimposed emotional disturbance. Hence, the issue becomes one of teasing out the data which appear to be relatively specific to a minimal brain dysfunction—not an easy feat! It is conceivable that many of the characteristics of SLD/MBD/HKS discussed previously (i.e., inadequate impulse control, inadequate integrative functions, especially at the conceptual level, defective self-concept, and narcissistic hypersensitivity) would also be produced by emotional factors. However, the manifestations of these characteristics are qualitatively different for the child with SLD/MBD/HKS as compared with the child with an emotional disturbance.

Below are listed a few of the *distinguishing factors* which may help to differentiate these two groups. These factors are not intended to be all inclusive, nor will the distinction between the groups hold true for every case; however, these factors are intended to serve as a general guide. Characteristically, the child with SLD/MBD/HKS relative to the child with an emotional disturbance:

(1) has greater difficulty with basic skill areas (e.g., visual and auditory perception and discrimination, visual and auditory sequencing, gross and fine motor coordination, directionality and laterality);

(2) shows a greater degree of improvement in performance on perceptual or conceptual tasks whenever structure is increased;

(3) may demonstrate a more immature level of language and conceptual development;

(4) may manifest greater unevenness of performance when the efficiency of different sensory channels is compared (e.g., visual versus auditory).

THE PSYCHOLOGICAL REPORT

After collecting and interpreting the data as described above, the final step of the assessment process is writing the report. The psychological report will serve as the primary means for communicating the findings and recommendations to those who are responsible for providing a remedial program. Consequently, as much careful consideration must be given to the report writing process as was given to the data collection process, so that the value of the data is not lost in a disorganized, poorly articulated, or incomplete report. Unfortunately, there is no guarantee that an excellent report will lead to a remedial program of similar quality; on the other hand, a poorly composed report may significantly limit the effectiveness of the remedial program which is, in part, dependent upon information from the cognitive assessment.

Format

The specific format which is used to organize the report and the extent to which details are elaborated will vary with the purpose of the assessment and the professional audience for whom the report is written. Also, with the inception of "right to know" legislation, parental requests for copies of such reports are more frequent. Consequently, unless two reports are written (one for the professional and one for the parents) the report should present the essential findings in a way which will guide the professional in developing a remedial program and which will be readily understood by parents who may not be familiar with esoteric, professional jargon.

Generally, consideration should be given to each of the following factors: intelligence quotients, subtest scores, intertest and intratest variability, patterns of variability (e.g., input versus central processing versus output, auditory versus visual), levels of functioning expressed in terms of developmental levels, response to structure, potential ability, assets, deficits, recommendations, diagnosis, and prognosis.

Other Suggestions

The remedial recommendations should be as specific and as age-appropriate as possible. There are several sources which provide suggestions for remedial activities, although these may require modification to be specifically applicable to the child's needs and level of sophistication. Some of the reference sources are: Bannatyne (1971), Blanco (1972), Farrald and Schamber (1973), Ferinden and Jacobsen (1969), Kirk and Kirk (1971), Searls (1975), Valett (1967).

CONCLUSIONS

In order to provide optimal guidance in the development of a remediation program, the assessment of children with SLD/MBD/HKS must reveal not only the blatant skill deficits, but also the subtle deficits and underlying factors which, although not readily apparent, may contribute significantly to learning and adjustment difficulties. Clinical behavior and diagnostic data must be examined systematically and almost microscopically. While standardized test procedures should be respected, they should not limit the scope of the assessment process. The developmental process approach which has been described above can enable the examiner to collect more informative data than might be otherwise possible were the assessment process limited to standardized procedures only.

This approach to data collection and interpretation can, of course, be applied to any area of assessment. In fact, such an approach or conceptual orientation should characterize the efforts of the professional team throughout the remediation period. The child's behavior and responses during the assessment session represent but a small sample of his daily behavior and response to all situations. The assessment of the child should not be limited to formal testing sessions, but should be ongoing, so that the treatment process can be continually modified in accordance with the child's current needs.

REFERENCES

Bannatyne, O. Diagnosing learning disabilities and writing remedial prescriptions. *Journal of Learning Disabilities,* 1968, *1*(4), 28-35.

Bannatyne, A. *Language, reading and learning disabilities.* Springfield, Ill.: Charles C Thomas, 1971.

Bender, L. *Bender Motor Gestalt Test: Cards and manual of instructions.* American Orthopsychiatric Association, Inc., 1946.

Blanco, R.F. *Prescriptions for children with learning and adjustment problems.* Springfield, Ill.: Charles C Thomas, 1972.

Bush, W.J. & Giles, M.T. *Aids to psycholinguistic teaching.* Columbus, Ohio: Charles E. Merrill, 1969.

Clements, S.D. *Minimal brain dysfunction in children: Terminology and identification.* Public Health Service Publication No. 1415, United States Department of Health, Education and Welfare. Washington, D.C.: U.S. Government Printing Office, 1966.

Dunn, L.M. *Peabody Picture Vocabulary Test manual.* Minneapolis: American Guidance Service, 1959.

Dunn, L.M. *Expanded manual for the Peabody Picture Vocabulary Test.* Minneapolis: American Guidance Service, 1965.

Farrald, R.R. & Schamber, R.G. *Handbook I: A mainstream approach to identification, assessment and amelioration of learning disabilities* (2nd ed.). Sioux Falls, South Dakota: ADAPT Press, 1973.

Ferinden, W.E., Jr. & Jacobsen, S. *Educational interpretation of Wechsler Intelligence Scale for Children (WISC).* Linden, New Jersey: Remediation Associates, 1969.

Frostig, M. & Maslow, P. *Learning problems in the classroom: Prevention and remediation.* New York: Grune & Stratton, Inc., 1973.

Gesell, A. & Amatruda, C.S. *Developmental diagnosis* (2nd ed.). New York: Harper & Row, 1967.

Hellmuth, J. (Ed.). *Cognitive studies, 2: Deficits in cognition.* New York: Brunner/Mazel, 1971.

Kirk, S.A., & Kirk, W.D. *Psychodiagnostic learning disabilities: Diagnosis and remediation.* Urbana, Ill.: University of Illinois Press, 1971.

Koppitz, E.M. *The Bender Gestalt Test for young children.* New York: Grune & Stratton, 1963.

Lerner, J.W. *Children with learning disabilities: Theories, diagnosis, and teaching.* Boston: Houghton Mifflin Co., 1971.

Rappaport, S.R. Behavior and ego development in a brain-injured child. *Psychoanalytic study of the child,* 1961, *16,* 423–450.

Rappaport, S.R. (Ed.). *Childhood aphasia and drain damage: A definition.* Narberth, Pa.: Livingston Publishing Co., 1964.

Rappaport, S.R. (Ed.). *Childhood aphasia and brain damage: Volume II. Differential diagnosis.* Narberth, Pa.: Livingston Publishing Co., 1965.

Rapaport, S.R. (Ed.). *Childhood aphasia and brain damage: Volume III. Habilitation.* Narberth, Pa.: Livingston Publishing Co., 1966.

Rappaport, S.R. *Public education for children with brain dysfunction.* Norristown, Pa.: Syracuse University Press, 1969.

Sattler, J.M. *Assessment of children's intelligence.* Philadelphia: W.B. Saunders, 1974.

Searls, E.F. *How to use WISC scores in reading diagnosis.* Newark, Delaware: International Reading Association, 1975.

Small, L. *Neuropsychodiagnosis in psychotherapy.* New York: Brunner/Mazel, 1973.

Smith, W.L. & Philippus, M.J. (Ed.). *Neuropsychological testing in organic dysfunction.* Springfield, Ill.: Charles C Thomas, 1969.

Terman, L.M. & Merrill, M.A. *Stanford-Binet Intelligence Scale.* Boston: Houghton Mifflin, 1960.

Valett, R.E. *The remediation of learning disabilities.* Palo Alto, California: Fearon, 1967.

Wechsler, D. *Manual for the Weschler Intelligence Scale for Children.* New York: Psychological Corporation, 1949.

Wechsler, D. *Manual for the Wechsler Preschool and Primary Scale of Intelligence.* New York: Psychological Corporation, 1967.

Wechsler, D. *Manual for the Wechsler Intelligence Scale for Children, Revised.* New York: Psychological Corporation, 1974.

CHAPTER 4

EDUCATIONAL ASSESSMENT, DIAGNOSIS, AND EVALUATION

BENJAMIN W. CHAMPION, Ed.D.

The analysis and so-called diagnosis of children with learning disabilities, from a psychoeducational standpoint, has been—and probably still is—based on superficial tests and observations ... What appears to be a more promising approach is the microscopic type of test ... (Such) analytical or diagnostic tests bring us closer than we have ever been to providing help in writing a prescription for teaching.

> —Samuel A. Kirk, *Selected papers on learning disabilities.*
> *Progress in parent information, professional*
> *growth, and public policy.*

With the passage of Public Law 94-142, on November 29, 1975, a written individualized educational program (IEP) has been mandated for all handicapped children, including learning-disabled students. The requirements for the IEP are consistent with the systematic approach to educational programming which will be discussed in this chapter. These requirements include (1) listing assessment data of the student's present educational levels, (2) establishing annual goals in basic skill areas and setting short-term instructional objectives relating to these goals, and (3) designating what tests, evaluative materials and/or procedures shall be used to determine mastery of the objectives and what the criteria of successful performance shall be. The sequence of assessment, determination of objectives, instruction, and evaluation of objectives mastered is to be evident in these requirements. Different states are, at the time of this writing, constructing their own forms on which to record the information which will comply with the requirements of PL 94-142. Some are not providing adequate space for complete recording of the data. One format which allows for flexibility in the amount of space needed has been published by The National Learning Resource Center of Pennsylvania and The Eastern Pennsylvania Special Education Regional Resource Center within the booklet, *An Introduction to Individualized Education Program Plans in Pennsylvania: Guidelines for School Age IEP Development.*

Public Law 94-142 requires written documentation of the individualized education program and provision for stipulated related services for appropriate educational programming within the "least restrictive environment." The term, "least restrictive environment," is used to indicate that all handicapped children are to be educated with children who are not handicapped to the maximum extent considered appropriate, and removed only to the degree that is necessary, based on the nature or severity of the handicap. The quality of the services provided and the results obtained are not covered by this law. The skill provided by the clinical and educational staff in assessing, planning, and implementing IEPs will, to a large extent, determine the quality and effectiveness of the educational program beyond the services and objectives required by PL 94-142.

Preceding the writing of goals and objectives for an IEP, testing must be done to establish current educational achievement levels. Therefore, the need for a foundational understanding of educational testing is especially important for the special educator but is also greatly needed for basic education teachers.

PURPOSES FOR TESTING

Testing has been associated with education in such an integral way that one may believe, as the song states, "You can't have one without the other." Tests involve questions, and a questioning attitude is an asset to the teacher, clinician, and researcher. Questioning helps us make judgments about many things, including what one knows and understands, what one can or cannot do and how well, and how one feels about persons, facts, or situations. In other words, through questioning, one can gain an awareness of another's knowledge, skills, and attitudes.

An early question to be asked about educational testing is one concerning the value of testing: "Why test students?" The answers may vary, depending upon what the examiner wants to know about

before a task at this level can be performed. For example, an arithmetic problem involving "carrying" requires sensory-perceptual abilities of visual discrimination between numbers, etc., and the percursory skill of being able to add numbers without "carrying."

Lerner (1976) presented these two ways of thinking about task analysis as: (1) the *modality-processing* approach, to evaluate and analyze the processing abilities that underlie the learning task; and (2) the *skills-sequence approach,* to analyze and evaluate what is to be learned, i.e., the task itself. The first analyzes the child, while the second analyzes the content to be learned.

These factors should be remembered when one considers a student's performance on a test or an instructional activity. Therefore, task analysis is a competency required for the clinician involved in educational diagnosis and for the learning therapist/teacher involved in clinical teaching.

TESTS AND ASSESSMENT

When deciding what to test and what instruments to use, the educational examiner is advised to begin with two interrelated questions: (1) what do I want the learner to know, to be able to do, and to become? and (2) what do I want to know about the learner?

Some of the areas in which information can be sought about SLD/MBD/HKS children are listed in Table 4.1.

Table 4.1
Important Areas of Educational
Information on SLD/MDB/HKS Children

Ability to relate and develop rapport with the examiner
Attitudes toward learning, school, and being tested
General interests
Ability to attend to tasks presented; degree of distractibility
Awareness of making errors and ability to self-correct
An estimated rate of learning
Accessibility to instruction
Levels of achievement in relation to age and intellectual functioning
Levels at which instruction could begin successfully
Visual and hearing acuity
Modality-processing strengths and weaknesses
Academic learning skills mastered and not mastered
General knowledge and comprehension

In assessing specific academic or learning skills to prepare an individualized education program (IEP) for an SLD/MBD/HKS child or adolescent, the key topical areas listed in Table 4.2 should be considered.

CLASSIFICATION OF TESTS

Tests may be classified a number of ways. The categories considered here are (1) standardized or norm-referenced, (2) criterion-referenced, and (3) informal measures.

Standardized tests, more recently called norm-referenced tests (NRT), result in grade level scores or developmental age level scores derived from comparing the performance of the testee with that of a normative population. Scholastic achievement tests and intelligence tests are examples of standardized or norm-referenced tests.

A *criterion-referenced test,* on the other hand, reveals what a student can do or cannot do or what one knows or does not know. Such a test is appropriate when the main information sought concerns which skills or learning objectives a student has mastered rather than how he compares with a group. Examples are the Prescriptive Reading Inventory (PRI) and the Diagnostic Mathematics Inventory (DMT) published by the California Test Bureau/McGraw-Hill.

Some attempts have been made to combine the aspects of norm-referenced and criterion-referenced testing. One test designed this way, the Key Math Diagnostic Arithmetic Test, provides a total test grade equivalent score and has instructional objectives operationally defined for each item in the test. More tests are needed, and can be expected, which provide information concerning how a student compares with a normative group, as well as the extent of his/her skill or knowledge in instructional areas, thereby establishing the assessment on which an instructional plan is based.

Informal measures are tests which can be teacher-made. The technique is an informal one in that specific methods are not standardized, and no norms have been established for performance to be compared with what other students can do (Johnson and Kress, 1965). A variety of informal measures are possible. Some of the possibilities have been suggested by Wallace and Kauffman (1973):

(a) seatword exercises emphasizing *one* specific task;
(b) orally administered exercises;
(c) informal teaching lessons assessing various skills;
(d) individually administered written assignments.

Table 4.2
Key Topical Areas for an
IEP Assessment of SLD Children

Language Arts

Readiness skills: visual discrimination between letters and words, letter recognition, rhyming, following directions, and sequencing.

Recognizing words as wholes: in isolation and in context.

Word attack skills: use of context, phonic analysis, and structural analysis.

Comprehension: from listening and from oral and silent reading.

Written expression: manuscript and cursive handwriting, spelling, sentence and paragraph construction, and capitalization, punctuation, and usage.

Mathematics

Content: numeration, fractions, and geometry.

Operations: addition, subtraction, multiplication, division, mental computation, and numerical reasoning.

Applications: word problems, missiong elements, money, measurement, and time.

Informal areas: geometric forms, counting skills, number writing, and monetary skills.

Speech and Language

Oral expression: syntax, phonology, morphology, semantic content (ideation sequencing), conceptual development, vocabulary.

Written expression: language – sentence development, syntax, sequencing, vocabulary, content, grammar, visual motor coordination.

Auditory Reception: directions – content, grammer, syntax, morphology, vocabulary, phonology.

General language development to determine age level: conceptual, vocabulary, comprehension, sequencing, visual-motor, following directions, general trend of information.

Auditory evaluation: acuity, discrimination, sequential memory, memory for content, blending, auditory sequencing (included in language evaluation).

Speech evaluation: oral peripheral evaluation, articulation test–isolation level, word level, sentence level.

CLINICAL TEACHING

Whether involved in assessment or instruction, clinical or diagnostic teaching is an important process in a student-centered approach. Both informal measures and instructional activities can be used. The purpose of clinical teaching is to observe how well the student can perform and learn when presented with tasks which are structured differently. The analysis and synthesis of impressions derived from these observations provide the examiner or teacher with conclusions regarding the rate of a student's learning as well as the preferred methods and degree of structure which appear to be efficacious for instruction.

This author feels that clinical teaching is so important that a diagnostic procedure which does not include it is incomplete in the data collected. Likewise, instruction for learning disabled students which does not involve close observation of the process and product of a student's performance lacks the diagnostic/prescriptive element necessary for optimal planning of instruction. The clinical teaching component of an instructional program is discussed in the chapter on educational remediation (see Chapter 15).

To illustrate the educational assessment procedure for SLD/MBD/HKS children and adolescents, four case studies from different age groups will be presented. The data outlined in Case Study 4.1 will be used to write an Individualized Education Program (IEP) in Chapter 15.

Case Study 4.1

An Educational Assessment of a Latency Age SLD Child

PERSONAL AND SOCIAL ASSESSMENT

Background History

Jimmy was an 8-year-old boy whose educational history suggested behavioral problems, hyperactivity, and aggressiveness. He began school in regular classes but was soon moved to a county program for emotionally disturbed and learning disabled children. His teachers were still not satisfied with his progress. Special school residential placement was recommended.

There was no history of fainting, convulsions, or seizures. No medication had been used. Jimmy had received psychotherapy, and it was recommended to be part of his residential habilitative program.

Behavioral Observations

Rapport was established easily with Jimmy, who knew his age and date of birth. He stated he likes school, especially being able to go fishing at his last school. Also, in this opening portion of the evaluation, he was asked to draw a picture of anything he wished to draw. In doing so he asked the examiner to draw some grass on one side of the paper while he drew on the other side. Throughout the evaluation he told the examiner a number of tasks he wanted the examiner to perform, sometimes manipulating with, "Unless you do . . . I won't work anymore." He also tried the shock value of a number of "dirty" words and sexual references, seemingly to observe the examiner's reaction. Although he frequently said, "I quit," when Jimmy experienced difficulty, he almost always finished what he was asked to do. It was the examiner's opinion that the results of this assessment seemed to approximate accurately Jimmy's optimal performance.

LANGUAGE ARTS ASSESSMENT

Tests Administered

Jimmy was given the following battery in this cognitive skill area:

A. Draw a Picture
B. General Orientation—Information—Sequencing Ability Quiz
C. Betts Ready to Read Tests
D. Informal Word Recognition Inventory—READ Series
E. Informal Reading Inventory—READ Series
F. Roswell-Chall Diagnostic Reading Test of Word Analysis Skills
G. Wide Range Achievement Test—Spelling—Level I

Discussion of Results

A. *Draw a Picture*. Jimmy drew a picture of a racing car that showed good proportion, including an accurate depiction of an American flag. When he tried to involve the examiner in the drawing, he was told that what was desired was his own drawing. He also correctly printed his first and last name.

B. *General Orientation—Information—Sequencing Ability Tasks*. While Jimmy knew the day of the week, he did not know the month or season. He also *knew* his birthday, which day comes before Friday, his right hand and left knee, two things that were behind him (without looking), counting backwards from 10 to 1, counting by 2s from 2 to 20, and counting by 5s from 5 to 50. He did *not know* his teacher's name, the months of the year, the seasons and which season includes January, the names of the days of the week in sequence, and the approximate time of day (without looking at the clock).

C. *Betts Ready to Read Test of Visual Discrimination*. Jimmy was able to visually discriminate eleven of fourteen upper case letters. The following were his errors: *C* for *S, V* for *U,* and *Y* for *W.* His visual discrimination of lower case letters resulted in thirteen correct responses out of 16 trials. The following were his errors: *b* for *d, p* for *q,* and he asked what letter the *u* is. Reversals were evident here.

Discrimination of combinations of letters between blends and digraphs and between words proved to be too difficult and frustrating for Jimmy, who said "I quit!"

When visually presented with the alphabet in capital letters, Jimmy made the following naming errors: *W* for *Y, V* for *U, Y* for *W* (then corrected), *H* for *N* (then corrected) and *L* for *J* (then corrected).

D. *Informal Word Recognition Inventory—READ Series.*

Level	Flash%	Untimed %
Preprimer	35	40

When presented with the task of reading individual words presented tachistoscopically, Jimmy responded with, "What's a guy gonna do if he can't read?" The examiner asked him to try anyway so what he could do and could not do could be determined to help teach him to read. The results indicated that Jimmy has few words in his sight vocabulary and very few word analysis skills. The only word he was able to identify when given an untimed presentation was the word *in;* when initially presented tachistoscopically, he said *it* for *in.*

E.   *Informal Reading Inventory—READ Series.*

Level	% Word Recognition In Context	% Reading Comprehension Oral Silent Average	% Listening Comprehension
Preprimer			
Primer	Unable to Read— Not Applicable		60
First			40

Due to Jimmy's lack of an adequate sight vocabulary at a preprimer level, he could not read enough words in context to receive a score and was not helped in word recognition by seeing the words in context rather than in isolation.

The listening comprehension at primer and first reader levels was below the 75% criterion for his being at an instructional level. His scoring below 50% at the first reader level in listening comprehension suggested he was functioning at a frustration level. He may have not scored any higher at these levels because of poor attention, but since these results indicate no discrepancy between listening comprehension and instructional reading level, it appears the prognosis for reading improvement is guarded. Comprehension and word recognition should, therefore, be emphasized in initial reading instruction with the comprehension being assessed in language-experience stories and listening comprehension activities.

F.   *Roswell-Chall Diagnostic Reading Test of Word Analysis Skills.* Jimmy was able to produce consonant sounds when shown the letter for all except the following, for which he said: the *v* sound for *z* (then corrected it), the sound *ah* for *l*, and the sound of *w* for *y*. He was unable to produce any sounds for consonant blends and digraphs, or do the following: (1) read single syllable words with short vowel sounds, (2) produce short vowel sounds when shown the vowel letters, or (3) read words with two vowels in the medial position.

G.   *Wide Range Achievement Test—Spelling Level I.* Spelling Grade Equivalent Score—1.2. Jimmy was to copy accurately eighteen marks as a readiness task within this spelling test. He was also able to spell his name but unable to spell any of the words presented. Although the grade equivalent score earned was 1.2, Jimmy should be given only those words for spelling which he can read, and he cannot yet read on a first reader level. The only exceptions to this principle would be in using a multisensory spelling approach like the Fernald technique for instruction in word recognition.

Summary of Results

A complete summary of Jimmy's pedagogical levels, assets, deficits in the language arts area can be outlined with prescribed methods of instruction.

A. *Pedagogical Levels*
   Instructional Reading Level—Readiness/Preprimer
   Instructional Spelling Level—Preprimer
   Listening Comprehension Level—Below First
   Written Expression Level—Preprimer

B. *Assets*
   1. Adequate visual discrimination between letters.
   2. Adequate pronunciation of almost all consonant sounds.
   3. Adequate recognition of almost all upper- and lower-case letters of the alphabet.
   4. Can print his name.
   5. Adequate oral expression.

C. *Deficits*
   1. Inadequate sight vocabulary at a preprimer level.
   2. Inadequate word analysis skills beyond pronunciation of single consonants.
   3. Inadequate spelling at a preprimer level.
   4. Inadequate cursive handwriting.
   5. Inadequate hearing comprehension at a primer level.
   6. Marginally accessible to instruction.

D. *Prescribed Methods of Instruction*
   1. Sight vocabulary at a preprimer level can be developed through language-experience stories and the READ basals.
   2. Instruction in word analysis skills can be introduced in relation to sight vocabulary words known, beginning with short and long vowels and consonant blends and digraphs, since he knows consonant sounds.
   3. Spelling instruction can be combined with reinforcement through writing of sight vocabulary words being learned.

4. The Lectro-Learn Handwriting Program can be used for instruction in cursive writing.
5. Opportunities for listening comprehension can be offered emphasizing his paying attention and visualizing while listening.

MATHEMATICS ASSESSMENT

Tests Administered

Key Math Diagnostic Arithmetic Test

Discussion of Results

Total Test Grade Equivalent—1.8.

Jimmy's total test grade score placed him about one year and two months behind his chronological grade level, third grade. His range among the subtests was from a beginning first to about a third grade level. He showed no erratic performance of missing easier items and correctly answering harder ones within the same subtest. Once he missed an item, he also missed the next two items, which ended the testing for that subtest, since a ceiling level of three consecutive errors was reached.

CONTENT

The content area focused on basic mathematic knowledge and concepts necessary to perform operations and make meaningful applications. Jimmy correctly answered four out of five items dealing with quantity, the most difficult of which involved counting the total number of items in a set of joined objects. He also was able to identify the number of objects in a subset when a set and a subset were given and to name an arabic numeral of one digit but was unable to give the quantity of the Roman numeral, VII. He correctly answered all items dealing with sequence of numbers including, "What comes after first, second, third?"

In fractions, he could demonstrate only an understanding of one-half. He correctly answered ten out of twenty items dealing with geometry and symbols including those requiring recognition of common shapes, their features, and identification of parts of objects. He correctly identified the symbols $+$, $-$, and $=$, but did not know $.

OPERATIONS

In addition to the four computational processes of addition, subtraction, multiplication, and division, this area includes subtests for mental computation and numerical reasoning. Jimmy could add a single-digit number to a single digit but could not correctly add when two-digit numbers were used or when regrouping (carrying) was involved. He could subtract *one* from *three, two* from *five,* and *four* from *eight;* he refused to do any subtracting problems beyond these. The only multiplication item he answered correctly was "How many are two 'threes'?" He was able to do only the first division problem which required dividing eight oranges evenly into four bowls.

In mental computation, Jimmy could answer only the following problems given orally: 1 plus 1 equals . . . ., and 2 plus 2 equals . . . . . The two items that he answered correctly in the category of numerical reasoning were like the following: tell me the number that goes in the red box: $2 + 1 =$ . . . . .

APPLICATIONS

This section of the test required putting content knowledge and operational skills into practice through subtests dealing with word problems, missing elements, money, measurement, and time. Jimmy correctly answered three word problems involving the addition of two single-digit numbers and had only one correct response to the items on missing elements; the second item which he could not answer was read to him as follows, "A farmer is paid $100 for each cow he sells. How much will he be paid for a truckload of cows? What information is missing?"

He gave the value of a dime, five pennies, and two nickels, was unable to read $47.10 on a check, correctly identified a ruler, knew that it was a six-inch ruler, gave the correct length for a three-inch line placed next to the ruler, identified a thermometer and knew that a pair contains two items, that a clock tells time, and that a wintery scene should occur in winter, and correctly identified a calendar.

Summary of Results

A complete summary of Jimmy's pedagogical levels, assets, and deficits in mathematics can be outlined for prescribed methods of instruction:

A.   *Pedagogical Level*
Mathematics Instructional Level—Mid-first.
B.   *Assets*
1. Can count backwards from ten.
2. Can count by 2s and 5s.
3. Can do addition and subtraction of single-digit problems.
4. Can understand the money value of coins.
5. Can understand simple measurement with a ruler and thermometer.
C.   *Deficits*
1. Inability to do addition and subtraction of two-digit problems.
2. Inability to do beginning multiplication and division problems.
3. Inability to handle mental computation for more than adding or subtracting two-digit numbers.
4. Inability to handle word problems involving two or more steps.

VISION SCREENING

Jimmy did not cooperate sufficiently well for a Keystone Telebinocular study to be valid. He said, "This machine will make me go blind." It was recommended that a visual function study be conducted, as outlined in Chapter 5.

SPEECH AND LANGUAGE ASSESSMENT

Jimmy was seen by an accredited Speech and Language Pathologist, who found him to be extremely hyperactive and distractible. He was able to respond to firm limits and was humorous, charming, and quite personable in general conversation.

Spontaneous speech revealed a few misarticulations. These did not interfere with intelligibility, and expressive language appeared generally adequate. A sample of written expressive language revealed many problems with spelling, grammatic, and syntactic skills. Noticeable problems with visual and auditory sequencing were also observed.

Tests Administered

Jimmy was given the following tests in this cognitive skill area:
A.   Audiometric Screening
B.   Oral Peripheral Examination
C.   Wepman Auditory Discrimination Test

D. Roswell-Chall Auditory Blending Test
E. Photo Articulation Test
F. Utah Test of Language Development

Discussion of Results

A. *Audiometric Screening.* Using a portable MAICO Audiometer in an ambient environment, for all frequencies at 20db ISO, Jimmy was found to have normal hearing bilaterally.
B. *Oral Peripheral Examination.* All physical structures and concomitant functions appeared adequate for Jimmy to execute normal speech production.
C. *Wepman Auditory Discrimination Test.* Using this measurement of Jimmy's ability to auditorily recognize the fine differences that exist between speech sounds, Jimmy's score of 22 indicated that his skills in this area were inadequate.
D. *Roswell-Chall Auditory Blending Test.* In this test to measure a child's ability to auditorily synthesize individual speech sounds into monosyllabic words, Jimmy's score of *18* indicated his skills to be inadequate in this area.
E. *Photo Articulation Test.* On this measure of his articulatory proficiency at a word level, Jimmy exhibited an inconsistent frontal lisp. He said he had had speech therapy and remembered his instruction, as self-correction was frequent. His speech was intelligible with no other remarkable deviations.
F. *Utah Test of Language Development.* Segments of this test were given with the following results: at the 4- to 5-year age range, Jimmy completed all tasks; at the 5- to 6-year range, he copied a square and identified all the vocabulary items but was unable to print simple words; at the 6- to 7-year range, he identified a penny, nickel, and dime, wrote numbers to thirty, told a familiar story, recited numbers one to fifty, and copied a diamond, but was unable to read pre-primer words; at 7 to 8, he identified all coins presented, repeated five digits, named the days of the week, and identified all the vocabulary items; beyond the 7- to 8-year age range, however, Jimmy was unable to complete any task.

Summary of Results

A summary of Jimmy's assets and deficits in speech and language can be outlined as follows:

A. *Assets*
  1. Able to be conditioned to work for a reward.
  2. Normal auditory acuity.
  3. Adequate oral peripheral mechanism.
  4. Knows monetary functions.
  5. Pleasant, somewhat cooperative.
  6. Able to self-correct his misarticulation.

B. *Deficits*
  1. Inadequate auditory perceptual skills: discrimination blending.
  2. Language development slightly delayed.
  3. Hyperactive and extremely distractible.
  4. Inconsistent frontal lisp.
  5. Slow processing time.
  6. Visual sequencing shows problems.
  7. Unable to read preprimer words.

CONCLUSIONS AND RECOMMENDATIONS

Jimmy was found to be a nonreader and slightly more than a year behind his chronological grade level in mathematics. No speech or language therapy was indicated, and it was recognized that a highly structured program of general language stimulation would be helpful. Although he consistently tested the limits of each examiner's structure during the assessment, Jimmy did respond to a firm, warm approach in holding him to appropriate expectations. In view of this response no medication was indicated.

Case Study 4.2

An Educational Assessment of a Late Latency SLD Child

PERSONAL AND SOCIAL ASSESSMENT

Background History

Sally was recommended for a private special education program after being evaluated by a psychologist at 4 years of age. After two years, she was moved to a self-contained special education class in the public schools. She has been in psychotherapy, and it is recommended for continuation.

Sally does not have a history of fainting, convulsions, or seizures and has had no surgery or significant injuries. She has been on medication only for allergies.

Behavioral Observations

Sally is an average sized youngster. She was neatly dressed and had a pleasant appearance. She is right handed.

Sally entered the examiner's office in a friendly manner. However, she acted impulsively and perseverated on some irrelevant questions. She responded well to verbal structure imposed on her by the examiner. Sally had some difficulty attending to task and will need a highly structured academic program in order to help her reach her full potential.

LANGUAGE ARTS ASSESSMENT

Discussion of Results

A.   *Informal Procedures—Writing Sample.* Sally was asked to write her name and to describe the scene viewed from the window in the examiner's office. She printed her name in legible manuscript with adequate letter formation and spatial alignment. She printed only one word for her description but was able to describe the scene orally.

B.   *General Orientation—Information—Sequencing Ability Tasks.* Sally knew the correct day, month, and season, named the days of the week but omitted October when naming the months, and was able to name the current season but had difficulty associating months of the year with corresponding seasons.

Numerically she performed as follows: counted to 14 by 2s and to 25 by 5s, and did not correctly complete the sequence of minute, hour, day. . . . Sally was able to say the entire alphabet and appeared to be aware of the concept of left and right.

C. *Wide Range Achievement Test—Level I. Reading*—Grade equivalent score of 2.2. As in an Informal Word Recognition Inventory, the student is asked to read a list of increasingly more difficult words presented in isolation. Sally appeared to have difficulty using word attack skills to decode unfamiliar words; she experienced difficulty with initial consonant blends and digraphs, e.g., read "book" for *block,* gave no response for *should, tray,* or *stalk,* and made errors involving vowels or vowel combinations, e.g., "spill" for *spell,* "awork" for *awake,* and "water" for *weather. Spelling*—Grade equivalent score of 2.0. This spelling subtest consists of three sections: (1) copying marks, (2) name writing, and (3) dictation of words. Sally printed her first name clearly in manuscript. Her letters were formed adequately, but her spatial alignment was somewhat immature.

D. *Roswell-Chall Diagnostic Reading Test of Word Analysis Skills.* Sally correctly produced consonant sounds in isolation, correctly produced consonant blends and digraphs and read C-V-C words with no difficulty. However, the fact that she could not produce any vowel sounds in isolation suggests that the C-V-C words were within her sight vocabulary. The remaining sections of this measure were not administered.

E. *Informal Word Recognition Inventory—READ Series.*

Level	Flash %	Untimed %
Preprimer	100	100
Primer	70	70
First	45	45

Sally's ability to recognize words immediately appeared to be adequate through the preprimer level, with a significant reduction in sight vocabulary at the primer and first levels. With unlimited time to apply word analysis skills to decode unfamiliar words, she did not raise her level of word recognition. The examiner feels that this indicates an inability to apply phonic skills.

F. *Informal Reading Inventory—READ Series.*

Level	% Word Recognition In Context	% Reading Comprehension			Oral Rereading
		Oral	Silent	Average	
Preprimer	86	80	100	90	Fail
Primer	72	66	83	74	Fail
First	73	Not Completed			

Some characteristic errors were: "want" for *when,* "can" for *do,* "work" for *word,* "fish" for *first,* and "of" for *for.* In the area of comprehension, Sally most often missed questions which required inferential thinking skills.

Summary of Results

A. *Pedagogical Levels*
   Instructional Reading Level—Approximately Preprimer
   Instructional Spelling Level—Approximately Primer
B. *Assets*
   1. Adequate sight vocabulary at the preprimer level.
   2. 70% sight vocabulary at the primer level.
   3. Adequate expressive language.
   4. Appears to have adequate attention span.
C. *Deficits*
   1. Scored 45% on word recognition test at the first level in both the timed and untimed section. Her apparent deficits in word attack skills severely restricted her ability to read fluently.
   2. Spelling deficits severely restrict written expression.
   3. Printing is immature and characterized by poor letter formation and spatial alignment.
   4. Made no response when asked to produce the short vowel sounds.
   5. Is currently functioning approximately five years behind her age-appropriate grade level in reading and written expression.

MATHEMATICS ASSESSMENT

Discussion of Results

A.   *Informal Tasks.* Sally was able to identify correctly coins of various denominations and their respective values. She required some prompting when naming a nickel and a quarter. Sally seemed to understand the process for making correct change.

Sally was able to count backwards from 10 to 1, to count to 14 by 2s and to 25 by 5s. She was able to write correctly the numbers 1 through 10 with adequate number formation but with somewhat immature spatial alignment.

The concept of time appeared to present great difficulty for Sally. An example of this was that, when she was shown a picture of a clock depicting three o'clock, she stated that the time was "twelve to three."

B.   *Standardized Tests.*

Wide Range Achievement Test—Arithmetic—Level I
   Grade Equivalent Score—3.2
Key Math Diagnostic Arithmetic Test
   Grade Equivalent Score—2.5

Summary of Results

A.   *Pedagogical Level*
Mathematics Instructional Level—Approximately Mid-Second

B.   *Assets*
   1. Writes numbers to at least 20.
   2. Demonstrated an awareness of the process of regrouping in addition and subtraction.
   3. Correctly completed one-digit word problems.
   4. Has an adequate awareness of money and corresponding values.

C.   *Deficits*
   1. Functioning approximately three years below appropriate age level.
   2. Unfamiliar with concepts of multiplication and division.
   3. Apparent difficulties with the concepts involved in telling time.
   4. Unfamiliar with many common units of measure.

VISION SCREENING

Keystone Telebinocular School Vision Screening

A. *Assets*
Simultaneous vision, posture, fusion, depth perception, and color vision were tested as being adequate for far point tasks.
B. *Deficits*
Usable vision for far and near point tasks was tested as being in retest area.
C. *Recommendations*
Because some subtest results were in a retest area, it is recommended that a complete vision analysis be conducted by the vision specialist.

SPEECH AND LANGUAGE ASSESSMENT

Behavioral Observations

Sally is a dark-haired, attractive 10-year-old girl. She was quite personable and cooperative, although somewhat distractible. Through general conversation, some slight language problems surfaced: noun-verb disagreement, word-finding difficulties, and some disorganization. These problems, however, were not so outstanding that they interfered with her communicative abilities. Written expression revealed immature but correct syntactic patterns.

Discussion of Results

A. *Audiometric Screening.* Results indicated esentially normal hearing bilaterally.
B. *Oral Peripheral Examination.* On observation, the physical structures and their respective functions appeared to be adequate for normal speech production.
C. *Photo Articulation Test.* Test results revealed the presence of an inconsistent distortion on some sibilants (*S, Z, /S/* blends). General conversation was found to be intelligible.
D. *Roswell-Chall Auditory Blending Test.* Sally's score of *29* indicated adequate auditory blending skills.
E. *Wepman Auditory Discrimination Test.* Sally's score of *21* in-

dicated that her skills in this area are inadequate. By this time in the session, Sally was quite tired and her concentration was somewhat limited.

F.   *Utah Test of Language Development.* Segments were administered, and Sally's language age on this test measured approximately nine years. This is one year, seven months below her chronological age.

Summary of Results

A.   *Assets*
   1. Cooperative and quite personable.
   2. Relates well with adults.
   3. Adequate auditory blending skills.
   4. Adequate receptive vocabulary.
   5. Adequate oral peripheral examination.
   6. Adequate auditory acuity.
   7. Can be structured to attend.
B.   *Deficits*
   1. Easily distractible, attention span short.
   2. Inconsistent /s/ distortion, but speech is intelligible.
   3. Inadequate auditory discrimination skills.
   4. Inadequate overall general language development.
   5. Expressive language reveals some slight syntax problems, word finding difficulties.
   6. Unable to read preprimer words.
   7. Written expression reveals immature language usage.
   8. Unable to write cursively.
   9. Poor auditory memory.

CONCLUSIONS AND RECOMMENDATIONS

Sally is a beginning reader who is, therefore, five years behind her chronological grade level and is three years behind in mathematics as well. Some slight problems with language reception and expression are exhibited by Sally, but these problems are not so remarkable that they cannot be handled by the general language program within the classroom. Speech therapy is not indicated for her at this time.

Sally appears to attend to task and adhere to routine when structure is imposed. Therefore, the need for medication is not indicated.

Case Study 4.3

An Educational Assessment of an Early SLD Adolescent

PERSONAL AND SOCIAL ASSESSMENT

Background History

Tommy has attended public school special education classes in which he made minimal educational progress, particularly in reading. He has had learning and behavioral problems in school since he entered kindergarten. The public school recommended a more intensive residential school program.

Tommy has had no illnesses and does not have a history of fainting, convulsions, or seizures, nor has he had any significant injuries. He had taken Ritalin and Cylert to help decrease hyperactivity, but no positive effect was noted by his teacher, and it was discontinued.

Behavioral Observations

Tommy was an attractive, dark-haired boy who related easily and was pleasant and humorous throughout this evaluation. He responded to the question of what he liked best and least in school by stating that he liked math most and reading least.

Tommy asked how long this part of the testing would be, and, after he was told that it would be two and a half hours, he said that was too long. Later in this testing, Tommy continually asked how much longer it would be until lunchtime. As he began to put less effort into later tasks, saying that he was doing so to get lunch quicker, he was told by the examiner that he would be allowed to go to lunch when he finished, even if that were after twelve o'clock, the scheduled finishing time.

The degree of cooperation and accessibility to assessment displayed by Tommy was adequate; therefore, the results of this evaluation seem to approximate accurately Tommy's optimal levels of performance.

LANGUAGE ARTS ASSESSMENT

Discussion of Results

A. *General Orientation—Information—Sequencing Ability Tasks.* Tommy was unable to name the months in correct sequence after July and tell which season January is in. While saying the alphabet in correct sequence, he missed *u* and *v* and said, "I always miss them two."

B. *Betts Ready to Read Test of Visual Discrimination.* While no errors were made on any of the subtests, on the one which required him to point to the one word which is different from the other four, Tommy's discrimination was slow on seven of the thirty items.

C. *Roswell-Chall Diagnostic Reading Test of Word Analysis Skills.* Tommy was able to produce the correct consonant sounds when shown the letters for most of the consonants. He was slow in producing the sound for *f*, made the sound of *z* for *v* and then self-corrected, and made the sound of *w* for *y* and then self-corrected. The following were incorrect sounds produced for consonant blends and digraphs: "sh" for *ch*, "fuh" for *fl*, "s-duh" for *st*, "w-huh" for *wh*, and no response for *scr*.

When the vowel letters were shown and Tommy asked to produce the short vowel sounds, he was unable to do this. Since the other subtests were more difficult than this, the test was discontinued at this point.

D. *Informal Word Recognition Inventory—Betts Series.*

Level	*Flash %*	*Untimed %*
Preprimer	80	85
Primer	40	75
First	35	40

At the preprimer level, Tommy was unable to recognize the following words presented tachistoscopically: *ride, me, have,* and *house.* When presented with a second exposure of these words, which was untimed, he correctly identified only the word *house.* A sharp drop in the percent of sight vocabulary occurred at the primer level; however, when applying word analysis skills, the percentage increased significantly. At the first reader level, the percentage of sight vocabulary remained low, and Tommy was unable to increase this percentage significantly when given the opportunity to apply word analysis skills.

E. *Informal Reading Inventory—READ Series.*

Level	% Word Recognition In Context	% Reading Comprehension Oral	Silent	Average
Preprimer	83	20	—	20

Informal Reading Inventory — READ Series	
Level	Listening Comprehension %
First	71
Second	60

Tommy was unable to meet the criterion in word recognition or in comprehension to be considered functioning at an instructional level in preprimer materials. When the mechanics of reading were removed by reading selections to Tommy, he still could not attain 75% listening comprehension (instructional level criterion) at either the first or second reader levels. He seems to be hampered by a lack of strength in vocabulary and background of experience, e.g., he did not know that a duck's or beaver's feet are described as being webbed. Also, the best description of dents in metal he could offer was "little round holes."

F. *Wide Range Achievement Test—Spelling—Level II.*
Spelling Grade Equivalent Score—2.2
The above spelling score was attained by correctly spelling his name and the word *cat*. On his third word, Tommy wrote "rat" for *run* and could spell no other words. His spelling words can be drawn from the preprimer and primer lists of words he is learning for sight vocabulary.

G. *Informal Written Expression Sample.* When asked to write three sentences, Tommy decided to write three versions of the same sentence: "My name is Tommy (plus his last name). My name is Tommy (middle initial and last name). My name is Tommy." The first two sentences were written in manuscript. Then Tommy was asked to write the third sentence in cursive, which he did legibly. His spacing, size, and slant of letters were all good.

Summary of Results

A. *Pedagogical Levels*
 Instructional Reading Level—Preprimer
 Instructional Spelling Level—Preprimer/Primer
 Listening Comprehension Level—Below First
 Written Expression Level—First
B. *Assets*
 1. Usually cooperative in an adult-student working relationship.
 2. Adequate visual discrimination between letters, blends, digraphs, and words.
 3. Adequate production of consonant sounds.
 4. Eighty percent of word recognition for isolated words at a pre-primer level.
 5. Legible handwriting in manuscript and cursive form.
 6. Can write sentences for written expression tasks.
C. *Deficits*
 1. Inadequate basic sight vocabulary at a primer level.
 2. Inadequate spelling at a primer level.
 3. Unable to demonstrate phonic skills in the knowledge of the sounds for some blends and digraphs and of all short vowel sounds.
 4. Inadequate listening comprehension at a first reader level.
 5. Inadequate written expression beyond the construction of simple sentences.

MATHEMATICS ASSESSMENT

Discussion of Results

KEY MATH DIAGNOSTIC ARITHMETIC TEST

 Total Test Grade Equivalent Score—3.8
Tommy's total test grade score places him slightly more than four years behind his chronological grade level, eighth grade. The range of his subtest performance was from around the middle of a first grade level in subtraction to around the seventh grade level in time concepts. However, the score on the subtraction subtest was spuriously low since, instead of subtracting, he added the last four problems.

Summary of Results

A. *Pedagogical Level*
Mathematics Instruction Level—End of Third
B. *Assets*
1. Tommy stated that he likes math best of all subjects.
2. Ability to count backwards from 10, to count by 2s to 20 and count by 5s to 50.
3. Highest performance was demonstrated on time concepts.
4. Understanding demonstrated for the four basic computation skills.
5. Numerical reasoning functioning was slightly above his mean math performance.
C. *Deficits*
1. Mental computation was significantly below his mean math performance.
2. Not paying attention to minus signs and then adding some subtraction problems.

VISION SCREENING

Keystone Telebinocular

Tommy displayed performance in the normal range of visual functioning on all distance vision tests and those at a reading distance. His eyes appear to work well in balance together and are coordinated to see a single image at both distances. On the tests of color vision, he could discriminate red from green and blue from violet.

SPEECH AND LANGUAGE ASSESSMENT

Behavioral Observations

Tommy is a handsome, brown-haired, brown-eyed boy of 13 years. He was cooperative and quite personable and seemed to relate well with this examiner. He spoke fondly of his family, his farm, and briefly mentioned his father's illness. He attempted all tasks presented to him, but exhibited reluctance on tasks requiring written and oral expression, i.e., writing three sentences, relating a familiar story. General conversation revealed a general language delay with some syntactic errors present. Speech was characterized by good articulation and a soft vocal volume. No problems with intelligibility were apparent.

Discussion of Results

A.   An audiometric screening using a portable MAICO audiometer was administered in an ambient environment. Testing was performed for all frequencies at 20 db ISO. Results indicate essentially normal hearing bilaterally.

B.   An examination of the peripheral speech mechanism was performed. All structures and their concomitant functions appeared adequate for normal speech production.

C.   The *Wepman-Auditory Discrimination Test* is a measure of a child's ability to auditorily recognize the fine differences that exist between similar-sounding paired words. Tommy's score of *28* indicates essentially normal skills in this area.

D.   The *Roswell-Chall Auditory Blending Test* is a measure of a child's ability to auditorily synthesize individual speech sounds into monosyllabic units. Tommy's perfect score of *30* indicates adequate skills in this area.

E.   The *Photo Articulation Test* measures a child's ability to correctly produce specific speech sounds when those sounds are embedded in words. No sound substitutions, omissions, or distortion emerged during this test measure or during his conversational speech. While his voice quality was somewhat soft, speech was generally intelligible.

F.   Segments of the *Utah Test of Language Development* were also administered. Tommy's approximated language age was eight years, three months. This is almost five years below his chronological age. Although communication appeared adequate, general language function did appear slightly delayed. Oral expression was halting with occasional syntactic errors. Additionally, at that age level, Tommy was able to read only eight of the twenty-four preprimer words presented. At the 7- to 8-year age range, he was able to identify a quarter, half-dollar, and dollar, repeat five digits, and name the days of the week. His receptive vocabulary at this age range was inadequate. At the 8- to 10-year age range, Tommy was able to repeat a sixteen syllable sentence, write cursively, rhyme words, and repeat four digits reversed. His receptive vocabulary was inadequate. No task at the 10- to 15-year age range could successfully be completed.

Summary of Results

A. *Assets*
   1. Adequate auditory acuity.
   2. Adequate articulatory skills.
   3. Adequate auditory blending skills.
   4. Adequate auditory discrimination skills.
   5. Cooperative, pleasant, easy to structure.
B. *Deficits*
   1. General language delay of approximately five years (UTLD).
   2. Disorganized cognitive process.
   3. Slow processing time.
   4. Oral expressive language, halting with occasional syntactical errors.
   5. Inadequate auditory memory skills.
   6. Receptive vocabulary is inadequate.
   7. Written expression is remarkably delayed.

CONCLUSIONS AND RECOMMENDATIONS

Tommy is a beginning reader who is functioning eight years behind his chronological grade level and around a 3.8 grade level in mathematics, which is slightly more than four years behind. Speech and language therapy are not indicated at this time. A language program within the classroom and emphasizing oral as well as written expression is recommended.

Attention and concentration appear to be adequate. No medication is indicated at this time.

Case Study 4.4

An Educational Assessment of an SLD Midadolescent

PERSONAL AND SOCIAL ASSESSMENT

Background History

Andy has a history of truancy from school because of fears and frustrations in learning situations. Relationships with peers have been poor, with some acting-out behavior.

Andy has had no physical problems, and there is no history of fainting, convulsions, or seizures nor significant injuries or surgical operations. No indication of the need for medication has been evident.

Behavioral Observations

Andy is a young man who is slightly shorter than the average 15-year-old but who is well built. He presented himself as a well-mannered youngster who appeared to be able to relate well to adults.

It is the examiner's impression that Andy is a warm sincere person who has been at a disadvantage in school due to his obvious learning disabilities.

In the learning situation, he appeared to be accessible to learning and instruction. He is right handed and works very deliberately.

LANGUAGE ARTS ASSESSMENT

Tests Administered

A. General Orientation—Information—Sequencing Ability Tasks
B. Roswell-Chall Diagnostic Reading Test of Word Analysis Skills
C. Informal Procedures
   1. Handwriting
   2. Oral Reading of a Paragraph
D. Wide Range Achievement Test—Level II
   1. Reading
   2. Spelling

E. Peabody Individual Achievement Test
1. Reading Recognition
2. Reading Comprehension
3. Spelling

Summary of Results

A. *Pedagogical Levels*
Instructional Reading Level—Approximately Mid-Second
Instructional Spelling Level—Approximately Second
B. *Assets*
1. Recognized and named all letters of the alphabet.
2. Sight vocabulary extends to mid-third level.
3. Spells words through mid-second level.
C. *Deficits*
1. Presently functioning approximately six years behind age—appropriate grade level in all aspects of language arts.
2. Has particular difficulty with initial consonant blends and digraphs.
3. Limited spelling vocabulary hinders written expression.
4. Andy's fund of general information appears to be substantially below age-appropriate levels.

MATHEMATICS ASSESSMENT

Tests Administered

A. Informal Procedures
1. Coins
2. Counting and Number Writing
3. Geometric Shapes
4. Time
B. Key Math Diagnostic Arithmetic Test
C. Wide Range Achievement Test—Arithmetic—Level II
D. Peabody Individual Achievement Test—Mathematics

Summary of Results

A. *Pedagogical Level*
Mathematics Instructional Level—Approximately Mid-Third

B. *Assets*
1. Writes numbers to at least 20.
2. Regroups in addition.
3. Mastery of some basic multiplication facts.
4. Awareness of basic concept of fractional parts.
5. Functional knowledge of money.

C. *Deficits*
1. Currently functioning approximately seven years below age-appropriate level.
   Wide range Achievement Test: Arithmetic—2.9 grade equivalent score
   Peabody Individual Achievement Test: Mathematics—3.7 grade equivalent score
2. Showed limited understanding of two-digit multiplication.
3. Demonstrated no knowledge of the process of division.
4. Demonstrated limited ability to add or subtract fractions.
5. Experienced difficulty when attempting to tell time to the correct minute, half-hour, and quarter-hour.

VISION SCREENING

Keystone School Vision Screening

A. *Results*

There were no outstanding deficits noted from this testing. However, usable vision for both eyes at near point was in the retest area.

B. *Recommendations*

Retest of near point vision.

SPEECH AND LANGUAGE ASSESSMENT

Behavioral Observations

Andy is a good-looking boy of 15 years of age. He tried all tasks presented, but often preceded these tasks with, "I don't think I can do this." Nevertheless, he did make the attempt and proved to be quite likable and cooperative.

Spontaneous speech was free of misarticulations, sound substitutions, and omissions. His voice was quite hoarse, and he indicated that he shouted frequently. Receptive and expressive language appeared appropriate for age and social background.

A sample of written expression revealed remarkable difficulty with syntactic and grammatic skills. Spelling and punctuation were likewise deficient.

Tests Administered

A. Audiometric Screening
B. Oral Peripheral Examination
C. Wepman Auditory Discrimination Test
D. Roswell-Chall Auditory Blending Test
E. Photo Articulation Test
F. Utah Test of Language Development

Summary of Results

A. *Assets*
   1. Cooperates and is pleasant
   2. Appears socially aware.
   3. Normal auditory acuity.
   4. Normal articulatory patterns.
   5. Expressive and receptive language appears appropriate for age and social background.
   6. Understands monetary values.
B. *Deficits*
   1. Inadequate auditory discrimination skills.
   2. Inadequate auditory sequential memory skills.
   3. Inadequate auditory blending skills.
   4. Unable to name days of week/months of year.
   5. Fearful of academic skills.
   6. Inadequate written expressive skills: grammar, punctuation, syntax, spelling.
   7. Hoarse voice.
   8. The score of 25 on the Wepman Auditory Discrimination Test indicates inadequate skills in that area.
   9. About six years behind in language functioning determined by an estimated language age of nine years on the Utah Test of Language Development.

CONCLUSIONS AND RECOMMENDATIONS

Andy's academic profile reveals a young man who is functioning approximately eight years below an age-appropriate level in many aspects of language arts including reading and is seven years below an age-appropriate mathematics level.

Neither speech nor language therapy is indicated at this time. A classroom program emphasizing general language development is recommended. Because of his hoarseness, Andy should be evaluated by an otolaryngologist to rule out vocal cord pathology.

Medication is not indicated, as there seem to be no significant problems in attending and concentrating.

SUMMARY

Educational assessment and evaluation help to determine the levels at which individual students are functioning in relation to where they should be in learning developmental skills and where one would like them to be in knowledge, understanding, and attitudes. Diagnosis has been defined in *Webster's New Collegiate Dictionary* as an investigation or analysis of the cause or nature of a condition, situation, or problem.

Assessment precedes instruction, and evaluation follows instruction; both determine what skills, knowledge, understanding, and/or attitudes a student has or does not have. Educational diagnosis, however, attempts to determine the cause or provide an understanding of why a student is experiencing learning problems. The usefulness of assessment, diagnosis, and evaluation is determined by the extent to which they are helpful in planning effective educational strategies.

Beyond what is learned quantitatively from standardized or criterion-referenced tests, qualitative information most strongly emerges from informal measures and the processes of clinical teaching and task analysis. Building on the firm foundation provided by the assessment and diagnosis, the teacher can proceed to the equally important facet of providing quality instruction (discussed in Chapter 15 below). Evaluation of the results of instruction completes the first cycle of the system and the process continues with a restructuring of objectives and priorities for instruction based on evaluation.

The system provides the model and structure for logical program progression; the professionals provide the human aspects of analysis, synthesis, enthusiasm, creativity, and caring. This combination of the system and its implementation by competent and caring persons offers hope for continually improving programs and services for children.

APPENDIX

Tests

Boehm Test of Basic Concepts. Psychological Corporation
Detroit Tests of Learning Aptitude. Bobbs-Merrill Co., Inc.
Developmental Test of Visual-Motor Integration. Follet Educational Corp.
Goldman-Fristow-Woodcock Auditory Skills Test Battery. American Guidance Services
Illinois Test of Psycholinguistic Abilities. University of Illinois Press.
Key Math Diagnostic Arithmetic Test. American Guidance Services.
Keystone School Vision Screening. Keystone View Company.
Metropolitan Readiness Tests. Psychological Corporation.
Peabody Individual Achievement Test. American Guidance Services.
Peabody Picture Vocabulary Test. American Guidance Services.
Photo Articulation Test. Interstate Printers and Publishers, Inc.
Roswell-Chall Auditory Blending Test. Essay Press.
Roswell-Chall Diagnostic Reading Test of Word Analysis Skills. Essay Press.
Stanford Achievement Test. Psychological Corporation.
Utah Test of Language Development. Communication Research Association.
Wepman Test of Auditory Discrimination. Language Research Associates.
Wide Range Achievement Test. Guidance Associates.

Addresses of Publishers

American Guidance Service, Inc., Publishers' Building, Circle Pines, Minn. 55014.
The Bobbs-Merrill Co., 4300 W. 62 Street, Indianapolis, Ind. 46206.
Communication Research Associates, P.O. Box 11012, Salt Lake City, Utah 84111.

Essay Press, P.O. Box 5, Planetarium Station, New York, N.Y. 10024.

Follett Educational Corp., 1010 W. Washington Blvd., Chicago, Ill. 60607.

Guidance Associates of Delaware, Inc., 1526 Gilpin Avenue, Wilmington, Del. 19806.

The Interstate Printers and Publishers, Inc., Danville, Ill. 61832.

Keystone View Co., 2212 E. 12 St., Davenport, Iowa 52803.

Language Research Associates, Box 95, 950 E. 59 Street, Chicago, Ill. 60637.

The Psychological Corporation, 757 Third Ave., New York, N.Y. 10017.

University of Illinois Press, Urbana, Ill. 61801.

REFERENCES

Bush, W.J. & Waugh, K.W. *Diagnosing learning disabilities* (2nd ed.). Columbus, Ohio: C.E. Merrill, 1976.

Ekwall, E.E. *Diagnosis and remediation of the disabled reader.* Boston: Allyn and Bacon, 1976.

Johnson, M.S. & Kress, R.A. *Informal reading inventories.* Newark, Del.: International Reading Assn., 1965.

Kirk, S. *Selected papers on learning disabilities.* Progress in parent information, professional growth, and public policy. Sixth annual conference of the Association for Children with Learning Disabilities. Fort Worth, Texas, March, 1969.

Lerner, J.W. *Children with learning disabilities* (2nd ed.). Boston: Houghton-Mifflin, 1976.

Otto, W.. McMenemy, R.A., & Smith, R.J. *Corrective and remedial teaching* (2nd ed.). Boston: Houghton-Mifflin, 1973.

Pennsylvania Department of Education, National Learning Resource Center of Pennsylvania, and the Eastern Pennsylvania Special Education Regional Resource Center. *An introduction to individualized education program plans in Pennsylvania: Guidelines for school age IEP development.* King of Prussia, Pa.: Author, 1977.

Popham, W.J. *Systematic instruction.* Englewood Cliffs, N.J.: Prentice-Hall, 1970.

Smith, R.M. *Teacher diagnosis of educational difficulties.* Columbus, Ohio: C.E. Merrill, 1969.

Wallace, G., & Kauffman, J.M. *Teaching children with learning problems.* Columbus, Ohio: C.E. Merrill, 1973.

CHAPTER 5

VISUAL FUNCTION ASSESSMENT

ARTHUR S. SEIDERMAN, O.D., M.A.

A human being survives to the extent that he adapts to an
environment which presents him, at the same time, with the
necessary materials for the satisfaction of his needs and
(with) the danger of destruction. For this reason everyone
needs to achieve sufficient understanding of the world and of
himself to be able to grasp the significance of the information
which he encounters and anticipate the results of his actions.

—Elaine Vurpillot, *The Visual World of the Child*

INTRODUCTION

The field of learning disabilities has grown rapidly during the past
fifteen years. Numerous disciplines have become involved in diagnosis
and remediation of learning disabilities in children, and many philoso-
phies and treatment techniques have been espoused in the process.
Perceptual development and training gained early attention of special
educators, reading specialists, psychologists, optometrists, and others
during this time. The work of Piaget (1952), Kephart (1960), Getman and Kephart (1957-59), Getman (1960), Frostig and Horne
(1964), Wepman (1964), Solan (1966, 1968), Barsh (1967), Ayres
(1965), and others suggested that sensorimotor and perceptual experiences laid the foundation for the later development of conceptual
and symbolic processes.

The profession of optometry began to explore a dynamic theory
of vision in the 1940s and 1950s through the work of Skeffington (1926–

68), Gessell *et al.* (1949), Getman and Bullis (1950–51), Getman and Kephart (1957–59), Apell and Streff (1961–63). Much of this work was pioneered at the Gesell Institute (formerly the Yale Clinic of Child Development) and the Optometric Extension Program. More recently, other optometrists, such as Solan (1973b), Flax (1974), Coleman (1968), Kraskin (1965–68), Greenspan (1971–72), Wold (1969), Kane (1969), Sherman (1973,) Furth and Wachs (1974), and Seiderman (1976b), have continued to elaborate on the existing foundations. Much optometric influence was evident in the writings of early perceptual motor theorists (Kephart, 1960; Barsh, 1967). As the concepts of developmental, functional or behavioral optometry evolved, a visual or perceptual component in the learning disabled child became evident.

Any discussion of vision and its relationship to learning should define *vision* and differentiate between *vision* and *sight*. Peiser (1972) defines vision as "the individual's ability to react to and interact with his environment on the basis of information received through the eyes" (p. 152). This is dependent upon clear acuity, past experiences, and the processing of information. Vision should not be confused with sight, which is defined as the ability of an eye to resolve detail and see as clearly as possible. The sight-oriented viewpoint frequently compares the eye to the optical system of a camera. Herein lies much of the controversy over the role of vision in learning disabilities. An optometrist seeks to find how the child functionally organizes and utilizes vision in learning. The sight-oriented practitioners are interested primarily in an organic and structural approach, i.e., if there is no pathology, lowered visual acuity, or overt muscle imbalance, then there is no eye problem. In contrast, the optometric approach addresses itself to the actual functioning of the eye in a learning situation (Seiderman, 1976a). Forrest (1962) explains,

> By vision we consider more than just eyes and eyesight. Since reliable sources indicate that 80% of learning occurs through the visual pathway, we must consider vision as a PROCESS that includes the retina of the eye as a sense receptor, the brain as a control center, and the muscles of the eye and the body as mechanisms to express the behavior responses triggered off by the sensory stimulations. This increases our scope to include vision and visual problems as part of the complete child as he performs in his everyday environment. (p. 299)

Gesell *et al.* (1949) defined vision as "a complex sensory motor response to a light source mediated by the eyes, but involving the whole action system." The developmental optometrist seeks to understand the development of vision from infancy in terms of the ever-changing demands on the visual system as well as newly acquired skills.

> Vision does not automatically, and once and for all, tell the infant where he is. At every stage of growth during infancy, childhood and youth, the visual mechanism undergoes changes which serve to reorient the ever-transforming individual. For him the space world is not a fixed and static absolute. It is a plastic domain, which he manipulates in terms of his nascent powers. He commands less space when he is a year old than when he is five— not because he is weaker and smaller, but because his total action system has occupied less operational territory. He was born with a pair of eyes, but not with a visual world. (Gesell *et al.*, 1949, p. 156)

Tyler (1968) reinforces the importance of development and learning in vision in still another way. He states,

> One continually adds to his visual models, and learning plays a significant role in visual recognition. An interplay can be seen between various psychologic mechanisms and our cognitive processes—perception, thinking, and learning; and these can significantly influence what is seen. Reception of visual stimuli is not a passive process; but, there is an active exploration of our world by our oculo-motor apparatus. How one looks becomes almost as important as how one sees when dealing with complex visual tasks. (p. 262)

In this vein, professionals studying developmental vision are very much concerned with the achieving as well as the underachieving child. The investigation of sight and vision is a matter of the greatest importance. Unfortunately, children in our educational system are routinely screened only for acuity. Children who demonstrate 20/20 sight on the Snellen wall chart are told that there is nothing wrong with their eyes. However, it is the interaction of the eye and the brain that allows for seeing. The child who has a school or learning problem should have a visual examination by a vision specialist who is interested in developmental vision and accustomed to investigating the function of the eyes as well as their structure (Seiderman, 1976a). This could be an optometrist (O.D.) or an ophthalmologist (M.D.). At the present time, one is more apt to find a developmental vision specialist among optometrists (Wunderlich, 1970).

FUNCTIONAL DISORDERS OF VISION

Traditional eye examinations are primarily aimed at answering the following questions:

(1) Is there any pathology?
(2) What is the "refractive state" of the eye? Are compensatory lenses necessary to improve visual acuity? How clearly can the individual see?
(3) Are the eyes straight? Is surgery necessary?

It is interesting to note that, with some minor exceptions, none of the aforementioned problems show a significantly greater incidence in a learning disabled population than in a "normal" population (Seiderman, 1973a; Sherman, 1973; Wold, 1971). In fact, there is a possibility that some refractive measurements actually represent an adaptive response in order to permit success in the school environment (Flax, 1968b; Forrest, 1962). Forrest explains this phenomenon as a response to stress. Each individual reacts differently to the stresses which arise normally in life situations (Selye, 1956) and has a different stability level to withstand them. If the total load of stress is intense, or persistent over prolonged periods of time, the normal adaptations become conditioned and cause structural distortions. In this case, a child who is unable to withstand a so-called "average" stress may well develop structural "eye defects" as an adaptation to the stress itself (Forrest, 1962). This variability in response to stress actually enables individuals' to achieve in spite of obvious physiological and/or perceptual deficits in visual functioning.

Binocular Fusion

It is of interest that, as a general rule, only casual attention, if any at all, is given to the individual's comfort and ability to sustain visual concentration in the learning or reading task. Sustained meaningful reading is dependent upon the ability to maintain an easy flow of information from what is contained on the printed page. Binocular fusion problems can create difficulties in these skills, resulting in any of the following behaviors:

Complaint of seeing double
Squinting or closing one eye
Head turned while working at desk
Resting head on arm while reading or writing
Holding head too close to desk while reading or writing
Complaining of words or letters running together
Frequent headaches from reading or watching television
Becoming tired and sleepy when reading
Eyes burning, itching, or tearing while reading
Inability to read and study for extended periods of time
Frequent loss of place when reading
Reading comprehension decreasing with time
Avoidance of reading
Difficulty catching or hitting a ball
Excessive eye rubbing or blinking
Eyes appearing red while reading
One eye appearing to turn either in or out
Print becoming blurry after prolonged reading, although initially
   clear.

Generally, any one or combination of these visual deficiencies will
not cause total failure at reading but will reduce the efficiency of the
reader and make reading much less desirable. For the individual with
poor binocular fusion, reading becomes quite laborious and frequently
is accompanied by symptoms of anxiety. Benton *et al.* (1972) have
reported that 77% of 115 children studied had binocular control
anomalies. Sherman (1973) found 92 percent with difficulties in
binocular fusion. It is interesting to note that the vast majority of such
children have adequate visual acuity and frequently are evaluated as
having no visual problem. It is not unusual for this type child to use
the defense mechanism of avoidance for all near point tasks. The
child may come to prefer outdoor type tasks or gross motor activities
to reading.

   In early elementary education (grades kindergarten through
third) binocular vision plays only a small role in effective visual performance, because the print is usually isolated and there is little demand
for sustained visual effort at the near point range. Emphasis at these
early levels of education is on sensory processing skills. Generally, at
around the fourth grade reading level, the print in books becomes

smaller and the emphasis in reading instruction gradually shifts from decoding to comprehension. To comprehend what one reads requires more concentrated near point work for longer periods of time (Seiderman, 1976a). Although some children learn to compensate very rapidly to near point stress, some will completely suppress vision in one eye, cover an eye, turn the head to one side, or develop amblyopia,[1] or strabismus,[2] combined with suppression. If only one eye is used, there will be no binocular stress. This paradox in the reaction of the visual system to stress points up one of the difficulties encountered in the literature concerning the relationship between visual processes and reading. In correlational studies, it is generally assumed that an individual with intact binocular function rates higher in visual efficiency than an individual with partial binocular function and that an individual with partial binocular function rates higher than an individual with no binocular function. In other words, the assumption is made that the requirements for successful reading co-vary with clinical visual measurements. Because of the reaction of the visual system to stress, a paradox exists here. This assumption is not necessarily true, since it is possible for an individual to read successfully with only one eye. An individual with mild instability in binocular function may, in fact, be more handicapped in reading than an individual with an actual turned or crossed eye. Yet, from a clinical measurement view point, partial ability to use both eyes would be considered better visual function than an inability to use both eyes together. However, when the demands of reading are considered, it may actually be advantageous to shut one eye totally rather than struggle to maintain inefficient two-eyed vision. This factor alone contributes to a great deal of confusion in the literature (Flax, 1968).

Performance in binocular fusion and its impact on learning and reading disorders have been reported by numerous researchers (Benton, et al., 1972; Benton, 1973; Robinson, 1953; Seiderman, 1973a; Sherman, 1973). Case study 5.1 below (Mitchell) clearly demonstrates the role of binocular coordination and learning disorders.

Accommodation (Focus Ability)

Another critical visual function is that of accommodation (focusing ability). Generally, a gross measure of accommodation will show

---

[1]Amblyopia is a reduction in visual acuity that cannot be improved with lenses nor attributed to disease.

[2]Strabismus is the condition in which the visual axes of the two eyes are not both directed toward the fixation point; the turning in or out of an eye.

adequate skill in this area. However, a dynamic functional appraisal of accommodative facility will show deficits in more than 70% of a learning disabled population (Sherman, 1973; Woolf, 1969).

Accommodative facility allows rapid and accurate shifts for visual inspection, with instantaneous clarity at different distances, such as from desk to chalkboard to teacher, as well as the ability to maintain clear focus at normal reading distance. Difficulties in this area may result in:

Difficulties in copying from chalkboard to paper at desk
Blurred vision while reading
Print in book blurring in and out of focus
Inability to clear vision at distance after reading
Fatigue or headaches while reading
Difficulty in sustaining effort in near activities, such as reading and studying

Many children cannot maintain clear close vision. Initially, difficulties in accommodation will not prevent a child from learning to read since the print is large and the attentional demands are low. However, when prolonged reading is attempted, children and young adults may experience asthenopia (symptoms of eyestrain or ocular fatigue) or use the defense mechanism of avoidance to deal with this stress.

To read a printed page, two oculomotor conditions are required: first, the convergence of both eyes so that they aim exactly at the same point and, second, small precise movements of the eyes (saccadic fixations) along the line of print. Failure to do this may result in loss of place, skipping of lines, omissions of words, and poor comprehension. The task is further complicated by the relationship between accommodation and convergence. While either system, tested independently, may function well, there must be a good relationship between both systems for efficient learning (Taylor, 1957). The eyes must focus precisely at the same point for which they converge. This linkage between accommodation and convergence is the only place in the body where the central and autonomic nervous systems must work in concert (Peiser, 1972). The act of reading is composed of rapid eye fixations, releases, and refixations on the words of a sentence as the eyes move from left to right across a page. As the two eyes sweep across the page, repeated tiny convergences of the two eyes are necessary as the eyes approach the midline, and repeated tiny divergences are necessary as the eyes sweep past the midline. If the focusing system of the eye is sluggish, there is no freedom to make these rapid, precise changes. As a result, poor readers who have poor accommodation/convergence skills read slowly, lose their places and have difficulty in comprehension (Seiderman, 1976b).

Visual Fixation and Control

Gesell *et al.* (1949) stated that fixation becomes the most primary visual function. Fixation is the directing or orienting of the organism so that a stimulus or an image falls in optimal relation to the visual receptor. All other visual functions are, in a sense, subsidiary to fixation or refinements of it. Kephart (1968) stated that a child who cannot hold a visual fixation for a reasonable period of time cannot maintain contact long enough to gather necessary perceptual data. Tyler (1968) noted that observations of visual fixation are important because of high correlations with attentional factors. The importance of attention becomes obvious when one realizes that perception depends partly upon differentiation among various sensory inputs.

Abercrombie (1964) reported that one of the most important functions of the eye muscles is searching or exploring the field of vision to find important targets, and he concluded that brain injured children whose eyes cannot accurately locate and fixate a target would be seriously handicapped in mental development. The significant relationship between visual skills, especially visual fixations, and attention, as well as distractibility, needs further exploration. Work in this area is now being done by Leisman as well as Ludlam.

Eye Movements

Inability to control accurately the speed and direction of eye movements is another factor which often contributes to reading inefficiency. This visual skill allows for easy shifting along the line of print in a book, a rapid and accurate return to the next line, and also quick and accurate shifts of visual attention between desk and chalkboard.

If eye movements are slow, clumsy, or not precisely coordinated, the following behaviors might be demonstrated:

Frequent loss of place while reading
Finger pointing or use of a marker to keep place
Frequent omission, substitution, or insertions of small words

Miscopying
Rereading of lines or phrases
Skipping words or sentences
Frequent movements of head while reading
Short attention span

The above observable difficulties will become more obvious as the child is forced to continue with a particular task, i.e., reading for any length of time. In addition, with dysfunctional eye movements, there will be a noticeable increase in fatigue and restlessness associated with all types of sustained visual activities.

The result, in general, is a reduction in reading speed and/or comprehension. Sherman (1973) found that 96% of learning disabled children have poor ocular motor efficiency, while Woolf (1969) found 70% of his population to have poor tracking abilities. Beltman *et al.* (1967) found that 54% of the poor readers and only 11% of the control group were unable to follow smoothly a diagonally moving target. It becomes apparent from the literature (Flax, 1968a; Goldberg and Drash, 1972; Wold, 1971) that defective eye movement skill, although perhaps not causative, is associated with the problem of reading disability.

Visual functions of binocular performance, accommodation, convergence, eye movements, and the accommodative-convergence relationship are generally referred to as end organ functions. It has been stressed that these end organ visual skills play a much greater role in reading and learning efficiency than they do in the basic aspects of learning to read.

Thus, we encounter again the paradox in the literature on vision and learning. Those who considered the physiological (functional) as well as the physical visual processes found relationships to exist between vision and learning. Those who restricted their testing largely to the physical segment found little or no relationship between vision and learning. However, all state that they are appraising vision (Bing, 1972).

VISION PROCESSING DISORDERS

It has frequently been observed that many learning disabled children demonstrate deficits in general perceptual-motor functioning. Possible explanations for the relationship between these deficits and school achievement has been postulated by Piaget (1952), Kephart

(1964), Barsh (1967), Strauss and Lehtinen (1947), Cruickshank *et al.* (1961), and others. In general, it has been hypothesized that perceptual-motor abilities are developmental in nature and prerequisite to the adequate development of higher level academic tasks. Since perception is the end-product of the total process of vision, the eye practitioner should be concerned with perception. Because perceptual abilities are important to a child's development and success in school, education and psychology are also concerned with perception. Each profession adds its own dimension toward a more comprehensive understanding of the child's perceptual abilities.

Children who display severe reading disabilities or who cannot learn to read at all show an inability to conceptualize form and direction. In particular, severely disabled readers experience difficulty in integrating both visual and auditory stimuli. Birch and Belmont (1965) reported a greater correlation between reading readiness and auditory-visual integration than between reading readiness and IQ, although both correlations were significant at the .001 level. These findings suggest that primary perceptual factors may be most important for initial acquisition of reading skill, but that factors more closely associated with IQ are more important in its elaboration.

Visual-Verbal Match

In beginning reading, when the child has to "break the code," he/she is required to make a visual-verbal match, i.e. to match the appearance of the word in print to its sound. The greater portion of the child's experiences during the first five years of life are oral and auditory. When he/she enters first grade, he/she should be able to make an intersensory shift from audition to vision. Birch (1962) suggests that reading disability may stem from an inadequate development of appropriate hierarchical organization of sensory systems and is, at least in part, the product of a failure in development of a visual system hierarchical dominance.

Ultimately, if a child's early sensory development proceeds well, he/she is able, by looking at an object, to acquire the information that would ordinarily be derived by touch, taste, or movement. In the neonate, multisensory exploration is brought about through reflex associations among sensory motor systems. Concomitant with maturation and development there must be an acquisition of intersensory equivalence. There must also be an ability to separate gradually one sense modality from another so that the need for redundancy in exploration is avoided.

Many learning disabled children exhibit difficulty in intersensory function and integration. It should be kept in mind that standard pedagogical programs assume the ability to utilize visual function independent of the opportunity for immediate tactile and movement support (Flax, 1968).

Figure-Ground Perception

Silver (1961) reported that nine out of ten children with reading disabilities had specific deficits in visual perception, particularly in figure-ground perception. These same children showed only occasional difficulty with tactile figure-background perception. Numerous researchers have reported figure-ground deficiencies in learning disabled children (Ayres, 1969; Cruickshank, 1967; Eisenberg, 1966; Seiderman, 1972; Silver, 1961; Solan and Seiderman, 1970). Normally, one has the visual ability to suppress background stimuli and focus on foreground. However, Eisenberg (1966) relates children's distractibility in part to figure-ground disturbance. Accompanying motor restlessness is analagous to distractibility in the perceptual sphere. These youngsters are at the mercy of every sight and sound and are overresponsive to sensory stimulation. In consequence, they are unable to sustain attention, fail to discriminate adequately between figure and ground, and are severely penalized in their attempts to learn. Their distractibility results in school performance that is inferior to that expected from their cognitive abilities as measured under optimal test conditions. As a result, these children may demonstrate behavior problems that are sometimes misdiagnosed as the primary difficulty, i.e., "He could do it if he wanted to." Resultant punishment and frustration frequently add to family friction that become self-feeding situations.

Children demonstrating figure-ground difficulties would be quite confused when faced with an arithmetic worksheet as shown in Figure 5.1. It would be beneficial for such a child if the teacher could isolate only a few problems, using several sheets of paper. Another suggestion might be the use of a cardboard window. This would allow the child to work on one problem at a time, while all others would be eliminated from the child's visual field of sight. Similarly, the child with a figure-ground deficit may experience difficulty in reading where there is too much visual stimulation. A case in point would be some comic books in which the characters have several verbal passages being spoken at the same time. This creates a type of "cluttering," which may result in confusion.

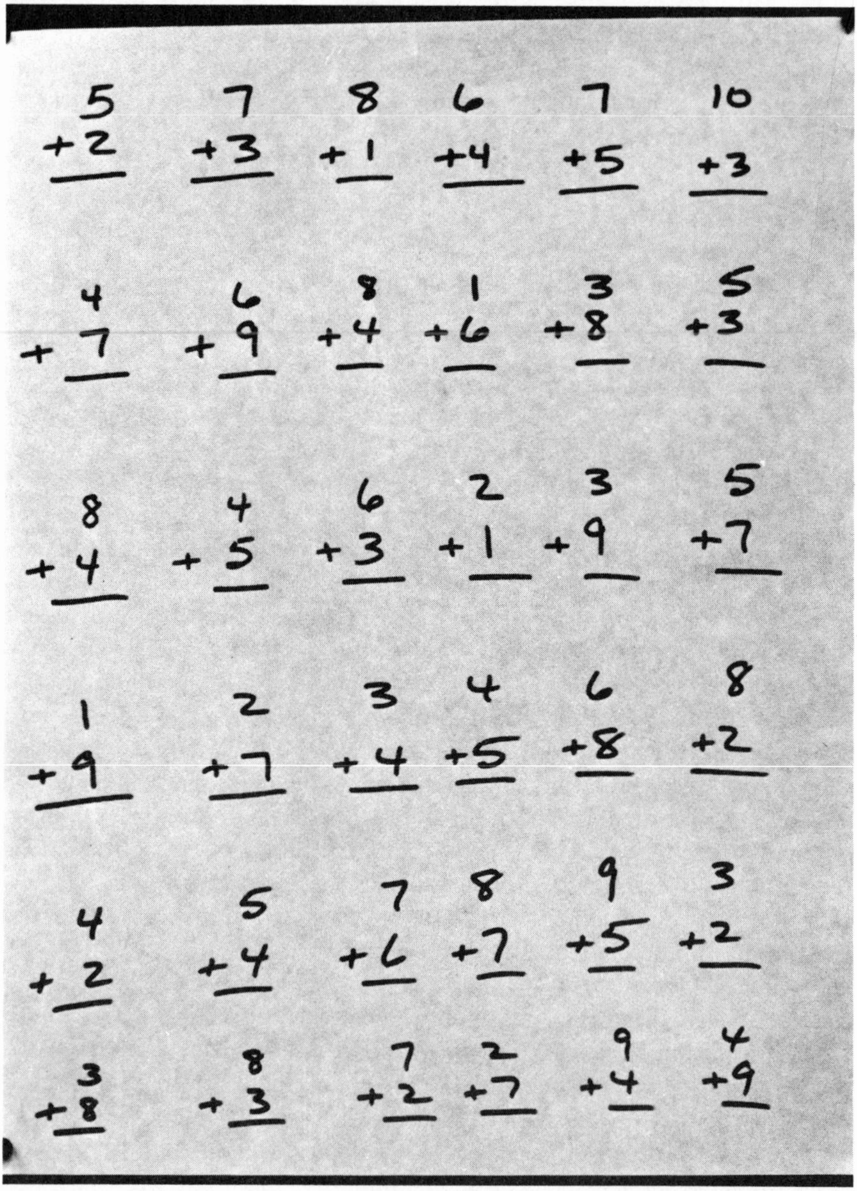

Arthur S. Seiderman, O.D., M.A.

Figure 5.1   This arithmetic worksheet may present a situation of overstimulation for the child with figure-ground difficulties.

Directionality in Space

Visual directionality is an important skill in academic learning, since, in our culture, letters and numbers are oriented on a left to right sequence. For a child to appreciate these visual directional differences, he/she must establish a set of internal visual coordinates in his/her own body, i.e., up and down, left and right, front and back, etc. A child supposedly learns these directional coordinates from his/her own body image (Abercrombie, 1964; Alexander and Money, 1967; Bryant, 1965; Ebersole, *et al.*, 1968), from general self-directed movement (Held, 1965), and from relating eye posture with general body kinesthesis (Gesell and Amatruda, 1947; Kephart, 1960). For example, the only visual difference between *b* and *d*, *p* and *q*, *u* and *n*, *N* and *Z*, *M* and *W*, *6* and *9* is simply directional orientation. Children who reverse letters and words (was for saw, on for no) have not developed visual directional skills to the point where they are sure of their own internal body coordinates (Alexander and Money, 1967; Bryant, 1965). Sherman (1973) and Seiderman (1973b) found in experimental studies that 76-78% of learning disabled children experienced difficulty with directionality. Woolf (1969) reported 60% failure among a similar population. Visual stimuli are not themselves directly related to directionality and space. However, these relationships are attributed to visual stimuli on the basis of kinesthetic awareness and subsequent translation through visual clues.

Directionality in space is projected from the organism outward. The mechanism for such projection in the visual field is the movement of the eyes (Kephart, 1960). Since a person cannot, with the hand, follow direction at a distance greater than arm's length, developing children must learn how to identify directionality in distant stimuli through some means other than the kinesthetic and tactual impressions from their hands. In effect, they substitute eye for hand. They move their eyes along the stimulus and match the pattern of eye movement to the kinesthetic memory patterns in their organism and the resulting projection develops (Hebb, 1949). Such a process implies that these children must have accurate control of the eyes, an accurate match between eye movements and the perceived visual stimulus, and an adquate interrelationship between movement of the eyes and movements of other muscle groups in the body. The primary pattern out of which the differentiation of left and right develops is that of balance. When experimenting with balancing problems, children must learn left and right. They must learn how to innervate one side of the body against the other, how to detect which side of the body must move, and how far, so that they may execute appropriate compensatory movements as their balance varies from one side to another (Kephart, 1960). Directionality, thus, depends upon laterality and balance, and until a solid laterality has been developed, the elaborations and extensions necessary for the establishment of directionality in space may well be limited and inaccurate.

As a child deals with the environment, he/she deals with spatial and temporal relationships rather than with absolutes. Therefore, the child must have a stable point of reference from which to organize one's impressions. This point of reference is one's own body. Body image is a complete awareness of the body and its possibilities of performance, including a knowledge of body parts and their relative positions, as well as an awareness of how much space the body occupies (Ebersole *et al.*, 1968).

Visual Form Perception

A critical visual skill involved in early reading is visual form perception (Cruickshank *et al.*, 1961; Spache, 1964), as letters obviously consist of a variety of shapes. Since adults can readily identify forms, one might think that this skill is spontaneous and natural. Visual form perception is, nonetheless, learned (Kephart, 1960). Arnheim (1969) states that in the perception of shape lie the beginnings of concept formation.

Visual-Motor Coordination

In their extensive work, Silver and Hagin (1967), reported that 92% of the dyslexic population show defects in the visual-motor area. Similarly, Sherman (1973) demonstrated a 90% incidence of eye-hand coordination deficits in a learning disabled population. Numerous other researchers have reported similar findings (de Hirsch *et al.*, 1966; Ilg and Ames, 1966; Koppitz, 1966). In the preschool child, it is normal for tactile and kinesthetic cues to reinforce eye aiming (hands guiding the eyes). Developmentally, at about the time that the child starts school, he should shift the relationship so that the eyes lead the hands. Various tests, utilizing the copying of geometric forms, are available for testing visual motor skills. In this type of test, the child, in effect, is being asked, "Can you reproduce with your hands what your eyes see?" Difficulties in visual motor coordination might be observed in some of the following behaviors:

Poor handwriting
Slowness in copying
Misalignment of horizontal or vertical columns
Inability to stay on ruled lines when writing
Turning or rotating paper in order to draw lines in different directions
Heavy reliance on tactual investigation of objects
Difficulty in closing buttons or tying shoelaces
Poor written spelling in comparison with oral spelling
Continued use of the fingers as a guide to steer the eyes while reading

Deficits in visual motor skills may also further manifest difficulties in putting thoughts down on paper, i.e., writing a letter describing a recent vacation.

Visual Imagery

One of the highest order visual skills is that of visualization or visual imagery. This is the ability to picture something which is not physically visible at that moment. For example, giving directions to a friend's house, dictating a letter, recalling the color combinations in the living room while shopping for a rug, etc. In attempting to spell a difficult word, how many times have people closed their eyes and attempted to draw a mental picture of the word, or written down two or three spellings of the word and said, "I have to see what it looks like—yes, this one looks correct." Visual imagery is an important skill in spelling. It allows us to deal with the inconsistencies and exceptions to phonetic spelling.

Piagetian philosophy of cognitive development tells us that the preoperational child (ages 2-7 years) is dominated by his/her visual perception (Flavell, 1963). If this is true, and if the child has deficits in visual perception, then we must conclude that his/her world is confused at best. According to Piaget, all thinking develops through the coordination of external actions. Coordination of body movements with sensory inputs is, therefore, a prerequisite to the application of body and sense activities to specific problems and tasks (Furth and Wachs, 1974). In the young child, thinking is still closely related to such activities, and they should be given a prominent place in our primary classroom. Piaget's theory reformulates the traditional distinction between activities of the mind and activities of the body. Movement and thinking are interdependent. Many children perform academic tasks inadequately because they have not mastered the movement control on which these tasks depend. As adults we may forget the complexity of what appear superficially to be simple movements, yet the majority of us tend to be somewhat clumsy when mastering a new physical task. Our performance often falls short of our expectations when we are neophytes. For example, merely memorizing the keyboard of a typewriter will not lead to fluent typing. Until the typist also learns the finger sequencing, movements will be slow, planned, and deliberate. Attention will be divided between *what* one is doing and *how* it is being done. After mastering the movement thinking control, one is free to concentrate exclusively on the material being typed. Similar problems are faced by the child when first given a pencil and asked to write (Furth and Wachs, 1974).

The early, simple games of childhood are intended to develop sense organs and motor systems. Children experiment with things, look at them, feel them from all angles, smell them, and tap them to produce sound. By the manipulation of things and of their own bodies in relation to things, they are performing the sensory-motor process and are learning to match sensory data. They need to take things apart and discover how they work and, later, perhaps even put them together again. Such experimentation needs to be, from our adult point of view, random. It must be child-centered, not adult-centered (Kephart, 1960).

In workshops, experienced kindergarten teachers have frequently asked the author, "Why is there such an increased frequency of visual motor problems in children today, as compared to twenty-five years ago?" Among other possible reasons, one answer may be the radical change in our society in the past twenty-five years. Technological advances have preempted many necessary developmental experiences for our children. Games such as bottle tops, jacks, wire ball, step ball, jumping rope, pen knife games (land), hit the penny out of the box with a ball, hop scotch, and the like are rarely seen today. Each of these is essentially a task of visual motor coordination. Today, however, marketing experts and game manufacturers have changed the basics of our young people's games. If a game or toy is not battery operated or electrical, it is not "desirable" to the child. Television is acknowledged as the universal instructor. Yet radio is far better for the development of visualization skills. Listening to The Green Hornet, Lux Theatre of the Air, Captain Midnight, and Let's Pretend certainly drew up mental images for the previous generation, thereby increasing visualization skills.

Many children are coming into our schools lacking in basic perceptual-motor skills. As a result of this basic lack, they are less able to participate in the formal educational activities which are arranged for them and they are less able to learn from these activities. They become slow learners in the classroom (Kephart, 1960), and it becomes necessary for the educational system and its auxiliary services to provide a program to develop these deficient sensory processing skills. Programs of individualized optometric vision therapy frequently incorporate sensory processing skill development when indicated. Such a program should be carried out at the child's developmental level, thereby building a series of successes and enabling the child to develop the necessary skills as well as build his ego.

Case Study 5.1: Mitchell (Age 8 years, 7 months) (Completing grade 3, traditional)

HISTORY

Mitchell was described by his parents as being a somewhat lethargic youngster who was easily distractible and had a short attention span. It was stated that he seemed to be lagging behind in his development, and something appeared to be wrong. He attended a private school for learning disabled children for two years. Mitchell is currently completing third grade in a traditional public school setting with no supportive services. Prenatal history revealed that Mrs. M. had difficulty conceiving and received hormone shots until four or five months prior to her pregnancy. Labor was induced and difficult. Perinatal history revealed that Mitchell ran fevers in excess of 105°F on two separate occasions. No convulsions or dehydration were noted. Motor milestones revealed frustration as early as the sucking response. New nipples were always needed on the bottle as he was not able to get enough liquid. He crawled, crept, and walked sequentially and in order. Mitchell first walked unassisted at approximately 16 months of age. Gross and fine motor development were described as poor. He had a great deal of difficulty learning to ride a bicycle, was always poor with puzzles, and his handwriting was poor. Language developed without delay. Occasional temper tantrums were reported.

Mitchell reported seeing double frequently. Frequent omissions, substitutions, and insertions of small words while reading were noted. Head movement while reading was observed, as well as the closing of one eye. Loss of place and rereading of lines during reading were also reported.

Visual Analysis

Near Point of Convergence=12 inches

Cover Test   Distance (20 feet) = $10^\triangle$ Exophoria
              Near (16 inches) = $14^\triangle$ Exophoria—Tropia

Visual Acuity at distance   Right eye 20/20—
                             Left eye 20/25—

Visual Acuity at Near   Right eye 20/25
                         Left eye 20/25

	Distance	*Near*
Phoria	$8^\triangle$Exophoria	$5^\triangle$ Exophoria
Divergence	13/5	10/6
Convergence	4/−2	3/−4
Vertical	Orthophoria	Orthophoria
Accommodation	−0.50 to blur	
	+1.00 to blur	

Cheiroscopic tracings showed left eye suppression.
Vectograph—No appreciation of stereopsis
            Continually closes right eye
Keystone Progress of Fusion showed left eye supression at both distance and near.
Eye Movement Skills—erratic, jerky, uneven, necessitates frequent head movement.

Tachistocopic Exposures 3 digits at .01 second showed 75% accuracy
or the equivalent of the 70th percentile of a grade one child.

Visual Sequential Memory (I.T.P.A.)=4 years, 10 months

Wepman Auditory Discrimination=Passed

Roswell-Chall Auditory Blending=Failed

Digit Span (WISC)=7 years, 6 months

Block Design (WISC)=5 years, 4 months (Raw score, 4)

Design C was reproduced ⎡R⎢R⎢R⎤
⎣W⎦

Piaget Protocol showed no appreciation of linear conservation, area
conservation, or reversibility.

Test of Spatial Orientation (using 6 colored inch cubes)—Used eleven
blocks to make reproduction which did not even resemble task.

Visual Copy Forms (Winter Haven) poorly reproduced and segmented—
see Figure 5.2.

Southern California Figure Ground Test=Less than the first percentile.

Divided Form Board—Only able to reassemble five of a possible six
forms in 180 seconds—performance almost entirely tactual—seemed
to use little if any visual input—equivalent to approximately early
kindergarten.

Tactual Angels—not able to raise his right hand and right leg simultaneously upon tactual stimulation only.

Directionality—on self, slow but correct; on the examiner when facing,
all responses incorrect.

Schilder Extension Test—right hand dominant.

Chalk Circles—unable to perform bilateral symmetrical.

Lateral Lines—on two separate attempts walks across the board.

Hopping: six times on each foot, good—not able to hop alternately
two times on each foot.

Ball Bouncing: able to bounce a nine-inch playground ball six times
with each hand—not able to bounce a ball alternately two times
with each hand.

Walking Rail: not able to walk a four-inch walking rail forward or
backward.

Keyed Pegboard: performance equivalent to a kindergarten child—
completes in 79 seconds—works from right to left—relies heavily
on tactual information.

Bender Gestalt (as reported from psychiatrist): Mitchell asked, "Do
you want me to copy them the way they really look? (see Figure

Figure 5.2. Mitchell's Visual Copy Forms (*Winter Haven*)

5.3), or do you want me to copy them the way they really are?"
(see Figure 5.4). Inspection of Figure 5.3 shows that Mitchell was
seeing them double, although he knew they really should be
single (Figure 5.4).

Reading Screen

Gray Oral Reading Check Test, Set 2, No. 1, was administered
in a telebinocular. Mitchell read the selection in 96 seconds while making 15 errors. All of the errors but one were due to omissions, insertions, or substitutions of small words. The norm for grade three is
one minute while making only three errors.
Metropolitan Achievement Tests, Primary 2 Battery

	Grade Level	*Percentile*
Word Knowledge	2.0	6
Reading	3.4	48
Spelling	3.6	50

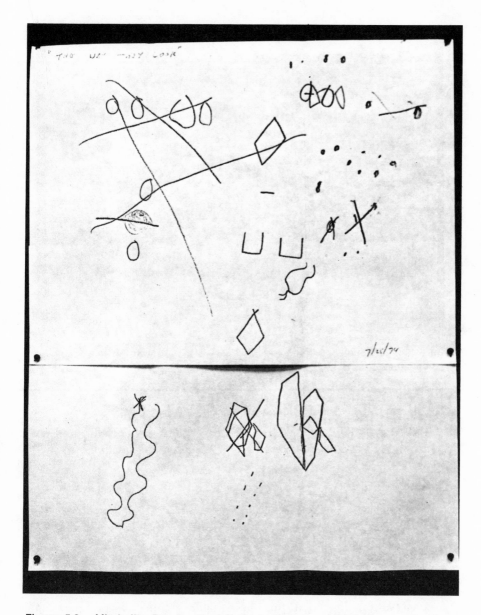

Figure 5.3. Mitchell's Bender Gestalt Test—"Do you want me to copy them the way they really look?"

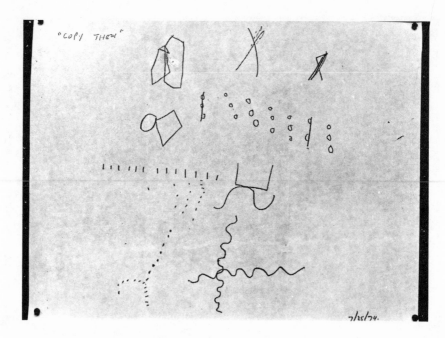

Figure 5.4. Mitchell's Bender Gestalt Test—"Do you want me to copy them the way they really are?"

Slosson Intelligence Test, mental age 10 years, 8 months, IQ=125; he showed most difficulty with questions relating to attention and concentration. His greatest strength was in the area of vocabulary.

DISCUSSION

Mitchell is a youngster of superior (verbal) intellectual functioning who demonstrated consistent difficulties in all areas of visual processing. The performance portion of the Wechsler Intelligence Scale for Children would most probably show a score of about ten to fifteen points lower than the verbal portion. In addition, the Piagetian tasks of conservation suggested that he is still within the preoperational stage, which is dominated by visual perceptions. Hence, it is reasonable to assume that his world is confused.

From the available data, it would appear that Mitchell's reading performance is hampered by his word recognition skills. An informal reading inventory and individual word recognition test would probably have given greater insight into Mitchell's reading performance, but these were not part of his psychoeducational assessment. However, his performance on the Gray Oral Reading Check Test revealed repeated insertions, omissions, and substitutions of small words. When this information is compared to the optometric findings, one notices erratic eye movement skills necessitating frequent head movements, double vision, and deficient visual processing skills. His visual compensatory mechanism is the frequent closing of one eye, confirming the observation that the "one-eyed" individual can function more efficiently than the individual who demonstrates difficulty coordinating the two eyes together as a team (see Binocular Fusion).

RECOMMENDATIONS

Mitchell would benefit greatly from a program of optometric vision therapy. Improved binocular coordination and sensory processing skills would tend to make Mitchell more receptive to his academic environment by eliminating the confusion which he presently experiences. In addition, visual concentration would be improved, reading and study type activities would become less laborious, and a program of remedial reading would be received with a higher degree of success and much less frustration. Mitchell should respond best to a combined program of optometric vision therapy (with a developmental optometrist) and a program of supportive and remedial reading (with a reading specialist).

Case Study 5.2: James (Age 10 years, 8 months) (Grade 5, completed)

HISTORY

James was referred because of school-related difficulties. While standardized achievement testing through the years has been good, his classroom performance has been consistently poor. The prenatal, perinatal, and postnatal histories were unremarkable. All developmental milestones were reported within the expected limitations. It was indicated that his coordination has been slow in developing, and he is not very athletic. He has difficulty in catching and hitting a ball and visually loses the flight of a golf ball. Jim was described as a "loner." He indicates that he experiences frequent brow type headaches, especially when watching movies or reading, and has occasional double vision. He wears glasses for all activities and holds reading material quite close. The classroom teacher reported that Jim tilts his head frequently, assumes unusual postures, and sometimes rests his head on his arm when writing.

Visual Analysis

Uncorrected Visual Acuity at Distance
    OD=20/50
    OS=20/40
Old Rx: OD=$+1.50-2.00 \times 45$
          OS=$+1.25-1.50 \times 142$
CNP=4 inches with Rx
Cover Test (Dist.) =$8^\triangle$ Esophoria
Cover Test (Near) =$5^\triangle$Esophoria (with Rx)
Static OD=$+1.25-1.25 \times 45$
       OS=$+1.00-1.00 \times 135$
Subjective OD=$+1.50-1.75 \times 43$ 20/30
           OS=$+1.50-1.25 \times 140$ 20/25

With Subjective	*Distance*	*Near*	*Near (With +1.50 Add)*
Phoria	$9^\triangle$ 11− eso	$10^\triangle$ eso	5–$7^\triangle$ eso
Divergence	0/−6	6/−12	14 to blur then suppress
Convergence	32/40/18	37/25	35/24
Vertical	Ortho	Ortho	Ortho

Accommodation	Accommodative Facility
−1.25 to blur	−2.50 ou fails
+3.00 to blur	+2.00 ou fails

Vectograph–Clown–No appreciation of depth perception
Cheiroscopic Tracings–fusion unstable–shows eso posture
Rx: OD=$+1.50-1.75 \times 43$
                         +1.25 ADD
      OS=$+1.25-1.25 \times 140$

Visual Perceptual Testing

Tachistoscopic Exposures 4 digits at a speed of .1 second = 60% accuracy. Some reversals were noted—performance equivalent to grade 3.

Motor-Free Visual Perception Test=9 years

Divided Form Board—completes in 153 seconds—relies very heavily on tactual reinforcement rather than visualization—performance equivalent to early first grade.

Handwriting Sample—James wrote, "I hate to write because it's so hard."

Chalk Circles—unable to draw reciprocally yolked circles on a chalkboard.

Hopping—Jim was able to hop on one foot. He was unable to hop alternately two times on each foot.

Frostig—Perceptual constancy subtest—age 9 years.

Intellectual Assessment

(Wechsler Intelligence Scale for Children)

Verbal	=	131
Performance	=	127
Full Scale	=	132

Jim scored at a very superior level on each of the subtests with the exception of the object assembly subtest, where he scored at an average level.

Personality Assessment

The clinical picture which emerged was that of a rather anxious youngster with poor impulse control. Human figure drawings resemble that of a much younger child. No overt personality disturbance was reported. Family dynamics were not unusual.

Educational Assessment

James' Word Recognition Test

Level	% Flash (Percent of words recognized correctly in flash of .2 second)	% Untimed (Percent of words recognized correctly with unlimited time)
Fifth	100	100
Sixth	80	95

Informal Reading Inventory (Temple University)

Pedagogical Level	Reader Level (Grade)
Independent	Fourth
Immediate Instructional	Fifth
Basic Instructional	Sixth
Frustration	Seventh

Wide Range Achievement Test

Subtest	Grade Score	Standard Score	Percentile
Reading	6.3	104	61
Spelling	5.0	93	32
Arithmetic	6.5	105	63

Gates-MacGinitie Reading Test

Subtest	Standard Score	Percentile Score	Grade Score
Vocabulary	56	73	6.8
Comprehension	59	82	8.1

In relation to his current grade placement, Jim displays no undue difficulties in relation to his reading comprehension skills, although he appears to be performing academically below his intellectual ability. He also demonstrated significant difficulties in spelling and handwriting.

DISCUSSION

James is a youngster whose intellectual functioning falls within the very superior range. Educational assessment, utilizing both informal and standardized tests, showed no apparent deficiencies. Personality assessment demonstrated an intact youngster with no unusual difficulties in the area of family dynamics. Yet his classroom performance was described as "consistently poor." It is also interesting to note that his coordination was described as poor and he is somewhat of a "loner."

Closer inspection of visual and perceptual functioning show a close relationship with the presenting problems. Difficulties in binocular coordination (a very definite tendency for the eyes to overconverge), accommodative facility, visual motor coordination, and visual synthesis were demonstrated. The use of bifocals for school-related and near point activities would improve Jim's ability to sustain effort. The fact that he consistently scores well on all tests suggests that he can "push" himself on given occasions, but on a day-to-day basis he cannot consistently perform at this level. Such a sustained major effort would probably result in headaches, eyestrain, and the like. James has stated that he frequently experiences headaches when reading, and that he also hates handwriting, another visual motor skill. A program of optometric vision therapy would help alleviate Jim's difficulty in athletic type endeavors, and possibly dispel his need to be a "loner."

The unusual postures and tilting of the head reported by the classroom teacher are not unusual for individuals experiencing problems in the physiological areas of visual development (see Binocular Fusion). These behaviors, as well as resting his head on his arm when writing, are Jim's visual compensations to eliminate the use of one eye, thereby functioning on a monocular basis. If one eye were patched (not advocated as a treatment procedure here, rather as a demonstration), many of the aforementioned behaviors, headaches, etc., would disappear. In effect, this is what Jim has done temporarily by resting his head on his arm or tilting his head to suppress vision in one eye.

This is an excellent case study of a child whose visual problem manifests itself as an educational one. Although visual problems usually are not the primary cause of learning problems, this is an exception to that rule. With the use of a bifocal and initiation of a program of optometric vision therapy, improved classroom performance can be expected.

Case Study 5.3: Peter (Age 7 years, 10 months) (Grade 2, Traditional)

HISTORY

Peter was first seen after 4 months of Grade 2. He was referred because "he can't read or write." Frequent reversals were reported. Peter was described as being easily distractible with a short attention span. The prenatal and perinatal histories were unremarkable. Postnatal history revealed that Peter ran a fever of approximately 104°F with pneumonia at age 5 years.

Motor milestones showed that Peter crawled, crept, and walked sequentially and in order. He first walked unassisted at approximately 16 months of age. He was described as being an extraordinarily large child at that time. Gross and fine motor skills were described as "poor." In fact, he just recently learned to tie his shoelaces.

Language milestones revealed that Peter first spoke single words at age 3 years. It should be noted that Peter's home environment is a bilingual one where both languages are spoken consistently.

Informal Word Recognition Inventory

Grade Level	Flash Percent Correct	Untimed Percent Correct
Preprimer	35	35
Primer	25	25

Metropolitan Achievement Test

Primary I Battery, Form F

	Grade Level	Percentile Rank (Beginning of Grade 2)
Word Knowledge	1.3	4
Word Analysis	1.1	2
Reading	Not administered	

Peter's performance on this test was not much better than a "guess score." It is sometimes misleading to assign an instructional level from standardized reading tests. This test suggests that Peter's performance in word knowledge and word analysis skills is at early first grade, when he is really a half step above a nonreader in a traditional second grade class.

Slosson Intelligence Test

Peter demonstrated a mental age of 7 years, 10 months which was equivalent to an IQ of 100. His greatest strength was in the area of vocabulary.

Visual Analysis

Peter's unaided visual acuity was 20/20 in each eye. Accommodative skills were adequate, as were fusional ranges of operation. All areas tested were within the expected range.

Perceptual Evaluation

Tachistoscopic exposures, 3 digits at a speed of .1 second = 25% correct and placed Peter in less than the 10th percentile of grade one.

Motor-Free Visual Perception Test revealed an age equivalent score of 5 years, 8 months.

Peter failed the Wepman Test of Auditory Discrimination.

Block Design Test of the Wechsler Intelligence Scale for Children = age equivalent score of 5 years, 2 months (raw score 4).

Southern California Figure Ground Test = 1st percentile.

Perceptual Constancy subtest of Frostig = 5 years, 6 months.

Geometric Copy Forms (Winter Haven)—performance equivalent to approximately a 6-year-old (see Figure 5.5).

Divided Form Board—completed this task in 174 seconds, equivalent to approximately a kindergarten child—relied heavily on tactual information rather than visual input.

Tactual Angels—Peter was unable to raise his left hand and left leg simultaneously with tactual stimulation only.

Figure 5.5. Peter's Geometric Copy Forms Test (*Winter Haven*)

Directionality was poor. He had no concept of left and right.
He was unable to hop six times on one foot.
Peter was unable to bounce a ball six times with one hand. He was
    unable to walk a four-inch walking rail backwards without
    stepping off.

DISCUSSION

Peter is a youngster of average verbal intellectual functioning. In
reviewing his performance one must ask the question, "Why is
Peter entering the fifth month of a traditional grade two class?" In any
assessment of a potentially learning disabled child, the most important
single question that must be answered is, "Is this child in an appropriate
class and school setting?" All of the supportive therapies known to the
field will be ineffectual if the child must return to the failure and frustration of an inappropriate classroom setting. Does the teacher of the
traditional classroom understand the exceptional child, his behavior, his

needs, etc.? Does the teacher understand that the hyperkinetic child has little or no impulse control? Does the teacher understand that his is not willful misbehavior?

RECOMMENDATIONS

Peter appears to need a special education environment, preferably a class for learning disabled children. If such a class is not available, then serious consideration should be given to placement in a private school experienced in working with learning disabled children. For all practical purposes he is a "nonreader" with many needs in the reading readiness area, especially the areas of visual perception. Early programming in his new school placement should include a heavy emphasis on the development of visual perception skills. The use of an optometric consultant would be helpful in coordinating such a program with the teacher and/or private therapeutic intervention. Without improved visual perceptual skills, Peter's foundations for future academic successes would be "shaky" at best. With a coordinated effort by the special educator, reading specialist, learning disability specialist, psychologist, and optometrist, Peter should achieve a greater degree of academic success and a positive school experience.

Case Study 5.4: Rhoda (Age 8 years, 2 months) (Grade 2, completed)

PARTIAL HISTORY

Rhoda was reported to have a very short attention span and a behavior problem in school. Difficulties in reading were also reported. She tends to read words better in isolation than in sentences. Psychoeducational testing revealed Rhoda to be a youngster of average intellectual functioning who was reading at an early to middle grade one level.

At age 6 years, Rhoda and her family were seen by a psychiatrist in family therapy. At age 7 years, Rhoda was seen by a psychologist in a behavior modification program. Rhoda is being seen by another psychiatrist, who is seeing her in individual psychiatric treatment. The latter psychiatrist suggested a program of concurrent optometric vision therapy. While language milestones developed without delay, Rhoda is hesitant to communicate verbally.

Visual Analysis

Near Point of Convergence= 5 inches

Cover Test Distance (20 feet) =Orthophoria
Near (16 inches) =Orthophoria

Visual Acuity at distance Right eye 20/25
Left eye 20/25

Visual Acuity at near Right eye 20/20
Left eye 20/20

	Distance	Near
Phoria	1$\triangle$ Esophoria	1$\triangle$ Esophoria
Divergence	5/2	10/14/6
Convergence	17/9	22/12
Vertical	Orthophoria	Orthophoria

Cheiroscopic tracings showed intermittent left eye suppression with slight vertical imbalance.
Vectograph—Poor appreciation of stereopsis.
Accommodative Facility——2.50 ou Doubles
+2.00 ou Fails 5 seconds
−1.50 to blur
+2.50 to blur
Eye movement skills—jerky, uneven, necessitates frequent head movement, difficulty converging on saccadic eye movements.

Perceptual Testing

Tachistoscopic Exposures 3 digits at .01 second showed 30% accuracy or the equivalent of the fifth percentile of a grade one child.

Piaget Protocol showed no appreciation of linear conservation, area conservation or reversibility.

Frostig, Perceptual Constancy—5 years, 6 months.

Visual Copy Forms (Winter Haven) poorly reproduced and segmented.

Southern California Figure Ground Test=Less than the first percentile.

Divided Form Board—only able to reassemble five of a possible six forms in 240 seconds—performance almost entirely tactual—seemed to use little if any visual input—equivalent to approximately early kindergarten—size judgments extremely poor.

Tactual Angels—not able to raise her left hand and right leg simultaneously upon tactual stimulation only.

Directionality—Unable to respond correctly to questions relating to left-right discrimination.

Chalk Circles—unable to perform reciprocally yolked circles.

Hopping—six times on each foot good—not able to hop alternately two times on each foot.

Ball Bouncing—able to bounce a nine-inch playground ball six times with each hand—not able to bounce a ball alternately two times with each hand.

Walking Rail—not able to walk a four-inch walking rail forward or backward.

DISCUSSION

Rhoda is experiencing very significant difficulties in both the physiological and perceptual aspects of visual development. Deficiencies were noted in accommodative facility (focusing) and depth perception, and fusion was quite unstable. Sensory processing skills showed deficits in figure-ground, visual closure, visual motor coordination, and motor planning.

The difficulties which were noted in Rhoda's performance in the areas of visual closure, figure-ground, accommodative facility, and fusional ranges of operation correlate well with her extremely short attention span. These factors and their relationship to the ability to attend and concentrate were discussed earlier in this chapter (see Visual Fixation). Rhoda does not seem capable of filtering out unessential stimuli in her efforts to concentrate.

Rhoda demonstrated that her present level of cognitive development was still in the preoperational stage of development. This stage is generally accepted to be characterized by the dominance of the child's visual perceptions (Flavell, 1963). If Piaget's philosophy of cognitive development is valid and Rhoda demonstrates such significant difficulties in visual perception, then we must conclude that Rhoda's world is confused. This may, possibly, explain why previous psychiatric and psychological intervention was unsuccessful. This case study in which treatment of the emotional factors in "isolation" proved unsatisfactory nicely demonstrates the need for multidisciplinary care. The question of which came first, confused visual functioning and perceptual skills or the emotional problems, is academic at this point. Treatment should include both psychiatric or psychological as well as optometric intervention. As Rhoda's visual understanding of the world around her improves, psychiatric counseling should be much more effective. As one or both of these treatment modalities are phased out or concluded, Rhoda's reading skills should be reevaluated. If skills in reading remain deficient, then work with a reading specialist should be initiated.

DISCUSSION AND CONCLUSIONS

Vision is the primary sensory modality for learning. When visual deficits exist and interfere with an individual's performance, therapeutic intervention is recommended. The role of optometric vision therapy is to teach the child proper use of the visual system in order that he/she may respond more effectively to standard academic teaching procedures—in other words, to provide a higher level of readiness for learning and/or to provide greater visual efficiency. The therapy should be individualized to the specific needs of each child at his/her developmental level. Physiological visual problems may range in severity from double vision (Case Study 5.1) to such discomfort that avoidance techniques are utilized. James (Case Study 5.2) displayed adequate reading skills in testing, but day-to-day classroom performance was poor. For this youngster, difficulties in binocular coordination resulted in headaches and eyestrain which he attempted to alleviate by unusual postures, head tilting, and resting his head on his arm. Perceptual disorders were evident in several case studies. Peter (Case Study 5.3) demonstrated significant difficulties in word recognition skills with associated sensory processing deficits. Rhoda (Case Study 5.4) experienced very significant deficits in perceptual development, resulting in a "confused state." Rhoda has been under the care of one psychologist and two other psychiatrists in the past four years. One must wonder what effect a combined psychiatric-optometric therapeutic approach might have had.

Another question is raised: can vision affect behavior? Actually, any physical or physiological deficit can do this. For example, consider a person who breaks an arm. Performance is altered, new compensations may be learned, and personality may be altered. In the same way, deficits in vision can alter personality, behavior, and emotional factors.

We tend to take vision for granted and assume that, if we can see clearly, our visual systems are functioning perfectly. The vast implications related to the functional aspects of our visual system should be more apparent from the presention of this chapter.

There are still many misconceptions and subtle inferences which remain. Two points should be made clear:

(1) Visual and perceptual training in isolation do not "cure" learning problems. If a child has a reading deficiency with an associated visual disorder, work with a reading specialist or special educator must either accompany or succeed visual training. The goal of optometric vision therapy is to make the child *visually* ready to learn and to respond more favorably to educational techniques.

(2) Many professionals fall into the trap of asking, "Which approach is more effective, the 'task oriented' approach or 'process training'?" By developing this artificial dichotomy, it is presumed the two regimens are mutually exclusive (Solan, 1973a). There is no reason why the two approaches cannot and should not be complimentary. If there is difficulty in both visual and perceptual functioning, as well as in reading, the child would benefit from therapeutic programming in both areas.

Unfortunately the role of visual training in a therapeutic regimen is frequently misunderstood and therefore discredited. This fact was clearly illustrated during a class in which the author was demonstrating visual, perceptual, and visual motor training techniques to a group of graduate students. One of the techniques designed to develop visual motor skills was a bean bag "pitch back" activity wherein the child throws a bean bag at the "pitch back" which, in turn, bounces the bag back to the child to catch again. One of the graduate students remarked that this game had been cited by another professor as an example of why visual training does not help children read better, whereupon the author replied, tongue in cheek, "Well we use red bean bags to improve word recognition skills, blue bean bags to improve reading comprehension, and yellow bean bags to improve arithmetic skills." Of course, this activity does *not* improve reading skills, for it is *not* the role of the optometrist to teach reading. It is the goal of optometric vision therapy to remediate any visual problems which might interfere with reading and learning. Does aspirin improve reading comprehension? Obviously not. But, suppose the child has a severe headache? Will that decrease his ability to read, comprehend and study? Yes, it will. If this child took aspirin and the headache dissipated, would his reading and study skills improve? Yes. Would we then say that aspirin improves reading comprehension? No, we would say that the aspirin relieved an interference to the child's reading. In the same way, optometric vision therapy is designed to relieve and/or improve visual and perceptual problems which may be interfering with reading, learning, or performance in general.

In this chapter, the role of vision and learning disorders has been discussed. The signs and behaviors frequently demonstrated have been reviewed. The effects of visual (physiological and perceptual) problems on learning and performance have been outlined. It is felt that a better understanding of vision and learning disorders will enable other professionals to work more comfortably with the developmental optometrist in the treatment of children with specific learning disabilities. The best interest of these children can be served by utilizing the services of many professions of which optometry is but one. No single profession, at this time, has all the keys to "unlock" all of the problems which SLD children experience. Therefore, we should attempt to understand and appreciate the contributions of each profession.

REFERENCES

Abercrombie, M.L.J. *The body image, clinics in developmental medicine* (No. 6). London: The Spastics Society, 1964.

Alexander, D. & Money, J. Reading disability and the problem of direction sense. The Reading Teacher, 1967, *20*.

Ames, L.B., Gillespie, C. & Streff, J. *Stop school failure*. New York: Harper & Row, 1972.

Apell, R. & Streff, J. *Child vision care.* A series of papers released by Optometric Extension Program, Duncan, Oklahoma, 1961-63.

Arnheim, R., *Visual thinking.* Los Angeles: University of California Press, 1969.

Ayres, A.J. Patterns of perceptual-motor dysfunction in children. A factor analytic study. *Perceptual and Motor Skills,* 1965, *20,* 335–368.

Ayres, A.J. Deficits in sensory integration in educationally handicapped children. *Journal of Learning Disabilities,* 1969, *2,* 160–168.

Barsh, R.H. *Achieving perceptual-motor efficiency.* Seattle: Special Child Publications, 1967.

Beltman, J.W., Stern, E.L., Whitsell, L.J., & Gofman, H.E. Cerebral dominance in developmental dyslexia. *Archives Ophthalmology,* 1967, *78,* 722–729.

Benton, C.D., Jr., McCann, J.W., & Larson, M. Dyslexia: A practical approach for the opthalmologist. *Journal of Pediatric Ophthamology,* 1972, *5,* 25–29.

Benton, C.D., Jr. Comment: The eye and learning disabilities. *Journal of Learning Disabilities,* 1973, *6,* 334–336.

Bing, L. Vision and the "right to read" effort. *Journal of Learning Disabilities,* 1972, *5,* 29–32.

Birch, H.G. Dyslexia and the maturation of visual function. In J. Money (Ed.), *Reading Disability.* Baltimore: John Hopkins University Press, 1962.

Birch, H.G. & Belmont, L. Auditory-visual integration, intelligence and reading ability in school children. *Perceptual Motor Skills,* 1965, *20,* 295–305.

Bryant, D.N. Characteristics of dyslexia and their remedial implication. *Exceptional .Children,* 1965, *31,* 197.

Coleman, H.M. Visual perception and reading dysfunction, *Journal of Learning Disabilities,* 1968, *1,* 116–123.

Cruickshank, W.M., *The brain-injured child in home, school and community.* New York: Syracuse University Press, 1967.

Cruickshank, W.M., Bentzen, F.A., Ratzeburg, F.H., & Tannhauser, M.T. *A teaching method for brain-injured and hyperactive children.* New York: Syracuse University Press, 1961.

deHirsh, K., Jansky, J., & Langford, W. *Predicting reading failure.* New York: Harper & Row, 1966.

Ebersole, M., Kephart, N.C., & Ebersole, J.B. *Steps to achievement for the slow learner.* Columbus: Merrill, 1968.

Eisenberg, L. The management of the hyperkinetic child. *Developmental Medicine Child Neurology,* 1966, *8,* 593–598.

Flavell, J.H. *The developmental psychology of Jean Piaget.* Princeton, New Jersey: D. Van Nostrand Co., 1963.

Flax, N., *The development of vision and visual perception: Implications in learning disability.* Presented at the 12th Annual Forum on Vision and Reading Optometric Association, Chicago, Illinois, November 9, 1968. (a)

Flax, N. Visual function in learning disabilities. *Journal of Learning Disabilities,* 1968, *1,* 74–78. (b)

Flax, N. *Vision and learning disabilities.* Lecture presented for Post-Graduate Courses, American Academy of Optometry, Miami Beach, Florida, December 1974.

Flax, N. Vision and learning disabilities: Optometry's contribution. In T. N. Greenstein (Ed.), *Vision and learning disability,* St. Louis, Missouri: American Optometric Association, 1976.

Forrest, E. Vision and the visual process. *Education,* 1962, *82,* 5.

Frostig, M. & Horne, D. *The Frostig program for the development of visual perception.* Chicago: Follet Publishing, 1964.

Furth, H. & Wachs, H. *Thinking goes to school.* New York: Oxford University Press, 1974.

Gesell, A., and Amatruda, C. *Developmental diagnosis.* New York: Hoeber, 1947.

Gesell, A., Ilg, F. & Bullis, G. *Vision: Its development in infant and child.* New York: Hoeber, 1949.

Getman, G.N. *Techniques and diagnostic criteria for the optometric care of children's vision.* Duncan, Oklahoma: Optometric Extension Program, 1960.

Getman, G.N. & Bullis, G. *Developmental vision.* A series of papers released by Optometric Extension Program, Duncan, Oklahoma, 1950–51.

Getman, G.N. & Kephart, N.C. *Developmental vision.* Post-Graduate Study Courses, Optometric Extension Program, Duncan, Oklahoma, 1957–59.

Goldberg, H.K. & Drash, P.W. The disabled reader. *Journal of Pediatric Ophthalmology,* 1972, *5,* 11–24.

Greenspan, S.B. *Research studies of visual and perceptual-motor training.* Optometric Extension Program Continuing Education Courses, Duncan, Oklahoma, 1971–72.

Hebb, D.O. *The organization of behavior.* New York: Wiley, 1949.

Held, R. Plasticity in sensory-motor systems. *Scientific American,* 1965, *213,* 84–94.

Ilg, F. & Ames, L.B. *School readiness.* New York: Harper & Row, 1966.

Kahn, D. & Birch, H.G. Development of auditory-visual integration and reading achievement. *Perceptual and Motor Skills,* 1968, *27,* 459–468.

Kane, M., Physiological theory of learning: The role of developmental vision in academic achievement and learning. In R.M. Wold (Ed.), *Visual and perceptual aspects for the achieving and under-achieving child.* Seattle: Special Child Publications, 1969.

Kephart, N.C. *The slow learner in the classroom.* Columbus: Merrill, 1960.

Kephart, N.C. Perceptual-motor aspects of learning disabilities. *Exceptional Children,* 1964, *31,* 201–206.

Kephart, N.C. Teaching the child with a perceptual-motor handicap. In Bortner, M. (Ed.), *Evaluation and education of children with brain damage.* Springfield: Charles C Thomas, 1968.

Koppitz, E. *The Bender Gestalt Test for young children.* New York: Grune & Stratton, 1966.

Kraskin, R. *Visual training in action.* A series of papers released by Optometric Extension Program, Duncan, Oklahoma, 1965–68.

Ludlum, W. *Learning disabilities.* Paper presented at College of Optometrists in Vision Development, New York, October, 1973.

Ludlam, W., Twarowski, C. & Ludlam, D. Optometric visual training for reading disability—A case report. *American Journal of Optometry,* January 1973.

Peiser, I.J. Vision and learning disabilities. *Journal of American Optometric Association,* 1972, *43,* 152–159.

Piaget, J., *The origins of intelligence.* New York: International Universities Press, 1952.

Piaget, J., *The mechanisms of perception.* New York: Basic Books, 1969.

Pierce, J., *The underachieving child.* Paper presented at American Academy of Optometry Post-Graduate Courses, Philadelphia, Pennsylvania, December, 1969.

Pierce, J.R. A clinical model for specifying relationships between vision function problems and academic underachievement. *Journal of American Optometric Association,* 1973, *44,* 152–156.

Robinson, H.M. *Clinical studies in reading* (Vol. 2). Supplementary Educational Monograph No. 77. Chicago: University of Chicago Press, 1953.

Seiderman, A.S. Motor planning and developmental apraxia. *Journal of American Optometric Association,* 1970, *41,* 846–857.

Seiderman, A.S. A look at perceptual-motor training. *Academic Therapy,* 1972, *7,* 315–321.

Seiderman, A.S. *Perceptual development program.* Title I demonstration under PL 89–313, Unpublished study. Wordsworth Academy, 1973. (a)

Seiderman, A.S. *Preliminary findings of a program of optometric vision therapy in an academic environment.* Paper presented at The Gesell Institute of Child Development, New Haven, Connecticut, June, 1973. (b).

Seiderman, A.S. An optometric approach to the diagnosis of visually based problems in learning. In G. Leisman (Ed.), *Basic visual processes and learning disability.* Springfield, Ill.: Charles C Thomas, 1976. (a)

Seiderman, A.S. Under scrutiny of optometry. *Pediatrics,* 1976, *57*(6), 980–981. (b)

Selye, H., *The stress of life.* New York: McGraw-Hill, 1956.

Sherman, A. Relating vision disorders to learning disability. *Journal of American Optometric Association,* 1973, *44,* 140–141.

Silver, A.A. Diagnostic considerations in children with reading disability. *Bulletin Orton Society,* 1961, *11,* 91.

Silver, A.A. & Hagin, R.A. Strategies of intervention in the spectrum of defects in specific reading disability. *Bulletin Orton Society,* 1967, *17,* 39–46.

Skeffington, A.M., Postgraduate Papers, *Optometric Extension Program,* Duncan, Oklahoma, 1926–68.

Solan, H.A. Physiological correlates of dyslexia. *American Journal of Optometry and Archives of American Academy of Optometry,* 1966, *43*(1).

Solan, H.A. Perceptual testing and training methods used in primary grades. *New Jersey Journal of Optometry,* May-June, 1968.

Solan, H.A. *An integrated approach to the diagnosis and treatment of language pathology.* Unpublished Paper, 1971.

Solan, H.A. Artificial dichotomy. *The Reading Teacher,* 1973, *27*(1). (a)

Solan, H.A. *The psychology of learning and reading difficulties.* New York: Simon and Schuster, 1973. (b)

Solan, H.A. & Seiderman, A.S. Case report on a grade one child before and after perceptual-motor training. *Journal of Learning Disabilities,* 1970, *3,* 635–639.

Spache, G.D. *Reading in the elementary school.* Boston: Allyn, 1964.

Strauss, A.A. & Lehtinen, L.E. *Psychopathology and education of the brain-injured child* (Vol. 1). New York: Grune & Stratton, 1947.

Taylor, E.A. The spans: Perception, apprehension and recognition. *American Journal of Ophthalmology,* 1957, *44,* 501–507.

Taylor, E.A. & Solan, H.A. *Visual training with the prism reader.* Huntington, New York: Educational Development Laboratories, 1957.

Tyler, R.H. Looking and seeing their relation to visual cognition. *Neuro-Ophthalmology,* 1968, *4,* 249–265.

Vurpillot, E. *The visual world of the child.* New York: International Universities Press, 1976.

Walker, R.N. & Streff, J. A perceptual program for classroom teachers: Some results. *Genetic Psychology Monographs,* 1973, *87,* 253–288.

Wepman, J.M. The perceptual basis for learning. In H.A. Robinson (Ed.), *Meeting individual differences in reading.* Chicago: University of Chicago Press, 1964.

Wold, R.M. *Visual and perceptual aspects for the achieving and under-achieving child.* Seattle: Special Child Publications, 1969.

Wold, R.M. Vision and learning: The great puzzle. I. *Optometric Weekly,* October 7, 1971.

Wold, R.M. Vision and learning: The great puzzle. II. *Optometric Weekly,* October 14, 1971 and October 21, 1971.

Woolf, D. Dyschriesopia: A syndrome of visual disability. In R.M. Wold (Ed.), *Visual and perceptual aspects for the achieving and under-achieving child.* Seattle: Special Child Publications, 1969.

Wunderlich, R.C. *Kids, brains, and learning.* St. Petersburg: Johnny Reads, 1970.

PART III

MANY PILLARS OF SUPPORT: INTERPRETATION AND PRESCRIPTION

We must work to escape shallowness, oversimplification, too quick acceptance of uncritical formulae which, by planting the mind against self-examination impair its capacity for a reasoned judgment.

—Justice Felix Frankfurter (1963)

INTRODUCTION

The central issue in this handbook is bridging the gaps. Too often clinicians are quick to construct shallow, oversimplified solutions for the complex emotional problems associated with specific learning disabilities. One can find, with little effort, a quartet of dichotomies from which our children are victimized (see Table A). These dichotomies, in philosophy and practice, widen the gaps in our delivery of service and in the quality of our educational/clinical intervention.

The philosophical backdrop of this Handbook has been to address the issues raised as dichotomies in Table A with a *both-and* point-of-view, rather than as *either-or* approaches.

Focusing on the whole-child concept from a genetic-dynamic-developmental viewpoint allows for the integration of the organic and functional, the educational and clinical, the special educational and mainstreaming classroom approaches, and for a rapprochement of symptom-related behavior modification therapy with individual psychotherapy focused on strengthening ego function, self-concept formation, and self-esteem.

Such a whole-child concept recognizes the significance of the child growing up in a family system within a subculture which serves as a unique environment for that child. The interaction, assimilation, accommodation, and integration of the biological, psychological, social, economic, and educational factors in the life of the developing child become the crucial processes in shaping the child's total personality. Recently, a Committee on the Needs and Rights of Children (Gause *et al.,* 1976) described the interactional and transactional nature of a child growing up in our culture in terms of five clusters of concern impacting in the matrix of six social systems (see Table B).

The Committee identified the five clusters of concern as follows: concern for intimate nurture, living conditions, learning and guidance, social interaction, and the realm of God.

It recognized that these five needs are being set and met in various social systems and institutions in our society, modulated according to the specific stage of development through which the child is progressing, shaped by the hierarchy of needs and the particular circumstances in which the individual is living, and influenced by the larger pressing realities of the time in history through which the child is growing and developing into adolescence and adulthood.

The Committee recognized and described six important social systems influencing the child's growth and the family's capacity to sup-

Table A
Children as Victims of a Quartet of Dichotomies

Organic	vs.	Functional
Educational	vs.	Clinical
Special Education	vs.	Mainstreaming
Symptom Focus	vs.	Dynamic Causes
(behavior modification)		(psychotherapy)

Table B
Interactional and Transactional
Forces in Growth and Development

	Five Clusters of Concern				
Six Social Systems	Intimate Nurture	Living Conditions	Learning and Guidance	Social Interaction	Realm of God
The Family					
Health Care					
Education					
Justice					
Economic					
Religious					

port or distort that growth. These social systems included the following: The Family System, Health Care System, Educational System, Justice System, Economic System, and Religious System.

Richmond (1971) developed and schematized a somewhat similar conceptual framework to highlight the relevant factors in psychosocial adaptation as a backdrop to the concept of the whole child (see Figure I).

Viewed from these larger sociocultural contexts, the petty dichotomies so often set up by workers in the field seem to pale and a sharper

FACTORS IN PSYCHOSOCIAL ADAPTATION
(Richmond, 1971)

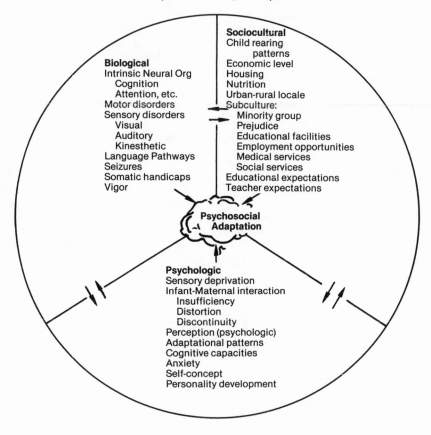

Figure A.

whole-child focus emerges to include the developing child in a family in a subcultural environment.

One of the strengths of this whole-child-genetic-dynamic-developmental approach is that it allows and encourages the investigator and clinician to place emphasis on certain types of clinical interventions according to individual needs and commensurate with the level of skill and background training of the intervenor.

In bridging the gaps of our knowledge about SLD, no one theory of clinical/educational intervention and no one treatment modality represents a panacea for all the clinical, educational, familial, and social problems brought into the SLD arena. With this in mind, several outstanding clinicians have been asked to author chapters related to their specific expertise and their area of emphasis in the unfolding dialogue of intervention strategies for the SLD population.

The initial discussion of treatment modalities focuses on Individual Psychotherapy from the genetic-dynamic-psychoanalytic-developmental model. Subsequent chapters will highlight, by the use of clinical case studies or clinical vignettes, the principles associated with Counseling with Parents, Group Psychotherapy, the use of the Life Space Interview and Time Out Process, Therapy Within the Family Constellation, Behavior Modification at School and at Home, The Creative Arts Therapies, and the pros and cons of the Medical Therapies so widely publicized in today's press, on television and in magazine coverage.

CHAPTER 6

INDIVIDUAL PSYCHOTHERAPY:
AN ILLUSTRATIVE CASE STUDY

WILLIAM C. ADAMSON, M.D.

The therapeutic process occurs as a unique growth experience, created by one person seeking and needing help from another who accepts the responsibility of offering it. This basic structure characterizes each potentially therapeutic setting irrespective of methods or techniques employed or of whether it is a child or adult who seeks assistance.

—Frederick H. Allen, *Psychotherapy with Children, 1942*

HISTORICAL PERSPECTIVE

The principles underlying genetic-dynamic psychotherapy with children and adolescents have been formulated by many clinicians in the field: Allen (1942), Adams (1974), Axline (1947), Freud (1946), Geleerd (1967), Klein (1932), Moustakas (1959), Pearson (1949, 1968), Rogers (1939), and Witmer (1946), to name a few. Principles more specifically related to the individual treatment process for children and adolescents with SLD have not been so well formulated. Part of the diffuseness or lack of clarity stems from the confusion in the field over the nature of the condition (SLD) being treated. More relevant, perhaps, is the historically pessimistic attitude of psychotherapists toward these children presumably handicapped by the "weakened ego" or "organic ego," felt to be associated with children functioning with the SLD symptom complex. Consequently, until the early

1960s, few psychotherapists of any persuasion were ready to invest time and energy in this population. Several striking exceptions to this general attitude were Strauss and Lehtinen (1947), Bender (1956), Pearson (1952), and Rappaport (1961), who invested their clinical time, energy, skill, and descriptive talents toward developing positive treatment models for these children.

Strauss and Lehtinen and their coworkers unlocked many mysteries associated with "brain-injured children" and wrote some excellent programs and publications for teachers and parents which continue to be incorporated in current prescriptions for today's SLD children. Bender provided a breakthrough in behavioral management when she recognized that the hyperactivity observed in these children can be seen as coming from three separate but related sources: the organic problem in the child, the constitutional inheritance, and the environment in which the child grows socially, emotionally, and cognitively. She proposed the use of the medications benadryl and amphetamine (see fuller discussion in Chapter 13) as adjuncts to the therapeutic intervention. Pearson made a significant contribution when he outlined a Classification of Learning Disorders which, quite remarkably, has stood the test of time. He sorted out the various causal factors for specific learning disorders and attempted by therapeutic intervention to alter those situations in which there was a major "psychological overlay" (see Chapter 1).

Pearson used a set of clinical vignettes to illustrate his insightful approaches in treating or mediating those emotional problems which were an integral part of the learning disorder. His descriptions are of such quality and depth as to make this article a classic in the literature on individual psychotherapy with SLD children. Rappaport (1961) made an equally significant contribution as one of the first clinicians to emphasize the fact that damage to neural tissue does not play the paramount role in the child's behavior. His thesis was that lack of intactness in the child's central nervous system fosters an equivalent lack of intactness in the primary autonomous ego functions (Hartman, 1939) of motility, language, perception, cognition, memory, concept formation, and intention (see Table 6.1). The result could be an unconscious lack of responsiveness in the pattern of mothering which interfered with Erikson's mutuality phase of ego development. Rappaport concluded that this pattern of deviant ego development in the child fostered an ongoing disturbance in the parent-child relationship. This disturbance, in turn, continued to interfere with the ego development of the child, setting up a vicious cycle of mutually reinforcing deviancy both

Table 6.1
Hypothesis of Ego Development in SLD Children/Adolescents*

Behavior disturbance is not due to damaged brain tissue
and is, therefore, reversible.

Lack of intactness of central nervous system affects
all primary ego functions.

These primary ego functions include: motor, language,
perception, cognition, memory, concept formation,
and intention.

Unconscious lack of parental responsiveness or over-
determined protectiveness interferes with the
mutuality phase of ego development.

Deviant ego development fosters vicious cycle of disturbed parent-child relationships and more deviancy
in the child or adolescent.

*After Rappaport, 1961.

in ego development and in the relationship between parent and child. In accord with these observations he established The Pathway School in Jeffersonville, Pennsylvania, for children with special learning disabilities.

The unique aspect of The Pathway School was the combination of a strong special education program with an equally strong clinical services program which provided individual and group psychotherapy for all the students and concurrent parent counseling for the concerned parents. A follow-up study by Frank and Abbott (1970) revealed the program to be effective with 65% of the student population, when effectiveness was defined in terms of placement in a normal or near-normal school setting, with passing grades in all or nearly all subjects, healthy peer group relationships with classmates and neighborhood children, and a reasonably comfortable interpersonal relationship with all members of the family system at home.

CONTEXTUAL FRAMEWORK FOR CASE STUDIES

Since this is a multidisciplinary handbook written for therapists, counselors, teachers, and other educators, as well as interested parents,

Table 6.2
Contextual Framework in Beginning Individual Psychotherapy
with SLD Children and Adolescents

Obtain a background history

Complete an initial psychodiagnostic evaluation

Engage parents or responsible surrogates through an interpretation conference

Help child establish basic trust in therapist

Recognize feelings stirred up in child about coming

Move toward some partial definitions of reasons for coming

Help child express and deal with resistances to treatment

Help child establish a lexicon of feelings

Develop a running thread of key issues to unite therapy sessions

Develop and maintain an interrelated movement process in working with parents concurrently with treating the child

all with different levels of training, experience, and sophistication, a Contextual Framework for Therapy applicable to any setting or discipline will be spelled out (see Table 6.2). This framework will include identifying the focal points in the beginning, middle, and ending phases of individual psychotherapy as presented in Case Study 6.1. Also, it should be recognized that an attempt has been made to "de-mystify" individual psychotherapy, while avoiding either oversimplification or overmechanization of the complex interpersonal relationship process which is central to individual psychotherapy.

Case Study 6.1

Latency Case in Long-Term Individual Psychodynamically Oriented Psychotherapy

HISTORY

Briefly, John was first seen when he was nearly 5 years of age. Pregnancy, delivery, and neonatal period were described as unremarkable except for a very pungent odor associated with perspiration. which persisted from the neonatal period into his fourth year. Following a gastrointestinal virus requiring hospitalization, the odor disappeared. Chromatogram studies for a generalized metabolic disturbance of the congenital type (e.g. hyperisovaleric acidemia) were negative, as were endocrine studies. There was a history of two febrile seizures with no residual EEG abnormalities.

Psychological evaluation at 5 years indicated he was functioning with some delay in gross motor coordination (three-and-a-half-year level), poor balance, a very short attention span, and considerable difficulty moving himself in space. Adaptive language on the Gesell Development Schedule was at a four to four-and-a-half-year level and language was at a four-year level. Social comprehension and judgment were mature beyond his age, yet he manifested considerable infantile and dependent behavior in social relationships. When he became tired in the testing situation, he threw himself on the floor, kicked his feet into the air, and screamed. He recovered quickly, but continued frequent mouthing of objects in the room in an anxious and resistive fashion. The Revised Stanford-Binet, Scale L, indicated a basal functioning level of four years with a ceiling at six years.

In the psychiatric evaluation at this time, John appeared to be a large boy for his age, nearer in height to a 6-year-old. His hands were pudgy, with hyperextensibility at the wrists, and hand dominance was not yet established.

John related to a train in the office. He was concerned that the train might be broken. As he made a circular track for the train, he commented that you could get a shock from the wires (an apparent reference to an electric train he had at home). He concluded his train play with the comment that "the shock will get on the caboose and go outch."

John's concern for the trains being broken and his fear of being injured by the "shock" probably represented his anxiety over his previous fall from a stone ledge, necessitating an X-ray to rule out any fractures. It also represented a less well-defined fear and apprehension about difficulties with his body, his inability to keep up with his peers in running, jumping, and playing games. Finally, it represented some of the retaliation and mutilation fantasies often associated with oedipal rivalry with the father for his mother's attention and affection.

His fears of separation from his mother and fears of body injury were verbalized in his initial interview:

> The boy is afraid the jet is going to take him to somebody else. He may leave his mommy . . . the alligator is biting off the little girl's head and she is crying.

The initial interview ended with some family doll play in which he restated his concern over being injured and recalled his separation from mother when she went to the hospital to deliver her second child.

> Don't let the train fall off the track as it goes up the mountain. The train is going to fall to pieces but daddy is not hurt. (The clinician asked the question "Is mommy hurt?") Yes. Where is the hospital? Mommy is sick in bed. She brings baby home to daddy.

Preparation and Inclusion in Therapy

Following the Interpretation Conference (see Chapter 2), John was prepared by his parents for coming to see the therapist once a week. They had shared with him that they loved him and knew he was unhappy about many things, seemed afraid he would be hurt or injured, and was afraid mother was going to leave him. They recognized with him that, although he was big for his age, he was upset when he couldn't keep up with his classmates in school and on the playground. Finally, his parents said they needed help to help him and that they knew a doctor who would be helping him with his fears about school and about things happening to him.

Generally, it is not considered helpful to tell a child he/she is "brain injured," as this frightens the child and often serves as an ongoing focus of self-doubt and a persistent barrier to growth. "I can't do it because I am brain-injured." On the other hand, there are times when a child can be helped by knowing that he/she is slower in developing, in learning, and growing up than other children. These children should be helped to know that this is through no fault of their own or anyone else. Rather, their growth is determined by nature's timeclock in their bodies and, to a large extent, centered in their brains, in the form of a little gland at the base of the brain as well as a larger gland located in their neck.

The children can be told that there are doctors, teachers, psychologists, and tutors who help boys and girls with these troubles in learning. Parents, at this point in the preparation process, can be helped to recognize that being slower in running, in school work, and in playing with other children can make children feel very upset inside, sometimes angry, sometimes sad, and sometimes just very confused and "down on themselves." Going to see a helping doctor or tutor can help these children feel better and, feeling better, to learn better in school and be happier at home.

Parents should be discouraged from the last minute approach in which they might say, "We are going for a ride and you are going to meet a nice man," or, "You are going to see a friend of ours who will be giving you some puzzles and toys to play with." Both statements represent a deception for the child and place the therapist in a less constructive role at the outset of therapy.

Preparation, on the other hand, should be done in a low-key, yet realistic way, focused on those areas of the child's growth and development which are of concern to the parents.

OVERVIEW OF BEGINNING PHASE

John was in kindergarten during his first year of once-a-week psychotherapy. For the first three months, he openly expressed his need to control the treatment hours unless the activity was anticipated and structured to his understanding and ability. He was overly sensitive about his size, his slowness, and his inability to move about quickly. He also showed great discomfort in any situation where teaching and learning were involved. He was able to express openly and fairly well his suspicion, then his warmth and acceptance, and, finally, his resistance to some of the therapist's directed activities in the treatment hours.

By the fourth and fifth months, he could express his anger and disappointment at the time limits of the treatment hours and at the destruction (removal by other children) of his various creations, which included an airport, a train station, and a filling station made of blocks. The therapist took a Polaroid picture of some of these constructions as a way of indicating his support for John's individuality and creativity, while building rapport, trust, and a positive therapeutic alliance. John allowed his feelings of hurt and chagrin to come into consciousness and verbal expression, and stopped using fatigue as an escape from the interaction in the treatment hours. By the sixth month, he could openly express positive and/or negative feelings toward the therapist and began to like himself more as a person. In one hour, as he jumped from chairs and windowsill, he said: "My body is too fat, but I can fly like an eagle and I can be a space man."

During the last half of this first year, John began to open up the conflicts he was having over his aggressive feelings. He began to show pride in his learning, especially his mastery of important elements in language, including syntax and phonics. He began to reflect an increasing self-confidence and readiness to leave his dependent, at times symbiotic, position with his mother and to move on toward greater interdependence. He had now reached well into the object constancy stage (Mahler *et al,* 1975) of development and was moving toward greater risk in peer group relationships.

Contextual Framework for Psychotherapy

Referring back to Table 6.2, it is important to observe the child's efforts to master age-appropriate developmental tasks while the therapist attempts to set several things in motion. These include some of the following factors:

HELP THE CHILD ESTABLISH BASIC TRUST IN THE THERAPIST

This can be done by the therapist at the first session by greeting the parent(s) in a warm and friendly manner, by responding to and introducing him/herself to the child, by defining for them the length of time the child will be seen, and by helping the child separate from the parent(s) to go with the therapist. Sometimes, with younger children, it is helpful to have the parent(s) walk into the office and not leave until the child begins to explore the room and feel more comfortable. The therapist can indicate to the parent(s) and child that he/she will be bringing the child back to the waiting room when the hands of the clock are in a very specific position. Being specific, pointing to a clock, and referring to the location of the big hand and the small hand, helps the anxious child focus on a familiar external object and partializes the separation experience so it does not seem that this first meeting with a stranger will last forever. Subsequently, at those times when the child may press to "go back to mommy," the therapist can point to the clock indicating exactly how many minutes are left until they will go. It is always most important to honor that time structure as a step toward establishing basic trust between the therapist and the child.

RECOGNIZE THE FEELINGS STIRRED UP IN COMING

Since genetic-dynamic therapy will continue to focus on self-awareness and mastery of feelings in interpersonal relationships, it is important to recognize with the child in the first hour the feelings which have been stirred up in coming. "You probably had some feeling about coming to see me today," or, "How did you feel about coming? I think you were pretty stirred up, maybe even a little scared in coming to see me."

Children often need to deny their real feelings until they become more comfortable in the situation. The therapist can recognize that some boys and girls like coming and some do not. Some are very angry and probably will tell (or already have told) mother and father they didn't like the whole thing.

MOVE TOWARD SOME PARTIAL DEFINITION OF REASONS FOR COMING

"John, it's good to see you today, and I wonder what mother and father told you about coming to see me?" is often a way for the therapist to begin the hour. Many times, children need to deny being told anything and will say they don't know. The therapist can accept this initial denial, recognizing the need to use the first visit to get acquainted. "Perhaps, as we talk together, we will get a clearer idea of the things that trouble you and have mother and father wondering how they can help you." As the visits unfold, the nature of the child's difficulties become clearer, and it can be helpful to "tag" those areas as "something mother and father may have wanted to help you with in your visits to see me."

With John, we were able to draw several large rectangles which we called his "freight cars" and which carried the things his parents thought he needed help with at this time.

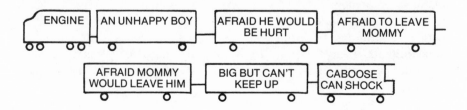

The therapist chose the freight car metaphor because of John's interest in trains and his fear of things happening to "his train." Symbolically, the train could be seen as related to his masculine assertiveness, his efforts to establish gender identity, and to aspects of his striving for initiative versus his fear of guilt and/or retaliation.

John's father had been concerned about his son's introspection and isolation from other children and perpetually sought to bring him, and the other members of the family, into wider sociocultural experiences. The father's pattern took the form of the instrumental orientation vis-à-vis the expressive function described by Parsons and Bales (1955) and extended by Johnson (1963) in his proposition that the instrumental orientation of the father allowed him to shape both his son's masculinity and his daughter's femininity in terms of the father's critical scanning of appropriate and inappropriate role behavior in society.

John responded well to the train metaphor in his treatment hours. He engaged on the issue of his size and slowness. At the same time, by identifying and externalizing several areas on which we would be working together, much of the "mystery" and fear of coming into a strange office to see an unknown person was dissipated. His anxiety lessened, and he became more trusting. The freight cars, with their captions, became areas for discussion and inquiry. As the weeks went by, we could redraw John's train, or create a toy train with plastic cars, and engage him in reflecting about the "unhappy boy" in coach #1 or the boy in coach #3 who is afraid to leave his mommy. It was in this contextual framework of awareness as to why he was coming that John became freer to express both his acceptance of and resistance to the more directed activities of the treatment hours.

HELP CHILD EXPRESS AND COPE WITH RESISTANCES TO TREATMENT

Aftr a period of establishing trust in the therapist, John became openly more verbal, more negative, and resistant to certain directions or suggestions brought into the hour by the therapist. Many times such resistances have been seen as defenses against treatment and as psychological manifestations which should be attacked or dealt with in a planned or preconceived way in order to "subdue" them or, at least, to provide immediate attenuation of the child's negative feelings and defensive attitudes. Children with the SLD syndrome and its emotional concomitants (see Chapter 2) frequently have developed passive-resistant personalities as a defense against continued reinjury to their narcissism and hurt pride. This was seen over and over again with John and has been observed as a lifelong issue in many other children and adolescents. Unless therapy with SLD children allows for the constructive expression of these negative feelings (felt as resistance), along with the positive feelings (felt as yielding), it becomes subjugation-dependency therapy rather than an ego-oriented growth therapy.

In recent years, analytic literature has attempted to make a distinction between defense and resistance (Gero, 1951; Sterba, 1951; Lowenstein, 1954), stressing that defense is the broader concept embracing all psychological processes, as both conscious and unconscious activity on the part of the ego, and not necessarily pathological in nature. Resistance, on the other hand, has come to embrace "all factors interfering with the goals of an analysis." Used within the context of therapy with children, resistance in the therapeutic process can be viewed more broadly as part of the emotional growth process in the child from which independence and individuality can begin to emerge, rather than always being viewed as a barrier to ongoing treatment.

HELP THE CHILD ESTABLISH A LEXICON OF FEELINGS

One of the ways dynamic-analytically oriented therapy differs from behavioral therapy is in its emphasis on feeling-awareness, feeling-life, and feeling-organization. Rather than focusing on the presenting symptoms *per se,* the emphasis is on how the child is reacting (with emotional feelings) from moment to moment in the treatment hour. The point of skill (science versus art of therapy) is to recognize that the child's feelings arise from and signal (1) the nature of the inner, intrapsychic conflict, (2) the child's emotional responses in interactional and interpersonal relationships in the present, and (3) the child's emotional responses to transactions between therapist and child in the therapy hours. Beyond this, the child's feelings and behavior in the hours reflect efforts to cope with, to defend against, and to master emotional issues associated with critical stages and developmental phases through which the child is growing at the time (See Chapter 2, Table 2.3). The therapist can "listen with the third ear," while keeping an eye on the child's developmental progression.

Listening and looking means to be aware of and to empathize with the feelings the child brings into the emerging treatment hours and the patterns the child uses to defend against those feelings. The listening and the looking are observational tools in the science of psychotherapy. How these observations are shared with the child in a helpful and growth-inducing way encompasses much of the art of psychotherapy. Good supervision remains the strongest way to teach both the science and the art of psychotherapy.

Therapy with SLD children is not very different from therapy with neurotic children, except that SLD children are often more sensitive to their failures, more narcissistically vulnerable, and appear to use denial and avoidance more frequently than other children. It is important, in either case, to help the child know what he or she is feeling, to be able to identify and label that feeling as part of the child's Lexicon of Feelings, and eventually to help the child find socially acceptable and age-appropriate ways of expressing those feelings. It is generally recognized that the highest social level will be attained through the verbalization of feelings in spontaneous and socially acceptable ways. Unfortunately, language usage and verbal expression are frequently areas of "detour" and disability in SLD children.

Initially, talking about feelings may frighten the child. By using the method of externalization to help the child displace internal feelings onto external play objects, such as family dolls, puppets, and other familiar objects in the world of childhood, the therapist helps the child gradually risk sharing these defended-against feelings with the therapist.

SLD children often respond to externalization through the use of the media of art, music, or dance (see Chapter 12). They can identify, for example, with faces drawn to illustrate feelings without feeling guilty or excessively anxious that they have revealed these feelings to the therapist. Nor does the therapist need to be an artist to illustrate the varied facial expression appropriate to feelings which can be represented by changing the eyes, nose, mouth and eyebrows in simple cartoon designs.

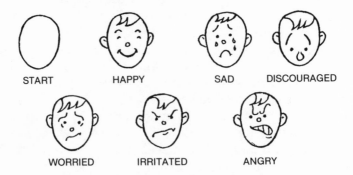

John did not have the fine motor skills to make these drawings himself. When they were cartooned for him, he did open up a great deal as he recognized it was safe and acceptable to have such feelings. It was his awareness and acceptance (owning) of these feelings as part of his emerging total feeling-life that signaled his readiness to move from the beginning into the middle phase of therapy.

DEVELOP A RUNNING THREAD OF
KEY ISSUES TO UNITE THERAPY SESSIONS

Perhaps one of the greatest points of clinical skill is the therapist's ability to help the SLD child establish a running thread from one therapy session to another around key issues in the growth and development of the child. This is an important characteristic that distinguishes a dynamically oriented process from therapy which comprises a series of unrelated sessions focused only on play, suggestion, persuasion, and motor and/or verbal abreaction.

Just as normal development follows a progression in which each successive phase develops out of and differentiates itself from the earlier phase, so, too, in dynamically oriented therapy, the therapist should help the child carry a thread of one or more specific issues from one hour to the next. For John, this meant picking up those moments when he was unhappy and helping him focus on the source of his unhappiness. Often it meant recognizing his repetitive fear of being hurt and helping him see that such a feeling seemed to be related to ideas he talked about in the earlier hours, when "being broken" was linked to his fear that something was going to happen to "his train," and when he felt that things happening to "his train" were really happening to him. By increasing the number of threads as common denominators in the therapy process, John became more aware of his emotional problems, of his strengths to deal with those problems, and of those areas about which he was less sure, which he avoided, or for which he needed more help from the therapist, from his parents, and from his teachers.

In short, therapy with such a focus, continues to emphasize that the growth potential of each successive hour is closely related to those mutual experiences between the child and therapist in the preceding hours. From such longitudinal observations of the past in the present, the therapist can sense (and titer by degrees of input and interpretation) what the next step into the future might be for the child. That is, what risks might the therapist support the child's taking in the next treatment hour, in school, in the home, or in the community, without rupturing the "thread of growth" in the child because of overexpectation or lack of readiness?

DEVELOP AND MAINTAIN AN INTERRELATED MOVEMENT PROCESS

The notion of interrelated movement between the child's use of therapy and the parents' involvement in concurrent counseling was one of the significant and worthwhile concepts of therapy with children in the early child guidance clinics (Dawley, 1939). Unfortunately, this concept and its related process have been lost in the decades of trying out new treatment strategies. The need to work with parents in a sustained and ongoing way has not changed. In fact, in the triangular model, where one therapist carries both child and parents, interrelated movement should not be difficult to sustain. However, when different personnel are seeing the child and parents separately, maintenance of this interrelated movement process may be difficult. More often, the effort is directed toward treating the parents and their neurosis separate and apart from the emerging needs and steps in growth of the child. When this happens, the therapist can unwittingly set up the child to be emotionally traumatized by the unprepared parents, who are out of step with or not yet related to this treatment phase. The process by which this interrelated movement continued to support John's social and emotional growth at home, in his school, and through the middle phase of his psychotherapy will be highlighted later in this chapter.

OVERVIEW OF MIDDLE PHASE

This phase of therapy lasted over a period of two years for John. It is the phase which, in analytic treatment, is centered around the process of "working through" (Fenichel, 1941), and which, with both children and adults, is usually the most prolonged phase. In John's case, as for most SLD children in intensive genetic-dynamic therapy, it can be helpful to divide this middle phase into a Series of Stages in which the therapist helps the child improve his or her ego function within a Contextual and Developmental Framework (see Table 6.3).

Ego function within this framework refers to that part of the mind which functions as an integrative, problem-solving agent, as well as the seat of sensations about oneself and the outside world (Waelder, 1960). Additionally, in working with SLD children, one should be mindful of the (primary) autonomous ego functions first described by Hartman (1939) and discussed as part of the evaluation process in Chapter 2.

In identifying these therapeutic stages in the middle phase

Table 6.3
Stages in the Middle Phase of Therapy

Stage 1	Ego Building and Assessing
Stage 2	Ego Risking and Assimilating
Stage 3	Ego Adapting and Integrating
Stage X	Ego Constriction and Fixation

of therapy, it is important to recognize that not all SLD children will struggle with these same issues to the same degree. Nor will each stage emerge in successive order. Rather, there can be overlap between the stages and a tide-like backing and filling during which the therapist and significant adults will see patterns in the child of growth and regression, insightfulness and denial, and risk of new emotional expressions, along with denial of these same emotions. Yet, in the treatment process, all SLD children will experience and will attempt to cope with some aspect or derivative of the developmental and therapeutic issues outlined in each of these successive stages.

Stage 1: Ego Building and Assessing

The middle phase of therapy for John began with opening up and assessing John's strengths and weaknesses. Before this Stage ended, John and the therapist covered many of the significant emotional concomitants associated with Specific Learning Disabilities. Table 6.4 outlines these issues. A large majority of SLD children struggle with similar issues and often need individual therapy to work through the intrapsychic and interpersonal conflicts represented. Following John's course through Stage 1 can be illustrative of these issues and the nature of the interaction between John, his therapist, and the larger environment which included his home, his school, and his community.

DISTORTED OR BROKEN BODY IMAGE

Nearly all SLD children will indicate early in the treatment process some aspect of their feeling about being different from other children without SLD. Often, they displace this sense of being different onto objects outside themselves, such as John's reference to the "broken train." As therapy moves into an ego building and assessment

Table 6.4
Stage 1: Ego Building and Assessing

Opening up strengths and weaknesses

Distorted or broken body image

Poor or inadequate self-concept

The family scapegoat

Aggression as a cover for depression

Anger as a by-product of failure

Passive resistance and opposition as a by-product of
extended failure

Poor impulse control: it gets worse before it gets better

To delay or not delay immediate gratification: That is the
problem

The accordion principle: Building internal controls from
outside resources

stage, the child will risk representing these feelings in human figure drawings similar to the drawing John made (Figure 6.1) with one arm larger and more distorted than the other. He also added the appearance of blood over different parts of the body.

Two important authorities on human figure drawings in children, Machover (1949) and Koppitz (1968), have essentially agreed that growth asymmetry of the limbs is found more frequently on the human figure drawings of children who have a history of neurological impairment. Machover also hypothesized that a general disturbance in symmetry on the drawings could reflect incoordination and physical awkwardness, as well as a neurologic dysfunction manifestation. In a more current study of 100 SLD children ages 6 to 12 years, Black (1976) reported a correlation between the actual height of the children and the height of the drawn figures. The investigator cautioned, however, against the use of the Draw-a-Person (DAP) figure and its size as an isolated screening procedure for emotional maladjustment. No mention was made in the study of body distortion or asymmetry, but Black concluded that, although the DAP figure may be an accurate reflection of the child's actual size, the study did not support the projective hypothesis of a direct representation of body image in human figure drawings. Machover (1949) had stated more categorically that the figure drawn *is* that person and that the paper on which the figure

Figure 6.1   Distorted or Broken Body Image before Therapy

is drawn corresponds to the environment into which the person projects himself or herself. (A fuller discussion of these issues related to drawing and art is found in Chapter 12.)

In John's case, there was a striking contrast between the first representation of himself and his "last picture," given as a present at the time of ending his treatment (Figure 6.2). The therapist did not comment on the distorted body image and the representation of a wounded, bleeding, and partially broken little boy in Stage 1 of the treatment process. However, a positive reinforcement of the dramatic contrast in the two drawings was shared with John as part of the ending phase of his therapy.

POOR OR INADEQUATE SELF-CONCEPT

John signaled the signs of distress in relationship to his poor and inadequate self-concept during Stage 1 of the middle phase of therapy, about the time he painted the first full picture of himself. Some educa-

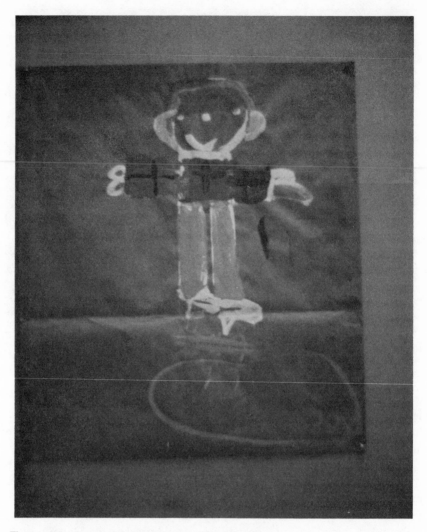

Figure 6.2   Improved Body Image after Therapy

tional authorities have raised the question as to how significant the self-concept is in the mastery of learning for SLD children. This issue could be added to the quartet of dichotomies in which self-concept development and the affective therapies are contrasted with an educational-prescriptive curriculum and behavior modification. The orientation for this Handbook is a *both-and* philosophy which is highlighted in John's case by the interrelated movement among John and his therapist, John and his teacher, John's therapist and teacher, John and his parents, his parents and their counselor, and the therapist, teacher, and parent counselor.

In this contextual framework, self-concept formation emerges from an integration of the educational prescription with the varieties of experiences in therapy, counseling, and the process of mutual collaboration. Coopersmith (1967) observed that a child's self-concept derives from social intercourse, private reactions to himself or herself, mastery in solving developmental tasks, and growing competence in coping with life situations. He noted that self-concept is both a social and physical abstraction about the child's activities, attributes, capabilities, and possessions. In the young, inexperienced child, it is a vague concept which tends to be highly localized in specific body parts. It is open to change but seems to be fairly resistant once solidified within the process of personality development. This section will attempt to describe the principles outlined above in ways that could be replicated within the provisions of PL 94-142, with the inclusion of clinical support services from psychology, social work, and psychiatry.

It is important to recognize that, in SLD children, the concept of self is closely related to the condition of the body, along with other determinants, inasmuch as any body distortion or sense of body difference from other children will influence the experience of the developing self (Langeveld, 1954). In John's treatment hour, he was experimenting with aspects of moving his body through space. He began by making rockets and testing them. As he became bolder, he began flying a toy airplane about the room. The rockets and plane were objects he could control and maneuver in space as he wished he might maneuver his own body. Suddenly and accidentally, the wings broke off from the plane. John panicked. "Fix it! Fix it!" he pleaded. Together, an attempt was made to fix the plane, but a period of waiting for the glue to dry was essential to the plane's continued flight. John could not tolerate the delay. "It has to fly! It has to fly now! Fix it!" And with that he fell to the floor, kicking and screaming. He unloaded all the emotions of his hurt pride, his sense of brokenness, his poor self-concept, and his sense of failure and frustration in trying to control the situation. John wanted to undo the "fact" of the broken plane, so painfully representing himself, and wished to make the plane whole and complete again.

The therapist cut through the kicking and wailing:

Johnny, you're upset because I haven't fixed your plane just like that (a snap of the finger). It is going to take time for the glue to dry, so instead of lying on the floor and acting like a little boy, why don't you stand up and tell me you're angry at me for not being an instant fixer?

John got up and took on a boxer's stance, as if he were ready to take on the therapist. That was a crucial moment. It was the moment when John moved from expressing his inadequate feeling by regressing to an infantile level in an effort to make the therapist treat him more like a baby to an active, more age-appropriate stance and emotional readiness to deal with the therapist and the situation. Reluctantly, John was able to leave the hour announcing that he wanted that plane fixed by Friday, the day of his next appointment.

At the next appointment, the plane was ready. John felt strong and confident until one of the mended wings came apart for a second time. He became upset again. He lay on the floor but did not cry. He kicked angrily at the desk, the chairs, and at the therapist.

John, you are really upset because you feel so much like that broken plane. Sometimes you fly through your reading and arithmetic and sometimes you crash. You just can't read the way you want to and sometimes you make mistakes in your arithmetic. I know these things really get to you.

John sat up. He seemed interested and ready for further interpretation and support. That support came from the teamwork between John's classroom teacher and the therapist and his parents and the parent counselor. When John made mistakes in arithmetic, he erased the errors to the point of tearing his paper. The torn paper, like the broken plane, sent John to the floor, crying and kicking at his desk. His conception of himself paralleled his reactions to the torn paper and broken plane.

The therapist talked with John about his feelings of being unable to deal with things that were broken and imperfect: that, by taking small steps in his reading and math, he could master them with time, patience, and good teaching. The teacher was included in helping John deal with his mistakes in less overwhelming and regressive ways. She helped him recognize that, when he tore the paper in his effort to wipe out the mistakes, it was like making him feel more torn and broken inside. John responded to the teacher in a more confident way, recognizing that the teacher, as well as his therapist, understood him. John's parents also shared in his shift from self-doubt to greater self-confidence. In their parent counseling, they had come to see the importance of lowering temporarily their academic expectations, while helping John accept that no one was perfect. As his parents, they knew that reading and arithmetic were difficult for him, yet they also could support his efforts, both successful and unsuccessful, with the shared recognition that, at his pace and in his time, he would master those subjects to the level of his innate and functioning ability.

Dubin (1972), in summarizing the literature on factors influencing the self-concept noted that all personality theorists who are concerned with the constructs involving the self accord great importance to the parent-child interaction in the development of the self-concept. This was clearly evident in John's gradual increase in his self-esteem and more positive self-concept in response to the multiple impact, *both-and* system of intervention, which included the integration of all the dimensions of his life experiences, rather than a dichotomized *either-or* system. Coopersmith (1967) has noted that self-concept and self-esteem are related but not interchangeable terms. Coopersmith quoted William James as having said that there is no good or bad level of self-esteem, but that the level is determined by the "ratio of our actualities to our supposed potentialities," such that, if a child perceives himself as presumably capable of some task but is unable to perform it, there will be a loss in his sense of self-esteem. Furthermore, it appeared that self-esteem could be high with regard to some areas of performance and low with regard to others, resulting in a self-concept which could reflect confidence and high motivation in some ways and not in others.

THE FAMILY SCAPEGOAT

John could have become the family scapegoat, as so often happens with SLD children. Fortunately, this did not happen, as his parents and siblings were supportive rather than destructive. In traveling to and from school, however, his peers made him a target for some scapegoating, as they recognized how easily he could be triggered off by teasing or taking his possessions. For John, taking his hat from him was like taking part of his incomplete body, leaving him less complete. The multiple-impact model helped him in this area, for, as he became more adequate and complete in his conception of himself, he became less volatile, vulnerable, and distressed at losing part of his possessions to his peers. He began standing up for himself and challenging his antagonists.

AGGRESSION AS A COVER FOR DEPRESSION

To be different from other children made John feel bad, no good, or a "reject," and sometimes he was pretty low and down on himself. Such a low sense of self-esteem and self-worth was often accompanied by feelings of depression and wondering why he had to be born like this. John frequently masked these feelings by becoming verbally negative and hostilely aggressive with his classmates and neighborhood peer group. If he couldn't keep up with them in other ways, he could use his size and weight to put them down, while discharging the nervous tension he felt over chronic failure.

This is a crucial time in therapy for the SLD child, who may attempt to act-out in ways which could hurt him/herself or others. Feelings of hurt pride, anger, and despair often have been bottled up so long that when they come out, while the child's inner emotional control is still tenuous and underdeveloped, they often result in loss of physical control.

The therapist, teacher, parents, and significant others need to be together at this crucial time in clearly supporting the SLD child's right to feel the way he/she does and, yet, holding him/her firmly to responsible expression of these feelings, within a healthy structure of relationships.

Initially, this means helping John and other SLD children to tell the therapist, teacher, and parents how it is and how they feel, often with tears and great emotionality. It may mean allowing them to beat on a pillow or on a Bozo-the-Clown object, as a way of discharging their rage upon an inanimate object. However, such a solution cannot and should not be the only one offered these children. They must be helped, through the multiple impact model, to verbalize their feelings in full, yet socially acceptable ways.

Often this means helping parents and teachers define which expletives they will allow and which are not acceptable. It means giving the children the verbal substitutes for more acceptable words in place of the emotionally loaded words which are unacceptable. Parents, teachers, and therapists differ as to what they will and will not allow the emotionally distraught child to say in these moments of frustration and failure, but it is important that they continue to support the child in the right to have and express these feelings (as they define those verbal expressions which are acceptable at home, in school, and in the larger community).

There is no magic in this important process of directing or channeling strong emotions into verbal expressions. Rather, our scientific body of knowledge has supported the concept that such verbalizations carry two important and essential components for emotional growth in SLD children as in all children:

(1) The strong feelings are channeled from a generalized fight or flight bodily reaction into a differentiated social response, namely, a verbal symbol which carries the total affect (feeling) without the threat of bodily harm to the sender or receiver.

(2) The involvement of the muscles of phonation (diaphragm, laryngeal, intercostal, and abdominal muscles) plus the muscles of articulation (buccal, pharyngeal, and tongue muscles) allow for a motor discharge of affect, along with the channeled symbolic discharge.

Much of this middle phase of therapy with John was focused on setting up this verbalization process within the multiple-impact model of intervention. One way to achieve some closure and uniformity in the signals given to the SLD child at this stage of therapy can be to plan a conference with the child which will include parents, parent counselor and therapist. (Chapter 7 will outline this process in more detail.) A similar three-way discussion can take place among the child, the teacher, and the therapist on these issues. The cautions for these conferences are very important and very specific, including the following:

(1) Wait until all parties have been helped to see the issues and are prepared to help the child find a healthy solution within the realities of the home and classroom.

(2) Spell out separately and clearly for parents, teachers, and child the ground rules for these conferences.

(3) Prepare the child carefully and be his/her advocate in a constructive and forceful way in the conferences.

(4) Do not allow the child to be attacked or emotionally traumatized in the interchange; the therapist should absorb the blows and abort the conferences if the ground rules are violated by any of the parties involved.

ANGER AS A BY-PRODUCT OF FAILURE

A great deal has been written about the short attention span and poor eye-hand coordination in SLD children, but surprisingly little has been written or spoken concerning the feelings of hurt pride or narcissistic hypersensitivity in relationship to situational failure which these children experience a hundred times or more a week and several thousand times a year. Each time the SLD child attempts to run or ride or jump, his/her effort is usually second best, or last in the family and peer group pecking orders. When asked tó follow a series of moderately complex directions, the central nervous system may garble the message, and, again, the child fails. When asked for an opinion or when excited about expressing a thought or an idea, delay in language processing and syntax often limits the SLD child's ability to verbalize at an appropriate age level. This is perceived as another failure. Finally, when compared to the nursery, kindergarten, or elementary school-aged student each SLD child is vulnerable to failure in one or more areas of cognitive and ego development, similar to those outlined in Chapter 2.

John had experienced such failures from nursery school on into the elementary grades in gross and fine motor coordination skills, in visual tracking, in left to right progression, in diagonal orientation, in eye-hand coordination, in language fluency skills, in seeing enough figure-ground to get a sense of general shape, and in mastering reading and arithmetic skills at a basic level. This mass of learning disability left John very vulnerable, very hurt, and very angry with himself, his family, and his teachers. He had built up a reservoir of angry feelings far greater than was his ability to cope with such internal pressure. Consequently, he could easily flare up, fling out at the nearest student, or cry out with a siren's wail when another moment of failure was imminent.

John's therapy hours were a beginning in helping him to see the cause and effect relationship between his hurt pride (at failing), his resulting anger (as a reaction to hurt pride, and his flaring-up, hitting, or wailing), and his behavioral expressions of this anger. He didn't like to talk directly about these things but could tolerate putting these thoughts onto imaginary astronauts and other fantasy figures in his play. This externalization of conflict allowed him to see more clearly the cause and effect relationship which seemed to happen when he was with his siblings or enroute to school. In the classroom, however, he defended against seeing these relationships and used so much mental energy to maintain this kind of defense that he siphoned off much of the mental energy that would have been available for learning. Hence, he recycled his academic failures by his internal psychological defenses.

PASSIVE RESISTANCE AND OPPOSITION AS A BY-PRODUCT OF EXTENDED FAILURE

John's years of failure in the classroom had moved him into a passive-resistant and oppositional personality pattern. His resistance to learning was especially evident in his refusal to read for his teacher or for the reading specialist. John had developed an assorted bag of failure-avoidant behaviors and was using them to continue his pattern of failure. In short, John's hurt pride had given rise to anger, which had now become partially internalized in a passive-resistant pattern which made him emotionally "unavailable" for learning.

The turning point for John came in a dramatic treatment hour in this middle phase of therapy. The therapist had recognized with him how hurt and angry John seemed to be over his failures in school. It seemed that John had never been told that much of his problem in learning was due to a specific learning problem over which he had no control and for which he was not at fault. He agreed he had not known or been told of this before. The therapist suggested that he must be pretty angry at all those teachers who had been saying to him through the last several years that he was lazy, or that he wasn't trying, or that he was just goofing off. For more than twenty minutes, John denied that he was angry or upset at these teachers. He asked why he should be angry at anyone when it was really his problem. Then he told the therapist he didn't like to talk about his angry feelings, as it made him all fuzzy and shaky inside when they discussed it together. The therapist agreed. He suggested that, if John could see that he had a reservoir of stored up, angry feelings toward the schools and teachers, he could begin to let some of this anger out of his tightly closed reservoir. Then he might feel less shaky inside. He might even do better in school!

With this last comment, John suddenly grabbed a hand puppet. "This is the first teacher I had," he said, and threw it on the floor. John jumped up and down on that figure, yelling and crying, "She said I was dumb! She said I was lazy!" Then he grabbed the puppet and threw it down again. "This is the second teacher. She said I wanted to fail to embarrass my family. I hate her! I hate her!" For twenty minutes, John unloaded his venom and anger on the rubber puppet. When he stopped, the therapist put an arm around him and told him he had just emptied that reservoir. Maybe he was ready to learn to read. Could he take a chance on letting the teacher help him? She would know and understand his problem in reading. She would let him use his "greasy finger" to follow the reading line and would not push him, but she would show him how to approach a new word he had not seen before. John was relieved. He smiled and left the hour like a different boy. Equally important, John's attitude in class changed radically from one of failure-avoidance and opposition to one of willingness to try with a persistence to learn and to master new words in reading. The change in John was truly dramatic.

Few clinicians write about reservoirs of anger in SLD children, yet all teachers, parents, siblings, and clinicians know they are present. Behavior modification gives the SLD child a new kind of spigot with which to turn the anger on and off. Genetic-dynamic therapy helps the child see cause and effect relationships, risk ventilating anger in a controlled, nonpunitive, or retaliatory relationship, and discover alternatives for handling anger which has been derived from hurt pride, while building confidence in the new teacher-student relationship. Such confidence allows for degrees of risk to balance out fears of failure.

POOR IMPULSE CONTROL: IT GETS WORSE BEFORE IT GETS BETTER

Once the stopper was out of the bottom of John's reservoir, he began to open up more and more. Opening up meant opening up more expressed hurt and anger. From a sluggish little boy, he became a slugging little boy, unloading old, as well as new, angry feelings on the nearest target at hand. "The therapist is making a monster out of that boy," the teacher commented. The parents wondered if, perhaps, they liked the sluggish John better than the slugger. This was a tough time for everyone! Finally, John's aggression was mobilized and beginning to be directed outwardly, hopefully into learning rather than into the back of his fellow students. The payoff would come in John's having more energy available for learning when less was tied up in suppressing his anger, more energy available for his bodily functions, which would speed up his response to the team's effort to assist his neuromuscular development, and more energy available to put into social relationships rather than turning the anger in on himself in a depressive and isolationistic style of living. Yet the clinical/educational team knew, and so informed the parents, that John's aggression and poor impulse control would get worse before it got better. This was a period when supportive parent counseling was essential for family survival and survival of the case in therapy. (See Chapter 7 on parent counseling and the interrelated movement between the child's therapy and the counseling with the parents.)

TO DELAY OR NOT DELAY IMMEDIATE GRATIFICATION: THAT IS THE PROBLEM

John's behavior, in and out of his therapy hours, had begun to change. He was much more responsive to both inner needs and outer stimuli. While this healthy step forward put him in greater contact with other people in his life, it posed another problem. With less voluntary suppression of feelings, less avoidance, and less unconscious denial of what he was feeling, John's strivings and assertive impulses were gaining in intensity. To delay or not delay the immediate gratification of his newly "experienced needs and impulses" became an important question for John. Feeling some initial success, John wanted immediate recognition for all his efforts, great and small. He became impatient when he found he couldn't go from a first level reader to a sixth level reader in six days. He could not wait his turn at bat once he consented to play ball. He wanted to sit in the preferred seat in the station wagon and not wait until his turn came up for that seat during the week. There were many such experiences during this phase of growth and therapy.

On one occasion, poor judgment mixed with his new sense of power could have resulted in a calamity. John wanted to see how strong he was. He wanted to test out his throwing arm. When he asked his father to go out and throw the ball with him, he was told that his father was busy and they would have to do it on Saturday. Unable to wait, John went out, found a stone, and wanted to see if he could throw it over a near-by car. It hit the top of the car, making a loud noise, but fortunately, it didn't scratch or dent the vinyl top roof. John could not delay his need for immediate gratification of the impulse to experience his new-found strength.

John did not progress very far on these issues in his individual therapy, pending his achievement of a healthier self-concept and a higher level of self-esteem, which would both allow him to share instead of demanding to be first in everything and enable him to wait until his environment could meet his need instead of forcing immediate satisfaction. Along this line, one also should be aware that many SLD children think more in concrete than abstract terms, so the Piagetian stage of concrete operations extends beyond the usual range of 7 to 10 years and often well into puberty and early adolescence. However, once the SLD child sees cause and effect relationships more clearly, he/she is more ready to postpone gratification in learning until enough of the basic skills have been mastered to allow for a greater gratification in the application of these skills to complex problems. Learning the multiplication tables would be a good example of this type of learning. The learner does not see the value in mastery of the times tables until asked to complete a problem which requires more extensive multiplication processes.

THE ACCORDION PRINCIPLE; BUILDING INTERNAL CONTROLS FROM OUTSDE RESOURCES

The concept of "structure" is not new in working with SLD children. For many years, the notion of "the same way every day" or setting clear limits and spelling out the steps to a task have been standard operating procedures. Less well known and adequately described has been the Accordion Principle of building internal controls from outside resources.

The main goal of this principle is to replace controls from without with controls from within. As seen in figure 6.3, there is a starting point from which two solid lines emanate. These lines represent

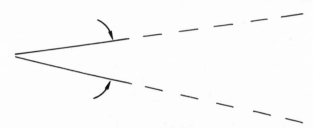

Figure 6.3   Diagram of the Accordian Principle

tight structure with no loopholes so far as direction and discipline of the SLD child are concerned. The two lines emanating from a single source represent the structure and definition put in by the adult person or persons (parents, teachers, and other significant adults) in the life of the child. The child may test limits but the answer is clear, firm, and consistent. The child can have strong feelings about these external limits and hopefully reasonable authoritarian control and should be encouraged to express these feelings verbally. All the adults in the child's hierarchy should be giving the same message concerning such Total-Life-Relationship Structure, while allowing the child opportunities for continuous verbal expression of negative feelings in response to the necessary limits placed on the child at this point in time.

The therapist may be the one to suggest to other adults how tight the structure needs to be and the degree of freedom (the amount of area between the two solid lines) the child may have to move spontaneously within those lines. These guiding and disciplinary lines may be seen as the fences for the child's developing emotional life. They are the fixed points, the more solid guidelines beyond which behavior would not be socially acceptable. However, within those lines, the child should be free to experience relationships, testing out, and interacting with all ages and at all levels of human emotional development.

SOCIALIZATION EXPERIENCES

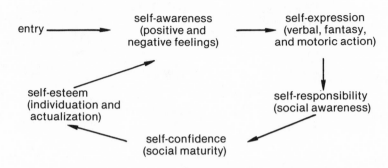

Figure 6.4   Spiral of Socialization Experiences

For John, at the middle phase of therapy, it was possible to widen the lines, and to allow him to monitor more and more of his behavior (represented by the extended dotted lines). The adults could widen or narrow the lines of control from moment to moment in response to the child's growth. Much of that growth follows a cycle, or more accurately, a spiral of socialization experiences (see figure 6.4).

The socialization process begins with a sense of self-awareness which characterized much of John's opening phase of therapy. The modes of self-expression were explored in the early part of the middle phase of therapy. Gradually, as self-responsibility and social awareness increased, John's self-confidence was also heightened. Finally, he began to reflect more and more positive feelings about himself, and his sense of self-esteem was high, with a great sense of pride that he had achieved so much in so short a time. This healthier sense of self-esteem allows the SLD child to increase his/her level of self-awareness. Reentry into the cycle of growth at a higher level reflects the spiral nature of the growth cycle, allowing for progression or regression in the ego adaptive functions, as well as in the primary autonomous ego functions. Through the interrelated movement process, which included John's teachers as well as parents, he became more comfortable moving along the socialization spiral, and this heralded his move into Stage 2 of the middle phase of therapy.

Stage 2: Ego-Risking and Assimilation

The processes of ego-risking and assimilation run through the entire treatment experience in a continuous fashion. There is no one static

Table 6.5
Stage 2: Ego-Risking and Assimilation

Continuation of interrelated movement

Projection of aggressive drives onto appropriate symbols:
    the goodies and baddies

Unloading on family, and fear of their retaliation

Masculine-feminine strivings and gender identity

Fear of sexual impulses in late latency and early
    puberty

Trial and error learning in peer relationships

or mechanical staging process in which these ego functions show greater ascendancy than in any other. However, for the purposes of highlighting the close parallel between the therapeutic process and the process of normal growth and development, the narrative has been written as a description of stages. Table 6.5 outlines some of the critical growth experiences frequently presented and worked through with an SLD/ MBD/HKS child, as part of an ongoing ego risking and assimilation process.

CONTINUATION OF INTERRELATED MOVEMENT

Whether the therapist is carrying the case alone, is seeing the parents at a separate time, or carrying the case with a colleague concurrently counseling the parents, it is important to keep in mind the child's level of movement in therapy in relationship to parental movement in supporting or resisting the cutting edge of the child's growth and development.

Johnny was reminded, from time to time, of the Bix Sixers who were backing him up in his growth and development (see Figure 6.5).

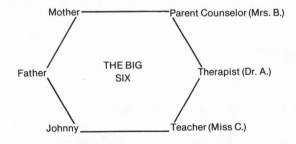

Figure 6.5   Adult Back-up Support for Child in Therapy

This was essentially true around times of decision making, of progress reports from school, of crises at home or school, and at the time of planning for an ending of therapy.

Periodically, the interrelated movement pin-pointed the need for parents, parent counselor, Johnny, and his therapist to meet together during one of Johnny's therapy sessions. Such meetings were planned several sessions in advance, and Johnny was always prepared by the therapist for such a combined interview: "Next week, Johnny, Mother and Father and Mrs. B. will join us in talking together about how we can help you handle some of those angry feelings that come out like a volcano at home or in school. You and I have worked together on helping you handle those upsets. We need to help Mother and Father know what they can do to help you, also. If there are things we have talked about that you do not want me to share with them, you should tell me what they are. I want you to know that what you have shared with me is private and confidential, and we won't be saying anything you want kept privately between us."

Johnny and his therapist then reviewed together the kinds of things that seemed to upset him, how these experiences were derived from feelings of being "broken" or "different," and how much he had already done to cope with the "inside" feelings and the "outside" problems (e.g. being teased on the bus, shunned by his neighborhood peer group, and occasionally set up for an emotional eruption by one of his siblings).

On the occasion of one such parent-child joint interview, John told the therapist in the earlier part of their hour about his most recent "volcanic" eruption at home. He was ready to illustrate the story with the play material in the office (see Figure 6.6).

He had been bossy and demanding at home, and when he was denied his way, he had thrown pots and pans around the kitchen. In his reenactment during the therapy hour, his play-fantasy was that he had run from the bedlam in the kitchen to the garage. He wanted to drive the family to Dr. A.'s office to tell the doctor his parents were not giving him what he wanted when he wanted it: namely, to be in control at home! In his therapy story, the car ran into the corner of his house. He laughingly commented, "See, I don't know how to drive yet!" The therapist recognized, with John, that although he wanted to be "in charge," to be the grownup, and to control Mother and Father (i.e. reversal of roles), he had driven into the house because he was scared. He knew he wasn't ready for that kind of "control-power." John wanted to share this story with his parents when they and the parent counselor came into the second half of the treatment session. His recounting of the story for his parents and parent counselor represented very healthy ego-

Figure 6.6   Use of Toys to Illustrate Child's Fantasies

risking for John, as he both admitted his need to control his parents and expressed an equally strong wish for them to be stronger than he to maintain their parental control and grown-up position.

Such interrelated movement usually can be sustained by open collaboration between therapist and parent counselor, and only occasionally will this conjoint interview strategy need to be used.

PROJECTION OF AGGRESSIVE DRIVES ONTO APPROPRIATE SYMBOLS: THE GOODIES AND THE BADDIES

Johnny was very adept at projecting all his negative feelings and what he called his "bad self" onto different toy objects in the therapy room. He would then follow this with "the good guy in the white hat" coming onto the scene to destroy the baddie. In this way, Johnny externalized his aggressive id drives (which he viewed as "bad") and brought into volitional action his ego and superego (which he viewed as "good") to neutralize and master his surging aggression. This was a very healthy expression of several key components of his personality structure.

At the same time, he needed to hear from the therapist that no one expected him to be "good" or "perfect" all the time and to know that he was supported in his right to express such hostile aggressive feelings in play and in fantasy. It would be all right if the "bad guys" won a fight or battle now and then.

For children and teenagers with SLD/MBD/HKS, the issue of allowing strong, hostile, aggressive feelings to surface in therapy is a critical one. How the therapist supports this emergence of strong feelings while helping the child or teenager move to increasing mastery of these drives and their derivatives through socially acceptable and age-appropriate expressions is a point of considerable clinical skill. For a therapist in training, the development of such skill often requires supervision by a therapist who has been successful in individual psychotherapy with SLD/MBD/HKS children.

Allen (1942) stated an important principle which should be remembered when working with SLD/MBD/HKS children who present major problems with their associated aggressive or passive-aggressive personality patterns.

> While on the surface these children give the impression of great strength and arrogance and of being afraid of nothing, actually they are, as a rule, children who are quite fearful and uncertain. They are afraid of any yielding since that involves giving in and using the strength of another rather than trying to eliminate the natural authority which is a part of all living. They are afraid of the more gentle positive type of feeling expression as this involves sharing and being related to another person on the basis of growth rather than on the basis of control. (p. 203)

UNLOADING ON FAMILY AND FEAR OF THEIR RETALIATION

Johnny became so comfortable sharing his destructive fantasies in his therapy hours that, on one occasion, he told the therapist a dream which he had had.

> He was riding in a trolley car with his mother and family. At one point, he became the motorman and was running the trolley. As they came to a hill, he told all the family except his mother to leave the trolley. When the trolley was half way up the hill, he let it roll down the hill. As it was rolling, he stepped off. He had planted a bomb on the trolley. When it went off, it blew up the trolley and his mother into little pieces that were so small you couldn't find them.

Initially, Johnny was scared by the dream, but, when he was encouraged to play out with the toys and family dolls the sequences he had dreamed, he did so with glee and gusto. As he went through the final bombing, the therapist recognized, with Johnny, that he had strong feelings of anger toward his mother, that he wanted to destroy her because he felt she was the cause of his learning problems. The therapist reassured him that he would not carry out his dream in real life but that he could express his wishes towards his mother in dreams, fantasies, and in the play of the hour and still not hurt her in real life. He was relieved and proceeded to reenact the bombing scene nine times. "My mother is like a cat," he said, "and I want to make sure I get rid of her nine times in this story."

For Johnny, that hour was a significant turning point. He became more openly ambivalent toward his mother. Meanwhile, during her sessions with the parent counselor, his mother was being prepared to accept John's right to be angry at her while he was being helped to find age-appropriate verbal expressions to convey those feelings. Gradually, the intensity of his ambivalence shifted and positive feelings toward his mother began to emerge along with the negative ones. He was then able to express this healthier balance of feelings when it was realistically appropriate to do so.

MASCULINE-FEMININE STRIVING AND GENDER IDENTITY

Up to this point in his development, Johnny had viewed his mother as the aggressive and powerful head of the family and his father as the less powerful and less effective adult. He was fearful of his mother's rejection and, as a defense, identified with her as the aggressor. This mechanism of defense had bound him into a passive, dependent position. Once freed from this pathologic tie to his mother, Johnny began to redefine his self-image and his self-concept. He chose to reduce his weight by dieting, and the reduction in weight allowed him greater control and fluidity of his body in space. He looked and felt like a different person.

In a developmentally predictable manner, Johnny went through a period of sorting out the difference between male and female, anatomically as well as in their generic and sociocultural roles. Occasionally, he expressed some anxiety about his maleness, but his overall trend was toward healthy masculine assertiveness. He went through an intense emotional phase in which he would denigrate one of the girl students in his class. This was a complex interaction arising out of academic competitiveness, sibling rivalry, provocations from the girl student, and displacement of residuals from the mother-son conflicts.

FEAR OF SEXUAL IMPULSES IN
LATE LATENCY AND EARLY PUBERTY

Although Johnny was at a stage of putting down peer relationships with girls, he developed a healthy "crush" on his classroom teacher. This experience turned on his motivation to learn, and he rapidly advanced academically to near-grade level in all subjects except mathematics, which was only slightly below grade level.

Once again, Johnny used his dream life to master those conflicts stirred by his libidinal attraction to his teacher.

> I dreamed I saw Miss C smiling at me. Suddenly I grew big and strong like the Six Million Dollar Man. I was getting into a racing car. The car was really moving, and I looked like a bird flying in the air. I crashed. There I was, looking like me, lying in a coffin. I thought I was dead. That was scary.

The therapist helped Johnny in a partial interpretation of the dream. He recognized John's wish to be strong and powerful to attract Miss C's love for him. This became scary since he didn't know how to handle such strong feelings of love for another person. Turning himself into a bird was one way to achieve protection. Unfortunately, it wasn't realistic enough, for boys are not birds. So his only "protection" (defense against his love for his teacher and more deeply his love for his mother) was to put these love feelings to rest, once and for all. That meant he had to put himself in a coffin, where he and the teacher would be safe from one another. It did not mean he wanted to die; he just wanted to slow down or put his love feelings to death until he was a little older and could cope with them. This dream fantasy was similar to the Snow White story in which the beautiful girl was put into a spell (the latency period) by the jealous witch and could only be awakened by the kiss of someone who loved her when she reached her adolescence.

Johnny was five to six years late in moving into the phallic-oedipal phase of psychosexual development. This delay, and Johnny's prolonged emotional dependency on his parents, was similar to the experimental observations of Adamson *et al.* (1961) that many late latency and early SLD/MBD/HKS adolescents have become partially fixated at a pregenital level of ego development. This pattern of delay seemed to be the result of constriction in the affective, cognitive, and conative aspects of personality development. For example, in the above study 36 MBD boys (10 to 22 years) were compared with 70 non-MBD boys in the tenth grade (ages 15 to 16 years) on the WISC, the WISA, and the Rorschach Personality Inventory. Comparative Rorschach data showed a higher mean F% response (57.5) in the MBD group than in the non-MBD group (45.0). There was also a reduction in the number of Rorschach movement and shading responses in the MBD as compared to the non-MBD group. The interpretation has been made that a high F% and a small number of movement and shading responses are associated with problems of ego-control in which constricting and suppressive/repressive mechanisms are utilized to limit the conscious expression of feelings, emotions, and impulses in age-appropriate patterns of behavior (Klopfer *et al.*, 1954).

TRIAL AND ERROR LEARNING IN PEER RELATIONSHIPS

Johnny's attachment to his teacher moved him into more age-appropriate late latency behavior. His peer group became more accepting of him and he of them. He began reaching out for a best boyfriend to travel with and to pal around with on weekends. However, new and unexpected situations continued to threaten him physically and emotionally, and he would allow himself only one close friend at a time. In this way, he felt in greater control of the situation.

Stage 3: Ego Adapting and Integrating Experiences

Throughout this entire middle phase of therapy, Johnny was involved in ego adapting and integrating experiences in his therapy, in his home, and in the classroom, which were carefully monitored by the therapist.

For a clinician trained to discern the developmental stages outlined in Table 2.3, it was clear that during his years of individual therapy, Johnny had made significant progress (Table 6.6). Using the more precise personality assay of Blanck and Blanck (1974), Johnny seemed to progress in his ego development as shown in Table 6.7.

The significant areas of growth in the development of John's ego are reflected in his partially resolved ambivalence toward the maternal object, the neutralized aggressive and libidinal drives, the growth into and through the phallic-oedipal period, the significant improvement in all areas of primary autonomous ego functions, and the shift in anxiety level from fear of annihilation and loss of object to the more mature fear of the superego.

Table 6.6
Comparative Developmental Levels Pre- and Post-Therapy

	Mahler	Freud	Erikson	Piaget
Beginning therapy	Rapprochement subphase	Oral dependency	Trust vs. Mistrust	Preoperational stage
	↓	↓	↓	↓
Ending therapy	Separation-individuation completed, object constancy	Phallic assertive and positive oedipal relationship and late-latency	Industry vs. Inferiority	Concrete operations

Table 6.7
Ego Development Pre- and Post-Therapy*

	Drive Taming Process	Object Relations	Adaptive Functions	Anxiety Level
Beginning therapy	Little differentiation of libido and aggression	Beginning endowment of objects with value	Weak primary autonomous ego functions	Fear of annihilation and of loss of object
	↓	↓	↓	↓
Ending therapy	Ambivalence partially resolved. Neutralized libido serves narcissism	Oedipal and post-oedipal	Stronger in all areas. Beginning synthetic and integrative functions	Fear of superego

*After Blanck and Blanck, 1974.

Table 6.8
Superego Development Pre- and Post-Therapy*

	Defensive Function	Identity Formation	Process of Internalization
Beginning therapy	Projection Denial Turning against self	Rapprochement subphase	Gradual disillusionment with omnipotent objects
Middle stage	Repression	Gender identity	Identification with phallic assertiveness
Ending therapy	Secondary autonomy. Defenses change in function and become adaptive	Increasing internalization by means of ego and superego identifications. Self-affirmation	Resolution of oedipus complex by identification with parent of same sex.

*After Blanck and Blanck, 1974.

Likewise, growth in the development of John's superego has been outlined in Table 6.8.

Stage X: Ego Constriction and Fixation

The inclusion of this stage is to signify that, in the therapeutic process, there will be elements of ego constriction and fixation which parallel those psychologic phenonema in normal growth and development. This particular X factor runs all through therapy from the beginning, middle, and into the ending phase. Hence, it is designated as Stage X, rather than a consecutive number. For Johnny, his constriction and inhibition kept him in an oral dependent stage beyond the normal period of expectancy and significantly retarded his psychosexual development. Rigidity and perfectionism continued to plague him, as he moved toward an ending phase of treatment. Equally crippling was his defense maneuver of "tuning out or controlling" the nature of his interaction and involvement with his peer group. This was particularly true when someone tried to reach him on a point which was emotionally charged. He called himself "chicken" about making more than one friend at a time. He spoke of being afraid of being laughed at, turned down, or rejected by his peer group.

Another rigidity which would be subsumed under Johnny's X factor of constriction, resistance, and fixation was his need to put down ethnic groups other than his own: "they are stupid people," "they don't know that much," and "they can't be trusted." Much of this content seemed to represent a projection of his residual wounded narcissism onto subcultural minority groups who seemed devalued, oppressed, or alienated from the larger cultural majority.

OVERVIEW OF ENDING PHASE

The ending phase of the treatment process is often minimized, loosely supervised, and rarely discussed at any length in the literature. For SLD/MBD/HKS children and adolescents, the ending of a therapeutic experience has many important ramifications. The issues of the narcissistic wound associated with being different, of difficulty in separation and individuation which leads to prolonged dependency, and of the chronicity associated with the SLD/MBD/HKS syndromes serve to make the criteria for their ending different from those of a neurotic child, for whom resolution of the neurotic symptoms would be a first criterion (Pearson, 1968). Other criteria proposed by Freud (1937, 1945) would be appropriate for both populations, the SLD/MBD/HKS syndromes and the neurotic group. They included the criteria outlined in Table 6.9.

Allen (1942) emphasized that the ending phase is an integral part of the larger growth process initiated in the early hours of treatment. Its essence is the child's affirmation of himself/herself as an individual, not in isolation but in relation to others.

Table 6.10 highlights some of the psychological issues which should be brought into focus as the plan for ending develops, along with the functions of the therapist during the ending phase of individual psychotherapy with SLD/MBD/HKS children and adolescents.

PARTICIPATING IN PLANNING AN ENDING

Johnny's ending was planned as he was (1) successfully moving into a normal classroom setting, (2) relating in a more age-appropriate way with peers and siblings, (3) reaching out in a more trusting way to his parents and teachers, (4) risking some tentative overtures to the opposite sex, (5) viewing himself more positively and with higher self-

Table 6.9
Criteria for Termination of Therapy*

Forward progression of ego and libido to age-appropriate
behavior and relationships

Undoing libidinal and ego fixations and regressions

Stability of parent-child-sibling interactions

*As summarized by Pearson *et al.*, 1968.

Table 6.10
Functions of Therapist in Ending Phase of
Individual-Psychotherapy with SLD/MBD/HKS Clients

Participating in planning an ending

Using calendar to structure reality of ending

Encouraging duality of feelings: sadness of separation/-
loss and joy of independence

Recognizing anxiety which generates 3 R's: Regression.
Repression, and Resistance

Allowing recapitulation of many symptoms and of
"work done" in therapy

Encouraging resynthesis and reworking-through conflicts
dealt with previously

Partializing ending by affirming continuous support, suggesting
ongoing open-ended communication and planned follow-up

Analyzing therapist's counter transference feelings

Accepting and understanding the meaning of the last gift,
the last picture, the last dream

esteem, and (6) sharing dream and fantasy material which reflected
healthy reality testing and age-appropriate ego/superego functioning.
His parents and the parent counselor participated in setting up the ending plan. A calendar was brought into the conjoint interview and a
date set which allowed for ending over a six weeks period.

ENCOURAGING MULTIPLICITY OF FEELINGS

Johnny was pleased and relieved to think of his "being free" after these years of coming once and sometimes twice a week to therapy. As the "graduation day" approached, however, the 3 Rs often associated with ending became more prominent. There was a recurrence of many of his old symptoms, patterns of regressive behavior at home and in school, much negative and angry feeling at the therapist "for throwing him out to the wolves" before he was ready, and frank resistance to the idea of leaving the sessions. Instead, he wanted the therapist to be his father and to live as the therapist's son in the office.

ENCOURAGING RESYNTHESIS AND REWORKING-THROUGH CONFLICTS DEALT WITH PREVIOUSLY

It was the therapist's support in allowing him both to recapitulate his earlier problems and to resynthesize and restate his more recently acquired ego skills in dealing with these historical problems which turned Johnny around and away from his partial regression and resistance to ending. In two therapy hours, he retraced 24 months of therapy and reaffirmed his readiness to make it on his own. It was at this point that he voiced most clearly the duality of feelings over ending: "I'm going to miss you as my friend. You know me better than anyone else. But I'm glad I'll be playing soccer this time next week and not coming to see my favorite shrink. Ha, Ha."

PARTIALIZING ENDING

For SLD/MBD/HKS children, as for all children ending therapy, it is especially important to partialize the ending experience. Often, patient and parental anxiety will give the ending process a finality which is not helpful or realistic. By suggesting ongoing support, communication, and follow-up, the therapist can help them perceive ending as carrying a degree of freedom to return in a planful way for periodic "pit stops" to check out "the mental battery," the "tread of the tires of human relationship," and "the internal combustion engine" to see if the child has sustained internal control and mastery of libidinal and aggressive drives, of cognitive and conative processes, and of ego and superego functions sufficient to deal with the residual emotional concomitants of their SLD/MBD/HKS situation.

ACCEPTING AND UNDERSTANDING THE LAST DREAM

In his last hour, Johnny told the therapist his "last dream."

I was on a deserted island. I was thrown off a ship by the crew who called me a "retard." I felt all alone, and you came up and asked if you could help me. I told you I was looking for some kind of treasure. I didn't exactly know where to look and what to look for. You told me where to dig. It seemed I was digging a long time and not finding anything. I was mad. I threw my shovel all over the place. You were very calm. You just said, "Keep digging, Johnny." Then I found the treasure chest. On the top were a lot of torn papers like the ones I tore up in school. Then I found some clothes. They didn't fit me; they were for girls. There was that broken airplane you fixed for me. I kept pulling out toys and missiles, even a machine gun. And do you know what I found at the bottom of that trunk? I found my Life, my new Life. It was a mirror, and when I looked at it I liked the boy I saw. He wasn't any Six Million Dollar Man. He looked just like me, and I knew I had found the treasure we were both looking for.

Johnny had given a parting gift as he affirmed his own self-hood. He had affirmed the therapist's role in helping him grow into manhood with greater confidence and greater pride in himself. Otto Rank would have referred to his gift as expiation of his "ethical" guilt, as distinct from moral guilt, for having taken help from the therapist. In recounting his last dream, Johnny had demonstrated clearly the therapeutic process as Allen (1942) had described it to a group of residents in training.

Therapy is an awakening process, but if the waking up is not in the world of immediate reality of people and events, it is not a waking up but a new medium to continue a dream existence. (p 295)

FOLLOW-UP: THREE YEARS LATER

Johnny had sustained much of his self-affirmation and had found an area of academic confidence in which he excelled. He was handling his strong libidinal and aggressive drives with an active fantasy and dream-life. His early narcissistic injury continued to color his current object relationships, since he still felt a sense of being different from many of his peers and remained fearful of risking himself in new social situations. However, he expressed a healthy desire for closeness with and acceptance from the opposite sex and suggested that he would like to see the therapist again for a couple of "pit stops" to talk about making friends with greater ease and confidence.

REFERENCES

Adams, P. *A primer of child psychotherapy*. Boston: Little, Brown, 1974.

Adamson, W., Hersch, A., & Creasy, W. Some psychological aspects of the management of the brain-damaged adolescent in a residential setting. *Journal Child Psychology and Psychiatry*, 1961, *2*, 156–164.

Allen, F. *Psychotherapy with children*. New York: W.W. Norton, 1942.

Axline, V. *Play therapy: The inner dynamics of childhood*. Boston: Houghton Mifflin, 1947.

Bender, L *Psychopathology of children with organic brain disorders*. Springfield, Ill.: Charles C Thomas, 1956.

Black, F. The size of human figure drawings of LD children. *Journal of Clinical Psychology*, 1976, *32*, 736–741.

Blanck, G. & Blanck, R. *Ego psychology*. Irvington-on-Hudson: Columbia University Press, 1974.

Coopersmith, S. *The antecedents of self-esteem*. San Francisco: W.H. Freeman, 1967.

Dawley, A Interrelated movement of parent and child in therapy with children. *American Journal of Orthopsychiatry*, 1939, *9*, 748–754.

Dubin, S. *The self-concept: A study in the relationship between a child's self-concept and the concept his parents have of him*. Unpublished master's thesis, Hahnemann Medical College and Hospital, 1972.

Fenichel, O. *Problems of psychoanalytic technique*. New York: Psychoanalytic Quarterly Publications, 1941.

Frank, B. & Abbott, R. *Follow-up study of SLD children in a residential school*. Unpublished report, The Pathway School, Audubon, Pa., 1970.

Freud, A. *The ego and the mechanisms of defense*. London: The Hogarth Press, 1937.

Freud, A. The indications for child analysis. *Psychoanalytic Study of the Child*, 1945, *1*, 127–150.

Freud, A. *The psychoanalytic treatment of children*. London: Imago, 1946.

Gause, E., Yolton, W., & Adamson, W. *On being a child*. Report of Consulting Committee on Needs and Rights of Children to the Program Agency, United Presbyterian Church, U.S.A., New York, 1976.

Geleerd, E. *The child analyst at work.* New York: International Universities Press, 1967.

Gero, G. The concept of defense. *Psychoanalytic Quarterly,* 1971, *20,* 565–578.

Hartman, H. (1939), *Ego psychology and the problem of adaptation.* New York: International Universities Press, 1958.

Johnson, M. Sex-role learning in the nuclear family. *Child Development,* 1963, 34, 319–333.

Klein, M. *The psychoanalysis of children.* New York: W.W. Norton, 1932.

Klopfer, B., Ainsworth, M., Klopfer, W., & Holt, R. *Developments in the Rorschach technique.* Yonkers-on-Hudson: World Book, 1954.

Koppitz, E. *Psychological evaluations of children's human figure drawings.* New York: Grune & Stratton, 1968.

Langeveld, M. The significance of one's own body for the child's experience of the self. *Psychological Research,* 1954, *5,* 206–220.

Loewenstein, R. Some remarks on defenses, autonomous ego and psychoanalytic technique. *International Journal Psychoanalysis,* 1954, *35,* 188–193.

Machover, K. *Personality projection in the drawing of a human figure.* Springfield: Charles C Thomas, 1949.

Mahler, M., Pine, F. & Bergman, A. *The psychological birth of the human infant.* New York: Basic Books, 1975.

Moustakas, C. *Psychotherapy with children.* New York: Harper & Row, 1959.

Parsons, T. & Bales, R. *Family, socialization, and interaction processes.* Glencoe, Ill.: The Free Press, 1955.

Pearson, G. *The emotional disorders of children.* New York: W.W. Norton, 1949.

Pearson, G. A survey of learning difficulties in children. *Psychoanalytic Study of the Child,* 1952, *7,* 322–386

Pearson, G. (Ed.). *A handbook of child psychoanalysis.* New York: Basic Books, 1968.

Rappaport, S. Behavior disorder and ego development in a brain-injured child. *Psychoanalytic Study of the Child,* 1961, *16,* 423–450.

Rogers, C. *The clinical treatment of the problem child.* Boston: Houghton Mifflin, 1939.

Sterba, R. Character and resistance. *Psychoanalytic Quarterly,* 1951, *20,* 72–76.

Strauss, A. & Lehtinen, L. *Psychopathology and education of the brain-injured child* (Vol. 1). New York: Grune & Stratton, 1947.

Waelder, R. *Basic theory of psychoanalysis.* New York: International Universities Press, 1960.

Witmer, H. (Ed.). *Psychiatric interviews with children.* New York: The Commonwealth Fund, 1946.

CHAPTER 7

PARENT COUNSELING

DOROTHY FISHER OHRENSTEIN, M.S.W., ACSW

It is difficult enough learning you have this child—what you want is to find out what you can do about it and that answer doesn't come forward very easily.

—From Parent to Parent. *The Exceptional Parent,* Vol. 1

INTRODUCTION

The principles and concepts stated in this chapter have developed out of the writer's experience in working with parents of children with SLD in a variety of interdisciplinary settings, e.g., a private day school, a residential school, an outpatient clinic, and private practice in collaboration with a child psychiatrist. The teams have included educators, psychologists, pediatricians/neurologists, psychiatrists, and other specialists such as speech clinicians, audiologists and child care workers. The philosophy, role, function, and techniques described here arise from the belief that the generic role of the social worker is the same when working in an interdisciplinary team, regardless of setting.

The approaches to parents described here have developed mainly in ideal circumstances; specialists to evaluate the child, appropriate educational settings, counseling services for parents on a regular basis, and psychotherapy for the child when needed have all been available and coordinated. The ideal as described here may not be possible at this time. However, it is the belief of this author that such programs should be viewed as exemplary and, one would hope, in time, will be available to all SLD children and their families.

A major piece of federal legislation was passed in 1975 which will have a profound impact on children with SLD and their parents. The enactment of Public Law 94-142, the Education for All Handicapped Children Act of 1975, mandates the public schools to provide free *appropriate public education* to all handicapped children with specific learning disabilities between the ages of 3 and 18 not later than September 1, 1978. Under the legislation, Individualized Educational Programs (IEP's) must be written for each child, reviewed at least annually, and revised according to the child's changing needs.

It is of particular interest to this writer that the law also mandates that parents participate in the writing of the IEP's, making official the fundamental thesis of this chapter, which is the conviction that parents must be involved and included if the child is to use fully those educational experiences made available to him/her. Growth in children takes place in relation to the family; therefore, any attempt to stimulate, enhance, or alter the direction of growth must involve the family. The new legislation makes official the foregoing thesis and assures the position of parents as partners on the team in relation to their child's educational planning.

School personnel will need to develop increasingly adequate and sophisticated skills in enabling parents to become full partners. Two issues need to be addressed: (1) to provide information to parents about their child's SLD and how he/she learns, and (2) to provide counseling services for these situations where parents need a better understanding of their feelings and behavior in order to cope with the problems posed by having a child with SLD (Freeman and Pearson, 1978).

The usual public school services, with only slight modifications, may be adequate to involve and support many parents of children with SLD: report cards, periodic conferences with the teacher, discussion of test results by the psychologist, and the availability of a guidance counselor. For the population of children with SLD/MBD/HKS, periodic group meetings for parents geared to education and support may be the only additional service needed and written into the (IEP's) for many parents.*

There are other parents who will require and/or may request or demand more individual help in order for them to be able (1) to support fully the growth of their child, (2) to work through their own feelings of having a child with SLD/MBD/HKS, and (3) to be able to derive a greater sense of satisfaction in their role as parents to a child with SLD. It is crucial that school personnel and professionals in diagnostic and mental health settings develop the knowledge and expertise to be able to offer services to these families with skill, understanding, and compassion.

Many health and mental health professionals are involved in counseling parents of children with SLD/MBD/HKS. Physicians, psychologists, and educators are the major professionals whose primary skills are in some way related to direct examination, assessment, evaluation, teaching, therapy, and tutoring of the child. They operate from a specific area of knowledge and expertise about some aspect of the child's functioning: learning, development, cognition, perception, etc. Their basic function in relation to the child and their usual role with parents may be viewed in terms of parent educator or parent advisor. As a rule, when they function as parent counselor, their primary identification is with the child.

The social worker as parent counselor functions specifically in relation to the parents; he/she is primarily identified with them. Although this chapter is written from the perspective of the generic role of the social worker as parent counselor, the same principles can be used by any professional person working with parents. It will, however, require a shift in the perception of the role and function and, more specifically, a shift in the identification from child-centered to parent-centered counseling.

---

*Group meetings with the focus on education and support may be a useful adjunct to individual parent counseling or, with some families, the main helping medium. Many parents are more comfortable with the educational atmosphere of a group, as contrasted to the more personal focus of counseling. Groups may also enable parents to feel less alone by exposing them to other families with similar problems. If possible, it is best to form groups with parents whose children are in the same age group, such as early childhood, latency, preadolescence, or adolescence. In this way, a perspective can be maintained on normal growth and development rather than the SLD/MBD/HKS *per se.*

KNOWLEDGE REQUIREMENTS

In order to be effective, a parent counselor must be knowledgeable about:

(1) SLD/MBD/HKS and the tools used to assess these deficits,
(2) normal child development,
(3) the impact of SLD/MBD/HKS on the developing personality,
(4) remedial approaches and techniques available through the educational-clinical modalities,
(5) techniques of behavior management with SLD/MBD/HKS children and adolescents, such as the use of structure, consistency, and positive reinforcement, and
(6) human behavior, personality and the various psychological mechanisms of defense.

BASIC ASSUMPTIONS

It is essential to start out with certain basic assumptions: (1) The child with SLD has a *chronic,* as opposed to *acute,* disability. He learns differently from the majority of children. Basic learning takes place over an extended period of time; therefore, there is no treatment or resolution possible in one day, one week, or even one month. The nature of the learning process requires thinking in terms of years: several years for the child to work out particular disabilities and master basic academic skills, and more years with struggles to understand what his/her learning disability was about and how it has shaped and affected not only learning, but also feelings about his/her own adequacy and selfhood. It is essential for the counselor to set this tone with the parents at the outset. (2) The problem, SLD, and the child are not synonymous. The child must be viewed first as a child, within the perspective of normal growth and development and with the same needs as any other child along with some special needs. There is a tendency for parents, as well as professionals, to focus excessively on the child's disability and, therefore, on his difference. The rise of special schools (and to some extent the development of special classes) has tended to contribute to this, as they set the child apart from his peers. The trend toward mainstreaming and equality of services for the handicapped under the new federal legislation should help to offset this trend. The child is like all other children his/her age in most characteristics, with needs identical to those of his peers: to grow and learn, to experience feelings of satisfaction and success within himself/herself, and to feel support from parents and acceptance from peers. (3) Diagnosis is a process which takes place over time, and it must be viewed as adaptable to new information and deeper understanding as new data are provided. The final prognosis of the child, that is, his/her "ultimate" learning level and "basic potential," is not fixed and known at any one time. Such knowledge unfolds slowly as the child continues to grow and to develop. (4) Counseling is a growth process. The parent counselor can facilitate the growth of parents and, through them, growth in the child by skillfully working to interweave the parents' growth with that of the child.

SPECIFIC FUNCTIONS/GOALS OF THE COUNSELING PROCESS

The essential function of the social worker as parent counselor is the same regardless of setting: school, community agency, or private practice. With the trend toward mainstreaming, the ideal setting is the school where the parent counselor can be a part of an interdisciplinary team and can function as a bridge between the team and the parents in behalf of the growth and well-being of the total family.

The social worker as parent counselor functions specifically in relation to the parent(s) to help them in the following areas:

(1) to understand how SLD affects their child's learning, development and behavior;
(2) to prepare their child for the educational experience and to support his/her use of that educational experience;
(3) to become aware of and understand their own feelings and reactions to the child;
(4) to integrate the knowledge and understanding of the child into their daily interactions in ways which contribute to the child's growth and which will be appropriate to the parents' individual personalities and their communication styles; and
(5) to feel satisfaction in their role as parents freely able to communicate with and contribute to their child's growth.

The goal of parent counseling is to enable parents to function effectively in their role as parents to their child, e.g., to be able to support actively the child's growth and to feel satisfaction in doing so. It is not to *treat* parents in the classical therapeutic sense, which is aimed at individual growth. Obviously, effective parent counseling can contribute to individual growth as well. At times, this issue can present a major dilemma for the parent counselor and pose an extremely difficult technical problem. The counselor's role is to identify with and assist parents in their growth as parents. However, where they are and where their child needs them to be may not and seldom will coincide. Nevertheless, these forces must somehow be reconciled and, in most instances, can be.

The parent counselor says to parents, "I am here for you, to help you develop as parents to your child. Let us work together on those kinds of interactions between you and John that are most uncomfortable for you." That is the basic approach. The parent counselor must, however, be fully attuned to and incorporate in the work understanding of the child's developmental needs. For example, the parents may want to work on the bedtime struggle first, and child may not be ready to deal with this issue. In such a situation, the parents need to be supported in their frustration, and the bedtime struggle may have to wait months to be worked on in the counseling hours.

Another example might be a situation in which the parent counselor may be working with the parents on their feelings of helplessness in relation to the child's demands. In treatment, the child may be working on impulse control. It is crucial, at that time, to involve the parents in the child's developmental needs and introduce that theme into the counseling sessions, helping parents to defer temporarily their own agenda. It is possible, however, that the parents' feelings of helplessness may not be immediately available to be worked on when the next opportunity presents itself.

This view of parent counseling, as opposed to individual treatment with parents of a child with SLD, must dovetail the work of the other team members with the child. The collaborative process among the parent counselor, teacher, and child therapist is crucial to maximizing growth for parents and child. The needs of the child provide the focus and usually predominate. Time is crucial, and each day that passes without growth puts the child further behind. The child's emotional needs within the guidelines of normal development must always be kept in mind. The child's educational needs must be understood. All professionals have to be clear about the diagnosis and family dynamics; they must be together in their understanding and focus for growth.

It is the responsibility of each professional person to be able, briefly and succinctly, to communicate to the others the essence of movement or change in the child's learning, therapy, and the parents' counseling, always keeping the focus on the interrelated movement between child and parents. Collaboration is a skill that can and must be learned. It is always demanding and frequently difficult. At times, it can be frustrating and uncomfortable, especially when differences of opinion arise. There may be differences in philosophy, understanding, and techniques, as well as the inevitable conflicts when several professional people representing different constituents have to keep the needs of all in balance. When practiced well, it can lead to maximum growth for the child and his parents and can be a challenging and creative experience for the professional partners involved.

THE COUNSELING PROCESS

From the beginning, an explicit contract has to be made between parent counselor and parents. The contract will spell out the purpose of the counseling sessions, their frequency, their focus, and who will participate. The contract will need to be defined and renegotiated during the course of the counseling relationship.

Ongoing counseling of parents at each phase needs to be handled flexibly. Often, it is appropriate to see father and mother together in the early sessions, for a number of reasons: to allow the counselor to see from what point each parent is starting, to allow the counselor to gain some impression of the relationship between the parents, and to ensure that both parents are involved from the beginning. This may require some extra effort on the counselor's part, in terms of evening hours to involve working parents, but it is unquestionably worthwhile. Diagnostically, the parent counselor must see both parents, and sometimes the entire family, to have any real understanding of the family dynamics and their effects on the child. SLD/MBD/HKS children need support from both parents, and parents need support from each other. Fathers who are not involved from the beginning are almost always somewhat behind in their understanding of and support of their child's program.

After the initial phases of counseling, it is appropriate to begin to see parents individually, particularly in phase VI below. Both parents have their own unique relationship with the child and their own "hang-ups." At times the presence of the spouse can be an inhibiting factor during some of the ongoing sessions.

Phase I: Diagnostic Assessment

The first task for the professional is to ascertain the parents' understanding of and feelings about their child. The most appropriate, direct, and productive approach is to ask where the parents have been in their struggle to know and deal with their child. What were the beginnings of their awareness that something was not quite right in their child's development? How did they search for answers and for a diagnosis? What did they feel when the problems did not disappear after the professional may have told them, "Don't worry, he'll outgrow it"? What was their struggle in coming to an understanding of their child's problem both cognitively and emotionally? What do they understand about how their child learns?

The beginnings of understanding can take place only when the counselor and parents have vicariously traveled the road together, when the counselor has listened to and shared the parents' experiences, their feelings of confusion, frustration, and fear, the anger, pain, and sense of loss. The literature includes many articles on the emotional impact on parents of having a child whose development is atypical. In the author's experience, most parents, to some degree, experience feelings of the loss of the idealized child (Olshansky, 1962). When parents can share experiences and feelings with the counselor and be "heard" with sensitivity and compassion, a relationship is created within which help can take place. These parents of SLD/MBD/HKS children today can be understood in the prospective of their yesterdays. The past is prologue to the reality of the present parent-child experiences.

Phase II: Relationship Building

Parents' Questions: (1) Who are you?
                        (2) How can you help me?

The counselor should begin at the beginning to establish a relationship. This may be obvious but cannot be taken for granted. It is necessary to convey acceptance and compassion to parents, being sensitive to their hurt, confusion, and pain. It is essential to be active in the early hours, so that parents may gain a sense that the counselor is someone who "knows" about SLD/MBD/HKS. If the diagnostic assessment has been adequately done, a good beginning has been made.

One must establish credibility as a knowledgeable helper and help parents experience counseling as a meaningful and helpful experience.

Phase III: Educational and Supportive

Parents' Questions:
(1) What is SLD?
(2) How does my child learn?
(3) How did this happen?
(4) What caused it?
(5) What did I do?
(6) Can it be treated?
(7) What is the cure?
(8) What is the outcome?

Begin at the reality level with an educational focus. Parents need to understand learning and how their child's way of learning is different. Counsel actively and regularly, consciously and consistently, gently and skillfully, to help the parents gain a perspective on meaning of SLD/MBD/HKS and how it manifests itself in their child. Provide an experience in which the parents may talk about the child, his or her behavior, and the impact of these behaviors on the life of the family. Provide an atmosphere where they can unload their feelings of frustration, fear, confusion, guilt, disappointment, sadness, and pain. Use the counseling sessions to enable parents to see their child in a more realistic perspective, not as an irrational, bad, uncontrollable, or hopeless child, but as a consistent, understandable human being who can become more predictable once the SLD/MBD/HKS syndrome and the child's patterns of reaction to it are more clearly understood. In this counseling context, as the parents talk about their experiences past and present and express their feelings about the child, they can begin to perceive the child differently. With the increase in their understanding, the parental anxiety begins to decrease.

Out of this dialogue between the counselor and parents based initially on education and support, a relationship and foundation of mutual understanding and trust will develop. Such a counseling relationship enables parents to begin to feel a greater degree of understanding and support for the child and for themselves. Such skillful counseling helps to offset the intensity of reaction to the diagnosis, which may have resulted in immobility, and leads quite naturally into the next major phase of counseling, geared to learning to "read" the child.

Phase IV: The Beginnings of Parent/Child Communication

IN RELATION TO THE DIAGNOSIS OF SLD

The goal of counseling is to enable parents and child to communicate together in mutually meaningful and satisfying ways. A beginning task in this area is to encourage parents to talk with the child about the nature of the problem, their understanding of it, and steps which will be taken to help with the difficulties, such as tutoring, a special class, a special school, a resource room, and, possibly, psychotherapy. Fortunately, we have come to a time when the diagnosis does not sound worse than the reality. Terms like "brain damage," "brain dysfunction," and "minimal cerebral dysfunction" were frightening to parents and children alike. The medical model of diagnosis (e.g., labeling) and prognosis forced upon the educational institutions the need to attempt to define cause as opposed to describing function: Specific Learning Disability (SLD), as an overall description, is a much more realistic and comfortable way to describe this population's problem.

One of the best ways to know where parents and child are in their communication about the child's SLD is to ask, "What have you told Johnny about the diagnosis?" The usual response is "Nothing," "I didn't know what to say," "I don't want to make him feel bad," and, occasionally, "He didn't ask."

If the counselor goes on to explore what indications the parent has gotten from the child about his/her awareness of the problem, parents may respond with, "He thinks he's stupid," "He gets frustrated easily," "He throws things when he can't do something," or, "He won't try anything new." It is inevitable that everyone in the family knows that something is wrong, but, often, no one knows how to talk about it. Therefore the problem looks larger, more frightening, and more formidable than it may actually be. Both sides, parents and child, are struggling in the dark while feeling helpless, frightened, and alone. Talking with a trained person does help. Helping parents to begin a dialogue with the child about their understanding of what is happening to the child and why it is happening is the beginning of help and growth for both parents and child. If the disturbing condition has a name, it does not seem to be as frightening. "If my parents can talk about it, maybe it's OK." Parents feel less helpless as they are able to put their feelings and knowledge into words and begin to help their child understand.

IN RELATION TO THE NEED FOR SPECIAL EDUCATION

The next task is to help parents prepare the child for the special services he/she may need. Whether the need is for a special class, school, or psychotherapy, it is the responsibility of the parents to sanction these programs and to endorse the teacher and/or therapist as someone they trust as a helping person. Without such help, parents may not be able to prepare the child adequately for and enable him to enter fully into a learning situation or a therapeutic relationship. The parent counselor must constantly be aware of the parents' understanding of and feelings about the Individualized Educational Program (IEP) and/or the treatment process in which their child is involved and their impressions about the teacher, school, or therapist. This area is frequently overlooked by educational and mental health professionals working with parents of a child whose IEP suggests that special class/school or psychotherapy is indicated.

The principles of preparing a child for any new experience are essentially the same. In the author's experience, services are made available to parents after the child has been admitted into a special education program. Little or no attention is paid to the needs of parents for help in talking with and preparing their child for the new situation. Parents need to be helped with their own understanding and feelings about their child's different way of learning, so that they can be ready to help the child begin to deal with his/her own difference. There are a number of critical issues to be kept in mind:

(1) Parents need to meet the child's teacher or therapist first, so that they can begin to establish their own relationship with him/her. It is unreasonable to expect parents to turn over their child to a stranger or to expect them to support blindly the child's use of an educational experience or psychotherapy. Parents need to hear how the teacher or therapist sees the child, e.g., the indications for, methods in, and goals of education or treatment.

(2) Parents need to *understand the nature of special education and/or psychotherapy* with children. In the case of psychotherapy, they need to understand the role of play and the meaning of a treatment relationship.

(3) Parents need to be helped to *support the educational experience*

and treatment in an ongoing way. Questions must be encouraged and carefully dealt with.

(4) Parents need to be helped to *express openly their own feelings* about the child's learning experiences or treatment to the teacher, therapist, and parent counselor.

(5) Parents need *feedback* from the teacher to provide them with some sense of "what is going on." In the school situation, this may be done by setting up a conference with the teacher and parents, including the child when appropriate. Whenever children are the subject of conferences, they must be told about it ahead of time by both parents and teacher. They need to feel that the responsible adults in their lives are working together to help them; they should not feel that the adults are "telling on" them and are creating a "conspiracy" against them.

An example of a particularly difficult issue between parents and child is homework. Parents must be clear about the teacher's expectations about homework and how they as parents are expected to handle this. Some of the possibilities are to work with the child directly, to hold the child to a certain time for homework with no television, and to leave the child totally on his own. In the author's experience, homework frequently becomes an emotional-laden issue, with parents feeling compelled to carry the role of teacher (one who expects specific performance) as opposed to parent (one who supports). It seems to be most advantageous for parent and child if the homework is an issue solely between the teacher and the child, allowing the parent freedom to be the parent and be available to listen to and be supportive of the child's feelings about school and the learning situation.

IN RELATION TO THE NEED FOR PSYCHOTHERAPY

In the case of psychotherapy, feedback can be done without violating the need for confidentiality between therapist and child. The focus is on sharing trends and process without sharing content. However, feedback from the parent counselor is not enough, and periodic conferences need to be set up between therapist, parent counselor and parents, sometimes including the child, as described in Chapter 6 above.

Parents may "understand" their child's needs for treatment and support such a plan while having various reactions to it, such as:

(1) feelings of failure because of the need for treatment,

(2) feeling the therapist is a rival for the child's affection,

(3) feeling the therapist is a more powerful influence on the child than they may be,

(4) feeling exposed by what the child may say about them to the therapist,

(5) feeling threatened by what the therapist may think about them, and

(6) feeling "judged," diagnosed," or "accused" by the therapist.

It is difficult and often painful to turn over one's child to another adult, to support the child's development of a trusting and close relationship with another adult, and to bear a sense of loss of one's own relationship with the child. Parents' feelings may be heightened if the therapist is of the same sex as the parent. This seems, to this counselor, at least, to be particularly striking in the feelings of fathers toward male therapists.

Years of experience in counselling parents suggest that the child grows in the direction set by parents and also in relation to the sanctions communicated to him/her by the parents. The child needs to feel that the parents know what they are doing and are in control of his/her life and growth. Finally, the parents must be able to state to the child that special education and/or psychotherapy is what they want for the child and clearly explain why the child needs this experience and that it is an expression of parental caring and concern for the child's educational or emotional growth. Their statement and explanation should convey their trust in the teacher or therapist, so that the child can trust as well. A similar preparation process should take place around all items written into an IEP for the child or adolescent.

Phase V: Coping and Learning to "Read" the Child*

Parents' Questions:
(1) Why does my child act that way?
(2) Why can't he/she behave like other children?
(3) What can I do?
(4) How can I help my child?

This phase is important in helping parents take an active part in the Individualized Educational Program plan and Clinical Prescription. At this point, parents have gained some degree of cognitive under-

---

*Cf. Rappaport (1969).

standing of SLD in general and specifically how it has affected their child in his or her learning and social behavior. They need to understand how the SLD/MBD/HKS process has affected their child's personality, how previous failures and negative experiences affect the child's feelings about himself/herself, and how the child defends against feelings of inadequacy and vulnerability. As parents learn to "read" the child, they can begin to anticipate precipitating events preceding outbursts. Parents can test their knowledge by getting "feedback" from the child, by asking how the child felt about a certain experience, or by acknowledging a reaction that seemed obvious. In this phase, counseling focuses on helping parents trust their own observations and knowledge of their child and, once doing so, to use these observations in ongoing interactions with their child.

The key is communication. It should have been established in the parent counseling relationship and then applied to the communication between parent and child. The counseling sessions must be a laboratory in which parents can test out their understanding of the child and his/her communication skills. Here, parents need to be helped to develop greater consistency in their expectation of the child, to develop routine, regularity, and repetition. They need to prepare the child for the unknown and for using those social/emotional skills which may be appropriate to the child's growth. Inevitably, changes will occur in the parent-child relationship, changes in expectation of the child's behavior, in setting limits, and in communication.

Parents need to learn how to change their own behavior with the child, so that the child is not frightened, confused, or made increasingly anxious. This can be done as parents learn to put child "on notice" that a change is about to occur. Parents need to be helped by the counselor to take responsibility for their own reactions to the child's behavior and communicate openly and directly with the child their positive or negative feelings. For example:

(1) Parents may acknowledge to the child that a certain kind of behavior is not acceptable.
(2) Parents may acknowledge to the child that, in past, they were accustomed to react or punish in a certain way, perhaps by yelling or spanking.
(3) They may now add that they do not feel that yelling is helpful.
(4) They may say that they are going to begin to deal differently with the child's feelings and behavior "starting tomorrow."

(5) They will spell out how they will deal with each situation as it happens.

(6) They will be consistent in their praise or their punishment.

As the parents learn to communicate, first with parent counselor and then with the child, they become positive models for the child, which supports a basic trust of the child's growth. Parents can do this when they feel ready to make changes and to deal with the needs of the child to test the new rules. Testing the new rules and the new dialogue will be inevitable and usually difficult for the child and parents.

When parents begin to experience a dilemma between what they "know" the child needs and their ability to be consistent in providing for these needs, they are ready to look at their own feelings which may be getting in the way of healthier role functioning as mother and father to an SLD/MBD/HKS child.

Phase VI: Coping and Learning to "Read" One's Own Feelings

Parents' Questions: (1) Why can't I do what I know?

(2) Why can't I be more patient?

(3) Why do I get so angry?

A word of caution: the parent counselor must be careful not to move too quickly into this phase of counseling before the parents are ready. The parents may become frightened and develop resistance to counseling, or they may become distrustful of the treatment or the educational program for the child. They may become skeptical of the diagnosis.

The key word here is *feelings*. Much of the work in the earlier phases was geared to education and support. Now the focus shifts in order to enable the parent to become aware of some of the deeper feelings which may be interfering with being able to respond to the child as he/she wants to respond.

In this phase, it is most productive to see each parent individually and focus on his/her own unique relationship with the child. Parents are ready to focus on themselves in this way when they themselves feel frustrated and uncomfortable about some aspect of their relationship with the child and want help in this area.

Interactions between parent and child which evoke feelings of discomfort in the parent must be carefully identified and fully experienced by the parent. The tasks are, then, to learn to sort out personal reactions and responses from those actually created or provoked by the child, to take responsibility for one's own feelings, and to handle these feelings so that they do not interfere with the relationship with the child.

As parents share their own feelings of anger, pain, inadequacy, and vulnerability, they may "regress" for a time during that phase of counseling. This regression on the part of one or both parents may express itself in the relationship with the child as increased feelings of helplessness, to which the child may react with panic or increased disorganized behavior. It is essential for the parent counselor to be in close communication with the child's therapist and teachers during this time. They always need to know which added stresses may be operating on the child, so they can understand and be supportive.

Phase VII: Parent As Full Partner

In this final phase, parents are able to function as fully contributing members of the team. They have developed the ability to understand the child, to "read" his/her behavior, to be aware of their own feelings which might get in the way, to communicate openly and effectively, and to deal with behavior both consistently and responsibly. As parents come to see themselves as adequate, responsible, and responsive, and as they gain satisfaction in being able to contribute to their child's growth, the focus on the counseling shifts. The time is spent on sharing experiences about the progress (or lack of it) the child is making at home, in school, and in treatment. The purposes are six-fold:

(1) to ensure consistency of approach,
(2) to continue to use the knowledge gained from psychotherapy to help parents stay focused on the road of growth and not get sidetracked,
(3) to give the therapist regular feedback on the home situation,
(4) to continue to support the parents in their frustration with the slowness or unevenness of growth and the inevitable losses as well as gains,
(5) to continue to support parents and deal with their fear about the outcome, and
(6) to share in the parents' feelings of joy in their child's growth and satisfaction in their own growing feelings of parental adequacy.

SUMMARY

Parents are an integral part of the educational-therapeutic team. They must be included, involved, educated, supported, and helped. Counseling services should be made available to them at every step along the way: e.g., in diagnostic settings, in schools, and in community mental health centers where they may turn for help. In this chapter, the author has defined a model of counseling parents of children with SLD that has developed from a social work perspective as part of an interdisciplinary team. However, the principles and techniques outlined can be used by any professional person working with parents. Knowledge, techniques, and skills are all essential for effective parent counseling, effective only when used with understanding and compassion.

REFERENCES

Adamson, W.C., Helping parents of children with learning disabilities. *Journal of Learning Disabilities,* 1972, *5,*(6), 327–330.

Barsch, R.W. Counseling the parent of the brain-injured child. *Journal of Rehabilitation,* May/June 1961, pp. 26–27; 40–42.

Berry, S.D. & Wegener, D.L. *Arlington Heights Public School District Number 25, Diagnostic Learning Center, final report—1966–1969.* Washington, D.C.: Office of Education (Department of Health, Education, and Welfare), 1969.

Brutton, M., Richardson, S., & Manuel, C. *Something's wrong with my child.* New York: Harcourt Brace Jovanovich, 1973.

Freeman, R.D. & Pearson, P.H. Counseling with parents. In J. Apley (Ed.), *Handicapped children: Aspects of management.* London: Heinemann/ Philadelphia: Lippincott, Spastics International Medical Publications, in press.

Gilmore, J.V. The effectiveness of parental counseling with other modalities in the treatment of children with learning disabilities. *Journal of Education,* 1971, *151*(1), 74–82.

Golub, R. & Gordon, S. *Recreation and socialization for the brain injured child.* East Orange, N.J.: New Jersey Association for Brain Injured Children, 1966.

Hersh, A. Casework with parents of retarded children. *Social Work,* 1961, *6*(2), 61–66.

Mandelbaum, A. & Wheeler, M.E. The meaning of a defective child to parents. *Social Casework,* July 1960, pp. 360–367.

Meares, P.A. Analysis of tasks in school social work. *Social Work,* 1977, *22*(3), 196–201.

Millman, H.L. Minimal brain dysfunction in children: Evaluation and treatment. *Journal of Learning Disabilities,* 1970, *3*(2), 89–99.

Minimal brain dysfunction: A new problem area for social work. Symposium presented at the annual forum of the National Conference on Social Welfare, Dallas, Texas, 1967. Chicago, Ill.: National Easter Seal Society for Crippled Children and Adults, 1967

Olshansky, L. Chronic sorrow: A response to having a mentally defective child. *Social Casework,* 1962, *63,* 190–193.

Rappaport, S.R. *Public education for children with brain dysfunction.* Syracuse, N.Y.: Syracuse University Press, 1969.

Shrier, D.K. Memo to day care staff: Helping children with minimal brain dysfunction. *Child Welfare,* 1975, *14*(2), 89–95.

Solnit, A.J. & Stark, M.H. Mourning and the birth of a defective child. *The Psychoanalytic Study of the Child,* 1961, *16,* 523–537.

Strickler, E. Family interaction factors in psychogenic learning disturbance. *Journal of Learning Disabilities,* 1969, *2*(3), 31–38.

CHAPTER 8

GROUP PSYCHOTHERAPY WITH SLD CHILDREN

WILLIAM C. ADAMSON, M.D.

The setting of a school for group therapy compared to a clinic often determines the nature and content of the group process. Schools (usually) will not tolerate grossly disruptive behavior; time and space are limited; there may not be free choice of group members; and administrators, teachers and group leaders are often bound into the issues of control of behavior and responsibility for cognitive learning . . .

—B. MacLennan and N. Felsenfeld,
Group Counseling and Psychotherapy with Adolescents

HISTORICAL PERSPECTIVE

A rather extensive review of group psychotherapy from 1970 to the present indicated very few articles on group psychotherapy with SLD children and even fewer papers reporting research studies on the effectiveness of group psychotherapy in an SLD population. It seemed apparent that, as interest in modified group process such as sensitivity groups, T-groups, transitional groups, marathon, and other forms of encounter groups peaked out in the early 1970s, interest in family therapy, social-community models, sex-therapy, and strategic therapies (matching treatment modality of choice more closely with the apparent need of the client and the client's psychological support system) moved into ascendancy.

Slavson (1943) wrote the classic work on group therapy with children, updating his work in the decades of the 1960s and 1970s

(Slavson, 1964; Slavson and Schiffer, 1975). Ginott (1961) and Glass (1969) wrote about task-focused groups for children, and Foulkes and Anthony (1968) authored a text on group analytic psychotherapy which included a discussion of a nursery school group, with illustrations from child and adolescent groups as well. Anderson (1968) described the group therapy process with "brain-damaged" children in one of the few manuscripts focused on group work with an SLD/MBD/ HKS population.

Yalom (1970) has written one of the most authoritative books of the past two decades on group therapy, and Sugar (1974), Illovsky and Fredman (1976), Schamess (1976), MacLennan (1977) and Anderson and Marrone (1977) have contributed significantly to the more recent literature on group therapy with children and adolescents. Few, if any, of these publications focused on the use of group therapy with SLD/MBD/HKS children, since these syndromes have not been defined clearly enough.

The concluding volume of each year's publication of the International Journal of Group Psychotherapy contains an excellent summary of all the literature published in this field for the preceding year or two and should be consulted by those working with groups of SLD/MBD/ HKS children and adolescents.

Rome (1972) summarized some of the issues related to group therapy in general. He recognized that, during the 1950s and 1960s, vast ideological differences developed in the practice of group therapy as the process was picked up in education, correctional systems, and organizational management. He noted that the essence of group treatment is its emphasis on interaction among the persons who comprise the group and that individual and collective affect, as experienced in the group, can produce change, because it is rooted in the reality of the here and now. Yet, he also observed a principle many group leaders know firsthand, "that when interaction is encouraged there is always the danger of acting out and the consequent exploitation of both the victim and the victimizer" (Rome, 1972, p. 7). Rome suggested the combined use of individual and group treatments as a safeguard against overly traumatic exposure to reality in a social context. His final point was that the technology of video-audio taped group sessions allows (1) for suitable study and control of the ongoing leader-to-group and group-to-group confrontation, (2) for a retrospective analysis and interpretation of what has happened in the group sessions, and (3) for a review of the individual's intention and motives vis-à-vis the intentions and motives of the group. Rome concluded by underlining the use of video replay as a method for the group leader to increase his/her skill through analyzing the taped interaction, the nature of the interventions, and the positive and negative strategies used in the role and function of group leader.

CHAPTER ORGANIZATION

To facilitate covering the material in a pragmatic, useful, and yet comprehensive way, this chapter will be organized in three sections, according to the age range and relevant issues for each age group. In each section, clinical examples from the author's experience will be presented in a descriptive narrative to illustrate ways in which the group therapy process may be used with each significant age group in the SLD population. Similar or contrasting methods reported in the literature will be presented in capsule form. Key issues from each age-group experience will be highlighted and discussed.

PRESCHOOL AND EARLY LATENCY SLD CHILDREN

The following example has been drawn from the author's experience with a latency-age group within a school for children with specific learning disabilities.

Composition

Four latency age day students (7 to 10 years) were selected from a class of eight for inclusion in the group. The two girls (A and B) and two boys (C and D) all showed clinical and educational signs of central nervous system dysfunction. In addition to some of the classic learning deficiencies, all showed attentional problems and some delay in social/emotional development, with behavior reflective of oral and anal fixations. Both boys showed conflicts in handling impulse control, assertiveness, and sibling rivalry and had difficulty accepting the authority of the teachers and parents. The girls showed fewer problems with impulse control but did have difficulty in verbal fluency and syntax, low levels of frustration tolerance, and aspects of provocative behavior more aggressive than sexual in scope and manifestation. All four were at a readiness level in reading, writing and arithmetic skills.

Selection

These four children were chosen because they appeared to have greater ability than they demonstrated in the mastery of learning. Their body image was uniformly poor; they all had a low sense of self-esteem in relationship to their peers and siblings; and their self-concept was equally poor. All seemed to be manifesting hostile-aggressive and angry feelings in response to their hurt pride at being different from other 7- to 10-year-olds (wounded narcissism), and all four had difficulty in their teacher-student and parent-child relationships.

Location and Time Allocations

The decision was made to see the group outside the classroom in a large activity room in one of the nearby residential cottages. They were seen for 35 to 40 minutes, twice a week, between 1:30 to 2:15 p.m. This was the last period of the school day and was chosen (1) because it paralleled recreational hours for the balance of the week and for students who were not selected for the group, and (2) because it was anticipated that some of the group content might stir up individual and collective conflicts which would momentarily interfere with prime learning time in the classroom and which could spill over in the form of group contagion once they returned to the classroom setting. Since the school day was completed at 2:30, all the students were in the process of preparing to leave the classroom and school in the 15-minute period between the time the group ended and the time the final bell sounded.

Method and Materials

The basic method was to use Gardner's, *The Child's Book About Brain Injury*. This small book was more recently included as part two in Gardner's (1973) book entitled, *MBD: The Family Book about Minimal Brain Dysfunction*.

In each meeting, the group leader read a chapter or part of a chapter to the group. The leader would stop while reading if there was a question or if he felt there should be a question. Each member of the group was asked if he/she had feelings or experiences similar to those described in the book. Role playing and modified psychodrama were used to help the group experience alternative behavior to those situations described in the text or described by the child as occurring in his/her life experiences in classroom and in the home. The group was given the freedom to talk or not to talk with the teacher, other students, parents, and siblings about the things they discussed. Very early in the group process, they all agreed that they would not talk to other students about most of the things that went on in the group, since they felt they were personal and private. They did, however, feel that they might want to talk with the teacher and their parents about some of the things that came up in the group, and this was supported. Actually, part one of Gardner's book is written expressly for parents and lends itself very well for use by a parents' group running concurrently with the child's group. An alternative model would have the parents of each of the children read, at home, the section for parents and discuss it between them, while being familiar with the content in the child's section, so that they could anticipate and answer any questions which would be raised from that portion of the text.

In addition to this resource book, the group leader had an easel with a large pad of newsprint and magic markers which were used by the students to draw out some of their ideas and feelings and by the leader to focus on certain words or to illustrate, in cartoon fashion, ideas about some of the topics discussed.

Finally, a reasonably large tropical fish aquarium, located in the recreation room, was used to allow for a focused break in the group discussions and to provide positive reinforcement for appropriate individual and group behavior during the group meetings when the group was permitted to watch or to feed the fish. On occasions, individuals in the group took turns feeding the fish, once the appropriate feeding time was established.

No other activities were available, apart from those which would be brought in from time to time by the therapist to illustrate some of the contents of the resource book or to reenact some of the conflicts which came up in the classroom or at home. This type of structuring of material and of the space in which the group took place is quite different from the group activity orientation described by most group therapists working with latency-age children. It is also different from the interpretive group therapy process described by Sugar (1974). The primary reason for this simplicity of structure was the fact that all of these children had very short attention spans, poor impulse control, and significant delays in their social-emotional development. By structuring the group in a fairly clear and somewhat "tight" fashion, it appeared possible to help them move toward the goals outlined below. A similar design would be to focus on one particular activity, such as art therapy, music therapy, or movement therapy, in which there would be some homogeneity of content, stimulation, and cognitive congruence expected from each group member. At the point where the individual group member's ego functions became more highly organized, the interpretive group therapy process could be quite appropriate.

Program Purpose and Goals

In discussion with the total team of parents and teachers, the following goals were formulated for the group:

A. To help each group member:
1. Gain a sense of increased self-awareness in terms of positive and negative feelings experienced in the group, in the classroom, and at home.
2. Gain a sense of increased knowledge about oneself and one's body in relationship to the significant SLD issues which are so critical for this population.
3. Gain a sense of increased self-responsibility in terms of the physical, fantasied, or verbal expressions of positive and negative feelings experienced in the group, in the classroom, and at home.
4. Gain a sense of increased awareness of the feelings and behavior of other persons, including peer group, siblings, parents, and teachers, and to develop an increased awareness of social relationships and their part in those relationships.
5. Learn coping mechanisms appropriate for the age group, constructive patterns of socially acceptable verbalizations, alternatives in social interaction through role playing and behavioral reinforcement as a result of group acceptance and rejection responses, and group and leader "shaping" of individual responses to real and simulated situations experienced in this small group.
6. Learn to delay immediate gratification or to transform an impulsive motoric behavioral response into an age-appropriate verbal response or some other planned and appropriate motoric response.
7. Learn to master attentional and intentional functions at an age-appropriate level through a small group social and emotional experience and through the social conditioning processes which all would experience in the leader-to-group and group-to-group interaction.

B. To help parents and families:
1. Experience a greater sense of family pride and success vis-à-vis a sense of family failure in response to their SLD child's increased socialization skills.
2. Experience a decompression of their SLD child's hurt pride, anger, and negative sense of difference from other children.
C. To help teachers of SLD children:
1. Increase the child's availability to learning.
2. Increase the child's internal control and decrease impulsive and acting-out behaviors.
3. Increase the child's attention span and intentional skills and reinforce the child's readiness for sustained learning.

Admittedly, these goals are idealistic and perhaps excessive for the limited clinical time involved (twice a week for approximately six months).

Description of Group Process

FIRST SESSION

Talked about the plan to meet as a group twice a week. Suggested purpose generally was to help each student understand more about himself/herself and why he/she was at the school, to allow the leader and group to help one another feel good about themselves, even though they did have some difficulty in learning, to give each one a chance to bring out his/her feelings about the school and the difficulty each had in growing up, to help them have more confidence in themselves in school and at home and, if it all worked out, to help each boy and girl make as much progress in the classroom as was possible during the next six months.

Presented Gardner's book and how we would be using it in each session to the group. Read the introductory chapter.

Group Response. A mixture of suspiciousness as to what the group was all about and pleasure at getting out of class twice a week.

SECOND SESSION

Presented Chapter 2: "What the Brain Does." Was at a level which turned on all four students. Each acted out the suggested brain functions in the text. Some expressed surprise that "their brains did those things." One (student D) became anxious and silly and tried to take over the group by clowning. The group leader recognized this was new information for all four, and D seemed shaken by it all. We would let him show us some of the things his brain could do, and then we would want him to settle down so we could go ahead with our discussion. He did.

Group Response. Great interest. Some anxiety. One student very silly but settled down. None had ever been helped to see so clearly the variety of functions of the brain; all seemed responsive and showed a sense of self and group pride that they were learning things other classmates did not know at this time; and all wanted to talk to "everyone" about what they had learned. The last five to ten minutes were spent discussing what they would say to parents, siblings, teachers, and classmates. They finally decided, as a group, that they would just talk about the things with their parents, when they wanted to, and maybe with their teacher.

THIRD SESSION

Presented Chapter 3: "People are Different in Many Ways." The chapter is well written, but it stirred up the basic conflicts over likeness (which was perceived as positive, good, and strong) and difference (felt as negative, bad, and weak). Much restlessness in the group. Used the structure of time to hold their attention for 10-minute segments and let them look at the differences in the tropical fish. How many different kinds could they count? Brought it back to how different were the colors of their hair, eyes, differences in their size, weight, and speed in running. Suggested that we could spend some time at the end of this session running some races to see how different each one was from the other in running. One student (B) remembered the story of the boy with the "green hair." Told this story as an illustration of the fear of difference and eventually the acceptance of difference. The group came to see they could understand and feel more comfortable with someone who was like them, felt they had something in common with one another, and also felt that, if they were alike in these obvious things, they were more likely to like one another. It was the strangeness in observed differences in other people that made those persons feel like "strangers" to them. And finally, they came to realize, as a group, that the stranger was someone they needed to get to know better, over time, because that person

did not have the obvious things in common with them that they understood and about which they felt comfortable.

Group Response. All four were very much engaged, stirred up, interested, and focused on a complex psychological phenomenon with
which they had lived for years but had never looked at in a dynamic and
interpersonal relationship framework. A knowledge of Rank's (1945)
discussion of likeness and difference was helpful for the group leader
in responding to some of the issues of this session.

Rank recognized that we develop a sense of individuality, in part,
by comparing ourselves to others. The earliest reaction to seeing oneself
as different from others who are valued persons is not only a painful
feeling, but a value judgment as well. "I should not be different from
but, rather, like you." The individual appears to suffer from this difference, this perception of his or her own individuality which is felt
to be bad and which carries a sense of being inferior to the object of
comparison. Rank felt the reaction was one of responding to the stronger
will of the other person, feeling that the person who is different may
have a stronger will than the perceiver. Thus, for Rank, the sense of
inferiority ultimately derives from what he called "will inferiority."

FOURTH SESSION

Presented Chapter 4: "What is Brain Dysfunction?" In the preface to his more recent book, Gardner explained that he was unhappy
using the term "brain injury," as he had done in the earlier edition
which had been used by the group leader. Fortunately, the group leader
and the school philosophy had been in the vanguard on this terminology
issue and had decided to use the concept of brain dysfunction, as
opposed to brain injury, even before it was widely accepted. The term
"brain dysfunction" was used with this group.

Gardner recognized, also, that the term learning disability has
become more commonly used, but, at the time he edited his book, he
felt it was misleading to use a more general term for this specific class
of disorders upon which his text was focused and which he viewed
as manifestations of organic neurologic dysfunction. At the time of
this group experience, the group leader was of a similar persuasion.
However, he has changed his opinion in the intervening years to feel
that there is a distinct advantage in using the concept of learning disorder or disability. There would appear to be less chance of injury to
the child's narcissism and self-esteem by referring to the more global

term, learning disorder or learning disability, while acknowledging that people learn at different rates.

For the group, this was a difficult chapter and topic. They alternately asked many questions or were very silent. The leader decided to approach the topic in slow motion fashion, taking only one or two pages of the seven total pages of the text in each of the next two sessions.

Group Response. Initially, a high level of anxiety, uncertainty, and questioning was mobilized. At the outset of the next meeting (fifth session), the group openly resisted getting into the discussion and wanted to spend the hour feeding the fish. This was viewed as a healthy individual and group ego defense against the anxiety which had mobilized the week before. The leader encouraged all four students to take turns talking about what that fourth session had meant to them. It was important to convey the nature of the group's response to the teacher and parents, and to encourage openness, forthrightness, and supportive reassurance with their child in the dialogue at home or in the classroom, should the child bring up a question or comment about it.

SIXTH SESSION

The rest of Chapter 4 was presented. The group was more settled, more accepting, and quite eager to ask questions related to causes, to eventual outcome, to issues of contagion, and to wonder when and how soon "they could expect a cure."

This kind of response gave the group leader an opportunity to review the first three sessions, the issues of differences among the four students, and the part parents, teachers, and their individual counselors and therapists had in helping them. The group leader focused on the team concept, which was the philosophy of the school, and the way in which the school brought together the teachers as educators, and therapists and helping persons as clinicians to help them move just as far and fast as they could in their learning and in their growing up socially and emotionally.

Group Response. A gradual psychological sophistication emerged. There appeared to be an increase in the sense of self, both as self-importance as well as a sense of self-difference. That is, they began to explore rather than deny their differences from one another, their differences from other students in the school classroom and, especially, their differences from other children at home. One student, D, became more open, conversant, inquisitive, and relevant in language content than he had ever been both at home and in school. His language shifted from an immature and defensive monologue, characterized by Piaget as a preoperational thought and language pattern, to social communication which was more clearly at the concrete operational level. Piaget suggested this occurs between ages 7 and 11 years. His content of thought changed from egocentric to social; his attention span and intentional focus in the classroom increased dramatically following these three sessions.

SEVENTH TO THIRTIETH SESSIONS

For purposes of brevity, the essence of these 24 group sessions will be summarized in a single paragraph or two.

Typical of a group process, paralleling that of individual development, this small group evidenced increasing resistance and, eventually, open negative feeling and opposition to hearing any more from Dr. Gardner and "that awful book." The confrontation to their narcissism and hurt pride was so strong that the group determined to decide on the topics to be discussed, so that we would go around the group giving each a chance to put a topic on the Agenda Sheet posted on the easel before them. This was the style used by Shaskin *et al.* in their analytically oriented group therapy in the military service.[1] The group responded by bringing in topics ranging from conflicts over food and eating habits, bedtime hours, sibling rivalry, and television programs at home to feelings of being mistreated, ridiculed, teased, threatened, and occasionally beaten up by other students in the class, en route to school, or on the playground. A role-playing and psychodrama model was used to suggest coping patterns, and the group cohesion and reinforcement process seemed to get the group process moving quickly from a resistance and resentment (negative) phase to an enthusiastic risk-taking and positive role-playing phase. Additionally, there was a positive carry-over from this small group, minilife experience into the wider circles of classroom, playground, home, and community.

Once this positive process was moving again, the group leader tied in specific chapters or pages from Gardner's book to some of the specific topic areas raised by the group. Gardner, for example, has short sections of relevant content (see Table 8.1) which, when read to the

---

[1]The author participated in groups run by Donald Shaskin, Eric Berne, and Harold Rashkis in the U.S. Army Bushnell General Hospital, Brigham City, Utah, 1944-45.

Table 8.1
Selected Topics from Gardner: Family Book about MBD (1973)

Most children get better as they get older.

Special schools and classes are helpful.

Things you can do to learn better.

Medicines sometimes help.

Worry about being retarded.

What you can do if children are cruel to you.

Things other children say may sometimes be true.

Things they say may not be true.

Bad names cannot hurt you.

Somewhere there are friends for everyone.

Children with brain dysfunction cannot always control
    themselves.

The fear of making mistakes.

Using brain dysfunction as an excuse.

You are not crazy if you have to see a therapist.

Talking with your parents about your problems.

group and illustrated according to the text, were both palatable and instructive to each group member.

THIRTY-FIRST AND THIRTY-SECOND SESSIONS

The last two sessions were used to bring closure to the group experience. The group talked about what they had gained from meeting
in this way, what they did that was fun and pleasant and what was
unpleasant and "turned them off," how they felt about Dr. Gardner
and his book, and how they felt about "Dr. A," their group leader.
These were noisy, active, and highly verbal sessions. They were short-
ened because the group found it difficult to focus on this type of verbal
recapitulation for longer than 30 minutes without becoming very highly
charged emotionally. Also, it was summer, and these last two sessions
were initially planned to be held outside. Though more pleasant for
them than the regular room without air conditioning, the number of
distractions for this type of child was so great that it was decided to
hold the sessions in the recreation room which had been their usual

meeting place. Serving lemonade and pretzels seemed to neutralize their strong feelings about moving indoors and rewarded them for their success in staying with the group for the 32 sessions.

Critique

No research design had been attempted to evaluate the effectiveness of the process described. Retrospectively, the group leader made several subjective observations in relationship to the original purposes and goals of the group.

(1) It seemed clear that within the limits of time and the school setting, many of the objectives were met to some degree in all four students; and contrary to what had been anticipated, the two male students and the more hyperactive and emotionally immature female student derived the greatest benefit.

(2) In all four students, a greater communication with parents was mobilized, and each student appeared to be viewed more positively by parents, siblings, and himself/herself.

(3) One of the four students showed significant carry-over into the classroom learning experience and was able to return to a regular school at the end of that school year. The other three showed sufficient growth in their learning skills and social maturity to move to a higher class grouping.

(4) An informal follow-up one year later showed that all four students had sustained both cognitive skills and interpersonal coping mechanisms appropriate, or nearly so, to the developmental age of the child.

Contrasting Methods

This review is not meant to be exhaustive, but to point up several contrasting methods which might be applicable to the preschool and early latency SLD child.

Interpretive Group Psychotherapy with Latency Children (Sugar, 1974)

Method is designed to facilitate the demonstration of intrapsychic and interpersonal conflicts, defenses, and fantasies through verbalization and play.

The author claims varying degrees of success with learning and behavioral disorders, as well as with children's symptoms including ulcers, asthma, transvestite tendencies, anxiety, and phobic reactions.

Therapist's role is to remain friendly and informal, not to be a parent substitute, a better parent, or to gratify children directly, but rather, to encourage children to seek other children in play which may then be interpreted on basis of the important unconscious themes, working from the most superficial levels of resistance, and what is conscious, troublesome, and can be managed, before interpreting more unconscious material. The author feels a clear-cut transference neurosis does not develop, but intense transference reactions are regularly present and should be interpreted at appropriate times in group process.

Sugar describes in some detail *logistics* such as composition of group, parents' part in supporting group process, playroom and suitable materials, and the possible content of the initial, middle, and termination process.

Group Suggestion in Learning Disabilities of Primary Grade Children (Illovsky and Fredman, 1976)

Method utilized 15-minute sessions of tape-recorded hypnotic suggestions given to groups of 9, 10, or 19 children, according to accommodation in the school, focused on suggestions for relaxation, ideas for coping with emotional problems, and suggestions for modifying attitudes towards learning. A total of 55 morning sessions were held, at which time a dot slightly larger than a fifty-cent piece was fixed on the front wall. Then the tape-recorder intoned in a monotonous voice the hypnotic suggestions. They returned to their home rooms to become part of a regular class, and all received remedial instructions in groups of 4 or 5 at some time during that same day.

The *population* comprised 48 children, between the ages of 6 and 8 years and from 3 public schools, who were selected to meet the criteria of short attention span, low frustration tolerance, hyperactivity, and poor learning motivation.

Pre- and posttest evaluations of the children's classroom behavior and attitudes towards learning were compared by their respective classroom teachers.

The authors claim 45 of 48 children functioned better in school, showing decreased hyperactivity and better than average performance in class. Significant correlations were found between the percentage of relaxation with increased attention span (r = .40) and the number of sessions with increased self-confidence (r = .46). The authors noted that no control group was used in this study and suggested that less than 40 sessions would be adequate to bring about the desired results.

Group Therapy in Public School Special Classes (Anderson and Marrone, 1977)

Method included introducing special education teachers to the concept of operating therapeutic group discussions, along with a trained therapist, using the following points: (1) the teacher is "in charge," (2) the setting is a circle of chairs for 8 to 10 children, (3) the ground rules include "not hitting the therapist or teacher," raising hands to be recognized, and a statement that confidentiality is to be respected by all members of the group, including teachers and therapists, and (4) that the topic for discussion should be decided by the students.

A study of 27 children (all boys), presenting emotional problems with varying degrees of specific learning disability, divided them into three groups matched for age, intelligence, and severity of emotional disturbance. The children in experimental group I were given an hour of individual therapy per week in the school in a room other than the classroom; experimental group II received an hour per week group therapy in the classroom with the teacher, teacher aid, and therapist as the treatment team; and group III served as a control, receiving no therapy in school, but seen in private or clinic treatment outside the school setting.

The nature of the *evaluating instruments* pre- and post- was not given in the article, but the authors stated that the evaluation of the program at the end of the school year "demonstrated the superiority of the group treatment in the classroom over other approaches."

Human Development Therapy (Bessel, 1970)

This approach has been called a packaged affective program. This author's (WCA) experience in a residential setting, as well as that of others (Anderson and Marrone, 1977), suggested that intellectual verbalizations about feelings are too easily substituted for dealing with real feelings, resulting in a distortion of the affective experience, rather than creating an environment in which spontaneous, interpersonal, affective experience and resultant learning may take place. Beyond this, the "Magic Circle" was a disaster with the hyperactive, poor impulse control children within the residential school experience who became extremely stirred up by the imposed, stereotyped content presented in the Human Development Therapy Manual.

LATE LATENCY AND EARLY ADOLESCENCE

This example was from the author's experience with a late latency and early adolescent group in private practice.

Composition

Eight boys (one 11 years, four 12, two 13, and one 14 years of age) were included in the group. Three had been in individual therapy with this therapist while attending a private school for children with learning disabilities and had graduated to other schools in the area. All three showed clinical and educational signs of a central nervous system dysfunction. They were struggling with the anticipated conflicts of early adolescence, including Erikson's (1963) role identity and role confusion and Freud's (1958) defense against sexual impulses by asceticism, intellectualization, and an uncompromising position. They were defending against attachment to another person of the same or opposite sex by regression, withdrawal of sexual feeling from the object back to the self with preoccupation of one's own body, or by denial, reaction formation, and reversal of affect. All three needed support in the transition from a special school setting into the regular classes of public junior high school or to private schools in the area. Each was functioning within a year or two of the expected grade level for his chronological age.

The remaining five boys were in five different junior high schools. Since the third and fourth grades, each had exhibited specific difficulty in reading, writing, and spelling to the extent that they were a year or two behind in these subjects, and were failing all courses which required reading comprehension and inference skills. Yet, each had an IQ in the bright-to-superior range. None presented the history or clinical or educational signs of the MBD syndrome or of a primary neurotic learning dysfunction (Sperry *et al.,* 1958; Ross, 1965). Emotional distress in each was a secondary rather than the primary source of the problem. Each fulfilled the characteristic SLD profile of low self-esteem, low frustration tolerance, failure avoidant behavior, hurt pride (narcissistic wounding), periodic turning in on the self of their feelings of failure, and feelings of anger at teachers who seemed to be critical and nonsupportive. This resulted in periodic depression and a high level of parental concern and positive support of their child.

All the families were intact and the family systems free from underlying psychopathology which might account for the specific learning disability.

Selection

Initially, the group was composed of six boys; later, two boys were added, one in the second month of the group process and the other in the third month.

The idea of enlarging the group was the outcome of the group's own thinking and desire to have what they determined "a revolving door policy." By this, they meant that any boy was free to drop out of the group at any time, and new boys could be added if they expressed an interest and had a need that met the criteria for group membership. None of the group wanted to drop out during the year, but two were eager to join in the second and third months.

These boys were chosen because they represented a partially homogeneous group in an active private practice so far as their learning disability was concerned; they all had different degrees of ego strength, which allowed for a healthy degree of heterogeneity in their social/emotional coping patterns; and all eight responded in a very positive way to the idea of a group experience vis-à-vis seeing the therapist in individual psychotherapy. They seemed relieved to find other teenage boys struggling with similar problems, and they attended weekly group meetings for an hour and a half each Saturday morning for the duration of the school year. In addition, each boy was seen in individual therapy once a month or, at his request, for an individual hour during the week which followed the group meeting. The individual sets of parents were also seen once a month, though they unanimously objected to being brought together as a parents' group when offered this option.

Location

The group was seen in a private office surrounded by a large grassy lawn which was used by the group as a touch football field, marked off in ten yard segments and covering approximately forty yards between goal lines.

Method, Materials, and Process

The basic method used was one which could be called "half talk and half action." Action took the form of developing individual and group leadership by asking the group to select two different team captains or quarterbacks each week. The captains then chose three players for each team from the remaining six members. Different captains were chosen each week until all eight members had a chance to function in that role.

Each team captain planned and called the plays for a touch football game which covered about half an hour of the group session. After the game, the group would critique the strengths and weaknesses of each of the team captains and how they could improve their leadership roles. The group leader functioned as the referee and linesman for the game and as the discussion moderator or coach for the critique that followed. A chalkboard was used to record the key concepts, to outline plays which the group felt had been responsible for the scores and the plays which failed.

The group leader helped the group shift its focus, first to reviewing aspects of active leadership and passive role following, then to good and poor sportsmanship on the playing field that morning, and, finally, to similar situations and feelings experienced by each member of the group at home, in school, and in his peer interaction in the community during the week which had passed.

Each member was encouraged to make his own "chalk talk" on the board in discussing the experiences and issues which had been either pleasant or very unpleasant. Role playing as a method of suggesting alternative ways of solving the problems which came up turned out to be a very effective process for both the group and for the individuals. Ventilation of conflicts and feelings was often hot and heavy. The group learned to make appropriate comments and inquiries into issues raised by individual members and clearly copied and, at times, emulated the group leader's style of interaction, intervention, and interpretation. Actually, the group leader often made only moderate initial interpretations which the group explored in more detail as they supported and confronted the various individual members on issues as they developed.

By the fourth month, the group had reached a high level of group cohesion and mutual concern for each other and for the individual differences which emerged. They were able both to affirm their sense of self-value as individuals and to accept the wide range of differences among themselves. The process of group cohesion and mutual support became so strong that, by the sixth month, several dramatic personality changes emerged. Two boys who had been passive, shy, and easily led became more assertive and more respected for their ability to analyze situations and to recommend constructive coping patterns for the problems which had been presented.

One interesting "resonance" phenomenon occurred in the sixth month. A group member who had been depressed at the outset over flunking three out of four courses began to make his move around the examinations at the end of the first semester. He had gained considerable self-confidence and poise through his leadership experiences in the group and had allowed this experience to carry over into the classroom. His grades had risen progressively in the daily work and he was surprised, and rather amazed, to find that, for the first time in his school experience, he did not "clutch" during his semester examinations. In fact, he did so well that, on the basis of his exam grades, he was eligible for the Honor Roll. However, his early failures in the first two marking periods lowered his average.

For the group, however, he became the "hero." It was the first time he had ever had such peer group acceptance and recognition. At the same time, a group contagion and group resonance effect followed. Several others felt they were as smart as this member in the touch football games and began to show healthier motivation for their own mastery of learning. Two who had strongly opposed tutoring at the outset of the school year agreed to be tutored in math and in foreign languages when it became clear that their basic skills in these areas were very low. They wanted to keep up with the others in the group who had been "turned on" in the classroom by the academic success of the "hero" member.

Two members who had ventured to take over the group in the fourth and fifth months were skillfully put down by the other group members, and, at the same time, they became less angry, showed less motoric activity, and took on more of the Piagetian formal operation process in their thinking. They evidenced a more thoughtful and less egocentric pattern, became more logical in their thinking, and were more able to delay immediate gratification in the group, in their homes, and in their community activities.

Interestingly enough, sex, girls, and dating did not become a central theme until the spring prom season in May and early June. It was the oldest (14) and youngest (11) members of the group who brought in this topic. Both had girlfriends and were proud of their dating accomplishments. All members became very excited, highly verbal, and initially quite anxious, as the group focused so exclusively on this area. Jokes, both dirty and clean, served as the icebreaker and equalizer for some of the other members, who were developmentally still in late latency and not yet ready for *Playboy* magazine, discussions of adolescent masturbation, and highly fantasized and exaggerated details of the dating games described by these two group members.

Outcome

Seven of the eight members showed significant improvement in socialization skills, significant shifts toward more positive self-esteem, a marked decrease in both hostile aggressive feelings (with heretofore periodic depressive episodes) and in the need for immediate gratification, and an equally significant improvement in classroom learning. Two made the Honor Roll by the end of the school year, after having begun the year with almost total academic failure.

Only one used the group in an ambivalent fashion. Although he had been a loner and a chronic school failure problem for three years prior to entering the group, he was momentarily viewed as a second group leader because he was the oldest (14) and the most street-wise. As his self-confidence grew, he began to reach out to a drug and mini-commune cult in the community. He became more comfortable in all his social relationships, but sought out school-age friends whose value systems were the opposite of those of his parents. He dropped out of school to live with a girlfriend, but continued to come to the group. One week he came in on a drug high, which was very disturbing to the group but resulted in their eventual acceptance and support. Later that day, he left town with his girlfriend. Nevertheless, although living in another city, he continued to keep in touch with the group by writing post cards telling them of his life away from home. The group, in turn, sent him a birthday card and a short summary of each of the group meetings. Several weeks after the group ended, he returned to his home and formed a positive attachment and healthier identification with his father. In his follow-up hour with the therapist, he chose not to continue in individual therapy. However, he said that he knew what sex, life, and making a living were all about. He wanted to make it on his own. At the same time, he acknowledged in a warm, friendly, and appreciative way that his experience in the group "had turned his life upside down." He could see things more clearly now, and, most important, he felt his father had some good answers which he had not appreciated before coming into the group. "Survival," he said, "was pretty damn tough for a 15-year-old trying to make it on his own with a second mouth to feed."

The group ended as the school year ended: each boy felt good about his progress and that of his friends. All felt a sense of loss and sadness that their friend (the 14-year-old) had chosen to opt for another community group and for another way of life. They accepted his need to do it that way but felt compassion and concern for what the outcome of his choice might be. All seemed relieved when they received a postcard from the group therapist indicating that their friend had returned home and seemed to be doing well with his father and family.

Critique

The original purposes of the group were these:

(1) to develop leadership skills to offset feelings of low self-esteem;
(2) to develop some alternative coping skills to deal with the problems associated with SLD and late latency/early adolescence;
(3) to develop greater insight into the feelings and conflicts over sex and aggression which are part of becoming a teenager, and to work out in a group setting age-appropriate ways of handling such conflicts;
(4) to improve communications and age-appropriate social functioning within the family systems represented by the individual members of the group; and
(5) to improve cognitive skills and to master academic learning at or near grade levels.

Although no evaluative or critical research design had been set up to measure outcome from the process described, the subjective responses from the group members, their families, and their teachers were uniformly positive. Even the 14-year-old prodigal son found a new relationship with his father through a limited positive transference with the group leader and from the acceptance and support he received from the group and the group process.

Finally, two things were striking. First, *all* members had reacted positively in the late 1960s to an experience which is now being referred to as "assertiveness training." The shifts in self-esteem away from a sense of self-pity, self-depreciation, and hurt pride (narcissistic wounding) were dramatic.

Second, the positive group contagion and subsequent "group resonance" phenomenon surprised everyone, including the parents, the teachers, the group leader, and the group members themselves. These two factors, along with the group balance and neutrality of the group leader, seemed to be the important factors in the success of the group process described.

Contrasting Methods

Kraft (1968) reviewed the literature on group therapy with adolescents up to that time. He indicated that the greatest number of papers dealt with group treatment of delinquent adolescents. Several authors reported on therapy groups for adolescent retardates, but only one paper was found which related to group therapy for children with minimal brain dysfunction (Anderson, 1968).

Key issues highlighted in Kraft's review included:

(1) the advantages and disadvantages of uni- or monosexual versus mixed sexual (coed) teenage groups (however, no paper presented actual experiences of group therapy with mixed sexes at this late latency or early adolescent age level);

(2) the importance of group selection in obtaining a balanced group with workable heterogeneous factors as opposed to a high density of acting out members;

(3) duration of sessions, optimally kept to a minimum of one hour and a maximum of one and a half hours (the life of the groups reported varied from four months to two years or more);

(4) the selection of therapists and the advantages and disadvantages of single-sex versus coed cotherapists (there were no final conclusions);

(5) unanimous opinion that confidentiality of the material produced needed to be maintained (otherwise, the group became "an instrumentality of the adults" in the individual adolescent's hierarchy, rather than a functional expression of the adolescents);

(6) guidelines for parental involvement, indicating approval of communication to the group those things which the parents may

have said without giving reciprocal information to the parents (this practice was at variance with the author's method of handling this issue in the group described above. No information from the parents was shared with the group. Rather, relevant information might be shared with the individual group member in an individual therapy hour. Likewise, the group was en-encouraged *not* to talk with anyone outside the group about *specific content* which came up in the group discussions but to feel free to speak or not to speak in generalities about the group activity, so long as these statements did not violate any group member's individual privacy. The group seemed very comfortable with these guidelines, and because parents were seen on a monthly basis they, too, were accepting of this process);

(7) use of a combination of individual and group psychotherapy (Garland *et al.,* 1962; Karmial, 1962) (however, it was not clear from Kraft's review how or if parents were included in the treatment model such as that described by the author);

(8) control of the groups, with focus on setting few limits, while emphasizing that no act which might result in bodily injury to self or others would be permitted, and on free and open verbalization (also, the group process was initially and periodically to be stated and interpreted to the members as a therapeutic process [Becker *et al.,* 1963]);

(9) utilization of interpretations with an ego orientation and the mastery of socialization skills as a paramount goal (Slavson [1962] asserted that a transference neurosis could not be worked through in group therapy).

In concluding his review, Kraft observed that evaluation of adolescent group therapy up to 1968 was more empirical and impressionistic than controlled and statistical.

In a more recent statement, MacLennan (1977) has indicated that, in late latency and early adolescence (12 to 15 years), boys and girls are highly self-conscious and so easily embarrassed or uneasy with the opposite sex that single-sex groups are preferable to coed or mixed sex groups.

Concerning content and group process, MacLennan suggested that this age group has more interest in discussing problems, and the majority of sessions may be verbal ones. He acknowledged the need for occasional breaks for exercises or games, but made no specific reference to the use of more organized games for leadership or assertiveness training, as was described in the author's experience. He also described the transitional activity/interview group process for adolescents who were reluctant to face or discuss interpersonal or emotional problems.

In such a process, the group would begin as any activity therapy group but would use a different selection of materials more suited to teenagers, such as a phonograph for background music or for dancing, more discussion at refreshment time, and the use of planned trips or camping as reinforcement experiences.

Finally, it should be recognized that there is a variety of programs in this age group which have focused on the development of survival skills through group camping, such as Outward Bound, and other programs which feature behavior modification as a core principle. This later topic will be included in the discussion in Chapter 11.

MIDDLE AND LATE ADOLESCENCE

Contrary to expectations, the author found that a group set up for this age within his private practice seemed to show the least progress for each group member in response to a group therapy approach. It had been anticipated, from the knowledge that middle and late adolescence is a period of greater stability and reduced aggressive and sexual conflicts, that a group with SLD at these ages would make significant use of the group therapy process.

Composition

Six teenage boys (two 16 years, two 17 years, one 18, and one 19 years of age) were included in the group. All six had been in individual therapy with the group leader, and three had worked with this therapist while attending a private school for children with learning disabilities. At the time, two of these three were attending a local high school, while the third had graduated with a high school equivalency degree and was not working. Of the other three, one was a high school graduate working full-time in a local industry. The three students from the private school setting showed clinical and educational signs of a central nervous system dysfunction significantly affecting their academic learning. Of the three remaining group members, one clearly showed a pattern of SLD extending back to fourth grade, with associated emotional problems which included moderate drug abuse, frequent school truancy, and several episodes of running away from home. The employed high school graduate presented problems with sustained motivation during his schooling, major problems in socialization which centered around introversion, egocentricity, reluctance to interact with groups of boys or girls, preoccupation with auto mechanics and sexy magazines, and a mother-son conflictual pattern extending back to an earlier age when the parents separated and eventually divorced. He was mentally bright, academically an underachiever, and could not be considered an SLD adolescent. The sixth member of the group had a severe mental illness a year before the group began and had been on homebound instruction for the last six months of the previous school year. He was beginning his senior year in high school at the time the group started. He had no specific learning problem but was included in the group because of his shyness and passivity. It was hoped that the group would help him increase his verbal fluency, make him more comfortable in a small group setting, and help him mobilize a degree of assertiveness and spontaneous aggressiveness which, up to this time, had always been turned inward, resulting in periodic episodes of depression, withdrawal, and isolation.

Coed Leadership

A female cotherapist was selected to share in the leadership role. Although not trained in a formal sense, she had attended several seminars on behavior problems of childhood and adolescence given by the group therapist and had worked as his assistant and executive secretary for several years in a teaching institution. Her role was defined as cotherapist and social director for the group.

Location

The group met one night a week, from 7:30 to approximately midnight, for 9 months, in a large recreation room in the home of the author, who functioned as one of the cotherapists. The room was set up with a record player, ping-pong table, several sofas, tables for chess, cards and checkers, floor lamps, and several comfortable chairs, placed in an informal way around a fireplace.

Method and Process

The format of the group was to follow a democratic agenda which was developed by the group. The process focused on a balance between recreation and group discussions aimed at developing a greater understanding of human emotions (in this age range), how each individual experienced these emotions at home, in school, on the job, in intimate and less intimate relationships with the opposite sex, and in relationship to one another in the group.

There was a shift in topical emphases from how a boy handles himself on a date to what girls expect from boys, to problems at home and at school, to discussions on what it takes to make it on your own in today's society (survival skills), to discussions of vocational employment and the workaday world, to special topics of interest to the group. Some of these included brief presentations and demonstrations by members of the group on electronics, auto mechanics, favorite rock groups, travel, the drug culture, how to play chess, and what it is like to work 40 hours a week in industry. Also, at a time when the group became interested in some of the headlines related to the United States and a planned détente with Russia, the group leader presented slides of a trip he had taken to Russia the summer before, and the group attended a conference on relationships between Russia and the United States given in a nearby city by the American Academy of Political and Social Sciences. The group had a chance to gain some background and perspective about Russia and the United States prior to attending the Academy presentation and then had the opportunity to critique the total presentation while returning home on the train that evening and at the next group meeting as well.

On some evenings, the group discussion would last two hours, and the group would then go out for refreshments. On other evenings, the group went bowling or played miniature and pitch-and-putt golf for the first part of the evening, returning later to the recreation room for refreshments and group discussion. The format was usually planned one week ahead by group discussion and a group process.

In the first and second meetings with the group, the coed leaders opened up the possibility of the group becoming a coed group. None of the members was ready for this step, which seemed surprising in view of their ages. They agreed to consider the possibility of inviting a date for a series of parties in the spring. Yet, as the time for planning such an event approached, only one of the six seemed ready to participate in such a coed evening.

A single day retreat at a cabin in a nearby resort was planned for the fall and a similar weekend retreat arranged for late spring or early summer. Interestingly enough, neither of these was very successful, with only three of the group participating in the fall retreat, though all six had been enthusiastic about the idea when it was presented. The reasons for the "no shows" varied from needing to work (on a Saturday) to traveling with the family to not wanting to spend two hours traveling to and from the resort area. The spring retreat was also attended by only three members, two of whom had participated in the fall retreat.

The discussions were sometimes very intense, lively, enthusiastically received, and seemed to evoke degrees of healthy insight. The presence of the female cotherapist seemed to be the magnet which attracted full attendance for the first four months. Role playing, psychodrama, and occasional educational or illustrative chalkboard talks were given by the cotherapists. Individual therapy was included with each member on a monthly basis, or more frequently if indicated or requested. The parents were also seen on a monthly basis by the senior cotherapist.

Subgroup Formation

By the fourth month, it seemed clear that, instead of reaching a degree of group cohesion, three subtle subgroups had begun to form. The 17-year-old senior and the two high school graduates developed a fondness for one another and became a core for planning and enjoying each other's company. Retrospectively, they seemed to be enjoying their adolescent experiences, wanting no part of dating but becoming more interested in and competitive for the attention of the female cotherapist. The 16-year-old junior stabilized his school attendance, became more cooperative at home, and increased his dating pattern. He pushed for making the group coed, and, when the group did not move on his needs and suggestions, he dropped out in the seventh month. He told the group he was enjoying his dating during the week more than he was enjoying his meetings with them. He did agree to participate in a family therapy process for the balance of the school year and used that experience quite well. This was in marked contrast to his abuse of his family during the family therapy evaluation sessions prior to the group experience.

The two youngest members, aged 16 and 17 years, had become well acquainted and carried that friendship into a social experience outside the group. Each was essentially a "loner" in his own right but felt increasingly comfortable as part of a "dyad" in the group for the first four months. At first, they enjoyed chess and checkers in round-robin tournaments with other group members; but as the discussions focused more on dating and on working, they pulled out and finally split off from the group entirely in the fifth month, continuing to visit with one another in the community on weekends. One remained in individual therapy, while the other decided to discontinue all contact with the therapist, although his parents continued in monthly parent counseling.

Critique

The format for this group was a new venture for the author. Consequently, the purposes and objectives were less clear and probably not as well stated at the outset. The group and cotherapist were included very early in the planning and development of the group's agenda. The purposes of the group were briefly stated to the members in their individual therapy hours prior to the first group meeting and again at that meeting, as follows:

(1) to learn to think better, to share ideas, and to enter into a give and take relationship with a small group of teenagers;

(2) to learn to communicate feelings and ideas more freely and with greater confidence in order to handle things better in school and at home;

(3) to get a better sense of boy-girl relationships and what was involved in dating and establishing a courtship (five of the six group members had had no more than a single date with a girl prior to entering the group; the 19-year-old had had very few dates and appeared to be functioning nearer a 14-year level than a 19-year level in his interpersonal relationships); and

(4) to discuss issues related to survival skills in the workaday world and in play, and to develop and practice, in a small peer group setting, ways of coping with the realities of the world in which they were living and growing.

No evaluative research was done on the process described. The subjective responses from the group members, their families, and teachers were highly variable. Two made significant progress in school but shifted very little in their basic characterological patterns. The remaining four continued to show essentially the same psychopathology at the end of the group experience as they had manifested at the outset. The single variable which showed the greatest change in all six members was their sense of group belonging and "other" relatedness. It could be fairly stated that, in the beginning, all six were essentially egocentric, self-centered, and had a minimum of social interaction skills, functioning nearer the 13- to 14-year social and emotional levels than at their stated age. All showed a significant increase in their sense of "other" relatedness, and, taking into account the subgroup process formation, each member demonstrated a healthier sense of group belonging. Apart from the two members who showed very definite increase in learning and cognitive skills, the remaining four members showed very little shift or change in their capacity to master learning within a school setting.

Although no personality studies were done in a pre- and posttest fashion, it seems clear, in retrospect, that, of the three groups described in this chapter, the individual members of this group presented more deeply internalized character patterns and more severely disturbed object relationship patterns, conflicts in masculine-feminine identification, and delayed socialization of aggressive and sexual drives than were present in the younger groups.

SUMMARY

An attempt has been made in Table 8.2 to summarize the key issues in planning for group therapy with SLD/MBD/HKS children and adolescents. The table covers the three sections described, including age range, group size, nature of the appropriate activities, and the key psychological issues which unfold through the group process.

The table highlights the importance of designing the group according to the age, developmental stage, and type of problem present in the population included in the group. The group process will be strongly influenced by the number and nature of the problems in the group members, the setting in which the group is held, the degree of structure and control exercised by the group leader, the philosophy and training of the group leader, as well as the kind and quality of leadership, including role modeling, benevolent firmness, and countertransference behavior activated by some of the group members.

Table 8.2
Issues in Planning Group Therapy
for SLD Children and Adolescents

Age Range	Size	Activity	Key Processes
Preschool and early latency (Section 1)	Small group (3-5)	Focused topic Tight structure Focused activity	Limited time Flexible format Use functional space Careful observations Identify ego mechanisms of defense within group setting Minimum interpretation Encourage mutual group support and constructive group confrontation Minimize scapegoating Follow-up Evaluative research
Late latency and early adolescence (Section 2)	Larger group (5-8)	Half-talk and half-action e.g. sports, music, art, and movement (See Chapter 12)	Develop leadership Group cohesion Role modeling Mutual concern for individual differences Acceptance of individual differences Moderate interpretations Group resonance Revolving door concept for new members Follow-up Evaluative research
Middle and late adolescence (Section 3)	Variable (5-8)	Coeducational (optional) Democratic agenda Shifting topical emphasis with opportunities for individual leadership Weekend retreats Survival skills (e.g. outward bound), vocational topics, and trips Practicing life skills	Co-leader model Role playing Balance verbal insight with appropriate recreational outlets Opportunities to work out aggressive strivings in socially acceptable ways Non-judgmental leadership which encourages open discussion of sexuality, dating patterns, and individual and social values Follow-up Evaluative research

REFERENCES

Anderson, J. Group therapy with brain-damaged children. *Hospital Community Psychiatry,* 1968, *19,* 175–176.

Anderson, N. & Marrone, J. Group therapy for emotionally disturbed children: A key to affective education. *American Journal of Orthopsychiatry,* 1977, *47*(1), 97–103.

Becker, B, Guare, R., & MacNicol, E. A clinical study of a group psychotherapy program for adolescents. *Psychiatric Quarterly,* 1963, *37,* 685–703.

Bessel, H. *Methods in human development therapy manual* (revised). San Diego: Human Development Training Institute, 1970.

Erikson, E. *Childhood and society* (2nd ed., rev.). New York: W. W. Norton, 1963.

Foulkes, S. & Anthony, E. *Group psychotherapy: The psychoanalytic approach* (2nd ed.). Baltimore: Penguin, 1968.

Freud, A. Adolescence. *Psychoanalytic Study of the Child,* 1958, *13,* 255–278.

Gardner, G. Problems of learning deficits in children. *Proceedings, Fifth Annual Conference of Mental Health,* Representatives of State Medical Association, Chicago, Illinois, 1958.

Gardner, R. *MBD: The family book about minimal brain dysfunction.* New York: Jason Aronson, 1973.

Garland, J., Kolodny, R., & Waldfogel, S. Social group work as adjunctive treatment for the emotionally disturbed adolescent: The experience of a specialized group work department. *American Journal of Orthopsychiatry,* 1962, *32,* 691–706.

Ginott, G. *Group psychotherapy with children: The theory and practice of play therapy.* New York: McGraw-Hill, 1961.

Glass, S. *The practical handbook of group counseling.* Baltimore: Behavioral Consultation Services, 1969.

Illovsky, J. & Fredman, N. Group suggestions in learning disabilities of primary grade children: A feasibility study. *International Journal of Clinical and Experimental Hypnosis,* 1976, *24*(2), 87–95.

Karmial, A. Some observations on concomitant individual and group treatment for adolescents. *International Journal of Group Psychotherapy,* 1962, *12,* 374–375.

Kraft, I. An overview of group therapy with adolescents. *International Journal of Group Psychotherapy,* 1968, *18,* 461–480.

MacLennan, B. Modification of activity group therapy for children. *International Journal of Group Psychotherapy,* 1977, *27*(1), 85–96.

MacLennan, B. & Felsenfeld, N. *Group counseling and psychotherapy with adolescents.* New York: Columbia University Press, 1968.

Rank, O. *Will therapy and truth and reality.* New York: Alfred A. Knopf, 1945.

Rome, H. Group therapy: Part II, introductory remarks. *Psychiatric Annals,* 1972, *2*(4), 7.

Ross, A. *Discussion of papers on learning problems in adolescence.* Presented at the meeting of the American Orthopsychiatric Association. New York, New York, March, 1965.

Schamess, G. Group treatment modalities for latency-age children. *International Journal of Group Psychotherapy,* 1976, *26,* 455–473.

Slavson. S. *An introduction to group therapy.* New York: Commonwealth Fund, 1943.

Slavson, S. Patterns of acting out of a transference neurosis by an adolescent boy. *International Journal of Group Psychotherapy,* 1962, *12,* 211–224.

Slavson, S. *A textbook in analytic group psychotherapy.* New York: International Universities Press, 1964.

Slavson, S. & Schiffer, M. *Group psychotherapies for children: A textbook.* New York: International Universities Press, 1975.

Sperry, B., Staner, N., Reiner, B., & Ulrich, D. Renunciation and denial in learning difficulties. *American Journal of Orthopsychiatry,* 1958, *28,* 98–111.

Sugar, M. Interpretive group psychotherapy with latency children. *Journal of American Academy of Child Psychiatry,* 1974, *13*(4), 648–666.

Yalom, I. *Theory and practice of group psychotherapy.* New York: Basic Books, 1970.

CHAPTER 9

THE TIME OUT AND LIFE SPACE INTERVIEW PROCESSES

WILLIAM C. ADAMSON, M.D.

All things move within your being in constant half embrace,
the desired and the dreaded, the repugnant and the cherished,
the pursued and that which you would escape ... thus your
freedom when it loses its fetters becomes itself the fetter
of a greater freedom.

—Kahlil Gibran, *The Prophet*

INTRODUCTION

There has been an increasing emphasis on controlling behavior
in children in educational and institutional settings in the United States
during the last decade (Schrag and Divoky, 1975). Behavior management and behavior modification have been placed next to medication as
prescriptions to control today's children, especially those with hyperactivity associated with SLD or impulsive acting out associated with
MBD. This chapter will deal with two procedures used to help children
and adolescents in their interactive dialogues and behavioral reactions
to the experience of growing up socially, emotionally, educationally, and
morally in our culture. These are the Time Out and Life Space Interview processes.

Case Study 9.1

SLD/MBD IMPULSIVE ACTING OUT AND THE
TIME OUT PROCESS

Jackie was an 11-year-old boy whose father left his mother when she became pregnant with him. She tried to interrupt the pregnancy early with a variety of chemical douches but without success. By the fourth month she decided to have the baby. Since it was a first pregnancy, labor was long (8 to 10 hours) and delivery somewhat difficult (occiput posterior). All postnatal signs in the neonate were within normal limits. However, Jackie's mother elected to place him for adoption by the third postpartum day.

Jackie was in five foster homes by the age of 9. He walked early at 11 months, but speech developed more slowly, and a psychological evaluation at the time of his admission to a residential treatment center revealed bright-normal mental functioning with scatter in both verbal and performance subtests, supporting the clinical impression of the MBD Syndrome. Neurological evaluation revealed several key "soft signs," and his EEG was read as abnormal due to generalized slowing and increased amplitude in all leads in response to hyperventilation and rapid photic stimulation. Emotionally, Jackie was an orally dependent boy who showed a great deal of oral aggressivity with feelings of being unwanted, defective, and very angry at the grown-ups in his life. The continual threat of being abandoned made him afraid of forming close relationships and kept him in the rapprochement phase of object relationships (Mahler *et al.,* 1975), with deep narcissistic needs which were never truly satisfied. By age 10 and 11, Jackie had begun to act out in destructive ways his anger, negativism, and feelings of rage in any situation in which he felt abandoned, unloved, or misunderstood. As a result, he became so unmanageable that repeated foster families requested he be relocated because of his destructive behavior. He was finally placed in a residential treatment center.

MISUSE OF FREEDOM ROOM

Every morning, between 8:00 and 9:30 a.m., Jackie would awaken in the treatment center and begin to go into his "Jackie maneuvers." These consisted of insulting the staff on duty, going on a rampage by upsetting or throwing chairs in his room, tearing his sheets, and using the corner of his room for his morning toilet. As a result, he was placed in the time-out or "freedom" room until all the other children were out of the unit and in school. While in this special room, Jackie continued to yell and soil, smear, and injure himself. Some days he came out by midmorning and had a good day. Other days, even with medication, he continued agitated, negativistic, and depressed to the point of attempting to injure and mutilate his body.

ANOTHER POINT OF VIEW

A field surveyor for the Joint Commission on Accreditation of Hospitals became aware of Jackie's situation in the process of evaluating the treatment center. Following a clinical hunch, the evaluator reviewed the facility's well-documented logs as to the time of day when the time-out room was most frequently used by Jackie and by a small number of other children who showed similar patterns of uncontrolled motoric activity which could not be managed.

Careful scrutiny of the logs disclosed that 90% of the "time-outs" in that unit occurred between 8:00 and 9:30 a.m. In discussing with the Child Care Staff the quality of the residential environment during that hour-and-a-half period, several factors were identified which seemed to have a direct bearing on the poor behavioral control seen in those boys, particularly Jackie, at that early hour in the morning:

(1) There was a change in shift of Child Care Staff around 7:00 a.m., so new staff came on as the night staff separated from the children.

(2) The unit was understaffed between 7:00 and 8:00 a.m., at a time when the children were awakening, most active, not yet fully in control of their mental faculties, and needing more rather than less personal one-to-one contact.

(3) The children did not eat breakfast until 8:30 a.m. and often were in a hypoglycemic phase of metabolism from the time they awakened at 7:00 a.m. until breakfast at 8:30 a.m.

(4) Finally, most of the children had developmental histories similar to those of Jackie, which included poor object relationship experiences, a lack of basic trust in the maternal caretaker, a sense of betrayal and abandonment by one or both parents, and an extensive feeling of hurt pride and narcissistic wounding which resulted in the failure of these children to reach satisfactority the rapprochement phase of object relationships de-

scribed by Mahler *et al.* (1975). This subphase of separation and differentiation allows for the melding together of the libidinal and aggressive drives in the process of personality development.

(5) The result was a tragic Double Destructive Pattern in which the children were separated from staff and peers at a time when they most needed acceptance and support, and they continued to be so wounded by this procedure that they established a chronic pattern of failure in this critical rapprochement subphase.

SOME POSITIVE SUGGESTIONS

Recognizing the metabolic and dynamic relationship needs being reenacted daily by the children and recorded faithfully by the staff, the surveyor made the following suggestions:

(1) Increase by one or two persons the coverage during the early morning hours.

(2) Give the early, hyperactive risers orange juice as they awaken, or nearer 7:30 than 8:30 a.m.

(3) If the time-out room must be used because of behavior dangerous to the child or to other children, arrange to have a staff person sit with the child rather than isolate and abandon him in a fashion which reduplicates the original and subsequent psychological insults.

OUTCOME

First, there was a significant change in the early morning behavior of Jackie and his hyperkinetic associates. Second, there was a marked decrease in the use of the time-out room. Finally, there was perceptible evidence of a greater response to individual and milieu therapy among those children who had been out of control, along with an increased readiness on the part of Jackie and the other children to bring their aggressive and sexual drives more into harmony with one another while moving toward the object constancy phase of differentiation and development.

USE OF THE TIME OUT PROCESS

In the interface between the expressions of individuality and the personal compliance necessary for socialization and acculturalization,

Table 9.1
Social and Learning Theory Models
Related to the Psychology of Discipline

Theorist	Area of Involvement	Key Issues in Discipline
Erikson	Ego Epigenesis	Basic Trust vs. Mistrust Autonomy vs. Shame and Guilt Initiative vs. Doubt
Freud	Ego Development and Superego Formation	Repetition-Compulsion Fixation Regression Identification and Internalization Fear of Retaliation or Mutilation Neutralization and Sublimation of Sexual and Aggressive Drives Resolution of Oedipal/Electra Complexes Reality Testing
Rank	Organization and Differentiation of the Will	Positive and Negative Will Separation and Guilt Will Struggle between Parent and Child Opposition and Collusion Assertion and Denial of Self Life Fear and Death Fear
Mahler	Separation and Individuation	Mutuality Practicing Separateness Interdependence Trust and Object Constancy
Piaget	Cognitive Function in an Interactional System	Assimilation by Action Omnipotence Egocentrism Preoperational and Formal Thought Processes Symbolic Representation in Language Moral Judgments in Rules and Games
Parsons	Ecological and Social Systems	Larger System of Interaction Tension Management and Pattern Maintenance Adaptation System-Goal Attainment Integration of Goals
Skinner	Operant Conditioning	Positive and Negative Reinforcement Contingencies Token Systems Aversive Methods Intermittent Reinforcement

Table 9.1 *(Continued)*

Theorist	Area of Involvement	Key Issues in Discipline
Hull	Systematic Behavior	Habit Formation and Strength Stimulus Intensity Incentive Motivation Generalized Habit Strength Reactive Inhibition Conditioned Inhibition Reaction Potential Evoked Response
Tolman	Sign Learning or Purposive Behavior Conditioning	Need Systems Belief Value Matrices Behavior Spaces Reward Expectancies Place Learning Latent Learning Confirmation vs. Reinforcement
Lewin	Field Theory of Interpersonal Relationships	Vectors in Life Space Distance and Direction Positive and Negative Valences Motivation Group Dynamics Time Dimension

there lies a whole matrix of complex psychological phenomena. What seems like a simple process of sending disruptive children to their rooms or fractious students to the principal's office (or Time Out room) actually represents an incredibly complex interchange between disciplining adults and the disciplined children. The content of Table 9.1 illustrates in outline form some of the psychological complexities involved in the presumably simple process of disciplining normal children. Hilgard (1948) has written a good description of the concepts of most of these theorists.

SLD/MBD/HKS children have the same need for discipline as normal children. Very often, however, they react to discipline with greater emotional intensity than normal children while struggling with a lesser capacity to cope with and handle the situations requiring discipline, as well as the discipline itself.

Case Study 9.2

SLD AND THE PSYCHOLOGY OF DISCIPLINE

The case study of Cheri elaborates on the relevance of the Social and Learning Theory Models to the psychology of discipline as presented in Table 9.1. Cheri was a slow developing latency girl who came from a family of high achievers, including two older siblings who were honor roll students (cf. Parson's pattern maintenance in a Family Ecosystem). She was a strong-willed little girl who, from an early age, had been struggling to affirm her own innate difference from her mother's expectations of her (cf. Mahler's separation and individuation and Rank's differentiation of will). The will struggle between mother and daughter peaked during the toilet training years, when Cheri became oppositional, negative, and withholding of both emotions and body wastes. After two years of battling with her mother, she developed feelings of guilt whenever she asserted herself (cf. Erikson's Autonomy vs. Shame and Guilt).

As she began her preschool and first grade experiences, Cheri had many problems. Because of some clumsiness in fine motor manipulation skills and a deficit in auditory discrimination of vowel sounds, she had great difficulty listening or taking directions from the teachers. No clear-cut case could be made for MBD, but she was clearly an SLD child. She felt the whole world should be centered around satisfying her needs (cf. Piaget's Omnipotence and Egocentrism) and was totally unable to risk new learning experiences because of the fear of failure and displeasing her teacher (cf. Erikson's Initiative vs. Doubt, Rank's Life Fear and Death Fear, and Freud's Fear of Retaliation). Increasingly, she became a tyrant on the playground and at home and a withdrawn dormouse in the classroom. She had been poorly programmed in all areas of Operant, Systematic, and Purposive Behavior Conditioning (cf. Skinner's Negative Reinforcement, Aversive Methods and Negative Shaping Behavior; Hull's Habit Formation, Stimulus Intensity, Incentive Motivation, etc.; Tolman's Need System, Reward Expectancies and Confirmation of Inadequacies vs. Reinforcement of her positive values). Finally, she had set herself as scapegoat to be punished at home and to fail and be ostracized at school (cf. Lewin's Negative Valences, disruption of Group Dynamics, and significant Vectors in Life Space; and Freud's Repetition-Compulsion in assuming a Masochistic, self-suffering position secondary to emotionally traumatic fixations at an earlier anal-sadistic level of development).

When Cheri entered a special school at age 8 years, she tested out the school environment, running the gamut of social, emotional, familial, and cognitive learning experiences through which she had lived in the prior eight years. She became demanding, aggressive, oppositional, negative, belligerent, defiant, and passively aggressive. She was a major management problem in the classroom. The question for the classroom teacher and supportive staff was how to help Cheri get back on a healthier developmental track with her family and, at the same time, help her become more accessible for learning. The Time Out process figured prominently in this reeducation process, along with individual psychotherapy for Cheri (see Chapter 6) and parent counseling for her parents (see Chapter 7). Some of the procedures suggested in the chapters on Behavior Modification (Chapter 11), Family Therapy (Chapter 10), and the Creative Art Therapies (Chapter 12) also might have been effective interventions.

The balance of this section will describe the concept of Time Out, indications for its use, some methods used in effecting the Time Out experience for a child, and some of the precautions for its use.

The Concept

Essentially, the Time Out concept is conceived as a means of enabling responsible adults to "call time" in the unfolding processes of our children's social, emotional, and cognitive development; that is, to call for or set in motion a period of time during which the intervention between guiding adults and responding or nonresponding children may be temporarily halted, or a time during which the direction and intention of the stimuli from the adults may be flexibly changed, reduced, or withdrawn. This may be accomplished by placing some physical distance between the interactive parties, by removing prior expectations placed on the reacting children, or by introducing new, nonconflictual content or action into the heretofore emotionally overheated interchange.

The Indications for Use of the TIME OUT Process

It is important for teachers of SLD/MBD/HKS children, parents of these children, and other educational and clinical persons to know and understand the indications for the use of the Time Out process. Table 9.1 serves as the conceptual framework from which this list of indications has been drawn.

The Time Out process should be used at home and in school for SLD/MBD/HKS children and adolescents for the following behavioral situations:

I.   To *register disapproval and disappointment* when unacceptable behavior persists in the face of admonitions and warnings.
     (a) *Reinforce verbally* that the behavior is not socially acceptable for the (social) age of the child or adolescent. For example, "You were acting more like a 4-year-old than a 14-year-old."
     (b) *Separate the feelings* for the child and disapproval of the behavior. For example, "I like you, but I don't like what you did, or said, or the way you acted."

II. To *decompress the situation* by allowing a cooling-off period, that is:
     (a) *time for controlled regression* of behavior in the service of the ego,
     (b) *time to save face,* dry tears, and momentarily leave the frustrating situation,
     (c) *time for reorganization of the Self,* which includes:
         (1) reestablishing basic trust and mutuality in responsible adults,
         (2) reestablishing a sense of autonomy and self-assertion,
         (3) reestablishing secondary process thinking (as opposed to more primitive, egocentric, primary process thinking) and improved reality testing. For example, "Maybe they are right. The next time, I should wait my turn and tell them how I feel, not spit in my brother's face because he got his dessert before I got mine."

III. To *break up an emotional impasse* with the adults involved, which would serve:
     (a) *to partialize or avoid a will struggle,*
     (b) *to alleviate* the fear of physical injury or retaliation by the adults,
     (c) *to alter* the established mental set of the adults and children involved (i.e., to undo elements of the repetition-compulsion in the disciplining adults and the disciplined child/adolescent).

IV. To *demonstrate a sense of fairness,* firmness, and flexibility, as well as an adult stance of sensitivity, strength, and personality style in handling the role of the responsible adult (i.e., shaping behavior through serving as a role model in the handling of assertive feelings and hostile-aggressive impulses which may have been provoked and/or aroused by the child or adolescent.

V. To *encourage age-appropriate action, assimilation, and integration* in the interpersonal relationship between adult and child, rather than allowing and reinforcing in the child a prolonged sense of omnipotence and egocentrism beyond age-appropriate levels for these behaviors.

VI. To *alter the existing pattern-maintenance* which has increased the tension with the adult-child dyad and/or within the larger eco-system of family, neighborhood, classroom, and school.

VII. To *allow adaptive responses to develop* through giving up old patterns and trying out new ones.

VIII. To *define and develop new constructive interpersonal relationship patterns* in response to conflictual issues and to discover new system-goal attainment objectives when that response is appropriate.

IX. To *reduce negative reinforcement* in learning experiences which have been characterized by continuous failure, and to reinforce appropriate responses in relationship to prior rules and previously stated contingencies.

X. To *alter the habit formation,* direction, and intensity of stimuli, and reintroduce new and familiar incentive motivation.

XI. To *assess the need systems* of both adults and children in conflict with one another; to restate and reformulate in less threatening ways the belief-value matrices and reward expectancies; and to attain between adult and child mutual confirmation of readiness to sustain growth on a developmental or learning issue.

XII. To *support the needs of the larger groups* (family, classmates, peer groups, and residential cottage populations) vis-à-vis the demands, disruption, and partial deterioration of socially acceptable behavior of the individual.

The Method

The method of applying the Time Out process is basically a three-step procedure:

(1) Warn or alert the child that his/her behavior is "out of bounds" and not acceptable.

(2) Set up degrees of separation, distance, and social isolation between the troubled child or adolescent and the adults, family members, or classmates with whom there is conflict. The degree of separation ranges on a continuum from partial separation and minimal isolation to total separation and isolation, as suggested in the outline below.

(3) After the Time Out period, work and dialogue with the child or adolescent in an emotionally controlled and low-key way to seek alternatives in his/her development, should the same interactive conflict or crises arise again.

I. *Partial separation* and minimal isolation is initiated by the responsible adult:

   (a) when the child is told to stand or sit in a separate part of the classroom or in the hall outside the classroom, to leave the dining room table at home and go to an adjoining room, or through the following contingencies:

      (1) "Until you are ready to settle down and rejoin the group without being upset," or

      (2) "Until I (teacher, parent, other adult) feel you are ready to rejoin the group."

   (b) when the child is partially separated from the group and receives a "fine" which must be "paid off," such as:

      (1) denial of watching television or of shopping privileges,

      (2) staying in the classroom for x minutes during recess or after school, standing apart from the group for x minutes, or going to bed x minutes earlier than usual.

   The key to remember is that many of the psychological issues outlined in Table 9.1 have become activated prior to and during the interaction that led to the need for such a Time Out process. It is important, therefore, to "read" the child's needs in relationship to these developmental issues before acting in an authoritarian or punitive way which will only aggravate rather than alleviate the interactive crisis.

II. *Moderate separation and isolation* is initiated when the teacher, parent, or residential counselor denies the child a privilege (recess or television) and removes the child from the classroom or family room to a previously designated area, such as the principal's office or to his/her own room. The door is kept open to allow an ongoing feeling of connectedness.

Behavior modification, as described in Chapter 11, would view this procedure as negative reinforcement and would attempt to set up contingency and token reward systems reinforcing socially acceptable interactive behavior while penalizing unacceptable behavior with lack of rewards.

III.   *Total separation and isolation* is initiated when the responsible adult places the child outside the immediate interactive area, usually in an isolation room designated as "the seclusion room," "the freedom room," "the Time Out room," or various other euphemisms. In the home, this may be the child's room with the door closed (but not locked).

In institutions and agencies where this degree of isolation is used, as in the case of Jackie (Case Study 9.1), very stringent and specific guidelines have been written to govern the use of such "freedom" rooms.

For example, the accreditation manual of the Psychiatric Facilities Serving Children and Adolescents of the Joint Commission on Accreditation of Hospitals (1974) states the following:

When seclusion is used, the facility shall have written policies which delineate the staff members who may authorize its use and the conditions under which it may be used. Seclusion shall not be used as punishment. Patients in seclusion shall be under frequent observation. Each use of seclusion and the condition or event necessitating its use shall be documented in the patient's clinical record. The written order of a physician, renewable every twenty-four hours, shall be required for seclusion for a period of longer than one hour. When specific areas have been designated to be used for seclusion, they shall take into account the needs of the patients and their human dignity. (p. 63)

The Division of Youth and Family Services (DYFS) of the New Jersey Department of Human Services has an equally clear and thoughtfully prepared document, "Behavior Management Room Statement," which delineates their policy. Briefly, the highlights of that statement include, the following topics:

(1) *Introduction.* Whenever the use of restrictive physical controls are imposed, the act in itself is potentially traumatic. The use of such controls must be applied with understanding and sensi-

tivity. A behavior management room may be used as a therapeutic tool to provide a child with firm, direct structure during
a time when he/she is seemingly out of control and poses a
threat to himself/herself or others; these rooms should not be
used punitively.

(2) *General rules to govern use of the room.* Person responsible for
supervising the child in the room must remain sufficiently close
to ensure the safety and well being of the occupant. Visual
checks should be made on the child every ten minutes, or more
frequently if necessary. No child shall remain in the room for
more than two hours in any twenty-four hour period. A report
utilization log should be filled out immediately following the
child's discharge from the room. When the room is not in use,
it should be locked to prevent unauthorized use. No more than
one child shall be placed in a behavior management room at
any one time, except when a staff member remains in the room
during the entire period of multiple occupancy, and children
placed in quiet rooms, unless constantly with staff, shall not have
belts, matches, knives, or any other objects with which to inflict
self-injury.

(3) *Objectives and criteria for use.* Essentially, these include what
has been described above as indications for use such as Time
Out for clearly defined, inappropriate behaviors, and confinement is limited to five minutes or less; calming the overly agitated or excited child, with the duration of confinement only as
long as the agitation and tension persists; and protection when
an extremely aggressive or apparently psychotic child poses a
threat to himself, to others, or to property. The duration of
such confinement should not exceed the length of time required
for counseling or for one of the available therapies to have a
calming influence.

(4) *Physical design of the behavior room.* The door of the room
must be interlocked with the building's fire detection system,
so that, any time the fire alarm is activated, the door unlocks
and opens. In the absence of this interlock, the door shall not
be equipped with a locking device of any kind, or a staff member
shall remain in the behavior management room during the entire
period of a child's confinement. The door shall be equipped
with a plexiglass window, large enough and suitably located so
as to provide visibility of the entire room. The room should
be large enough (eight square feet), with lights mounted so as

to prevent tampering by the room's occupant. There should also be adequate ventilation in the room, including a one-inch space at the bottom of the door and a ceiling-mounted exhaust fan capable of moving a minimum of 150 cubic feet of air per minute. The exhaust fan and the light shall be operated by the same key-activated switch, mounted on the outside of the door. There shall be carpeting or padding on the floor and on each wall up to a six-foot level, and the wall should be completely free of objects.

(5) *Reporting on use of the room.* A utilization log giving name, date, time in and out of the room, the reason for the room's being used, and the initials of staff members making ten-minute obsrevations, along with a sentence describing the child's condition, will be included in the entry into the log.

(6) *Authority for use of the room.* The New Jersey agency does not require that the physician sign the order, but suggests that the decision to place the child in a behavior management room may be made by the child care worker with the approval of the agency head or other supervisory personnel. A report of each incident requiring isolation is to be prepared and signed by those staff members involved. The report is to include a summary of the incidents leading to isolation and those attempts which were made to resolve the situation prior to isolation. A copy of the report is then entered into the child's record as well as into the utilization log for the room.

Precautions for Use of the Time Out Process

While the Time Out process, as outlined, can be an effective method of supporting growth and change, it carries several pitfalls which should be recognized. Therefore, before relying on this process in working with SLD/MBD/HKS children and adolescents, the following precautions should be kept in mind:

(1) *Remember that any break in the interactional dialogue* between adults and students or children which results in a Time Out action will invariably be felt as punishment by the disciplined children and adolescents, rather than as support through an interactive crisis.

While some adults may wish that the message of punishment be conveyed to the children, greater emotional growth and stability will ensue if such an action is viewed as creative discipline (i.e. training, teaching, and guiding) rather than as a punitive "put down." Encouraging a positive reconnection with the children after the Time Out and suggesting other more adaptive behaviors will go a long way toward reestablishing basic trust, identification, an increased sense of self-esteem, and a continuing interactive dialogue between the concerned adults and developing SLD/MBD/HKS children.

(2) *Recognize that few parents, teachers, and clinicians can know and be aware of the manifold subtle and complex psychological* issues being hammered out on the anvil of the Time Out process. These were outlined in Table 9.1 to point up the complexities and to underline the thesis that the Time Out process is far more complicated than is generally realized.

Looking for some of the psychological issues discussed in this chapter, listening to children and adolescents before, during and after a Time Out, and talking with other teachers, parents and clinicians about mutual experiences in using the procedure will raise the level of awareness and sophistication which the adult will bring to this process.

(3) *Remember that the Time Out represents more than a behavior management technique* to control unruly children. Dynamically, it usually represents the authority of adults putting down, squelching, and often punishing the unacceptable and threatening assertiveness of children and adolescents without offering other alternatives to the unacceptable behavior. In short, it is a process which can quickly generate in SLD/MBD/HKS children a great deal of hurt, anger, disgust, guilt, fear, shame, hostile-aggressive fantasy formation, and crippling self-doubt, unless applied with sensitivity, understanding, support, and without rancor or bitterness.

It is essential, therefore, that all three steps outlined in initiating and following up the Time Out process be acted upon by those who choose to use this procedure.

(4) *Realize that there are many problems associated with the use of the seclusion* or locked Time Out room, as highlighted in the case of Jackie (Case Study 9.1). In a conscientious effort to control life-threatening, program-threatening, and self-threatening behavior, hasty use of the Time Out process could mean overlooking critical issues which may have a significant impact on the interactive behavior and dialogue between the disturbed children/adolescents and the responsibly concerned adults.

(5) *Finally,* since the Time Out process has become an integral part of many Behavior Modification and Operant Conditioning programs *it is important to critique* very briefly *the thrust of behavior modifica-*

tion in establishing discipline *in the home and in the classroom.* This topic will be covered more fully in Chapter 11.

Tyler (1976) has emphasized that conditioning is a necessary and important type of learning. To eliminate it from an educational system would be disastrous. From Tyler's point of view, the inadequacy of conditioned response-learning lies in the fact that it does not furnish a model to guide the education of developing generations in such a way that they will be able to deal with the rapidly changing socioeconomic environment, to gain and use new knowledge, skills, attitudes, and deeper understanding, and to form and strengthen new relationships between men and society. Within the conceptual framework of this handbook, we would paraphrase Tyler's observations: as SLD/MBD/-HKS children and adolescents gain improved self-concept and self-actuation and develop their own character structure and conscience, the rewards that arise from ongoing interpersonal-interactive-developmental dialogues and from learning who they are and what they believe are more to be preferred than rewards that depend solely on the favor of others.

LIFE SPACE INTERVIEW PROCESS

The increasing emphasis on the Time Out Seclusion Room process, along with behavior modification as an essential tool to control the actions and thoughts of SLD/MBD/HKS children and adolescents, is in marked contrast to that of the late 1950s and early 1960s, when the focus was on understanding the feelings behind disruptive and unacceptable behavior and on identifying, if possible, the nature of the internal or external conflict from which the behavior-provoking feelings arose.

It was the genius of Redl (1959) which led to the development of the Life Space Interview (LSI) process as a practical method for bringing such a dynamic point of view into the classroom, as well as into residential treatment centers.

Redl recognized the LSI concept as a renaming of the "marginal interview" which a child might need for a specific incident or type of behavior and which would be held around the immediate event by the teacher, a child care worker, or by the child's therapist, even though the material concerning the incident would eventually get back into the individual's treatment process.

Redl described two goals and tasks essential to life space inter-

Table 9.2
Goals and Tasks for Life Space Interviewing*

A. Clinical Exploration and Exploitation of Life Events

---

1. Reality Rub-in by Staff Adults

   Immediate confrontation of inappropriate behavior

   Huge script of more age-appropriate behavior for socially nearsighted children

   Repetitive focusing of child's misinterpretations and distortions of real life experiences

   Helping the child crack the code of ego alibiing and self- or object-conning-rationalizations

2. Symptom Estrangement

   Enlist part of self-awareness (insight) to liberate part of child's pathology

   Reinforce symptom estrangement by consistent staff rub-in

3. Massaging Numb Value-Areas

   Stimulate and reawaken value sensitivity to codes of fairness, loyalty, caring, and sharing

4. New-Tools Salesmanship

   Demonstrate inadequacy of tools used to solve problems

   Promote new adaptation skills (ego defenses) for old problems

5. Manipulation of Boundaries of the Self

   Help child avoid being put in "sucker" role, set up by group suction or scapegoating process

   Encourage child to widen concept of boundaries of selfhood to include his/her group, benign adults, the classroom, and larger institutions: to gain sense of group acceptance and belonging

---

*After Redl, 1959.

viewing. The essence of each has been summarized in the accompanying tables using his own unique vocabulary of descriptive phrases.

Clinical Exploration and Exploitation of Life Events

Table 9.2 focuses on five goals which were effective with a population of children and adolescents with poor impulse control. The techniques were essentially ego adaptive, cognitive, reality-oriented strategies which have been equally effective with SLD and MBD children. The concept of *reality rub-in* is central to helping these children establish controls from within. The immediate, here and now *confrontation* of inappropriate behavior without condemnation, supported by clear, open, nonretaliatory suggestions of more age-appropriate behavior, allows for increased socialization, cognitive assimilation, and hopefully, Id-Ego-Superego integration. *Repetitive refocusing* of misinterpretations and distortions of real life experiences increases the reality testing processes while shaping behavior and cognition toward more concrete and, eventually, more formal thought processes. This learning experience can be critical for SLD and MBD children who have great difficulty in generalizing new coping mechanisms from situational and concrete-specific experiences to wider interpersonal and intrafamilial relationships.

Redl recognizes that many impulse-ridden children have sufficient ego strength to set up an ego alibiing scheme which features conning themselves and others into believing rationalizations which deny reality or which support suppression and avoidance of dealing with the critical internal and external conflictual issues.

As a consequence, Redl focuses on this ego alibiing process in a way reminiscent of the cryptographer's cracking the code of a secret message which is designed to be understood by some (the unconscious mind) but withheld from others (the conscious mind).

The explanation of *symptom estrangement* can be interpreted as a splitting of the ego into an observing ego and an affective ego (behavioral pattern in response to feelings), and also as a shifting of an ego syntonic symptom into an ego alien one, which can then be sublimated, neutralized, or dealt with by isolation, intellectualization, and reaction formation. Both of these processes seem to "liberate" the symptom from the child's psychopathology.

The *massaging numb value-areas*, promoting *new tool salesmanship*, and the *manipulation of boundaries of the self* are strategies directed toward ego and superego functions readily adaptable to working with SLD and MBD children.

In summary, Redl describes the five goals to illustrate a Life Space Interviewing process rather than defining a system which would be binding to the LSI process. The real goal, he says, is for the life space interviewer to make constructive use of an immediate, negative, or problem-filled experience in order to draw out of it something that might be of use for more long-range therapeutic goals and/or the psychological processing of an emotionally corrective experience.

Emotional First Aid on the Spot

The elaboration of the concepts of *Emotional First Aid* in Table 9.3 is sufficiently full to give the direction and flavor which Redl originally brought to this LSI concept. In his summary about these five strategies, he suggests that many or all of these goals can be combined into one Life Space Interview, or that the goals might be switched as the interview process unfolds. In any event, emphasis should be placed on the importance of tying the content of each LSI into the ongoing individual treatment and of relating its origin (stimulus) and outcome (social response) to the socialization and learning processes taking place in the classroom and in the home or residential cottage.

Critique of Process

Bernstein (1963) wrote an interesting critique on the Life Space Interview in the school setting which is still timely and applicable for classroom teachers of SLD and MBD children, as well as for the principal, unit supervisor, child care worker, or therapist to whom the disturbed child may be sent at a moment of emotional crisis. She suggested nine points which might be useful and appropriate at the time of an LSI in the school setting.

(1) *Be polite.* Demonstrate mature and appropriate behavior for the child. Don't interrupt child's discourse unless it represents manipulation and control.

(2) *Don't tower over a little child.* Put yourself at eye level with the child to enhance eye-gaze and mutual communication.

(3) *Use "Why?" sparingly.* It is difficult to explore reasons and almost impossible for a troubled child to expose motivations for unacceptable behavior so that the principal or other staff person can dissect them.

(4) *Get description of what happened.* Listen to what child says and keep focus on the actual situation.

(5) *Help child to put into words* what he/she was feeling but can't verbalize. "You are angry because——, aren't you? You wanted that badly and couldn't wait, could you? You seem to be still testing us out to see how strong and how fair we can be." Bernstein pointed out that interchange should not be confused with the amateur practice of psychiatry.

Table 9.3
Goals and Tasks for Life Space Interviewing*

B. Emotional First Aid on the Spot

---

1. To Drain Off Frustration

   For children with low frustration tolerance.
   Hurt pride, anger, acting-out, and overaggressive patterns.

   Sympathetic communication avoids adding hostility to original reservoir of hurt and hate.

2. To Support Management of Panic, Fury, and Guilt

   Many SLD/MBD/HKS children do not know what to do with such states when involved in them.

   Help for individual child or group when heavier quantities of emotions are stirred up than can be handled.

   Adult availability can "put things back into focus and proportion" after an emotional blow up.

3. To Maintain Communication in Moments of Relationship Decay

   Passive-resistant SLD/MBD children pull back into avoidant, obstinate, noncommunicative, withdrawn patterns.

   Keep communication channels open between supporting adults and troubled children.

4. To Regulate Behavioral and Social Traffic

   Avoid moralizing, preaching, or lecturing on the do's and don't's.

   Remind child and sound a warning about basic rules of social interaction.

   Strengthen internal control and concept of rules at moments of frustration, impulse to action responses, or impending loss of internal control.

5. To Umpire Services

   For decision crises between dictates of the healthier versus destructive sides of child's self.

   For the time of a fight or quarrel, clarification of game rules, and conflicts between peers or staff.

   For management of "loaded transactions" such as borrowing, trading, swapping, or appropriating property.

---

*After Redl, 1959.

(6) *Help child with plans for specific steps to improve the situation.* Reassure child to allay anxiety and support the naturalness of the provoked feelings, but help child think about other alternatives for expressing those feelings under similar circumstances.

(7) *Give child opportunity to ask you questions.* "Is there anything you want to tell me?" or, "Is there anything I can do for you?"

(8) *The return (reentry) to class is important.* Allow teacher enough time to cool down and get class under control. The child has had a chance to talk out his or her strong feelings, but the teacher has not. The teacher can be upset by seeing a smiling child reappear when the iron of teacher frustration and anger is still hot.

If you cannot take the child back to the classroom, a note to the teacher is an imperative. Read it to the child or let the child read it. Say exactly what you mean. Say it clearly enough for the child to understand. Do not expect the note to take the place of a follow-up conference with the teacher. Although finding a time for such a follow-up is difficult, it is essential to a constructive LSI process and to helping both child and teacher.

(9) *Teachers have their pride.* They may resent having to ask for help, since it might imply a lack of competence. Support the right of teachers to seek out and use an LSI process without guilt or feelings of self-doubt. At the same time, the teacher should not look for and expect observable punishment, for the aim of the LSI is not punishment but guidance, direction, and counseling to improve the SLD/MBD/HKS child's availability for learning and his/her personal and social coping skills in an arena which has been fraught with successive failures.

Long (1963) wrote a critique of the use of the LSI process by a group of teachers especially trained in the method. Thirty classroom teachers of "normal" children were included in the follow-up study, and nearly all agreed on the following points: (1) the children responded quickly to this approach; (2) these "normal" children presented many complex problems over which they had little or no control; (3) without guidance, counseling support, and ongoing supervision in the method the teachers felt more and more inadequate and became depressed about the method; (4) many of the teachers' colleagues were openly unsympathetic and critical of the LSI approach; (5) 26 of the 30 teachers changed their attitude over the year of teaching and decided not to use the LSI process; and (6) all 30 teachers agreed that the LSI procedure was useful but required total support of the school staff, could not be employed successfully in isolation, and bi-weekly group supervision focused on the handling of the behavior of selected students would have been sufficient to reinforce their efforts and keep the LSI as a viable procedure.

Morse (1963, 1965, 1966) has been one of the strongest and most articulate exponents of the LSI process. It has been his set of guidelines, along with Bernstein's (1963) nine points described above, which the author has found to be most helpful in training educational and clinical staff in the use of the LSI procedure. A well-written statement of the LSI process following the precepts of Redl and Morse was prepared by Lindgren (1967), but little evaluative research on this procedure has been reported since these early descriptions of the process.

LIFE SPACE INTERVIEW (LSI) GUIDELINES

These guidelines attempt to integrate the concepts of Redl (1959), Bernstein (1963), Morse (1963, 1966), and Lindgren (1967).

I. The *first goal* is to help the teacher and residential child care staff to a *greater understanding of and empathy for* SLD/MBD/HKS children and adolescents. This includes:
   (a) *Increasing* the responsible adults' *capacity for behavioral appraisal*. For example, what brings on the emotional distress and misbehavior? and how can these students be taught to cope with external and internal pressures and conflicts?
   (b) *Training* adult educational and clinical staff to perceive and describe *the way the world looks* to SLD/MBD/HKS children and how these children may be feeling, what behavior may ensue from these feelings, and what the response of the peer group and other adults to this behavior will be.
   (c) *Preparing* teachers, child care workers, and clinicians to use these learned behavior appraisal skills *to provide immediate help* to disturbed children in the classroom or cottage under the given limitations of both settings.
II. The *second goal* is *to help SLD/MBD/HKS children and adolescents* with the educational, social, and emotional problems which are interfering with learning and socialization. This includes:
   (a) Recognizing that no attempt is being made to make amateur psychologists or psychiatrists out of the teachers or child care staff.

(b) Using either the Learning Theory (Behavior Modification) Model or the Developmental Interactive Model, or a combination of both. The LSI process uses the latter Model to reinforce self- and other-awareness, interpersonal relationships, value systems, and ego-adaptive behavior. The former model is used to reinforce socially acceptable and age-appropriate behavior which emerges from an LSI.

III. The *third goal* is *to develop total support* within the school system, classroom, or residential program for such a crisis intervention LSI Model. This includes:

   (a) *Adequate training* and supervision in its usage.

   (b) *Regular in-service* training to introduce new staff to the LSI procedure and to clarify its strengths and weaknesses within that educational/clinical setting.

   (c) *Continued monitoring* for the top administration of the effectiveness of LSI procedures and support for teachers in seeking other ways to augment its usefulness.

IV. The *fourth goal* is to develop and *establish a workable LSI system* within the school, institution, or agency. This includes:

   (a) Defining who will be called to do the LSI. Will the teacher carry this function? If so, will it be inside or outside the classroom? Will the principal or guidance counselor carry any part of the LSI? If so, where? Who will supervise the process? How will the LSI be coordinated with a Time Out process should that intervention be necessary?

   (b) Defining the system according to the nature of the students' needs. At one residential school, two types of LSI processes were developed: one was a "disciplinary" LSI in which the principal or an assistant would be called to help aggressively acting-out students leave the classroom when necessary to "cool-off" in the principal's office. The second was an "affective" LSI for which the students' therapists or residential counselors were called when it seemed clear that psychological conflicts within the students were being expressed in unacceptable and disruptive behavior. It was not always easy to make such a distinction until the personality of the students became better known to the teachers.

V. The *fifth goal* is to *know and be skilled in the LSI procedure* once the system has been developed.

   This procedure includes some or all of the eight steps in Table 9.4. These were formulated by Morse (1963) and Lindgren (1967).

Table 9.4
LSI Procedure

Step 1. Ask *what was happening* and how it happened, *not* why did you do it? (i.e. nonjudgmental and nonpunitive).

Step 2. Ask *what else* the student was feeling and what else was happening at home or school? (i.e. what other possibilities and realities might have affected the behavior?).

Step 3. Ask *what the student feels should be done* about the situation? (i.e. a test of the student's reality orientation, readiness to change or to avoid realistic resolutions, and some indication of the student's ego-superego function or value system).

Step 4. Ask *what the student understands* about the ground rules of behavior in the classroom or cottage, and make some helpful observations about what seemed to be happening.

Step 5. Ask *how you can help,* now that you both know what was going on (i.e. a readiness to set up a helping alliance).

Step 6. Ask *if the student is ready* to handle feelings differently when he/she is returned to the classroom or cottage program? (i.e. placing some responsibility for emotional control on the student, while allowing the teacher or other adult involved time to "cool-off" and to regain a positive leadership role in the classroom or cottage).

Step 7. Ask *what we will do if this situation happens again?* (i.e. a second testing of the student's readiness to change or to seek realistic resolutions).

Step 8. Ask the *teacher and student how things went* after the reentry. If the teacher conducts the LSI, he/she should record this observation for the total team. Share with the team members any observation which will be helpful without violating the confidentiality of the information. If the student is involved in one of the treatment modalities, encourage the student to bring up the incident, if he/she is ready to work on it in that part of the helping process.

VI. The *sixth and final goal* is to know and *be alerted to the possible pitfalls* of this procedure. Briefly, these include the possible reward for negative behavior, setting up the procedure to get out of the class on a regular basis, the possible implication, often felt by teachers, that he/she is unable to handle behavior problems, and the possibility that two different systems may be confronting the child: an educational versus a mental health system and an authoritan-control versus a permissive-expressive system.

REFERENCES

Accreditation manual for psychiatric facilities serving children and adolescents. Accreditation Council for Psychiatric Facilities for the Join Commission on Accrediation of Hospitals. Chicago: Joint Commission on Accreditation of Hospitals, 1974.

Bernstein, M. Life space interview in the school setting. *American Journal of Orthopsychiatry,* 1963, *33,* 717–719.

Division of Youth and Family Services (DYFS), *Manual of standards for residential child care facilities: Purposes, procedures, regulations.* Supplement on behavior management: Room statement. Trenton, N.J.: Department of Institutions and Agencies, 1976.

Erikson, E. *Childhood and society* (2nd ed., rev.). New York: W. W. Norton, 1963.

Freud, A. *The ego and the mechanisms of defense.* London: The Hogarth Press, 1937.

Freud, S. (1923) *The ego and the id* (Std. ed., Vol. 19). London: Hogarth Press, 1961.

Gibran, K. *The prophet.* New York: Alfred A. Knopf, 1923.

Ginsburg, H. & Opper, S. *Piaget's theory of intellectual development.* Englewood Cliffs, N.J.: Prentice-Hall, 1969.

Hilgard, E. *Theories of learning.* New York: Appleton-Century-Crofts, 1948.

Lindgren, H. *Educational psychology in the classroom.* New York: Wiley, 1967.

Long, N. Some problems in teaching life space interviewing techniques to graduate students in education in a large class at Indiana University. *American Journal of Orthopsychiatry,* 1963, *33,* 723–727.

Mahler, M., Pine, F., & Bergman, A. *The psychological birth of the human infant.* New York: Basic Books, 1975.

Morse, W. Working paper: Training teachers in life space interviewing. *American Journal of Orthopsychiatry,* 1963, *33,* 727–730.

Morse, W. Intervention techniques for the classroom teachers of the emotionally disturbed. In P. Knobloch (Ed.), *Educational programs for emotionally disturbed children: The decade ahead.* Syracuse: Division of Special Education and Rehabilitation, Syracuse University, 1965.

Morse, W. Standards for the preparation of teachers of brain-injured children: Emotional problems. In W. Cruickshank (Ed.), *The teacher of brain-injured children: A discussion of the basis for competency.* Syracuse: Syracuse University Press, 1966.

Parsons, T. *Social structure and personality.* New York: Free Press, 1964.

Rank, O. *Will therapy and truth and reality.* New York: Alfred A. Knopf, 1947.

Redl, F. The life space interview. *American Journal of Orthopsychiatry,* 1959, *29,* 1–18.

Schrag, P. & Divoky, D. *The myth of the hyperactive child: And other means of child control.* New York: Pantheon Books, 1975.

Skinner, B.F. *The behavior of organisms.* New York: Appleton-Century-Crofts, 1938.

Tyler, R. Learning: An overview and update. In K. Hansen (Ed.), *A report of the chief state school offices: 1976 Summer Institute.* Washington, D.C.: U.S. Office of Education, 1976.

CHAPTER 10

THERAPY WITHIN THE
FAMILY CONSTELLATION

FLORENCE W. KASLOW, Ph.D.

And a woman who held a babe against her bosom said, Speak
    to us of Children
And he said:
Your children are not your children.
They are the sons of daughters of Life's longing for itself.
They come through you but not from you,
And though they are with you yet they belong not to you.

You may give them your love but not your thoughts,
For they have their own thoughts.
You may house their bodies but not their souls,
For their souls dwell in the house of tomorrow, which you can
    not visit, not even in your dreams.
You may strive to be like them, but seek not to make them like
    you.
For life goes not backward nor tarries with yesterday.

You are the bows from which your children as living arrows are
    sent forth.
The archer sees the mark upon the path of the infinite, and He
    bends you with His might that His arrows may go swift
    and far.
Let your bending in the archer's hand be for gladness;
For even as He loves the arrow that flies, so He loves also
    the bow that is stable.

—Kahlil Gibran, *The Prophet*

INTRODUCTION

As Gibran stated so eloquently, "Your children are not your children. They are the sons and daughters of Life's longing for itself." They are longed for as the embodiment of one's sweetest dreams, loftiest goals and ideals—as the perfect extension and expression of the couple's love and caring.

Thus, it is easy to understand why parents react strongly when they are informed that their child has a learning disability. This realization brings shock and dismay, grief, disbelief or anger, and, always, a sense of narcissistic injury.

Parents' handling of the child's idiosyncratic behavior and learning style prior to the diagnosis, their reaction to the handicap once it is defined, and their coping with their own and other family members' perception of the child's "specialness" will all influence the child's learning pattern and self esteem. Because the child lives within a family system and is vitally affected by his/her important others, either conjoint family therapy or concurrent parent child treatment may often constitute the "treatment of choice."

In this chapter, the extant small body of literature is alluded to when pertinent. The efficacy of concurrent parent child therapy and conjoint family therapy when a family member has a learning disability are explored. Family dynamics and structure and the impact of the disorder on the family's functioning are highlighted, specific interventive strategies discussed, and several case illustrations utilized. The underlying framework is a dynamic, developmental, holistic one, predicated on the tenets of psychoanalytic ego psychology (see Chapter 2) and organismic theory and attending to both intrapsychic and interpersonal factors. The overall approach is biopsychosocial, encompassing Goldstein (1959) and Angyal's (1965) views of the importance of the person in the situation and of body-mind unity.

Starting from a launching pad of psychoanalytic ego psychology as articulated by Hartman, Kris, and Lowenstein, (1949) one can view the basic functions of the developing personality as the functions of the developing ego, functions which play a crucial role in the child's adaptation to life. The cognitive and executive functions of the ego, which include reality testing, memory, thinking and analysis, and synthesis of perceptions and data, are the sine qua non of psychological existence. Anything which interferes with development of the ego and its functions and with healthy mechanisms of defense (Freud, 1937) will negatively influence the child's total adaptation, including his/her capacity for learning (Pearson, 1954). A child's sense of self, his/her physical being and boundaries, and the way he/she is perceived by others essential to well being and survival develops initially in the context of the family, whose early views and handling leave an indelible imprint. Thus, complete understanding of the child's needs, behavior, personality, and self-concept are only possible when one adopts a family systems perspective, appreciates the structure and dynamics of the primary family unit, and understands the mutual interaction which occurs. The child's ego development is affected by the environment in which this development takes place; and the learning disability, whatever its etiology, exercises a profound effect on the total family gestalt (Abrams and Kaslow, 1976).

THE IMPACT OF THE LEARNING DISORDER ON THE FAMILY

Something is wrong, but what? The child who was so desired does not seem quite "right" or "normal" somehow, and no one seems able or willing to identify the malady. When the difficulty is subtly manifested as clumsiness and a lack of coordination, the concerned parents are often assured, by friends and relatives, as well as the pediatrician, that their child is just more awkward than most and may be slow in physical development and that they should not be unduly worried or pushy. If the child is lagging behind in the area of acquiring vocabulary and good word pronunciation, kindhearted friends again may use a differential developmental rate explanation. However, when the sensitive and loving parent ultimately believes the inner nagging sense that all is not well, or when the signs of difficulty become more clearly manifested, then the parents seek the advice of professionals to allay their fears or to ascertain the nature of the perplexing difficulty.

In the emotional preparation for a child about to be born, expectant parents usually fabricate a glamorized image of their baby which involves the fantasy of a perfect child, a kind of ego-ideal. The parents may desire, either overtly or covertly, a youngster who has all the qualities they admire in themselves but who will not possess the characteristics they dislike in themselves. Even with healthy, normal babies, there is usually some discrepancy between the parents' dream child and the real child. To accept and resolve this disparity is a developmental task of parenthood. When the incongruity is too great, as in the birth of a baby with a noticeable handicap, or when the parents' wishes are too unrealistic, a crisis ensues.

The healthy child's acquisition and mastery of basic ego skills during infancy and early childhood evokes parental responses of happiness and pride. The child is frequently perceived quite literally by the parents as their "product" and represents a personal accomplishment. However, when the child is learning disabled or lags behind in developing normal functions, the responses may be quite different, and parents wonder how they could have produced this defective, unappealing child.

Formerly, it was thought that, because of her more intimate and total role in the gestation process, the mother might have a greater narcissistic investment in the child than does the father, that any discrepancy between her illusions and the reality presented by the infant would threaten her pride and sense of self worth more severely, and that the child's appearance as "slow" or "different," in the absence of an obvious physical defect, would increase the degree of her fear and fantasy (Abrams and Kaslow, 1976). More recently, however, as a result of responses from numerous caring fathers of learning disabled children, it has become clear that they also experience a deep narcissistic wound and are greatly troubled by their child's disorder. As more husbands become involved, along with their wives, in preparation for natural childbirth, participation in the delivery room, and moving quickly into active fathering with their infants, one can expect greater similarity in how they experience the realization of their child's "differentness" and come to grips with the fact that this particular child is likely to need and demand more from them for a longer period of time than a normal child would, while giving less return for the emotional and energy investment. The cherished future "my son the baseball slugger, football quarterback, or Phi Beta Kappa" is not present in this child. Nor can they visualize their daughter gliding along a runway to the melody of "Here She Comes, Miss America" or donning the robes of a judge.

The sequential phases leading toward ultimate acceptance of and the ability to cope with the child's condition appear to be somewhat analogous to the process of grief and mourning that sets in when one learns that death is imminent for a loved one. Upon recognizing or being informed that their child is handicapped, parents suffer a sense of loss of the fantasied "perfect" progeny. First, there is denial of the problem, the grasping for rays of hope, the searching for a doctor who will give them a more favorable diagnosis and prognosis. When the handicap is repeatedly confirmed, anger ensues. Beseechingly, the parents may ask of anyone who will listen, "Why did this have to happen to me? Is this punishment for some transgression? What did we do to deserve this wicked blow?" Myriad fantasies and frustrations filter into consciousness, as the parents struggle with their ambivalence and sense of helplessness and futility toward the child and with their fury at God, the doctors, and other external forces.

Frequently, there is an attempt to bargain with or mollify the powers that be, to promise to act in a certain way if only the child will be made whole; but this, also, is destined to fail. Only when the remnants of the wished for child can be discarded and mourned can the real, defective child be permitted to live and develop to the fullest extent with encouragement, and even love, from his/her parents. The acceptance of the youngster as he/she is and can become, within the parameters circumscribed by his/her own potential, is necessary before parents and child can make headway.

These observations on the process parents undergo after being apprised that their child is minimally brain damaged or otherwise learning disabled concur with those described in a Group for the Advancement of Psychiatry report (1963) on *Mental Retardation: The Therapeutic Role of the Physician*. This report indicates that the initial reaction of the parents involves the psychological defense mechanism of denial; they either insist that the wrong baby has been given to them, that the problem simply does not exist, or that the doctors are mistaken in what they are saying. Accompanying the denial is the inevitable guilt, and the doctor is often the recipient of the anger and hostility they feel. In this torturous period of readjustment, any means of reducing guilt and allaying anxiety, including projection, is utilized. Keeping in mind that the GAP report is dealing with the mentally retarded and not the more minimally learning disabled child, it is still instructive to grapple with their contention that many parents have secret thoughts of "killing" their unappealing baby. Then, since this is intolerable, a reaction formation sets in and the pattern becomes one of overcompensatory caretaking of the youngster.

Similarly, after a diagnosis of specific learning disability (SLD), minimal brain dysfunction (MBD), or hyperkinesis (HKS) has been tendered, there is bewilderment over causality. The parents experience strong mixed emotions which trigger untenable feelings of guilt and shame. The rage and anger invariably felt toward the child cannot be tolerated by their superegos, and barriers against consciously recognizing these impulses are erected. To compensate, at least partially, for the intense guilt over their hostility, parents often become overprotective and overindulgent. However, their defensive maneuvers deprive the child of important chances for growth and development of adaptive secondary ego functions, and the child instead becomes facile at using the disorder as a way of controlling his/her parents.

> In a very real sense, he becomes the dependent despot. It is this manipulative overdependency which plays a large role in the power struggles which are set up between parent and child. . . . the same kind of behavior which ultimately is displaced onto the school and becomes a problem between teacher and child. (Abrams and Kaslow, 1975, p. 8)

FAMILY DYNAMICS AND STRUCTURE

Given the constellation of feelings described above, it becomes obvious that many of the parent-to-parent and parent-to-child interactions may become unduly governed by the presence of the disorder. Instead of perceiving and relating to the whole child, including what is "right" with him/her as well as what is "wrong," the problem engulfs many parents and seems to become for them the totality of the child. Such families exist in an aura of pathos as if a cloud of sadness and sorrow perpetually engulfs them.

Although it is true that the parents may be responsible for exacerbating their child's problems by their inept handling and extreme reactions and that many parents lack insight into the whys and wherefores of these difficulties, this does not encompass the whole of parent-child relations. The parents have usually struggled through a long period of uncertainty and confusion in relation to their disabled child, the nature of his/her affliction, and the prognosis, and have no doubt received much conflicting advice. To compound the problem, the very nature of the child's ego weaknesses makes it quite difficult for the parents to cope with the daily problems he/she presents. With no choice but to deal with these ego defects as effectively as they can, the parents invest a tremendous amount of energy and often become weary, anxiety-ridden, and enraged. Ultimately, this fury accumulates, with each spouse in some way projecting the blame onto the other, until their interactions soon cease to express much besides irritability and recrimination. Thus, at the point of greatest need for mutual support and compassion, they are unable to face one another in their shared devastations, and the marital bond becomes severely strained.

One parent may begin to see himself/herself as the child's only protector and move into an alliance with the child against the other parent. These two, thereby, become overly attached and enmeshed, in a symbiotic sense, effectively shutting out the other parent and erecting additional barriers to successful resolution of the pain and to formulation of an acceptable and sensible plan for (and with) the child. The extruded parent may escape into work, a flurry of activities, or an affair to offset the disappointments and loneliness. The overly invested parent manifests a self-sacrificial devotion so that a fusion of parent (usually mother) and child ensues which does not allow for individuation. In some instances, both parents become completely invested in the child, and rivaling for his/her attention and affection may become a major preoccupation, supplanting the parental roles of caregiving and role modeling and the spouse-lover interaction bond.

Usually the term "learning disability" is used to connote a condition in which there is a specific learning disorder; this disorder has often been assumed to exist in and of itself, relatively independent of environmental influences. However, as stated earlier, this chapter is written utilizing a conceptual framework which posits that one must take into consideration the total functioning of the person including, but not limited to, biopsychosocial and familial factors. For instance, there may be conflicts in the child's home situation which have a debilitating effect upon his/her learning capacity. Parental arguments, addiction, or a critical illness can certainly prove devastating. If the child is preoccupied with worries about family quarrels, monetary difficulties, or exposure to potential or actual seduction, it is unlikely that he/she will be able to concentrate on learning activities.

As with other preschoolers, parental attitudes toward these SLD children are crucial determinants of their receptivity to learning. If their families have infantilized or overprotected them, their problems will be compounded, and a lack of readiness for school will be evidenced. If the parents place undue emphasis upon the necessity for school achievement, the children rapidly perceive that receipt of affection from one or both parents may be contingent upon good achievement in school, especially in middle- and upper-class families who place a premium on educational attainments. When children begin to realize they can never totally gain parental approval, they may simply withdraw from the futile effort. Since parents are too hard to please and only criticism is forthcoming no matter what the child does, it is senseless to try. So he/she gives up and internalizes a failure concept.

The significant influence of marital discord when accompanied by maternal rejection in the etiology of some kinds of learning disabilities has been pointed out (Harris, 1961). It is not clear which is more up-setting for a young child, chronic quarrels within the family or a mother who is often inaccessible because she is either physically or emotionally out of the home. When both parental dissension and an absentee mother are situational components, the effect on the child is disturbing. Harris, who called this combination *double disorganization*, found that the percentage of nonlearners coming from such homes was almost three times as high as that for nonlearners coming from families where this combination was not present. It stands to reason that, if both parents are out of the house most of the time and argue continually when there, the child will be preoccupied with frightening thoughts of abandonment, rejection, parental separation, and disruption of the family unit. This is certainly not conducive to maximizing concentration ability or to mobilizing the child's energy for intellectual mastery.

In addition to the cumbersome load described above, the family must assume a heavy financial burden. Visits to neurologists, psychologists, and other specialists are costly and time-consuming. Ambiguity and contradictory diagnoses from professionals compound the turmoil, the mea culpa syndrome, and/or wish to take flight felt by many parents. They may fluctuate between being permissive and re-jecting, between banding together on behalf of the child or despising each other for conceiving a handicapped youngster. If the child is demanding and constantly in motion, the parents may need periodic time away from the youngster; yet they may be unable to find a sitter willing and able to deal with the child's hyperactivity. Sometimes, enmeshed parents may refuse to go out without the afflicted child, thus creating their own narrow prison. Ultimately, the rage accumulates to volcanic proportions, erupts, and the frustrating cycle of resentment, guilt, over-protectiveness and permissiveness is reactivated, to the disadvantage of all. A youngster caught in such a web has little energy free for the adventure of learning.

Eventually, a troubled or pathological family may project onto the handicapped child the blame for all of their difficulties. This youngster, therefore, becomes the index patient, if and when the family decides or is advised to seek professional psychological or psychiatric help. In the role of scapegoat (Ackerman, 1961), he/she is the target of all the family's frustrations, and because this jeopardy is insured in his/her handicap, he/she becomes the overt symptom bearer for them all. In such a family scenario, the learning disabled child deflects attention from parental conflict and other sources of turmoil so that underlying contributory problems are often masked and are unlikely to surface if the child is treated in individual therapy. Meanwhile, they continue to percolate underground, never getting resolved. In this way, the child assumes a peculiar function: he/she becomes the negative bond holding the parents together, the living symbol of a conception for which they are mutually responsible and from which neither can, in good conscience, escape. Despite lack of gratification in and from the marriage, it must continue at all costs for the child's sake, because leaving one's mate to cope alone with such a weighty burden is personally and socially unacceptable, as a general rule. Therefore, added to the child's task of learning despite his/her neurological impairment may be the task of serving as the link between the two disgruntled parents.

The feelings, reactions, and behavior of other members of the family are also salient considerations in any assessment of the family dynamics and functioning. When parents are informed that the child has SLD/MBD or HKS, the other children are usually not present. Parents frequently relegate this information to the "secret" category, partly out of shame and embarrassment, partially to protect them from the "awful truth," and also because they can not articulate their pain and its source. Normal brothers and sisters are often not included in the planning for the disabled youngster. Generally, this is done by the parents, possibly with the advice of a physician or the counsel of a psychotherapist, and sometimes in collaboration with school personnel. By withholding information about the disabled child's status from normal siblings, the parents cloak the malady in mystery, making it unspeakable and, therefore, blowing it out of proportion. They thereby foreclose the siblings' understanding and do not provide them an opportunity to come to grips with the situation, raise their questions, and ultimately share in the loving, caring for, and planning about their special sibling. The kind of family strength derived from solidarity, from a feeling of "We are in this together," does not have a chance to blossom, and everyone suffers from the veil of silence. The continuing mystery surrounding what is wrong fosters heightened anxiety and fantasy (Silver, 1974). Only when the parents can be honest about the nature of the affliction and can convey a positive attitude are the other children able to make peace with the differences of a member of the family.

The sisters and brothers of learning disabled youngsters are vital people for them and vice versa. They can relate to them rather spontaneously and with a high degree of caring, or they can respond in a rather tense, attacking, or avoidant way.

They may be plagued by guilt for feeling relieved that it is not *their* impairment. Siblings often resent such a child because he receives a disproportionate amount of parental time and attention. In addition, he causes them embarrassment, and they are ashamed to bring friends home or be seen in public with their handicapped sibling. Parents may intensify the animosity by harboring unrealistic expectations that the children should not argue, thereby suppressing normal conflict expression and resolution. (Abrams and Kaslow, 1976, p. 37)

Not to be forgotten are the grandparents and other relatives in a closely knit family. They can be a cause of added strain, voicing their distress and engaging in weeping and/or too much sympathy, or they can be a reservoir of support and strength and a source of relief, providing respite for the tired parents through babysitting, comforting attitudes and statements, and possibly financial assistance.

INTERVENTIVE STRATEGIES

In several earlier works, a continuum of differential treatment approaches to the learning disabled child and his family have been delineated (Abrams and Kaslow, 1976, 1977). The treatment of choice depends on such factors as the specific symptomatology, the family dynamics, the facility in which treatment is sought, the skills of the staff, and the nature of the educational setting. Potential interventive approaches include:

(1) *educational strategies*—here special education techniques are utilized with the child from a reasonably happy home environment whose learning disorder does not seem complicated by emotional problems (see Chapter 15);

(2) *learning therapy*—when the experienced special education teacher supplements her teaching endeavors with psychotherapeutic activities and handling;

(3) *individual child therapy*—utilized when the child's problems have already been internalized and personality restructuring appears advisable, and when there is no strong indication that the parents need to be in treatment (see Chapter 6);

(4) *parent group counseling or group therapy*—when the parents get along and are functioning well, yet exhibit a desire for some involvement with their child's school and can benefit from educative and interpretive counseling and support from an interchange with other parents confronted by a similar situation (Loeb, 1977);

(5) *parent tutoring*—here parents are encouraged to become extensively involved in the school as aides or resource specialists in a partnership relation with the teacher; as they become involved in this setting, their knowledge about and skill in dealing with learning disabled youngsters is increased, so that their sensitivity to and effectiveness with their own child's problems will be enhanced;

(6) *child therapy plus tutoring*—when the parents either do not require therapy or are deemed inaccessible, and when the usual classroom instruction needs supplementing;

(7) *concurrent therapy of parents and child with separate therapists*;

(8) *concurrent therapy with the same therapist*; and

(9) *conjoint family therapy* for the entire nuclear family.

It is on the latter three approaches that the remainder of this chapter will focus, since the other strategies are dealt with elsewhere in this book.

CONCURRENT THERAPY OF PARENTS AND CHILD WITH SEPARATE THERAPISTS

As indicated earlier, feelings in a family with a learning disabled member are likely to be conflicted and the tension level quite high at the point at which they first arrive requesting therapeutic help. They may each need to have a cooling off period provided by their own separate therapist and a private space in the therapist's office which the other party(s) in their family drama do not enter. Thus, when child and parent desire help but each needs the treatment and therapist alone, they should be seen by different therapists who collaborate closely. This model is likely to constitute the "treatment of choice" (1) when parents are too enraged or distraught to be seen jointly with the child, (2) when the family is characterized by an "undifferentiated ego mass" (Bowen, 1961), (3) if the parents need support of their right not to immerse themselves totally in the child, (4) when the child is so emotionally empty that he/she can not tolerate sharing the therapist's time and attention, or (5) when the child needs to be protected from the onslaught of criticism he/she would receive if the parents were present. If any of the people involved are somewhat paranoid, then the therapist's pledge of confidentiality will fall on deaf ears, thus making the assignment to different therapists a critical ingredient for a potential therapeutic alliance. The therapist may make constructive suggestions regarding (1) such home management of the child as establishing a more fixed routine to reduce his anxiety and confusion and to augment predictability, (2) how to handle normal developmental tasks with equanimity to avoid precipitating a crisis, and (3) coping with community pressures and prejudices. Yet if, in the presence of the child, these suggestions would be construed as criticisms by the parents, this should be viewed as an additional sign that concurrent treatment with different therapists is the preferable arrangement. By way of illustration:

> Mrs. J. called and sounded quite agitated. The teacher had been in frequent touch with them about their 7-year-old son who was quite disruptive in the classroom because of his fidgeting and hyperactivity. He was mirror writing, always tripping over himself and others, and generally making a nuisance of himself. She had recommended that he be evaluated quickly by the school psychologist and considered for placement in the special education class. His mother was angry at the teacher and furious at her son for not behaving properly, as they had tried to teach him. Her husband was chagrined at their frequent embarrassment over the child's clumsiness and difference; it was interfering with their social life at the country club, and he was unable to accept the fact that the child could not act better simply by trying and learning to be obedient.

> It was suggested that Mr. and Mrs. J. could be seen within the week, as she seemed quite distraught and an early appointment would give her a chance to clarify the situation and ventilate some of her concerns. When asked if they wished to bring son Bobby along, the mother declined forcefully, indicating that they would not feel free to talk in front of him, that they were too "uptight" where he was concerned, and that this was something for adults to handle. It was apparent during the first visit that they had probably been ignoring signs of minimal brain damage for quite a while and were now angry at the school for forcing them to recognize the existence of a definite disorder. They had been badgering Bobby to "be a good boy and everything will be fine," and now they needed to reorder their feelings. It was clear that, had he been present, they would not have settled down and utilized therapy productively but would have spent the time scapegoating him (Bell and Vogel, 1968). Thus it was recommended that the psychologist see them weekly and that Bobby have a complete psy-

chological plus a neurological examination to help determine the best educational-treatment plan for him. The parents concurred and proceeded in that manner.

By the time the examination reports came through, they were ready to accept the fact that Bobby indeed belonged in a special class in a school in which he could be mainstreamed at a later time, if this seemed advisable, and that their son also needed therapy to help him build a better self-concept and get over the sense of failure which had become ingrained in him.

In sum, such a format affords an opportunity for parent(s) and child each to deal separately with his/her reactions to the learning handicap and its accompanying problems with feelings toward each other and with the need to learn more productive attitudes and interactive behaviors. During the course of their treatment, the parents can confront the frustrations, disappointment, and recriminations which emanate from the child's impairment and be encouraged to differentiate between those dilemmas which stem from the child's condition and those which are an expression of marital conflict. The possibility of their identifying and working through the marital conflict is much greater when they are seen in tandem minus the child, than when they can focus on the unruly child as the index or identified patient. When such conflict becomes evident, marital therapy might prove more advantageous than parent counseling on how to understand and cope with the child's behavior and their own reactions.

CONCURRENT THERAPY WITH SAME THERAPIST

Sometimes parents and child reveal a need for separate time with a therapist but do not appear to be particularly embroiled in a battle. They are not symbiotically enmeshed nor so competitive that they are unable to share the same therapist. There are decided advantages in such an arrangement. When one therapist sees everyone, there is no danger of two therapists working at cross purposes or of family members sabotaging therapeutic gains by playing them off against one another. A single therapist can acquire a more complete picture and can interweave the progress in treatment of his several patients. Knowing all family members, he is in a better position to help them modify the daily routine to accommodate everyone's needs and achieve a more satisfying and dynamic equilibrium.

Besides having all of the merits mentioned in the prior approach, this option has the added value that parents and child sense that they are all endeavoring to improve the situation; the momentum is reenforced. Since the same therapist is seeing their child, the parents assume he/she knows their problems first hand and are more open to his/her ideas about how to help their child become more self-reliant, independent, and successful as a student.

CONJOINT FAMILY THERAPY

The field of family therapy dates back to the early 1950s. Many therapists with training and experience in a one-to-one treatment model were becoming disenchanted over the slowness of the results they achieved. Frequently, improved functioning seemed insured, only to be undermined by other family members who seemed to need a dysfunctional person in the home to maintain the status quo. Numerous bright therapists, separately and in small groups, reasoned that if one saw the family in unison and could gain a fuller perspective on what transpired, he/she could minimize and perhaps eliminate the sabotage (Satir, 1964). Thus, pioneers like Ackerman, Bowen, Haley, and Satir began to conceptualize the idea of the family as a system, with its members as interdependent parts. Other theoretical premises undergirding the evolving new approach include: (1) that the patient unit comprises the whole family system and, therefore, all members should be seen simultaneously; (2) that these systems have and attempt to maintain a homeostatic equilibrium which must be changed to alleviate the pathology; (3) that the symptomatic member or identified patient is the symptom bearer, carrying the problems of the entire family; (4) that the person assigned to be the symptom bearer is selected, albeit unconsciously, because of his/her special sensitivities and vulnerabilities; (5) that if the original index patient improves but the family needs to have an identified patient, the pathology will float; (6) that most families are governed by fairly rigid rules by which their interactions are patterned; and (7) that most families have a secret that needs to be opened up and confronted before therapeutic progress can occur (Kaslow, 1973). The role of the therapist entails: (1) entering the family system in order to serve as an active change agent, (2) dealing with its secrets, rules, and myths, (3) assessing its dynamics and structure, and (4) working with interactional as well as intrapsychic material. In the past 25 years, the field has matured and expanded and family therapy has become a well-recognized treatment modality.

Specifically, in the family with a learning disabled child, each member is likely to respond to that child as the identified patient, and perhaps the family scapegoat, in his/her own idiosyncratic manner. Maximum therapeutic benefit can be derived when the family is seen as a unit. Once family members can look squarely at the nature of the impediment, their emotional reactions to it, their regrets, and their fears, then they can go through the necessary process of grieving for the idealized perfect child they do not have, if they have not already done so. Next, they can be helped to see their real child as he/she is, strengths and weaknesses, problems and potentialities. The normal children can be given a chance to end the mystery by asking questions and can be allowed to express whatever they feel—confusion, jealousy over the extra time and energy the handicapped member requires, shame, and, ultimately, some tenderness. Then the therapist can help them look at techniques for home management of the child, enlisting all members in appropriate ways to share the responsibility of caring for the child and helping him/her become as self-sufficient as possible. In this way, the bound energy released can encourage a synergetic buildup to propel the family in a positive, forward direction. Grandparents, neighbors, and friends can be invited by the family to contribute in any ways they can as part of the nuclear family's extended support system. This kind of thrust flows with rather than against the family's loyalty bonds (Nagy and Spark, 1973), avoids becoming fixated in a whirlpool of guilt and self-pity, and is conducive to setting in motion a creative life process for the family as a whole and its individual members. Almost invariably, the presence of a learning disabled child has disturbed the family's equilibrium, contributed to its disorganization, and placed its coping mechanisms under severe stress. Family therapy, by healing some of the narcissistic injuries and enabling the family to cope more effectively, affords an opportunity to reduce the chaos and turmoil and begin to function as a unit at a satisfying level of existence. With these as its treatment goals, family therapy appears to be the most suitable approach for enhancing awareness of and preparedness for all events in the drama that comprises the family's life cycle.

A milieu is created in conjoint family therapy which enables all members to gain a deeper awareness of themselves, each other, and their interactions. By seeing everyone simultaneously the clinician has a superb opportunity to obtain a family history from a multifaceted perspective and to assess the actual nature of feelings and interactions in vivo. During the assessment process with a learning disabled child, the family should be seen as a unit, its dynamics and functioning evaluated, and a family diagnosis made as a foundation from which education and treatment planning will be launched (Friedman, 1973). Distortions are reduced, since the problems are acted out in therapy, replacing subjective perceptions which are filtered through memory and recounted by one member. A case in point:

> Jerry, age 9, had become increasingly inattentive in class and had ceased doing his homework. He was constantly "in trouble" with his fourth grade teacher. She had been keeping him in from recess and prodding him to do his work, using such ploys as having him write on the blackboard 100 times: "I should do my work every day." In the lower grades, he had been in the top reading and arithmetic group, had done well in art, and had sometimes been "teacher's pet."

> The parents had consulted a therapist 3 years earlier when his older sister, Karen, now 12, had been "giving the mother a rough time" in the form of whining and disobeying. Since 6 months of family therapy had improved relationships, the G.'s decided to reenter family treatment.

> With the four of them together, the interaction was much clearer than trying to sketch it in from the descriptions of only one or several members. Mr. G., though less passive than several years earlier, was still quite dominated by his outspoken, controlling wife. She had maintained some therapeutic gains, but the neurotic perfectionism was far from resolved. She had transferred her nagging for excellent grades from Karen to Jerry, determined to have one child an outstanding student. During the earlier course of therapy, she had cut back from working full time as an X-ray technician to working part time in order to be home after school when the children arrived and to ease up on the pressure for them to perform inappropriate household chores for which she did not have time. However, she had returned to work, full time, at the beginning of the preceeding school year.
> When asked how he reacted to this, Jerry expressed his resentment of his mother's inaccessibility after school, when he most needed someone to talk to him over milk and cookies, someone to chauffeur him to Hebrew school and scouts. He had to fend for himself much more than he was ready to do. With Karen now 12, they saw no need for a sitter or mother's helper, so the children were left to their own devices, Jerry feeling neglected and sad. He also told his mother in no uncertain terms, "All you do is nag, nag, nag—just like my teacher." Mr. G. chimed in that he felt his wife's resumption of full-time employment was premature, to which she

jumped in defensively with, "No one cares what I want and need." At this point, Jerry walked over to sit near and cuddled up next to the therapist, obviously seeking a nurturing mother, and his body tension relaxed visibly.

Since family therapy appeared to be the therapy of choice, it was agreed that they should be seen weekly, with a focus on trying to see how they could all get their needs met, but not at each other's expense. Mr. G. felt that he had some flexibility in his work schedule and could get home early two days a week. Mrs. G. then said she could not work late one evening and come home early that day. The children agreed that they could manage on their own the other two days. The strong push for educational achievement was explored, and Mrs. G. realized she wanted to go back to college for an advanced degree but felt she could not, so the goal was being projected onto Jerry. Some long-range planning as to when she could live out her plan for herself was undertaken.

But, even with the pressure diminished, Jerry continued to have difficulty at school. A full battery of psychologicals was requested. Although his full score IQ on the WISC was in the high average range, there was a good deal of scatter between tests. Also, on the Bender Gestalt, many soft signs of MBD showed up. Because of his brightness and delightful manner, he had done well in the lower grades, just showing difficulty mastering handwriting. But as the work became more complex, no matter how hard he tried, he could no longer keep up with the top group because of the undiagnosed learning disability. The family was helped to accept this, reduce their pressure and revise their expectations, and interpret the diagnosis to the teacher and school counselor, who then requested and had a meeting with the parents, child, and therapist.

In this case, the learning problem was exacerbated by the pressure of an achievement-oriented mother. Child therapy alone might have enabled Jerry to understand and live well with his disability and to cope with the stress he felt from his parents, but family therapy enabled them to all get a sense of how their expectations, arguments, demands, and loyalties converged to make Jerry a "problem child" and the index patient and to move jointly toward a more harmonious family system which allowed space for each to fashion his/her own identity.

To recapitulate, conjoint sessions provide a continuous opportunity for involving the family in joint problem solving and for confronting each other's troublesome attitudes and behaviors honestly in the "here and now," while also enabling them to be mutually supportive. Because they are all engaged, the possibilities of sabotage are diminished. Members can reinforce each other's progress, since they are attuned to one another's needs and goals. By opening up the communication network, working through family secrets, and promoting greater honesty, the therapist helps the entire family to achieve a more satisfying life style. By empathetically tuning in to intrapsychic, deep-seated conflicts, as well as interpersonal problems and stresses, the therapist simultaneously works to understand and improve two levels of personality functioning.

For those seeking the services of a competent family therapist, there are a number of avenues to travel. In many geographic areas, they are listed in the yellow pages of the phone book under Marriage and Family Counselors. The American Association of Marriage and Family Counselors maintains an up-to-date list of qualified practitioners (clinical members and fellows) by states. Their membership currently totals close to 5000 (June 1977). In many metropolitan areas, there are Family Institutes which will make available names of their members for referrals. One can also check with the local Psychological and Psychiatric Associations to see which of their members specialize in family therapy. In addition to these private resources, competent family therapists may be found in the public sector on the staffs of Family Service Agencies and Community Mental Health Centers.

CONCLUSION

No one can encounter and work with SLD/MBD/HKS children without being impressed by the myriad factors that have contributed to and sustained these problems. To endeavor to help such children in a static, mechanistic fashion when dynamic approaches and innovative possibilities exist seems unprofessional and unfair. One must, instead, focus constantly on the interplay of many factors—physiological, psychological, social, familial, and environmental—which interact to produce and perpetuate the handicap.

The emphasis in this chapter has been on the overall functioning of these children as they attempt to deal with their frequently oppressive environment and, equally, on the family dynamics and functioning as these influence and are influenced by the special children.

Concurrent and conjoint family therapies have been described and recommended as viable approaches to dealing with people caught in the sad saga of a specific learning disability. These are not panaceas, but they do offer many possibilities for alleviating stress and confusion, mobilizing the family support system, and normalizing the family's life-style to the extent possible. In pondering and experimenting with its efficacy, the reader is encouraged to think of these approaches as strong possibilities and to determine when and how to use them in combination with other treatment approaches elaborated in this handbook.

REFERENCES

Abrams, J.C. & Kaslow, F.W. *The learning disabled child and his family: Differential diagnosis as the key to effective intervention and treatment.* Paper presented at the Association for Children with Learning Disabilities (ACLD) Annual Conference, New York, February 1975.

Abrams, J.C. & Kaslow, F.W. Learning disability and family dynamics: A mutual interaction. *Journal of Child Clinical Psychology,* 1976, *5*(1), 35–40.

Abrams, J.C. & Kaslow, F.W. Family systems and the learning disabled child: Intervention and treatment. *Journal of Learning Disabilities,* 1977, *10*(2), 86–90.

Ackerman, N. *Exploring the base of family therapy.* New York: Family Service Association of America, 1961.

Angyal, A. *Neurosis and treatment: A holistic theory.* New York: Wiley, 1965.

Bell, N & Vogel, E. The emotionally disturbed child as the family scapegoat. In N. Bell and E. Vogel (Eds.), *A modern introduction to the family.* New York: Free Press, 1968.

Bowen, M. The family as a unit of study and treatment. *American Journal of Orthopsychiatry,* 1961, *31*(1), 40–60.

Freud, A. *The ego and the mechanisms of defense.* London: Hogarth Press, 1937.

Friedman, R. *Family roots of school learning and behavior disorders.* Springfield, Ill.: Charles C Thomas, 1973

Gibran, K. *The prophet* (1923) New York: Alfred A. Knoff, 1975.

Goldstein K. Organismic approach. In S. Arieti (Ed.), *American handbook of psychiatry, II.* New York: Basic Books, 1959.

The Group for the Advancement of Psychiatry, Report #56, *Mental retardation: The therapeutic role of the physician.* 1963.

Harris, I.D. *Emotional blocks to learning.* New York: Free Press of Glencoe, 1961.

Hartman, H., Kris, E. & Lowenstein, R. Notes on the theory of aggression. *Psychoanalytic Study of the Child,* 1949, *3/4,* 9–34.

Kaslow, F. Family therapy: Viewpoints and perspectives. *Clinical Social Work Journal*, 1973, *1*(3), 196–207.

Loeb, R.C. Group therapy for parents of mentally retarded children. *The Journal of Marriage and Family Counseling*, 1977, *3*(2), 77–83.

Nagy, I.B. & Spark, G. *Invisible loyalties: Reciprocity in intergenerational family therapy.* Maryland: Harper and Row, 1973.

Pearson, G.H. *Psychoanalysis and the education of the child.* New York: W.W. Norton, 1954.

Satir, V. *Conjoint family therapy*, Palo Alto, Calif.: Science and Behavior Books, 1964.

Silver, L.B. Emotional and social problems of the family with a child who has developmental disabilities. In R.E. Weber (Ed.), *Handbook on learning disabilities.* Englewood Cliffs, New Jersey: Prentice-Hall, 1974.

CHAPTER 11

BEHAVIOR THERAPY: APPLICATIONS WITHIN THE HOME AND SCHOOL

ROBERT GAMACHE, Ph.D.

Behavior modifiers have to address the question of whether the behaviors they seek to change are the behaviors that will receive some reinforcement in the natural environment at a later date, or whether they are simply behaviors which allow the teachers and educational systems to maintain some immediate control of their constituents.

—K. Daniel O'Leary and G. Terence Wilson,
Behavior Therapy: Application and Outcome

This chapter focuses on the modification of the learning and behavioral problems commonly associated with children diagnosed as learning disabled. More specifically, it offers a review of classroom behavior therapy techniques and examines the importance of including parents of learning disabled children as behavioral change agents.

Traditional views of learning disabled children have been concerned with diagnosing emotional problems, perceptual-motor deficits, and organic impairments, and with other similar approaches which attempt to provide information about the etiology of the behavioral problem. In contrast to the traditional approach, behavior therapy is concerned with the programming of situations and contingencies to alter an individual's response to environmental stimuli. The behavior therapist largely ignores etiological speculations of problem behaviors, believing that diagnostic labels do not help in the development of sound teaching or clinical approaches (Kazdin and Craighead, 1973), and concentrates instead on the behaviors for which the label is applied. Once a target behavior has been defined, the therapist seeks to determine the conditions under which the behavior occurs or fails to occur. By then altering environmental events, the frequency of the behavior can be increased or decreased. This is the basic tenet of behavior therapy.

A basic measurement procedure of behavior therapy provides a sound way to demonstrate causal relationships when only one subject is being studied. This procedure, called a reversal (ABAB) design, has four components: (1) a baseline [A] condition in which behavior is measured prior to the institution of therapeutic techniques, (2) a treatment [B] condition in which treatment procedures are instituted, (3) a second baseline [A] condition in which the treatment procedures are discontinued, and (4) a reinstatement of treatment [B] conditions. For behaviorists, the changes in behavior resulting from this manipulation of conditions demonstrates the presence of a cause and effect relationship.

Although the legitimacy of diagnosing learning disabilities has been called into question, the fact that there are children whose activity and attention patterns provide a problem to their parents, their teachers, their peers, and to themselves is undeniably real. Behavior therapy offers a practically oriented conceptual model that enhances the effectiveness of the teachers and parents who must deal with these problems. Certainly, the increase in the number of research reports attests to the rising popularity of behavior therapy. The following represents an overview of the most widely accepted therapeutic approaches of behavior modification in the classroom and the home as they pertain to the problems commonly associated with children having a learning disability: inattentiveness, hyperactivity, oppositional behavior, immaturity, academic underachievement, peer difficulties, and low self-esteem.

BEHAVIOR THERAPY IN THE CLASSROOM

Extinction

The withdrawal of reinforcement from a response weakens that response, and this decrease in behavior strength under nonreinforcement conditions is referred to as extinction (Bandura, 1969). Jones (1971) used an extinction procedure to eliminate the arguing behavior in a fourth-grade boy. The youngster, labeled brain damaged and learning disabled, was being tutored some 6 hours a day in several subject areas. Arguments would ensue when the boy was corrected for a mistake, with as many as four arguments recorded in a 30-minute period. The arguments proved to be quite disruptive and seriously impeded the youngster's academic progress. After carefully observing the tutoring sessions, Jones hypothesized that the tutor was inadvertently reinforcing the arguing behavior by her responsiveness to the protests. In order to test this hypothesis, the tutor was asked to ignore all contradictions. Such disregard had the effect of reducing the arguing behavior to zero in just four tutoring sessions. Allen *et al.* (1970) used an extinction technique to eliminate the tantrum behavior of a preschool child, Townsend. Observations of Townsend revealed that, during temper outbursts, he was physically comforted and restrained by his teachers. The investigators, assuming that such attention was reinforcing, decided that all tantrums should be ignored, regardless of intensity. Under extinction conditions, Townsend's first tantrum lasted 27 minutes, and each successive tantrum episode decreased in duration. The final tantrum, lasting just 4 minutes, occurred on the third day of the therapeutic program.

Extinction does not always occur so rapidly. Carlson *et al.* (1968) report that it took several months of therapeutic effort to eliminate the tantrum behavior of Dianne, an 8-year-old girl who would attack other children, scream profanities, throw chairs, and run wildly about the room. When a tantrum occurred, the usual procedure had been to take Dianne to an office where, although removed from peer support, she received attention from her teacher, the secretaries, the social worker, and the principal. In an effort to eliminate much of this attention, a program was established whereby Dianne was not removed from the room under any condition, and her classmates were given a candy treat when they successfully ignored her tantrum behaviors. Characteristic of behaviors which are no longer reinforced, Dianne's tantrums reached a deafening intensity and then decreased gradually in both intensity and frequency. Initially, Dianne was very sullen following a tantrum and covered her ears so as not to hear the other children enjoying the candy they had earned. During periods when no tantrums occurred, however, she seemed happier, and she played more with the other children. After nearly three months, the incidence of tantrum behaviors had been reduced to zero, cooperative play increased dramatically, and she was now described as a "happy, cheerful" child.

There are behaviors other than the target behavior which are affected by extinction procedures. Sajwaj *et al.* (1972) found that, when a teacher ignored the inappropriate conversation of a 7-year-old boy, the frequency of other behaviors also varied. Wayne had been referred to a remedial class for gross inattention to tasks and lack of academic progress. Although Wayne did not attend to academics, he did appear to be constantly around his teacher and reportedly tried to engage her in inappropriate conversation. On the other hand, he seldom played with the other children, and when he did play with them, he used girls' toys and assumed traditional women's roles, e.g., housewife. The target behavior initially selected for modification was Wayne's inappropriate speech. In an effort to reduce conversations to more acceptable levels, the teacher no longer responded to his initiated speech during recess. As expected, when the speech was ignored, there was a decrease in the behavior. Interestingly, the use of girls' toys also decreased, while initiated speech to children, cooperative play, and disruptive behavior increased. It can be seen that, although the extinction procedure may be effective if given enough time, the absence of reinforcement can result in emotional responses such as agitation, frustration, and increased motor activity. Also, during the later phases of extinction, alternative patterns of behavior emerge. Bandura (1969) has suggested that the types of behaviors which emerge during extinction are determined by the response options available. An individual will tend to behave in ways which have previously been successful. If, as Bandura indicates, the emerging behaviors are inadequate, then the change agent may be faced with the choice of extinguishing a long succession of inappropriate behaviors.

There are other characteristics which may make the extinction process an undesirable therapeutic technique under certain conditions. One is the apparent situational specificity of the suppression effects. For instance, Carlson *et al.* (1968) reported that tantrum behaviors were suppressed only as long at Dianne remained in the treatment setting. When Dianne was transferred to a new school, her tantrum behavior not only returned but was also strengthened through the inadvertent action of the school staff. Additionally, there is the problem of identifying and removing all reinforcements which maintain the maladaptive behavior. This may be very difficult, considering that many behaviors are reinforced by intrinsic effects, self-reinforcement, and subtle contingencies on complex schedules (Kanfer and Phillips, 1970). The principal disadvantage of extinction, however, would appear to be the inability to control or predict which new responses will replace the one being extinguished. In order to control for the emergence of these responses, adaptive behaviors must be reinforced. It is this modification of behavior resulting from the reinforcement of incompatible responses which will be reviewed next.

Reinforcement of Incompatible Behavior

An event is reinforcing if it increases the strength of the behavior it follows. The only way to determine if an event is a reinforcer is to observe its effects on the behaviors it follows (Hall, 1971). Basically, there are two types of reinforcers, primary (e.g., food) and conditioned (e.g., praise, attention, and approval).

When food is used as a reward, it is generally paired with a conditioned reinforcement. In a study by Shafto and Sulzbacker (1977), contingent food and praise were compared with methylphenidate (Ritalin) in controlling the hyperactive behaviors of a preschool child. The child, Byron, continuously moved around and rarely spent more than a few seconds at any given task. In one phase of treatment, Byron was given 5-mg. and later 15-mg. doses of Ritalin a day. In the other phase of the treatment, he received a piece of sweetened cereal and was praised following each 15 seconds of continued appropriate play. The results indicated that there were fewer free-play activity changes during the contingent reinforcement. In contrast, the medication had the effect of increasing attention to tasks but decreasing the intelligibility of speech and responsiveness to the teacher. It would appear that, if a behavior is reinforced, it displaces the inappropriate behavior with which it is competing. The study conducted by Allen *et al.* (1970) adds credence to this assumption. Contingent attention was used to modify the unintelligible speech of a young girl. Observations revealed that the girl's speech was almost totally unintelligible and that the teachers tended to ignore her attempts at appropriate speech. The teachers were, therefore, instructed to ignore Doreen's unintelligible verbal behavior and to give attention to appropriate verbalizations. Under this program, appropriate verbalizations increased steadily until they dominated verbal output.

The reinforcement of incompatible behavior can prove to be a very powerful behavior-changing technique. In a comparison of classroom behavior control methods, Madsen, *et al.* (1968) used rules, praise, and extinction to control the behavior of two classrooms. Teachers told students the rules for behaving in class, praised students who worked on assignments, answered questions, and ignored disruptive behaviors which interfered with learning. By systematically varying the control techniques, the investigators were able to show that providing rules and ignoring disruptive behavior did not noticeably affect this behavior.

Disruptive behavior decreased only when appropriate behavior was praised.

In describing the properties of a reinforcer, emphasis has been placed on the reinforcing stimulus. Premack (1965), in his investigations, placed emphasis on the reinforcing response. According to the Premack Principle, the opportunity to engage in a high probability activity can be made conditional upon the performance of a low probability behavior. For example, Hughes and Gregerson (1971) used playing with a toy (high probability behavior) to reinforce the classroom quiet time (low probability behavior) of a first-grade student. Programs in applied settings make extensive use of the Premack Principle. In one study utilizing this principle, Brooks and Snow (1972) used free time as a reinforcer for academic work. Bill, aged 9, was doing so poorly in school that he was being considered for special class placement. Although his IQ was 128, parents and teachers had low academic expectations for Bill, and peers considered him "dumb" and "stupid," an opinion which he himself shared. In an effort to keep Bill in the regular class, a behavior modification program was established. Within this program, free time was earned through the successful completion of arithmetic problems. Initially, the number of arithmetic problems which Bill had to complete was only 5. Over time, the criterion of performance necessary to earn recess was raised to 35 arithmetic problems. By the end of the program, Bill was successfully performing at near grade levels. As important spillover effects, his skills in spelling, writing, and social studies also showed significant improvement. Additionally, Bill's concept of himself improved, and his parents and teacher began to view him as bright and capable.

Behavior therapy is not limited to the modification of maladaptive behaviors. There have been a number of studies which have successfully used behavior therapy principles to accelerate the acquisition of academic skills. Harris and Sherman (1973) used consequences to motivate students in social studies and mathematics. The students' overall performances in these two academic areas had been described as deficient. In one phase, social studies students were simply asked to complete homework assignments according to traditional procedures. In a second phase, social studies students who had answered 80% or more of homework correctly could leave school 10 minutes early (later changed to 15 minutes early). Similar procedures were established in a mathematics classroom. The investigators reported that the assignment of homework alone had little effect on classroom performance. However, in both the social studies and the mathematics classrooms, the use of consequences for accurate completion of homework significantly improved academic performance in the classroom. The management of an entire class can be difficult, if only from a logistic point of view. The use of positive consequences, intermittently applied, can significantly reduce management demands and improve student academic performance. In a kindergarten class, the effects of intermittently applied consequences on the quality of printing was compared to a feedback procedure (Salzberg *et al.,* 1971). In the feedback phase, children were taught printing through detailed instructions and then graded on the quality of performance. In the contingency phase, the children were instructed and guided, but they also had to meet a predetermined level of performance before being dismissed for recess. If a student did not reach criterion, he/she was required to repeat the assignment until it was satisfactory or not participate in recess. The students were intermittently reinforced so that, on a given day, half the children were graded while the other half were released to play immediately upon completion of the assignment. It was reported that grading alone did not increase printing accuracy, but when grading was paired with access to play, printing accuracy improved significantly for every child.

Token Economies

Perhaps no other conditional reinforcer has received as much attention as the token. A voluminous part of the behavioral literature deals with these reinforcers and what has come to be known as token economies. A token is an object (e.g., a poker chip, point, or star) that can be exchanged for back-up reinforcers from which it obtains its value. When tokens are earned for a variety of behaviors and used to purchase a variety of back-up reinforcers, then a token economy is said to exist (Kazdin, 1977).

In one of the first studies to utilize token economy principles in the classroom, O'Leary and Becker (1967) were able to improve academic performance and reduce disruptive behaviors in a class of 17 children with behavioral problems. The class had a reputation for being hard to manage, and, indeed, it had been observed that 76% of the classroom behavior was disruptive. Interestingly, it had been reported that several of the children had not completed a class assignment in 2 years. Essentially, their program involved a set of rules about the appropriate behavior to be rewarded. Token reinforcers were then given at the end of each academic period commensurate with classroom performance, both academic and behavioral. These tokens were later exchanged for back-up reinforcers varying in value from 1¢ to 29¢. The investigators reported that, following the introduction of the token program, the average rate of disruptive behavior fell to an average of only 10%. Additionally, the students who had had difficulty completing papers were now completing class assignments at near perfect accuracy.

In another study, Ayllon *et al.* (1975b) found that token reinforcers could provide a feasible alternative to medication (Ritalin) for controlling hyperactivity. These school children, diagnosed as chronically hyperactive, were all receiving drugs to control such hyperative behaviors as gross motor activity, disruptive noise, disturbing others, and blurting out in class. Throughout the study, these hyperactive behaviors were measured, as were arithmetic and reading performance. In Phase 1 of the study, the students were observed for 17 days while on medication. During Phase 2, the students were observed while off the medication for a 3-day "wash out" period. In Phase 3, a token reinforcement system was introduced in which check marks, later exchanged for a variety of back-up reinforcers, were earned for arithmetic performance. Phase 4 was similar to Phase 3, except that both reading and arithmetic were now reinforced. No medications were used in these last 2 phases, and each phase lasted for 6 days. When medication was discontinued, the levels of hyperactivity doubled or tripled above those observed during Phase 1. However, when token reinforcement was administered for academic performance, the level of hyperactivity once again decreased to levels observed in Phase 1. Most important, although the average of correct performance for arithmetic and reading was only 12% when the children were taking medication, it was 85% under the token program. Thus, this study demonstrated that token reinforcement programs can offer justifiable alternatives to the use of medication for hyperactive children.

One criticism often leveled against academic behavior therapy programs and, in particular, token programs is that, when the teacher uses extrinsic rewards, she is really "bribing" the child. Unfortunately, such a choice of words implies that the teacher is applying contingencies for her own benefit, and not the child's. The real fear is that the extrinsic rewards are replacing the intrinsically motivating factors of learning. Once extrinsically rewarded for classroom performance, the child will expect to be so rewarded in the future. As a result, when the reinforcers are withdrawn, performance will deteriorate below the levels observed prior to the token program. It should be pointed out that the weight of research evidence does not support such a proposition

(Kazdin, 1977). Performance does not tend to return to baseline levels following the withdrawal of token reinforcers. One way to help insure that performance is maintained above baseline levels is for the teacher to utilize natural or intrinsic reinforcers when withdrawing the token and back-up reinforcers. Chadwick and Day (1971) illustrate how it is possible to maintain performance levels even after extrinsic reinforcers have been withdrawn. After establishing a point system which was paired with social reinforcers to improve academic performance, the researchers terminated the point system while continuing with the social reinforcers. The results showed that, with combined token and social reinforcers, percentage of academic work completed and performance accuracy increased significantly. After termination of the point system, the students under the social reinforcement program continued to complete academic work at the same high rate and at the same high accuracy level. The only performance decline noted when the points were withdrawn was in total work time. The withdrawal of extrinsic consequences, thus, does not necessarily have to result in a concomitant drop in performance. This is especially true when response maintenance is planned, rather than assumed to be an automatic consequence of the program.

In summary, it should be noted that token reinforcers are used only when students lack self-motivation or when intrinsic reinforcers are not effective. Token systems may serve to initiate behavior that more natural consequences can later control through careful planning and programming.

Group Consequences

With the exception of the Carlson *et al.* (1968) study, the programs presented so far have been individualized. There are a number of programs, however, that employ group consequences. A principal advantage of utilizing group contingencies is that the influence of peers can be a powerful factor in bringing about desired changes. Another reason for using group contingencies is that it may teach the child to be more responsive to others.

There are basically three kinds of group contingency approaches (Safer and Allen, 1976). In the first kind, one child earns rewards or punishments for the entire class. Brooks and Snow (1972) utilized this approach when Jim, a 10-year-old boy, was referred because of stealing, leaving the classroom without permission, and leaving the group when it was engaged in activities outside the class. To modify these behaviors, the teacher told her class that they were going to help Jim change his behavior and that Jim would earn points whenever he followed the classroom rules. When Jim earned 10 points, the entire class was awarded an extra 15 minutes of free time. If Jim's behavior was inappropriate, the entire class lost 1 minute of a desired activity. The results were immediate. Jim completed all academic work and was now performing at a level consistent with his ability. Additionally, the number of times Jim stole and left the class or group was reduced to zero. In another study (Evans and Oswalt, 1968), an entire fourth grade class would be dismissed early for recess when an underachieving student correctly spelled selected words. However, if the word was misspelled, the class continued with their work until the customary dismissal time. Similar procedures were implemented with other under-achieving students in arithmetic, social science, and general science. Compared with control subjects, the treated subjects' weekly test scores increased to a statistically significant degree.

In the second kind of group contingency program, each individual separately earns rewards for the entire group. For example, in a study by Packard (1970), a class was given access to a play activity or given points for back-up reinforcers when all of the students attended to task for a preestablished period of time. This procedure was compared to a control method in which the teacher reminded the students to attend. By contrast with the control condition, which produced relatively low and variable levels of attention, the group contingency condition consistently resulted in nearly 100% attention level. Group contingency programs sometimes exert greater control over the student than do programs directly focusing on the student alone. Alexander *et al.* (1976) reported that students were more likely to attend classes when reinforced as a group. Seven high school students who had a high incidence of school truancy were initially given a dollar for each day that they had attended. In the next phase, a student was given a dollar only when all 7 students achieved perfect school attendance for a particular day. The researchers reported that the group contingency was significantly more effective than the individual contingency system. More important, 2 of the students who were unresponsive to individual contingencies attended classes regularly under the group contingency condition. Peer pressure appears to have been the single most important factor affecting this behavior change. It is possible that such pressure can create additional problems for the learning-disabled youngster. The child can become a loss of reinforcement for everyone and, therefore, is likely to become an unpopular group member. This could adversely affect his/her already low self-concept.

The third kind of group contingency program involves competition between groups, with the reward going to the winning group. This type of program is often referred to as the "good behavior game." Barrish *et al.* (1969) used this procedure to modify the behaviors of 24 fourth-grade children. The class was reported by the principal to be a general management problem. Observations of the classroom revealed substantial behavior categorized as talking out (e.g. laughing, talking to classmates, whistling) and out-of-seat (e.g., standing or walking in the room without the teacher's permission). To deal with these problems, the teacher divided the class into 2 groups and told them that they were going to play a game. According to the game's rules, when a member of a group broke a class rule, his/her entire group got a point for the infraction. At the end of the week, the group with the fewest points received various classroom privileges, including an extra 30 minutes of free time. The game had the immediate effect of significantly reducing disruptive out-of-seat and talking-out behaviors. It seems that the ability to earn classroom privileges did much to motivate a youngster in a group. What may have been more reinforcing, however, was the opportunity to brag about being on a winning team. Comments such as, "My team beat yours again today," and, "Can't your team do anything right?" are apparently common in good behavior games. It should also be noted that, at one point in the program, one boy announced that he was no longer going to play the game and despite peer pressure, became so disruptive that he had to be dropped from the group. A similar episode happened in another class using the good behavior game (Harris and Sherman, 1973). In the middle of the game 3 students who were members of a group announced that they were no longer going to play and became very disruptive. To deal with this disruptiveness, a new group was formed of the 3 disruptive students. A procedure was also instituted whereby the losing group now had to remain for 5 minutes after school for each point earned over a criterion level. The new group had to remain after school for 15 minutes on the first day of the revised program. Thereafter, no group had to be kept after school, and, towards the end of the study, the 3 students asked to be and were returned to their original groups. It would thus appear that some youngsters are minimally, and in some cases adversely, affected by peer pressures. In such instances, more individualized programs may have to be implemented by the teacher.

Punishment

Three punishment techniques will be reviewed: time out, response cost, and overcorrection. The first, time out, is the removal of all reinforcement *for a specified time interval* (Bandura, 1969). To illustrate, a time out procedure was used to modify the tantrum behavior of Dicky, a young boy diagnosed as brain damaged (Wolf *et al.*, 1964). During a tantrum, Dicky would bang his head, whine, and cry, and his tantrums became so violent that he had to be put in restraints. To modify this behavior, the investigators isolated Dicky in a room for 10 minutes, contingent upon the onset of a tantrum. After 2½ months, Dicky's tantrums, which initially had occurred at almost a continuous rate, dropped to near zero.

It is important that time out be therapeutic. It should not exceed effective durations. The effects of time out durations have been investigated by White. *et al.* (1972). Children who displayed aggressive and tantrum behaviors systematically received 1, 15, and 30 minutes of time out in a research design that counterbalanced time-out duration order. Within this framework, a child was placed in a time out room for the specified durations, contingent upon the occurrence of disruptive behavior. The researchers reported that time outs of 15 and 30 minutes' duration produced a 35% decrease in disruptive behavior, with little difference in effectiveness noted between the 2 time out periods. Howver, the effectiveness of the 1-minute time out period proved variable and dependent upon whether it preceded or followed the other 2 time out periods. Unfortunately, the students participating in this study were not learning disabled, and, thus, the time-out durations may have to be adjusted to fit the particular needs of learning disabled students. For instance, a 15-minute time out may have little effect upon a learning disabled child who has difficulty in making temporal discriminations. Clearly, addtional research is needed in this area.

As with extinction, positive reinforcement is commonly used in conjunction with time out. Bostow and Bailey (1969) utilized these procedures in controlling the aggressive behavior of a 7-year-old boy. The boy, Dennis, would attack staff and other children and, as a result, was often tied to a hallway door. In order to modify Dennis' inappropriate behavior, it was decided to reward him with a piece of cookie for each 2-minute period containing no aggressive behaviors and to punish him by placing him in time out for 2 minutes following an aggressive act. Over the course of therapy, Dennis' aggressive responses decreased from a high of 75 in a session to a low of zero. The principal advantage in using positive reinforcement is that it enhances the suppressive effect of time out and helps insure that a desirable behavior will take the place of the undesirable behavior.

Chapter 9 above has also discussed some of the psychological implications in the time out process.

Response Cost

Response cost is the removal of a reinforcer, contingent upon the display of undesirable behavior.

Kaufman and O'Leary (1972) instituted a response-cost procedure in a remedial reading class of 16 adolescent students with long histories of disruptive classroom behavior. The cost procedure involved the loss of tokens, contingent upon a broad range of disruptive behaviors. Each student was given a behavioral rating at the end of 15 minutes (3 per 45-minute class) and was then told how many, if any, classroom rules he had broken. A token was taken away for each rule violated, with the remaining tokens being exchanged for back-up reinforcers. It was reported that the cost procedure markedly reduced disruptive behavior and had the concomitant effect of improving reading performance.

Burchard and Barrera (1972) compared the effectiveness of response cost to time out. Boys with histories of antisocial behavior were involved in 4 different time-out/response-cost conditions within a token economy. The youngsters were either fined (5 or 30 tokens) or placed in time out (5 or 30 minutes), contingent upon disruptive behavior. It was found that the punishment procedures at both high values (30 tokens or 30 minutes) were significantly more effective in reducing disruptive behavior than at the lower values (5 tokens or 5 minutes). Also, the time out and response cost of higher value were increasingly more effective over time, unlike those of the lower value. There was little difference in effectiveness, however, between procedures of similar magnitude. Burchard and Barrera point out that, in choosing between these punishment techniques, one should be aware of two advantages favoring the use of response cost. The first is that response cost does not remove the student from the opportunity to engage in desirable behavior; the second is that, by not being removed from the learning situation, the student is given the opportunity to choose between continuing with his/her disruptive behavior and behaving in a more acceptable fashion. When students are allowed to control their own behavior, they develop greater independence and trust in their own decision-making ability.

In another comparison of procedures, McLaughlin and Malaby (1972) found that ignoring inappropriate verbalizations while reinforcing (giving points for) quiet behavior was more effective in modifying student behavior than a response-cost procedure. Furthermore, like many punishment techniques, the response-cost procedure produced many undesirable emotional side effects, such as student agitation and a sharp increase in disruptive behavior. Although these emotional responses were only temporary, it was quite obvious that the students found the loss of points aversive. Thus, the teacher should be cognizant of the possibility that emotional side effects can result from the use of response cost.

Overcorrection

Overcorrection is a behavioral procedure designed (1) to overcorrect the situational consequences of an inappropriate act and (2) to require that the disruptor thoroughly practice the correct form of behavior (Foxx and Azrin, 1973). The method of having the offender achieve the first objective, referred to as restitutional overcorrection (Foxx and Azrin, 1972), requires that disruptors correct the consequences of their misbehavior by having them restore the situation to a state vastly improved over that existing before the disruption. For example, a student might have to scrub clean the whole classroom door, even though he/she had written on, or marked up, only a small portion of it. The second objective is achieved by having the disruptor practice the correct or appropriate behavior. This is referred to as positive practice. For example, if students speak out in class without permission, they are given extensive practice in raising their hands and asking for permission to speak. Generally, when no environmental disruption is created by a misbehavior, the restitutional overcorrection procedure is not applicable, and only the positive practice procedure can be employed.

In implementing the overcorrectional procedures, the teacher should be aware of certain guidelines. In overcorrecting the misdeed, the offender should exert effort. Overcorrection is work, and active participation is required. Also, as a punishment procedure, overcorrection should be related to the misbehavior. If it is not related, then the punishment may be viewed as "arbitrary" and "punitive" (Foxx and Azrin, 1972). In addition, it is important that a reward not be given the disruptor while he/she is rehearsing the correct forms of behavior. As negative reinforcement, the appropriate behavior is learned in order that punishment might be avoided (Kazdin, 1975). The first overcorrectional study to use restitution procedures was conducted by Foxx and Azrin (1972), who developed programs to modify the behaviors of 3 institutionalized adults. They are reviewed here because of their direct applicability to the classroom. Ann had been institutionalized primarily because she damaged property by throwing or overturning beds, chairs, and tables. These behaviors were modified by having Ann turn the overturned beds to their proper position and remake them, as well as straightening out all the other beds on the floor. When she turned over a chair or table, Ann was required to straighten all tables and chairs on the floor, wipe off all furniture with a damp cloth, and empty all trash cans. Ann was also required to apologize to the individuals whose beds, tables, or chairs had been overturned and to the other residents present on the ward. The authors reported that, in 2 weeks, Ann's abuse of furniture had been reduced from an average of 13 disruptions per day to only 1 per day. The throwing behavior was completely eliminated after 11 weeks.

Patricia was the second resident to participate in the study. She was a 56-year-old female who had suffered extensive brain damage in a car accident. Patricia's major behavioral problem was screaming. She often would scream for hours, both day and night, and, understandably, this caused much agitation among the other ward residents. In the treatment program, whenever Patricia screamed, she was required to go to a remote bedroom area and lie quietly in her bed for 15 minutes. Following the 15-minute quiet period, Patricia was taken back to where she had screamed, and, there, she had to apologize repeatedly to everyone present for having screamed. After a week of training, Patricia's screaming episodes were reduced by 80% and were nearly eliminated after 2 weeks of training.

The third resident to receive overcorrection training was Joan. Joan's major behavioral problem was her physical aggression. She would often grab or bite staff and residents. This behavior was modified by having Joan clean her mouth with oral antiseptic immediately following a biting episode. She was also required to wash the bitten area of her victim, apply an antiseptic solution, bandage the area, and help the staff complete a hospital incident report. As a result of the overcorrection program, Joan's attacks were reduced from an average of 6 per day during baseline to a near zero level after 2 weeks.

Positive practice overcorrection has been evaluated as a method of eliminating classroom disturbances (Azrin and Powers, 1975). Six students who were frequently disruptive in class participated in the study. Initially, the students were only warned and reminded of the classroom rules when disruptions occurred, as well as praised and given verbal approval for constructive classroom work. In the next phase of training, a student lost the right to go out for recess when he/she talked or left his/her seat without permission. In the third phase of training, a child who broke the rules was required to stay in the classroom over recess and practice the positive behavior of asking permission either to talk or to leave his/her seat. Finally, in the fourth phase of training, a student was required, as in Phase 3, to practice the positive behavior of asking for permission, this time immediately after violation of the rules. Azrin and Powers reported that, when compared to the initial phase of training, the loss of recess had the effect of reducing disruption by about 60%, the delayed positive practice phase by 95%, and the immediate positive practice phase by 98%. Clearly, the positive practice procedures (both delayed and immediate) were more effective. Exactly what effect the early phases of training had on later performance is unclear.

It would appear that overcorrection, as both restitution and positive practice, is a potentially powerful therapeutic tool. The overcorrection studies offer initially impressive and encouraging findings. However, the paucity of overcorrectional classroom research warrants the caution that further research on the efficacy of the technique and theory is still needed before any definite claims for overcorrection can be made.

It can be concluded that, whatever the technique, the teacher should be aware of several factors which maximize the effectiveness of punishment: (1) the greater the punishment strength, the greater the response suppression (Burchard and Barrera, 1972); (2) punishment is more effective when it is given every time the maladaptive behavior occurs, rather than intermittently; (3) the effectiveness of punishment is greater when it immediately follows the maladaptive behavior, rather than being delayed (Azrin and Powers, 1975) and; (4) punishment is most effective when a student is being reinforced for appropriate behavior while being punished for maladaptive behavior (McLaughlin and Malaby, 1972).

BEHAVIOR MODIFICATION IN THE HOME

Rationale

A major concern of the behavioral clinician is that gains made in the office or classroom be maintained in the child's natural environment. Researchers have developed a number of procedures to insure the maintenance of behavioral gains. These procedures include, among others, the development of target behavior in the child's natural environment, the substitution of intrinsic reinforcers for extrinsic reinforcers, and the use of intermittent reinforcement to replace continuous reinforcement (Kazdin and Bootzin, 1972; Kazdin and Craighead, 1973). Ultimately, however, if behavior is to generalize across settings and be maintained across time, it is most important that the parents be considered as change agents, since in most cases, the parents are in the best position to control the type of reinforcement, as well as the schedule of reinforcement, in the child's environment. As Wahler *et al.* (1965) point out, parental training often eliminates the very contingencies which have helped to support the child's deviant behavior and provides new contingencies which produce and maintain more adaptive behavior.

Parents as Change Agents

Many of the behavioral techniques used in training parents to modify disruptive home behaviors have been reviewed above. These techniques are generally taught within the framework of 3 parent-training models. Two of these, described by Walder *et al.* (1969), are individual consultation and controlled environment. In the individual-consultation model, the clinician observes parent-child interactions in the therapist's office and provides feedback to the parent on better ways of dealing with the child. Generally, the therapist shapes parental competence in behavior modification, reinforces desired parental behaviors, and instructs the parent on the importance of accurately observing and recording behavior. One of the earliest and simplest applications of this model was reported by Williams (1959), who instructed parents on the use of extinction procedures to eliminate the tantrum behaviors of their young son. Before treatment, the child would yell and scream when his parents left the room at bedtime and continue until they returned to the room. The parents then had to remain in the room until the boy fell asleep. In order to prevent these tantrums, the parents were counseled to ignore the disruptive behaviors. In the home application of the extinction principle, the parents simply put their son to bed, left the room, and closed the door. The child screamed for 45 minutes the first time he was put to bed. The duration of the crying decreased gradually over successive occasions until, by the tenth occasion, the child no longer fussed when his parents left the room. Interestingly, the tantrum behavior did not occur again until a visiting aunt put the child to bed. The child immediately began to cry when the aunt left the room, and this behavior was reinforced when the aunt stayed at the youngster's bedside. After the aunt's visit, it became necessary to extinguish the behavior a second time. There were no reported tantrums at bedtime during the next 2 years following the second extinction series. Green *et al.* (1976) taught parents to modify maladaptive behaviors through instructions provided in the clinic. Parent-child interactions were videotaped, and, with the aid of these videotapes, the parents were taught how to ignore deviant behaviors, use time out, and attend to appropriate behaviors. In one study, the deviant behaviors of a young girl decreased from an average of 24% before training to 6% during treatment. Further, the gains obtained in the clinic were maintained 6 months later, when it was reported that disruptive behaviors occurred at a frequency of less than 1%. Thus, the individual consultation model would appear to be a viable training model for instructing parents on the use of behavioral management techniques.

In the controlled-environment model, the interactions of parent and child are again carefully structured, but much of the clinician's time is now spent in the home, observing and providing instructions to parents. Wahler (1969a) instructed parents on the use of behavior management techniques in the home. The parents were taught how to use a time out technique and how to attend to appropriate behavior while ignoring inappropriate behavior in an effort to control the oppositional behavior of 2 elementary-school-aged boys. The boys had been described as uncooperative and negativistic. To insure that the behavioral principles were appropriately applied, Whaler carefully monitored interactions as the parents implemented the contingency program. Any misapplication of behavioral principles was quickly brought to the attention of the parents. After only a few weeks, it was reported that the parental program had effected a significant reduction in their children's oppositional behavior. Just as important, the parents' interactions with their children were more positive. For example, the parents described themselves as enjoying their children and were observed smiling more frequently and having more physical contact with them. Wahler's second study (1969b) replicated these findings. In addition, he reported that the therapy effects did not generalize across settings. Although the disruptive behaviors were evident in both the school and the home, as the disruptive behaviors decreased in the home, they remained unchanged at school. In order to affect school behaviors, a contingency program had to be implemented in that setting. This demonstrates, again, that generalization should not be expected to occur naturally; it has to be programmed.

Working with a mother, O'Leary *et al.* (1967) used a home token economy and a time out procedure to modify the disruptive behavior of a 6-year-old boy, Barry, who had been diagnosed brain damaged and was described by his psychiatrist as "seriously disturbed." Observations revealed that Barry was hyperactive, refused to follow parental instructions, fought with other children, and destroyed his or other children's toys. Initially, the therapist carried out a home token economy, with the parents playing only an ancillary role. In the second phase, a time out procedure was added, and the mother worked alongside the therapist. The mother was trained to use behavioral principles, with hand signals being used by the therapist to indicate their application. Over time, the therapist faded into the background, and the mother assumed more and more responsibility for implementing the program. It was found that Barry's disruptive behaviors were greatly reduced under the behavioral program, and they remained at a low level even when social reinforcers were later substituted for the extrinsic token reinforcers.

Combining elements of both the individual-consultation and controlled-environment models, Engeln *et al.* (1968) helped the parents of a very disruptive boy to gain awareness of the relationship between their behavior and that of their child. Mr. Jackson, the father, rarely responded to his children, except to punish them when he found them irritating. To appease the children, he would promise to take them hunting or fishing, but on the scheduled morning of these trips, he would sneak out of the house before the children awakened. Mrs.

Jackson, on the other hand, had spent some time in a state mental hospital and appeared totally inadequate in dealing with either her husband or her children. The Jacksons had been referred to the clinic because of the oppositional behavior of their 6-year-old son, Jacky, who was described as out of control by his parents. When he did not want to do what was asked of him, Jacky would engage in violent temper tantrums involving hyperactivity, swearing, and physical aggression. He would also scream and cry out for extended periods and often physically attack his younger sister. To modify these behaviors, a therapist first instructed Mrs. Jackson on behavior modification principles in the clinic, while a second therapist went into the home and gradually established a good rapport with the initially hostile Mr. Jackson. A third therapist, working with Jacky in the clinic, shaped compliant behavior by reinforcing the youngster's responsiveness to commands. Following the sixth session, Mrs. Jackson joined the therapist working with her son and helped shape compliant behaviors while ignoring inappropriate behaviors. As Mrs. Jackson become more proficient in applying behavioral contingencies, she instituted a home token economy. Gummed stars, exchangeable for various toys and treats, were given, contingent upon appropriate behavior. As a result of the program, Jacky's disruptive behaviors had been markedly reduced, and Mr. Jackson indicated that communication between him and his wife was much improved. A follow-up after 6 months revealed that Jacky's behavior continued to be manageable, although the communication between Mr. and Mrs. Jackson had returned to pretreatment levels.

Miller (1975) borrowed elements of both the individual-consultation and controlled-environment models to develop a parent training program holding much promise. For convenience, each of the steps in this training program is presented in outline form in Table 11.1.

A third training model outlined by Walder *et al.* (1969) is the educational group. This model has been utilized by Tams and Eyberg (1976) with large numbers of parents. In the program, parents of children with moderate to severe behavior problems meet as a group and discuss methods of dealing with disruptive behaviors. With the help of a trained professional, the group develops problem solving skills and behavior management skills. The principal advantage of the educational program is that it provides opportunities for parents to see that other families have similar difficulties. At the same time, it allows them to give support as well as receive it. Salzinger *et al.* (1970) instructed 15 families on the use of behavioral principles and guided

Table 11.1
Intervention Strategy

Steps	Purpose
Screening	Assess appropriateness of parent training as treatment of choice.
Baseline	Document the frequency and intensity of the disturbing behavior patterns identified in the screening interviews.
Intervention 1	Assess and improve the parents' understanding of basic social learning concepts with videotape observations, behavioral rehearsal, and home observations used in each intervention phase.
Intervention 2	Develop parents' abilities to discriminate and respond appropriately to their child's behavior.
Intervention 3	Help parents develop and implement a home contingency program.
Intervention 4	Train parents in the use of discipline procedures.
Intervention 5	Counsel parents on problems which interfere with treatment progress and continue working on the home interventions (maintenance training and follow-up).

the parents in the application of those principles. All participants in the program were parents of brain-damaged children who had volunteered for the training. Initially, the parents were asked to observe and record their child's disruptive behavior while attending lectures and group discussions on behavior modification principles. After a year of such instruction, the parents were asked to construct home management programs. Only after a program had been written out and checked were parents given permission to carry it out in the home. Through continued instruction and group discussion, the families were guided in the implementation of their programs. The parents reported that the behavior modification programs had successfully changed their children's behaviors. Unfortunately, the investigators did not validate these claims through home observations.

Parents have also been involved in classroom contingency programs. For instance, Sluyter and Hawkins (1972) were able to modify the disruptive classroom behaviors of Tim. Tim had been observed shouting, talking out of turn, and disturbing other children and the teacher in the classroom. In an effort to shape more appropriate behaviors, the teacher sent a written note of praise home whenever Tim's inappropriate behaviors fell below a predetermined criterion level. The parents would follow up these notes with verbal praise and inexpensive toys. The investigators found that, with the institution of the parent-managed reinforcement program, there was a statistically significant decrease in disruptive classroom behavior. When the program was extended to 2 other students experiencing academic difficulties, similar findings were reported. Children who had experienced academic difficulties showed significant improvement when parents reinforced daily classroom achievement. Several other studies have recently replicated these very interesting findings (Ayllon *et al.,* 1975a; Schumaker *et al.,* 1977).

Another interesting aspect of parent training is the apparent ripple effect. When parents are trained to apply contingencies and begin to treat the maladaptive behavior of one family member, the behavior of siblings also changes. Lavigueur *et al.* (1973) found that, when a mother praised her son's appropriate behavior and punished inappropriate behavior, the rate of acceptable behavior, not surprisingly, increased. Most interestingly, the mother's behavior towards her daughter, who was not considered a behavior problem, paralled the handling of her son. As a result, the frequency of the daughter's appropriate behavior increased, while the frequency of inappropriate behavior decreased. The mother differentially reinforced the daughter's behavior, even though no specific treatment plan had been developed to modify it. Similar findings have recently been reported by Resick *et al.* (1976).

Perspective on Ethics

A justifiable concern of the behavioral clinician is ethics. Every clinician should be concerned that behavioral principles taught to parents are being appropriately applied. It makes little sense, for instance, to spend only a few days instructing parents, or any non-professional, on the use of learning procedures without taking the time to evaluate the practice of those principles (Stein, 1975). The clinician must follow up training sessions with direct supervision or, at least, with weekly consultations on the application of the learning procedures. The consequences of a failure to supervise adequately may be unfortunate. When a therapist trains parents in the use of behavioral procedures, especially those involving some kind of punishment, he/she makes a commitment to the family, a commitment which should include a guarantee of adequate supervision. Even when such supervision is provided, suitable follow-up procedures are often lacking (Howlin *et al.*, 1973). Too often, a telephone conversation suffices as a check on posttherapy progress. Such a follow-up procedure is weak, at best, and it ignores the real possibility that parents may lie, if only to avoid continued therapeutic involvement. It also ignores the possibility that there may be significant discrepancies between actual and perceived changes in behavior (Schnelle, 1974). Clearly, more adequate follow-up procedures are needed if the long-term effects of parent training are to be known.

One other ethical issue involves the use of punishment. Bernal *et al.* (1968) recommended that a mother use spanking as one means of controlling her son's disruptive behaviors. However, it was reported that, on a few occasions, the mother had become so frustrated in dealing with her son that she spanked him severely. The therapist should train parents in the use of procedures which cause the least amount of pain to the child; e.g., spanking should be considered as an alternative only when other behavioral management techniques fail.

Let us now examine some important aspects of parent training which are in need of investigation. Elaborate procedures have been established for interviewing and initiating parent training programs (Holland, 1970) and for evaluating parental skills during training (Gardner, 1975). However, little or no attention has been given to the question of the best way to terminate training or the best way for the therapist to sever contact with the family. Considering the obvious importance of adequate supervision and follow-up, this is not an insignificant matter.

Consideration should also be given to the best parent training methods. Looking into this question, Gardner (1972) found that role playing was more effective in teaching behavior modification principles to nonprofessionals than was a lecture method, while Kovitz (1976) found little difference between individual and group methods. Certainly, this question merits further investigation. Another important issue in parent training is the determination of which parents make the better change agents. Lovaas *et al.* (1973) have pointed out that not all parents make equally good behavior modifiers. Those who are willing to use strong contingencies throughout the entire day seem to be the most successful. Salzinger *et al.* (1970) found that parents with educations beyond the high-school level tended to achieve greater success as behavior modifiers than did parents with less formal education. An empirical investigation is needed, however, before any definite statements can be made.

SUMMARY

This chapter reviews the current status of behavior therapy in the classroom and the home. Emphasis is given to behavior modification principles which can assist teachers and parents in dealing with the many problems of the learning disabled child. The applicability of each principle is examined, with special attention focused on the issue of the long-term effectiveness of behavior therapy. Theoretical as well as ethical issues are also considered, particularly as they pertain to working with families in therapy.

REFERENCES

Alexander, R.N., Corbett, T.F., & Smigel, J. The effects of individual and group consequences on school attendance and curfew violations with predelinquent adolescents. *Journal of Applied Behavior Analysis,* 1976, *9,* 221–226.

Allen, K.E., Turner, K.D., & Everett, P.M. A behavior modification classroom for Head Start children with problem behaviors. *Exceptional Children,* 1970, *37,* 119–127.

Ayllon, T., Garber, S., & Pisor, K. The elimination of discipline problems through a combined school-home motivational system. *Behavior Therapy,* 1975, *6,* 616–626. (a)

Ayllon, T., Layman, D., & Kandel, H.J. A behavioral-educational alternative to drug control of hyperactive children. *Journal of Applied Behavior Analysis,* 1975, *8,* 137–146. (b)

Azrin, N.H. & Powers, M.H. Eliminating classroom disturbances of emotionally disturbed children by positive practice procedures. *Behavior Therapy,* 1975, *6,* 525–534.

Bandura, A. *Principles of behavior modification.* New York: Holt, Rinehart & Winston, 1969.

Barrish, H.H., Saunders, M., & Wolf, M.M Good behavior game: Effects of individual contingencies for group consequences on disruptive behavior in a classroom. *Journal of Applied Behavior Analysis,* 1969, *2,* 119–124.

Bernal, M.E., Duryee, J.S., Pruett, H.L., & Burns, B.J. Behavior modification and the brat syndrome. *Journal of Consulting and Clinical Psychology,* 1968, *32,* 447–455.

Bostow, D.E. & Bailey, J.B. Modification of severe disruptive and aggressive behavior using brief time out and reinforcement procedures. *Journal of Applied Behavior Analysis,* 1969, *2,* 31–38.

Brooks, R.B. & Snow, D.L. Two case illustrations of the use of behavior modification techniques in the school setting. *Behavior Therapy*, 1972, *3*, 100–103.

Burchard, J.D. & Barrera, F. An analysis of time out and response cost in a programmed environment, *Journal of Applied Behavior Analysis*, 1972, *5*, 271–282.

Carlson, C.S., Arnold, C.R., Becker, W.C., & Madsen, C.H. The elimination of tantrum behavior of a child in an elementary classroom. *Behavior Research and Therapy*, 1968, *6*, 117–119.

Chadwick, B.A. & Day, R.C. Systematic reinforcement: Academic performance of underachieving students. *Journal of Applied Behavior Analysis*, 1971, *4*, 31–32.

Engeln, R., Knutson, J., Laughly, L., & Garlington, W. Behavioral modification techniques applied to a family unit—a case study. *Journal of Child Psychology and Psychiatry*, 1968, *9*, 245–252.

Evans, G.W. & Oswalt, G.L. Acceleration of academic progress through the manipulation of peer influence. *Behavior Research and Therapy*, 1968, *6*, 189–195.

Foxx, R.M. & Azrin, N.H. Restitution: A method of eliminating aggressive-disruptive behavior of retarded and brain damaged patients. *Behavior Research and Therapy*, 1972, *10*, 15–27.

Foxx, R.M. & Azrin, N.H. Dry pants: A rapid method of toilet training children. *Behavior Research and Therapy*, 1973, *11*, 435–442.

Gardner, J. Teaching behavior modification to nonprofessionals. *Journal of Applied Behavior Analysis*, 1972, *5*, 517–522.

Gardner, J. Training nonprofessionals in behavior modification. In T. Thompson & W. Dockens (Eds.), *Applications of behavior modification*. New York: Academic Press, 1975.

Green, D.R., Budd, K., Johnson, M., Lang, S., Pinkston, E., & Rudd, S. Training parents to modify problem child behaviors. In E.J. Mash, L.C. Handy, & L.A. Hamerlynch (Eds.), *Behavior modification approaches to parenting*. New York: Bruner/Mazel, 1976.

Hall, R.U. *Behavior management series: Basic principles*. Lawrence, Kansas: H & H Enterprises, 1971.

Harris, V.W. & Sherman, J.A. Use and analysis of the "Good Behavior Game" to reduce disruptive classroom behavior. *Journal of Applied Behavior Analysis*, 1973, *6*, 405–418.

Holland, C. An interview guide for behavioral counseling with parents. *Behavior Therapy*, 1970, *1*, 70–79.

Howlin, P., Marchant, R., Rutter, M., Berger, M., Hersov, L., & Yule, W. A home-based approach to the treatment of autistic children. *Journal of Autism and Childhood Schizophrenia*, 1973, *3*, 308–336.

Hughes, F. & Gregerson, G. Reduction of irrelevant talking-out in a fiirst grader through the use of magic (slate). In R.V. Hall (Ed.), *Behavior management series: Applications in school and home.* Lawrence, Kan.: H & H Enterprises, 1971.

Jones, S. Extinction of arguing behavior in a fourth grade boy. In R.V. Hall (Ed.), *Behavior management series: Applications in school and home.* Lawrence, Kan.: H & H Enterprises, 1971.

Kanfer, F.H & Phillips, J.S. *Learning foundations of behavior therapy.* New York: Wiley, 1970.

Kaufman, K.F. & O'Leary, K.D. Reward, cost and self-evaluation procedures for disruptive adolescents in a psychiatric hospital school. *Journal of Applied Behavior Analysis,* 1972, *5,* 293–310.

Kazdin, A.E. *Behavior modification in applied settings.* Homewood, Ill.: Dorsey Press, 1975.

Kazdin, A.E. *The token economy.* New York: Plenum, 1977.

Kazdin, A. & Bootzin, R. The token economy: an evaluative review. *Journal of Applied Behavior Analysis,* 1972, *5,* 343–372.

Kazdin, A.E. & Craighead, W.E. Behavior modification in special education. In L. Mann & D.A. Sabatino (Eds.), *The first review of special education* (Vol 2). Philadelphia: Buttonwood Farms, 1973.

Kovitz, K.E. Comparing group and individual methods for training parents in child management techniques. In E.J. Mash, L.C. Handy, & L.A. Hamerlynch (Eds.), *Behavior modification approaches to parenting.* New York: Bruner/Mazel, 1976.

Lavigueur, H., Peterson, R.F., Sheese, J.G., & Peterson, L.W. Behavioral treatment in the home: Effects on an untreated sibling and long-term follow-up. *Behavior Therapy,* 1973, *4,* 431–441.

Lovaas, O.I., Koegel, R., Simmons, J.Q., & Long, J. Some generalization and follow-up measures on autistic children in behavior therapy. *Journal of Applied Behavior Analysis,* 1973, *6,* 131–165.

Madsen, C.H., Becker, W.C., & Thomas, D.R. Rules, praise, and ignoring: Elements of elementary classroom control. *Journal of Applied Behavior Analysis,* 1968, *1,* 139–150.

McLaughlin, T.F. & Malaby, J. Intrinsic reinforcers in a classroom token economy. *Journal of Applied Behavior Analysis,* 1972, *5,* 263–270.

Miller, W.H. *Systematic parent training.* Champaign, Ill.: Research Press, 1975.

O'Leary, K.D. & Becker, W.C. Behavior modification of an adjustment class: A token reinforcement program. *Exceptional Children,* 1967, *33,* 637–642.

O'Leary, K.D., O'Leary, S., & Becker, W.C. Modification of deviant sibling interaction pattern in the home. *Behavior Research and Therapy,* 1967, *5,* 113–120.

O'Leary, K.D. & Wilson, G.T. *Behavior therapy: Application and outcome.* Englewood Cliffs, N.J.: Prentice-Hall, 1975.

Packard, R.G. The control of "classroom attention": A group contingency for complex behavior. *Journal of Applied Behavior Analysis,* 1970, *3,* 13–28.

Premack, D. Reinforcement theory. In D. Levine (Ed.), *Nebraska symposium on motivation* (Vol. 13). Lincoln: University of Nebraska Press, 1965.

Resick, P.A., Forehand, R., & McWhorter, A.W. The effect of parental treatment with one child on an untreated sibling. *Behavior Therapy*, 1976, *7*, 544–548.

Safer, D.J. & Allen, R.P. *Hyperactive children: Diagnosis and management.* Baltimore: University Park Press, 1976.

Sajwaj, T., Twardosz, S., & Burke, M. Side effects of extinction procedures in a remedial preschool. *Journal of Applied Behavior Analysis*, 1972, *5*, 163–176.

Salzberg, B.H., Wheeler, A.A., Devar, L.T., & Hopkins, B.L. The effect of intermittent feedback and intermittent contingent access to play on printing of kindergarten children. *Journal of Applied Behavior Analysis*, 1971, *4*, 163–172.

Salzinger, K., Feldman, R.S., & Portnoy, S. Training parents of brain-injured children in the use of operant conditioning procedures. *Behavior Therapy*, 1970, *1*, 5–32.

Schnelle, J.F. A brief report on invalidity of parent evaluations of behavior change. *Journal of Applied Behavior Analysis*, 1974, *7*, 341–343.

Schumaker, J.B., Hovell, M.E., & Sherman, J.A. An analysis of daily report cards and parent managed privileges in the improvement of adolescents' classroom performance. *Journal of Applied Behavior Analysis*, 1977, *10*, 449–464.

Shafto, F. & Sulzbacker, S. Comparing treatment tactics with a hyperactive preschool child: Stimulant medication and programmed teacher intervention. *Journal of Allied Behavior Analysis*, 1977, *10*, 13–20.

Sluyter, D.J. & Hawkins, R.P. Delayed reinforcement of classroom behavior by parents. *Journal of Learning Disabilities*, 1972, *5*, 20–28.

Stein, T. Some ethical considerations of short-term workshops in the principles and methods of behavior modification. *Journal of Applied Behavior Analysis*, 1975, *8*, 113–115.

Tams, V. & Eyberg, S. A group treatment program for parents. In E.J. Mash, L.C. Handy, & L.A. Hamerlynch (Eds.), *Behavior modification approaches to parenting.* New York: Bruner/Mazel, 1976.

Wahler, R.G. Oppositional children: A quest for parental reinforcement control. *Journal of Applied Behavior Analysis*, 1969, *2*, 159–170. (a)

Wahler, R.G Setting generality: Some specific and general effects of child behavior therapy. *Journal of Applied Behavior Analysis*, 1969, *2*, 239–246. (b)

Wahler, R., Winkel, G., Peterson, R., & Morrison, D. Mothers as behavior therapists for their own children. *Behavior Research and Therapy*, 1965, *3*, 113–124.

Walder, L., Cohen, S., Breiter, D., Daston, P., Hirsch, I., & Leibowitz, J. Teaching behavioral principles to parents of disturbed children. In B.G. Guerney (Ed.), *Psychotherapeutic agents: New roles for non-*

professionals, parents and teachers. New York: Holt, Rinehart & Winston, 1969.

White, G.D. Nielsen, G., & Johnson, S.M. Time-out duration and suppression of deviant behavior in children. *Journal of Applied Behavior Analysis*, 1972, *5*, 111–120.

Williams, D.C. The elimination of tantrum behavior by extinction procedures. *Journal of Abnormal and Social Psychology*, 1959, *59*, 269.

Wolf, M.M., Risley, T., & Mees, H. Application of operant conditioning procedures to the behavior problems of an autistic child. *Behavior Research and Therapy*, 1964, *1*, 305–312.

CHAPTER 12

THE CREATIVE ARTS THERAPIES

MYRA LEVICK, M.Ed.
DIANNE DULICAI, M.A.
CYNTHIA A. BRIGGS, M.M.
LISA BILLOCK

The creative process is the process of change, of development, of evolution, in the organization of subjective life . . . In order to create, one must yield to the . . . indeterminate fullness and activity of the inner life. For it is organic, dynamic, full of tension and tendency. What is absent from it . . . is determination, fixity, and any commitment to one resolution [in preference to] another of the whole complex of [life's] tensions.

—Brewster Ghiselin, *The Creative Process*

INTRODUCTION

In the preceeding chapters, the utilization of traditional psychotherapeutic techniques with specific learning disabled (SLD) children has been discussed. These include individual, group, and family concepts from a psychoanalytic and behavior modification theoretical framework.

This chapter will address the utilization of art, movement, and music therapy with this population. While some of the case material presented here will replicate the age groups described previously, the emphasis is on the unique intervention and efficiency of the nonverbal modalities. Becker (1976) describes the child with minimal brain dysfunction as one who is very likely to be under considerable emotional distress and often unable to articulate his "anxieties, confusion and understandable feeling of insecurity." The directors of the Creative

Arts in Therapy (CAT) program at Hahnemann Medical College and Hospital in Philadelphia have worked with numerous populations of children with SLD and have supervised CAT students on field placements in schools, both public and private, with such populations. They have learned that not only do the children have difficulty articulating their feelings and thoughts, but so do their families and even sometimes their teachers.

The creative arts therapists contributing to this chapter primarily view development from the genetic-dynamic-psychoanalytic model. However, in diagnosis, intervention, and treatment, the examples given will demonstrate the adaptation and modification of this model and, where necessary, the use of other treatment approaches to meet the needs of the child in question.

Art, music, and movement therapists who see themselves primarily as therapists rather than as teachers must first be skilled in the use of either art materials, musical instruments, or dance and movement notation. They must be able to translate the therapeutic goal into an appropriate activity and be able to teach the child how to express himself/herself through art, music, or movement in order to accomplish this goal. These therapeutic goals must be consistent with those of the other members of the therapeutic team (Levick, 1975).

Definitions of each of these modalities follows:

Art Therapy:

Art therapy can be considered as a prescribed substitution of creative activity to replace neurotic symptoms, to strengthen defenses used successfully by the patient before illness became acute, and to establish a prescribed relationship with the therapist.

There are a number of goals the art therapist must keep in mind, i.e., strengthening of the ego and catharsis, or the ventilation of feeling. Other goals include making diagnosis from color and forms, from what the patient says and the associations he/she makes with his/her artistic productions; reducing guilt, uncovering anger, helping develop control of impulses, helping develop an ability to integrate and relate; and finally, helping the patient use art as a new outlet during his/her incapacitating illness (Levick, 1967).

The above definition was originally formulated while the author (art therapist) was working with a population of adolescent and adult emotionally disturbed inpatients. These goals have been consistently applicable to a variety of populations and are concomitant with those described in the case material for diagnosis, intervention, and treatment of SLD children.

Dance/Movement Therapy:

This is the psychotherapeutic use of dance/movement as a process for the purpose of physical, emotional, and cognitive growth (American Dance Therapy Association, 1966). Movement therapy has addressed itself predominantly to the emotional aspects of the individual and incorporates the body movements of the patient as well as verbalization and secondary elaboration. This combination of mind/body processes in the therapeutic session allows for extensive intervention with the SLD child.

Music Therapy:

Music therapy is the use of music in the accomplishment of therapeutic aims: the restoration, maintenance and improvement of mental and physical health (National Association for Music Therapists, 1977). The professional music therapist participates in the analysis of individual problems and in the systematic application of music to bring about desirable changes in behavior.

Music therapy can be beneficial to individuals by providing a means for nonverbal expression, by encouraging verbal expression, by promoting the aim of cognitive skills through different learning channels and methods, and by fostering greater insight and under-standing of self.

BROAD APPLICATIONS TO EDUCATION

Many problems still exist regarding diagnosis and differentiation of organic versus functional learning disorders. It is our purpose to examine ways in which creative arts therapies can contribute to the resolution of this major area of concern.

Creative arts therapists have a broad knowledge of normal stages of development as they relate to their own disciplines, especially in the area of nonverbal communication, with its inherent value for correlating chronological, cognitive, and emotional levels of functioning. Space does not permit a comprehensive literature review, but some well-known literature from each field will be cited to give an indication of the body of knowledge which provides a basis for this understanding.

Findings and Application to SLD

ART

In the field of psychology, Machover (1949) and Koppitz (1968) have contributed much to the recognition and understanding of body image projections in the human figure drawings of children and adolescents. Kellogg (1970), Kellogg and O'Dell (1967), and DiLeo (1973) have collected data and demonstrated the universality of children's drawings from age 1 through adolescence. For example, every child aged 1 to 2 begins to scribble in definite patterns. By age 3, the child begins to enter the stage of outlining shapes. Circles, ovals, squares, rectangles, triangles, and crosses begin to appear in a variety of ways. From these initial outlines, shapes, structured forms and shapes-within-shapes are produced.

During ages 4 to 5, the pictorial stage of development occurs. Structural designs begin to look like something adults can identify. In the early pictorial stage, human figures, animals, trees, etc., are only suggested; in the later stage, they are more clearly defined (Kellogg and O'Dell, 1967). All children move through these stages sequentially, and differences in the ages at which they occur vary according to genetic factors and environmental stimulation.

Kramer (1958) and Naumburg (1966) describe the manifestation of intrapsychic conflict in children's drawings. They and other well-known art therapists have demonstrated that spontaneous drawings of both children and adults reveal normal and pathological evidence of fears, fantasies, thoughts, and affects stimulated by internal and external pressures, ego strengths and weaknesses, id derivatives, and normal and abnormal defense mechanisms. It has also been demonstrated that unconscious material can be made conscious and that both mastery and resolution of conflicts can often be obtained through expression in graphic and plastic productions.

Through looking at children's drawings, the trained art therapist can guide the therapeutic team in pinpointing developmental motoric, perceptual, or emotional problems that may interfere with learning. For example, in a pilot study conducted at a residential school for children classified as "mentally retarded," Kohn (1973) compared scores as seen on the Draw-a-Man test, a semistructure test designed by the researcher, and interpretation of the free drawings of 40 retardates aged 5 to 65, with IQs of 40 to 85. Kohn was originally interested in developing a method for predicting maladaptive behavior in "acting-out retardates." While some of the subjects did manifest psycho-pathology that correlated with their behavior, others drew pictures that suggested problems not observable clinically. In addition to demonstrating clearly that signs of retardation are discernable from functional signs in drawings of retardates, the study presented considerable evidence that IQ tests may not be a valid measure for intelligence. This latter finding carries profound implications for SLD/MBD/HKS (learning disabled/minimal brain damaged/hyperkinetic) children.

Another study compares the art work of four adolescent readers, functionally disabled by the influence of obsessive-compulsive defenses on both art and reading performances and referred to a reading clinic, with that of four readers disabled by SLD/MBD/HKS and four normal adolescents. The findings of this pilot study suggest that the defenses of functionally disabled readers are more rigid and, therefore, less effective in binding anxiety than those of the other populations (Shaw, 1976). While further research is necessary in this area, the implications for therapeutic intervention are manifold.

Vogler (1973) specifically examined the use of art therapy as a measure for exploring the emotional problems of the severely retarded. In her pilot study, she found several advantages for the use of art therapy as a diagnostic tool in situations where standard testing materials proved difficult or inadequate:

(1) It eliminates the need for verbalization.
(2) It permits retardates' (and other handicapped persons) to function at their own level within their own limitations.
(3) It eliminates the need for abstract thinking.
(4) It gives no rules for right or wrong in production.
(5) It provides a personal means of expression which can also be a nonverbal experience fostering socialization.

DANCE/MOVEMENT

North's work (1972) in the field of dance/movement therapy focused on normal development and the correlation of movement patterns to intellectual growth. This seminal work confirmed the relationship between personality, IQ, and nonverbal communication during a 12-year longitudinal study of children with average intelligence. This original work was the necessary starting place for investigation into disruption of development from a movement focus.

Kestenberg (1965), while doing considerable work on the developmental stages of movement, focused also on emotional problems as manifested in movement patterns.

A child first learns through kinesthetic experience of his/her own body and remains rooted in the concrete physical world until age 7 or 8 (Ginsberg & Opper, 1960). Even language acquisition is supported by kinesthetic cues: synchronous gesturing of the parent and physical manipulations of the face and jaw.

The emotional aspects of the child's development have long been recognized as dependent on the nonverbal behavior of child and parent during the first five years (Kestenberg, 1975). Attachment, separation, body boundaries, body image, regulation of drives, and clarity of autonomy are all evidenced in the physical realm. Dance/movement therapists are trained to address the developmental, cognitive, and emotional issues manifested in the movement patterns of children, enabling them to diagnose, treat, and support growth in both areas in a concrete clinical manner.

Posey (1976) studied six children, 9 to 15 years of age, in a residential facility for the mentally and emotionally handicapped. Movement assessments and interpretation of drawings were made separately by art and movement therapists. Comparison of these assessments indicated that a significant correlation exists between the evaluations of nonverbal material from different modalities. Posey, like Kohn (1973), found that these evaluations were inconsistent with the results of standard IQ tests.

Levine (1976) developed specific movement games and demonstrated that they can be effective as diagnostic measures for children with learning and/or emotional disabilities. Her pilot study was conducted with children who were patients at a short-term crisis intervention clinic with both outpatient and inpatient units.

MUSIC

Research in stages of development of musical abilities and related behaviors has been done by Ostwald (1973), Noy (1968), Meerloo (1961), and McDonald (1970). All these authors begin with prenatal influences, specifically the mother/child heartbeat and intrauterine vibrations and rhythms.

Ostwald also emphasizes the infant cry, with its normal versus pathological parameters. Meerloo and Ostwald both discuss the concepts of vocal contagion and mental contagion of sounds in the first years of life. McDonald discusses the young child's use of humming and repetition of tunes to soothe himself/herself and to serve as a "transitional tune." As the child moves into second year of life, his/her ability to vocalize and mimic increases (Ostwald), and by age 2, he/she can begin to put together song patterns. Toward age 4 to 5, the child's singing voice, pitch manipulation, and rhythmic ability steadily improve (Ostwald, 1973).

The SLD child is characterized by hyperactivity, distractability, spatial and temporal distortion or disorientation, communication disorders, and memory impairment. In working with these children, trained music therapists not only recognize impaired musical abilities and related behaviors, but also address themselves to the levels of development in which these problems first manifested themselves, regardless of chronological age. To date, little has been reported in this area.

Helping the SLD Child Learn Through Creative Arts

As stated above, art, music, and dance/movement therapists do present themselves primarily as therapists. However, their unique skills and knowledge in the areas of nonverbal communication enable them to develop avenues for learning not possible through traditional methods. Rubin (1975) affirms that expressive arts therapists increasingly recognize that the goals of therapy and education, while not identical, overlap considerably. In addition, however, their knowledge of psychosexual development and therapeutic techniques makes it possible for them to achieve their goals more quickly and effectively. Such expertise is especially valuable, since we cannot assume that any specific artistic activity is relaxing for everyone. Artistic productions cannot be forced from the patient without his/her willingness to participate in the artistic media (Levick, 1967).

Lyons challenged Cruickshank's theory (in Lyons, 1971) that learning disabled children should rarely be asked to draw a picture on their own. As a teacher in a private school for children with learning disabilities, she collected data for one year and demonstrated conclusively that this theory does not hold true. To begin, she removed the cubicles the children had been assigned and arranged the room for more peer interaction; she conducted art sessions on a regular weekly basis; such media as crayons, magic markers, and colored pencils that provided structure and control were used; freedom of expression was encouraged. All the children's productions were highly valued and were displayed on classroom walls. The school year was concluded with a puppet show presented to the school by the children, who wrote, staged, and acted it themselves. Her results raised many questions for future art therapists and teachers, demonstrating that art can be a stimulus and an aid to ego function in a classroom for learning disabled children.

Boyle (1973) devised a method of teaching brain-damaged children between the ages of 5 and 6 to know the names of shapes which they previously had been unable to recognize. At the same time, there was an improvement in body image. Unexpectedly, Boyle found that, as the children's drawing skills improved, it became possible to detect emotional disturbance within their drawings which had not been demonstrated in their previous work.

Kruger (1973) and Shaw (1976) demonstrated in their pilot studies with learning disabled preadolescent children that art therapy is effective in improving self-esteem and can be used to foster learning by uncovering and working through conflicts associated with reading disabilities and obsessional behavior.

Bush (1976) studied five public school children between 10 and 12 years of age who had been placed within the school in special classes for academic and behavioral problems, more specifically defined as "acute learning problems." A graduate art therapy student, Bush met with these children at least once a week, individually or in groups of three. The pilot study covered a period of eight months, and some improvement in both areas was observed. One child in particular began to disclose thoughts and feelings about the death of his father, which had occurred three years prior to this study. Neither the school counselor, teachers, nor his mother had realized how traumatized the child was by this event. During the art therapy sessions, he began to work through some of this. He improved in his school work and was encouraged to continue to deal with this trauma with the school counselor.

In a therapeutic nursery setting, Dreby (1976) investigated the correlation between the growth of movement repertoire and speech development in three preschoolers who were undergoing movement therapy over a period of four months. The results revealed a general trend toward higher developmental usage of both language and movement as movement therapy progressed.

In literature related to music and SLD, emphasis has been placed on ways in which music and its elements can be used both to improve the LD child's listening, motor, and speech skills (Phipps, 1975) and to organize the SLD child in his educational areas of deficit (Welsbacher, 1975). Another concept discussed is that of using music as a background modifier, programming the best music for each child to hear while working in the classroom (Campbell, 1972).

Music educators and music therapists consistently rely on the fact that rhythm is an organizer and that music, by its elements, can provide structure, self-organization, and interpersonal relations (Sears, 1968). The rhythms and phrases of music can be easily adapted to aid in teaching skills unrelated to music itself. By incorporating concepts in song, cognitive skills such as numbers, animals, colors, syllables, and prefixes can be taught in a flexible, enjoyable structure in which rhythm and melody organize the process of learning and memorizing.

Specific music therapy activities, or a thorough breakdown of the most useful approaches, may reveal further applications, especially since work with learning disabilities is a relatively new field for the music therapist.

Recognizing both that music is useful as a teaching tool by making learning fun while aiding concentration, attention, and memory, and also that music can mobilize strong feelings and lend strength to the ego in dealing with them, Adamson (1977) suggests that a technique combining therapy and education through music should be effective in working with children whose conflicted psychological processes inhibit their learning.

ART THERAPY CASE MATERIAL

The following two examples of the utilization of art therapy with children referred to a reading clinic for SLD students were provided by Karen L. Greene, art therapist and teacher at the Temple Laboratory School, Temple University, Philadelphia, Pennsylvania.

Case Study 12.1

Becker (1976) states that children with SLD may see themselves as clumsy and inept. For example, they may have difficulty riding a bicycle, playing ball, tying their shoelaces, or even engaging in the usual noncompetitive, playful games of childhood.

This is an appropriate description of Joey, aged 10, who was transferred to this school after moving from the country to the city with his parents and one younger sibling. From the time he arrived, it was clear that he was having difficulty adjusting both in his new home and in his school environment. Relationships with peers were poor; he was reluctant to participate in classroom, art room, and schoolyard activities. In fact, he appeared unable to engage in any play activities with his peers and was indeed clumsy and awkward.

All the children in this school meet with the art therapist at least once a week in a group, and those with special problems are referred either by the director of the school, the psychologist, the social worker, or the child's teacher for weekly individual art therapy.

Joey's first drawing (Fig. 12.1) suggested severe poor body image in the incomplete figures, i.e., stumps for arms in both figures, only the top of the figure drawn at the right, and half of one leg missing on the figure at the left. Stumps for limbs often appear in drawings made by children of a much lower chronological age. The lines are drawn with a sureness that would be absent if there were organic impairment. Therefore, the picture suggests considerable evidence of emotional disturbance causing learning disorders. When he completed the two figures, he proceeded to cross them out. In conversation, he seemed well oriented to his surroundings, but his representation of the human figure was bizarre and unrealistic. He was referred for individual art therapy.

The art therapist/teacher decided to structure the art sessions by suggesting topics that were familiar to this child and gave him media that would provide controls, such as crayons, pencils, magic markers. In this way, she hoped to develop his cognitive skills through a pleasant experience and improve his body image through mastery of his surroundings and awareness of his role within them.

Figure 12.2 is a picture he did only two months later, depicting the scenery he passed on his way home on the bus. This drawing is realistic and almost age-appropriate. Concomitantly, his classroom work had greatly improved. As the rapport between therapist and child grew, supported also by her helping him learn to play ball during recess, she

Figure 12.1 Restricted Use of Space and Poor Body
Image at Beginning of Therapy

Figure 12.2 Realistic Drawing of Landscape after
Two Months in Art Therapy

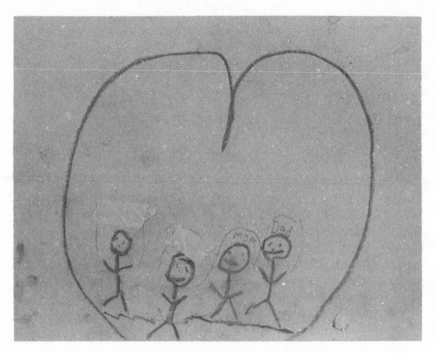

Figure 12.3   Family Picture at End of Art Therapy Sessions

lessened the structure of the sessions and attempted to engage him in more dynamically oriented art therapy.

The progress made by this child was interrupted by two anxiety provoking situations. His parents considered moving again, and his writing teacher (a graduate student) left. Regression was observed in his drawings and classroom work even before these events were known to the staff. He refused to play with his peers or attend art therapy. The staff met and decided that the art therapist should continue to work with him in his homeroom in an effort to reestablish their previously productive relationship and provide him with every possible opportunity to express his feelings. In addition, when notified of his behavior the writing teacher volunteered to return, and his parents did not follow through on plans to move.

Before the end of the year, Joey asked to return to art therapy sessions with a friend. The art therapist viewed this as a healthy attempt not only to make peer relationships, but also to master the separation anxiety he had experienced at the threat of the two real losses. In the closing sessions, he was encouraged to work with his friend and to prepare with him for the end of the school year. Figure 12.3 is a picture he did of himself, his sister, and his parents. Note the stick figures, frequently drawn by children between the ages of 7 and 10, the wide use of space in comparison to the restricted use in Figure 12.1, and the ability to contain the image rather than obliterate it as in Figure 12.1.

Case Study 12.2

Becker (1976) discusses the clowning behavior of some SLD children, and cites Gardner (in Becker, 1976) who reports that MBD children often act as if they see themselves as freaks, not because they are, but because they have chosen to be freaks. This provides these children with a perceived power to play whatever roles they choose, and to turn them on or off at will.

Greene describes Rose, 11 years of age, as "angry, hostile, dependent, clinging, silly." Rose described herself as a "clown." To prove her point, she drew the same clown head over and over again in art therapy group sessions. Figures 12.4, 12.5, and 12.6 are examples of the many she produced, for several months, without bodies.

While accepting these repetitive, obvious self portrayals, the art therapist did question who was under the clown mask. Rose said she herself was under the mask and agreed to "unmask" the clown. The day this was to occur, the child reported a nightmare to Greene. Realizing that the child was not yet ready for the unmasking but making no interpretations, the art therapist suggested they continue to paint the same clown face as in the past. Rose readily agreed. For Christmas, she made a clay head wall-hanging as a gift for her "art teacher." Several weeks later, she drew herself with the clown hat and ruffle. By the end of the school year, she gave her clowns complete bodies and talked of designing clothes for people and clowns. She also moved up one level academically.

This is a good example of how the therapist's knowledge of defensive patterns manifested in images and of psychotherapeutic tech-

Figure 12.4   Rose's First Clown Head Drawn Without a Body

niques helped her to discern and challenge a defense for which the child had no replacement. At the same time, her knowledge and sensitivity helped her to support the defense until the child was ready to relinquish it in favor of something more productive.

These brief examples indicate that the goals of art therapy sessions with SLD children should be established to meet the needs of each child in the area of cognitive and emotional growth. The art therapist's

Figure 12.5   Rose's Repetitious Drawing of Self as a Clown

knowledge of graphic media, psychosexual development, and psychotherapeutic techniques enable him/her to establish these goals consistent with the child's level of development and emotional strengths
and weaknesses, regardless of chronological age.

Figure 12.6   Rose's More Elaborate Drawing of Clown Head Without a Body

MUSIC THERAPY CASE MATERIAL

The following two examples of music therapy with an SLD population are taken from the files of the author (music therapist).

Case Study 12.3

Metzler (1973) used music therapy with behavior problem and learning disabled children in a learning center that focuses on returning the child to his/her regular school as soon as the child is able. Using behavioral techniques, the music therapist focused on providing success experiences for the children and employed music to help achieve specific behavioral objectives for each child. Congruent with the center's rules structure, the music therapy setting required that children must "earn" entrance, must have impulse control to move into instrumental work, and must conduct themselves appropriately to remain.

Case Study 12.4

In a private agency setting for LD children, music therapy, recreational therapy, and speech therapy were provided as adjuncts to classroom situations that leaned mainly toward behavioral techniques. Music therapy focused largely on allowing a successful, creative experience that channeled hyperactivity and encouraged impulse control. Additional emphasis was placed on allowing children to use their creativity, fantasy, and imagination in a focused, acceptable way. Music therapy involved the use of adapted Orff-Schulwerk (Bitcon, 1976) rondos, acting out of original and familiar songs, group and solo singing, and moving to music and rhythms.

Adapted Orff-Schulwerk (Bitcon, 1976) and the rondo form provide a rhythmic structure for activity for the unorganized SLD child. Structuring "hellos," conversations, and fantasies encouraged group process and cohesion and expression at the same time.
Examples:

>   I've got a name and it
>   Goes like this . . .

Or: There is a telephone on the wall.
       If you had a telephone,
       Who would you call. . . .   (Bitcon, 1976)

Group singing with actions or sections for individual solos provides a structure with an appropriate opportunity to gain attention from the therapist and peers. Writing a group song with everyone contributing a line similarly encourages creativity, sharing, group interaction, and group identity/unity.

One of the most successful group activities is the use of Orff-Schulwerk structure to allow movement and imagination, beginning with rondos like:

>   Choo choo choo choo choo
>   The train stops for you
>   Where will we go and
>   What will we do?

Or: We're going to the store
       It's just down the street
       We don't have to ride
       We can go on our feet.   (Bitcon, 1976)

The children can march, imitate a train, choose a peer and a destination and pretend to take their train to that destination. Similarly, they can march, skip, or hop to the store and imagine what they would buy if they were free to choose anything. Once the children learn the framework, it is easy for them to write their own.

The best process for a music therapy session is to start with a name activity that allows each child to play, sing, or in some way respond to his/her name, move into an activity that fits his/her "state," try to impose a structure to modify hyperactivity, and *always* close with a group song or rondo.

The goals of the music therapist in working with SLD children are: (1) channeling hyperactivity into acceptable and appropriate musical expressions, and (2) structuring appropriate ways to allow the children to use their imagination and fantasy in a creative, expressive, ego-strengthening way.

MOVEMENT THERAPY CASE MATERIAL

In the following example of a 5-year-old child in a treatment clinic setting, the authors (movement therapists) present: (1) a movement evaluation of the child, (2) the therapist's interpretation of the profile in terms of cognitive and emotional development, and (3) treatment goals for the movement therapy sessions.

Case Study 12.5

This child, Tom, was treated at a clinic for emotionally disturbed children for symptoms of autism in addition to organic retardation. He could not speak, rarely gave evidence of understanding speech, and manifested eating disturbances and avoidance of contact with others in his environment.

Movement Evaluation

Using Laban's methodology (Laban and Ullman, 1969), the movement therapist examined Tom's movement repertoire, consisting of body attitude, dynamic level, use of space, weight, time, and phrasing. The following interactional components were found:

Rare use of eye contact
Inability to accept entrance of another into his kinesphere

No gestural initiation to others
No molding or accommodation of body
No synchrony with other person
Active avoidance of physical contact

None of the above categories shows sufficient development to assess this child's functioning at age-appropriate level. Actually, the severe deprivation of the repertoire suggests that disturbance began in the first year of life. During that period, the ability to scan the crib visually or focus directly on an object in the crib provides the beginning underpinnings of differentiation of self and object. One suspects, therefore, that there were also nursing problems which, in turn, affected his need satisfaction.

After the vertical position is attained (sitting, walking, etc.), the task of differentiation becomes more intense. The normal child deals with weight (his own and that of objects), viscosity, and his effect on the environment (pushing away, pulling, etc.). Yet this child had no grounding or body center, leaving him to pass through the "terrible twos" without sufficient developmental tools with which to function. His emotional development was effectively stopped. Chronologically, he has reached 5 years with the attendant physical drives and the added burden of parental expectation of developmental progress unattained.

Placing this child in a classroom situation where direct focus is necessary for short periods of time while being seated would serve only to frustrate the child, parent, and teacher. He has weathered a series of failures to meet expectations which date back to earlier failure in relational process of individuation, specifically from his mother. Additionally, he has since added failures which, at 5 years, have rendered him immobilized with fear of failure itself.

Cognitive Aspects in Movement Therapy

Learning, for a disabled child such as Tom, becomes a monumental undertaking. Observation of the child's body movements provides the assessor with clear keys to his levels of cognitive functioning. The movement observer focuses first on this child's use of the space around him. It is important to note that he seems to confine himself to one area of the room in which he is working. Attempts to venture out of his small space result in extreme disorientation and ensuing hyperactivity. He is unable to move directly through space with purpose and follow-through. Even if there is purpose involved in his initial decision to move from point *a* to point *b,* it is not easily discernible by the observer.

On a playground with "normal preschoolers," one might see the children moving from one activity to the next, e.g., going up and down the sliding board, running to the swings, and swinging. It may be done with quickness, and time may not be spent on one activity alone. However, one can see the purpose, the intention, and the planning that go into their schema. Here we are talking about a concept known as motor planning. For normal children, this develops predictably and concurrently with growth in other areas. For SLD/MBD/HKS children, motor planning must be externally structured, and careful consideration of the environment in which the learning is to take place must be made. Without the development of motor planning, these children become disorganized, fragmented, and unable to make sense out of their world. Tom shows not only an inability to carry through a movement strategy, but also a lack of differentiation between space at close proximity and far space. Such children must first learn to process the space around them before they will be able to take in and process the information needed to learn.

The movement observer looks next to the child's concept of his/her own body. Observation of Tom reveals his lack of clarity concerning his own kinesphere, as defined by the space directly around the child's body as far as the limbs can reach. One sees hesitancy in SLD children, for example, in using the area behind them. They function as though they were unaware of this back space. They are uncomfortable lying prone or doing activities which require reaching backwards. Consequently, we see these children constantly in an upright position, often vertical, and rarely relaxed. Knowledge of one's own kinesphere not only facilitates exploration of the world around one, but it also provides options for accommodating to the stress which compounds the disorganization of children with SLD/MBD/HKS.

Knowledge of kinesphere plays a large role in the area of language. These authors (movement therapists) have observed many times that movement through space and utilization of the child's own body space facilitate understanding of the verbal symbols. For example, rocking with a child back and forth while labeling the action aids the child in making a connection which previously has been confusing. Tom clearly has difficulty in making verbal connections to the actions around him. Gesture and movement, combined with the spoken word, clearly help him to do so.

In this study, we have observed a child who functions restrictedly with the space around him and with his own body. It follows that he is also unable to adapt his body intensity appropriately to any given situation. For example, he jumps on a bouncing board repeatedly throughout the session; however, he is unable to change the speed at which he jumps. It appears that the child is unable to find release through the activity; he is unable to stop. Implications are that he will have great difficulty in concentrating for any period of time. The child's attention span is practically nonexistent at this point. He also lacks body modulation.

We have seen the therapist attempting to intervene, to help the child organize himself, to suggest more control. The concept of a beginning and an ending to any one activity must be a long-term goal for a child such as Tom.

It is only after the issues of modulation, spatial relations, and body space have been addressed that the child may begin to understand the ingredients required to process information, to learn. Once the child is aided in sequencing the material, he/she will then be ready for the more complex sequencing techniques needed to read and to write.

Movement Therapy Goals

These would be the goals for the movement therapy sessions with Tom:

(1) To use the movement repertoire of the child to begin the process of communication between therapist and child, with emphasis on:
   (a) molding
   (b) reciprocal accommodation
   (c) modulating sequencing of drive discharge
   (d) improvement of spatial clarity
(2) To allow avoidance behavior to a partial degree and then paralleling and integrating parental limit-setting rules in the therapy sessions.

COLLABORATIVE CREATIVE ARTS THERAPY

This next example of case material reflects the collaboration of a dance/movement therapist and art therapist.

Case Study 12.6

An 8-year-old boy with a diagnosis of hyperactivity and MBD was referred for movement therapy by the school psychologist. He had been placed in an MBD classroom. As movement therapy sessions progressed, the therapist raised questions regarding the basis (organic or functional) for the MBD diagnosis. The child was asked to do two drawing tasks: (1) draw a house very quickly and (2) draw another house, taking as much time as he wished (top and bottom of Figure 12.7). The art therapist concurred with the movement therapist's evaluation: that under stress this child appeared loose and disorganized, with minimal evidence of motoric and perceptual impairment. However, when allowed to go at his own pace, there was no evidence of any organic problems. The child's emotional component produced the most interference with learning.

After weekly movement therapy sessions, this child has been returned to a normal classroom and has completed the year with a *B* average.

CONCLUSION

While this chapter has presented only a brief introduction to the utilization of the creative arts therapies with SLD children, the potential for diagnosis, intervention, and treatment is enormous.

However, much work still needs to be done to educate the community. As stated in the introduction, teachers and parents must also be helped to deal with their feelings so that they, in turn, can provide more support to the SLD child.

The creative arts in family therapy is not a new combination, but little has been reported in this area with families of SLD children.

In a private school for the minimally brain damaged, Dubin (1971) had a small group of children draw pictures of themselves. She then had the parents of these same children draw pictures of their children. The results of this pilot study were most interesting: the poor self-image of the child was repeated by the parents. This suggests the tremendous influence which the parents' nonverbal communication has on the child's development of self-esteem.

Cohen (1975) writes of her experience in introducing art therapy into a school system in a Southwestern city. The project was funded for

Figure 12.7   (*top*) House Drawn Quickly
(*bottom*) House Drawn More Carefully

only six to eight months, and while many problems combined to make success impossible, one is particularly relevant here. Before she could even begin to work with the children, she found it necessary to conduct art therapy sessions for the teachers and administrative staff. Cohen seriously recommends that whenever plans are made to incorporate creative arts therapies into a regular school program, intensive in-service training should be planned and given not only to school faculty and staff, but also to the administration, psychologists, and counselors. She feels strongly that the entire school system must be educated.

The authors of this chapter concur with Cohen: the team approach is essential. The creative arts provide an efficient, economical, and effective part of the bridge to better understanding and treatment of the SLD child.

REFERENCES

Adamson, C.K. *Effects of prescribed music therapy on the psychological development of disadvantaged preschool children.* Unpublished masters thesis, Hahnemann Medical College, Philadelphia, 1977.

American Dance Therapy Association, *A.D.T.A.* (pamphlet). Columbia, MD: Author, 1966.

Becker, R. The neurology of childhood learning disorders: The minimal brain dysfunction syndrome examined. *Therapeutic Education,* reprinted from *Journal of the Association for Therapeutic Education,* 1976, *4*(1).

Bitcon, D.H. *Alike and different: The clinical and educational use of Orff-Schulwerk.* Santa Ana, CA: Rosha Press, 1976.

Boyle, B. *A study of the relationship between body image and shape recognition in brain damaged children.* Unpublished masters thesis, Hahnemann Medical College, Philadelphia, 1973.

Bush, J. *Art therapy: Its use in effecting change in school age children with acute learning problems.* Unpublished masters thesis, Hahnemann Medical College, Philadelphia, 1976.

Campbell, D.D. One out of twenty: The L.D. *Music Educators Journal,* April 1972, pp. 38–39.

Cohen, F.W. Introducing art therapy into a school system—Some problems. *Journal of Art Psychotherapy,* 1975, *2*(3/4).

DiLeo, J.H. *Children's drawings as a diagnostic aid.* New York: Brunner/Mazel, 1973.

Dreby, R. *A pilot study of the relation of movement and language in movement therapy for pre-schoolers.* Unpublished masters thesis, Hahnemann Medical College, Philadelphia, 1976.

Dubin, S. *Self-image and the image parents have of the child.* Unpublished masters thesis, Hahnemann Medical College, Philadelphia, 1971.

Ginsberg, H. & Opper, S. *Piaget's theory of intellectual development.* Englewood Cliffs, N.J.: Prentice-Hall, 1960.

Kellogg, R. *Analyzing children't art.* Palo Alto, CA: Mayfield Publishing, 1970.

Kellogg, R. & O'Dell, S. *The psychology of children's art.* Del Mar, CA: CRM Associates for Random House, 1967.

Kestenberg, J. Role of movement patterns in development. *Psychoanalytic Quarterly,* 1965, *34.*

Kestenberg, J. *Children and parents: Psychoanalytic studies in development.* New York: Jason Aronson, 1975.

Kohn, D. *Study of free drawings in predicting behavior of retardates.* Unpublished masters thesis, Hahnemann Medical College, Philadelphia, 1973.

Koppitz, E. *Psychological evaluation of children's human figure drawings.* New York: Grune & Stratton, 1968.

Kramer, E. *Art therapy in a children's community.* Springfield, IL: Charles C. Thomas, 1958.

Kruger, L. *Art therapy as a means to strengthen the self-esteem of the early adolescent disabled reader.* Unpublished masters thesis, Hahnemann Medical College, Philadelphia, 1973.

Laban, R. & Ullman, L. *The mastery of movement* (Rev. ed.). Boston: Plays, 1969.

Levick, M. The goals of the art therapist as compared with those of the art teacher. *Journal of the Albert Einstein Medical Center,* Philadelphia, 1967, *15.*

Levick, M. Art in psychotherapy. In J. Masserman (Ed.), *Current psychotherapies* (Rev. ed.). New York: Grune & Stratton, 1975.

Levick, M. The goals of the art therapist as compared to those of the art teacher. *Journal of the Albert Einstein Medical Center,* 1976, *15,* 157–158.

Levine, L. *Effectiveness of movement games in treating children with learning and/or emotional disabilities.* Unpublished masters thesis, Hahnemann Medical College, Philadelphia, 1976.

Lyons, S. *Art applied as a stimulus and an aid to ego function in a classroom for learning disabled children.* Unpublished masters thesis, Hahnemann Medical College, Philadelphia, 1971.

Machover, K. *Personality projection in the drawing of the human figure.* Springfield, IL: Charles C. Thomas, 1949.

McDonald, M. Transitional tunes and music development. *Psychoanalytic Study of the Child,* 1970, *25,* 503–520.

Meerloo, J. A. M. Rhythm in babies and adults. *Archives of General Psychiatry,* 1961, *5,* 77–83.

Metzler, R.K. Music therapy at the behavioral learning center. *Journal of Music Therapy*, 1973, *10*(4), 177–183.

National Association for Music Therapists. *A career in music therapy* (pamphlet). Lawrence, KS: Author, 1977.

Naumburg, M. *Dynamically oriented art therapy: Its principles and practices.* New York: Grune & Stratton, 1966.

North, M. *Personality assessment through movement.* London: McDonald Evans, 1972.

Noy, P. The development of musical ability. *Psychoanalytic Study of the Child*, 1968, *23*, 332.

Ostwald, P.F. The sounds of emotional disturbance. *Archives of General Psychiatry*, 1961, *5*, 97–102.

Ostwald, P.F. *Soundmaking.* Springfield, IL: Charles C. Thomas, 1963.

Ostwald, P.F. Musical behavior in early childhood. *Development of Medicine and Child Neurology*, 1973, *15*, 367–375.

Phipps, M.F. Music education for learning disabilities. In R.M. Graham (Ed.), *Music for the exceptional child.* Compiled for The National Commission on Instructions, Music Educators National Conference, Reston, VA, 1975.

Posey, P. *Psychological development as reflected in drawings and body movement of handicapped persons.* Unpublished masters thesis, Hahnemann Medical College, Philadelphia, 1976.

Rubin, J.A. On education: How the arts can help. *High Fidelity/Musical America*, May 1975. (reprint)

Sears, W.W. Process in music therapy. In E.T. Gaston (Ed.), *Music in therapy.* New York: Macmillan, 1968.

Shaw, B.A. *The relationship between obsessive-compulsive defenses and reading disabilities in adolescence, as observd in the process of art therapy.* Unpublished masters thesis, Hahnemann Medical College, Philadelphia, 1976.

Vogler, S. *Art therapy: Its use in exploring the emotional problems of the severely retarded.* Unpublished masters thesis, Hahnemann Medical College, Philadelphia, 1973.

Welsbacher, B. Music for the learning disabled. In R.M. Graham (Ed.), *Music for the exceptional child.* Compiled for The National Commission on Instructions, Music Educators National Conference, Reston, VA, 1975.

CHAPTER 13

MEDICAL THERAPIES

WILLIAM C. ADAMSON, M.D.

There is an overriding need for social and even ideologic research into current practices (in prescribing medications). We need to know not only what should be done but what is being done, with what justification, by whom, to whom, for how long, with what expectations, and with what long-term outcome.

—Roger D. Freeman, *School Review*

INTRODUCTION

On July 4, 1970, the Huntley-Brinkley television news report picked up and reported a *Washington Post* story of doctors in Omaha, Nebraska, who had been giving behavior-modifying drugs to control children's behavior in the classroom. On the anniversary of America's independence, these newscasters raised the question: does such medical therapy improve behavior or infringe on individual liberty?

In journalistic style, Schrag and Divoky (1975) brought this problem to the attention of the reading public with their popular book, *The Myth of the Hyperactive Child.*

CRITICAL ISSUES

From a clinical and educational point of view, Freeman (1966, 1976) has continued his ten-year pursuit of objectivity, clarity, realism, irrationality, and absurdity in evaluating the effects of drugs on learning in children. The following fourteen critical issues can be highlighted from Freeman's most recent and compelling presentation:

(1) The lack of useful criteria to delimit the nonsynonymous SLD, MBD, and HKS groups of children has led to confusion in the field.

(2) Better delineation of appropriate diagnostic procedures will require clarification of the boundaries of these entities and more comprehensive observation and research on the various homogeneous subgroups.

(3) Valid data on the prevalence of SLD, MBD, or HKS in North America are not available. The study by Rutter *et al.* (1970a, 1970b) on the Isle of Wight population found less than 0.5 percent of hyperkinetic disorders in 9- and 10-year-olds. Bax (1972) found no hyperkinetic 5-year-olds in that population.

(4) Labeling, to some extent, is tied to existing cultural trends, fashions, and expectations and has powerful effects for good or ill in the population labeled.

(5) Learning disability, per se, is not an indication for medication. Pharmacotherapy may be helpful for deficits in attention and impulse control which lead to severe overactivity. Drugs act as an adjunct to other interventions and do not alter behavior patterns directly and/or permanently.

(6) A combination of drug administration and behavior modification may be more effective than either alone (Christianson and Sprague, 1973).

(7) Little is known about the metabolism of stimulants and other psychoactive drugs in children. More sophisticated methods are needed to compare a child's behavior with the level of free drug in the body, which cannot be equated with the dose administered orally.

(8) There is general agreement that education is a basic necessity for all children with SLD, MBD, and HKS and that all should have the benefit of a competent psychological assessment (see Chapter 3 above) and a diagnostic educational assessment (see Chapter 4 above).

(9) Teachers and school administrators must develop a critical attitude toward the use of medications, since it is often school behavior which stimulates the prescription of drugs as well as the accusation that they are being misused.

(10) Physicians are often not well informed in pharmacotherapy for

children. Many do not utilize school observations in evaluating and monitoring drug therapy.

(11) The follow-up study by Weiss *et al.* (1975) of the stimulant drug treatment of HKS children indicated that, while short-term benefits were evident, later outcome showed no difference between the control group and children receiving methylphenidate (Ritalin) and chlorpromazine (Thorazine).

(12) There is no epidemic in the field of SLD, MBD, and HKS conditions among children. Instead, there has been an unfortunate episode of progressive medicalization of deviant or troublesome behavior.

(13·) Two factors play supporting roles in the burgeoning of prescriptions for these children: (1) huge profits for the manufacturers of psychotropic drugs, and (2) the government's increased concern for the control of deviancy which might lead to anti-social behavior in later life.

(14) In the use of medication for these children, our society has accepted a series of questionable assumptions. It is time to examine more critically and accurately the social side-effects of our present treatment approach.

MEDICATION IS *NOT* THE ONLY TREATMENT

Currently, the pendulum is swinging away from the traditional medical model in dealing with SLD, MBD, and HKS populations. This appears as a more general trend throughout our culture. For example, the right to treatment or the right to refuse treatment has been recognized by the Supreme Court of the United States (O'Connor v. Donaldson [No. 74-8], June 1975) as resting in the hands of the individual patient, rather than in the prescription of commitment by the physician. In this case, the traditional medical model has given way to a legal system model.

In the epidemiology and psychopathology of mental disease, the individual's subcultural environment and family system may be more significant than the more traditional cellular and organ-function-dysfunction system. Here, the medical model has been partially replaced by the social systems model.

In the economic system, the rising costs of medical care and the multimillion-dollar medicare and medicaid programs under the Social Security Administration are pushing the traditional medical service delivery model toward a bureaucratically administered National Health Insurance.

Finally, and most relevant to our present study, there has been an equally strong trend in the educational system to shift the management of SLD, MBD, and HKS populations, with their associated personality disorders and behavioral problems, away from a medical to an educational model (Table 13.1). It seems clear that the pendulum has been swinging toward the educational system since Kirk and Bateman (1962) refocused the issues of learning disability as the principal concern of the then-designated population of "brain-damaged" and "hyperkinetic impulse disorder." This shift from a medical to an educational emphasis culminated, in 1975, in the passage of the Education for All Handicapped Children Act, PL 94-142.

INTERDISCIPLINARY TREATMENT AS A CORE MODEL

The disciplines of clinical psychology, child psychiatry, and social work have provided clinical support and back-up services for SLD, MBD, and HKS children at home and in the classroom. These disciplines have joined hands with teachers and offered guidance to puzzled parents from the earliest recognition of these problems, irrespective of changes in terminology or which model, educational or medical, was in the ascendancy in prescribing the program for remediation. All disciplines have been in agreement that medication, per se, does not alter the emotional conflicts in these children, conflicts which are played out in one or more of the emotional concomitants to their disability, as outlined in Chapter 2 above.

Invariably, the feelings and conflicts of these children become roadblocks to social and emotional growth, as well as being obstacles to the mastery of learning. Unfortunately, the end point of the accumulation of these untreated conflicts is, all too often, a passive-aggressive-resistant personality or a passive-dependent-depressive personality. Both patterns, without vigorous clinical intervention, can lead to chronic failure in the classroom and in the employment world, to social isolation and withdrawal into fantasy, to cripplingly inappropriate social behavior, and to a lifetime of self-doubt, self-denigration, and self-defeat.

The emphasis of this handbook has been on the integration of the clinical and educational disciplines and on the need for a healthy balance among educational, medical, and interdisciplinary models, rather than on an overemphasis of one to the exclusion of the others. The critical weakness of PL 94-142 is in its exclusion, to a great extent, of

Table 13.1
Interrelationship of Medical and
Educational Systems

Date		System
1896	Morgan wrote first descriptive study on congenital word blindness (dyslexia).	Medical
1923	Ebaugh described brain damage in epidemic encephalitis.	Medical
1934	Kahn and Cohen suggested organically driven behavior associated with brain stem lesions.	Medical
1937	Bradley observed improvement in children's behavior with amphetamine.	Medical
1937	Orton described reading, writing, and speech problems in children and their relationship to cerebral dominance.	Medical and Educational
1947	Straus and Lehtinen developed concept of specific behavior disorder with brain damage.	Medical
1957	Laufer, Denhoff, and Solomons described hyperkinetic impulse disorder.	Medical
1962	Kirk and Bateman focused on learning disability in this population.	Educational
1966	Clements emphasized organic components in etiology and suggested Minimal Brain Dysfunction Syndrome terminology.	Medical
1973	Cohen proposed EBD: Etiology Be Damned.	Educational
1973	Sprague emphasized use of behavior modification in MBD.	Educational
1974	Feingold suggested allergic responses to food additives.	Medical
1975	Congress passed The Education for All Handicapped Children Act: PL 94-142.	Educational

the clinical support systems which may be effective in helping SLD, MBD, and HKS children, their families, and their teachers to work through the crippling conflicts and behavior disorders invariably associated with learning disabilities.

Medication may be helpful once an Individualized Education Program (IEP) has been written, as mandated in PL 94-142, for each educationally handicapped child. In order to carry the prescriptive role, it is imperative that physicians ordering the medication must have complete knowledge about the use of such medication. Parents, school nurses, teachers, clinical psychologists, residential counselors, child care workers, and social workers should have sufficient knowledge about drug therapy in order to be more sophisticated observers of the effectiveness of these medications and their possible side effects.

Among the central issues with which a physician should be familiar are the following:

How do drugs work and where?
What principles should be followed in prescribing drugs?
What drugs should be given? For what symptoms? How much and how often?
What side effects should be anticipated?
How can physicians, teachers, and parents work together to monitor medication?
What are some of the new treatment ideas? How effective are they? How can a physician evaluate the effectiveness of psychotropic drugs from articles in the professional literature? That is, how can he/she become a critical consumer of research articles on the use of drugs and other therapies on SLD, MBD, and HKS children?

HOW DRUGS WORK AND WHERE

Freeman (1976) emphasized that little is known about how drugs work and where they work, especially in children. Some knowledge is being accumulated which is helpful to the prescribing physician in clinical practice. Figure 13.1 presents a simplified diagram of what is known about drug metabolism today. First, all drugs introduced into the body pass through the liver, which serves as an additional screening organ. The liver contains enzymes and other biochemical products which break down or modify the drug's chemical structure into simpler forms which differ in biochemical activity. Enzymes in the plasma, the lungs, and other tissues also appear to play a part in the metabolism of some drugs, altering their chemical structure and restricting their biological function. Some drug binding takes place in the blood plasma, and the free drug remains in the extracellular fluid. Subsequently, the simpler substances, or metabolites, are carried with the free drug to specific ·sites of drug action or are excreted through the kidneys. The lungs also function as an important route for the excretion of drugs.

HOW DO DRUGS WORK AND WHERE

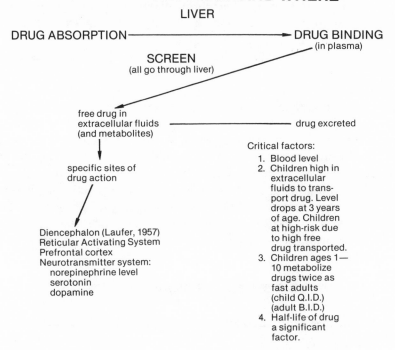

LIVER

DRUG ABSORPTION————————————————→ DRUG BINDING
(in plasma)

SCREEN
(all go through liver)

free drug in
extracellular fluids ————————————— drug excreted
(and metabolites)

Critical factors:
1. Blood level
2. Children high in
   extracellular
   fluids to trans-
   port drug. Level
   drops at 3 years
   of age. Children
   at high-risk due
   to high free
   drug transported.
3. Children ages 1—
   10 metabolize
   drugs twice as
   fast adults
   (child Q.I.D.)
   (adult B.I.D.)
4. Half-life of drug
   a significant
   factor.

specific sites of
drug action

Diencephalon (Laufer, 1957)
Reticular Activating System
Prefrontal cortex
Neurotransmitter system:
 norepinephrine level
 serotonin
 dopamine

CRITICAL FACTORS IN DRUG METABOLISM

From the explanation of drug metabolism as represented in Figure 13.1, several critical factors emerge:

(1) The blood level of the drug is going to determine how much free drug may reach the drug-action site and how much may react

in other body tissues to produce untoward side effects.

(2) Young children are high in extracellular fluids to transport drugs throughout the body. At age 3 years, the extracellular fluid level drops sharply. Therefore, children under 3 years of age are at high drug-risk due to the high level of free drug being transported.

(3) Children ages 1 to 10 years metabolize drugs twice as fast as adults. Therefore, the prescription for the child should be smaller amounts of drug more frequently, e.g., Q.I.D. or four times a day, as compared with larger amounts for adults, B.I.D. or twice a day.

(4) The half-life of the free drug in the extracellular fluid is the most significant factor in determining the duration of the drug effectiveness. Unfortunately, this is difficult to determine in the laboratory and is not available to the practicing physician. As laboratory sophistication develops, the Physicians' Desk Reference (PDR) may eventually designate the half-life of drugs within certain age ranges.

PRINCIPLES IN PRESCRIBING DRUGS

The clearest and, perhaps, the most authoritative statement on the basic principles of prescribing drugs for children was made by Eisenberg (1968). These principles are outlined in Table 13.2. As such, they should become an integral part of the prescribing physician's knowledge and treatment regimen. They should also be shared with and understood by school nurses and nonmedical adults working with children receiving psychotropic medication.

Each of these ten principles should be part of the conservative position taken by the medical profession in the use of psychotropic drugs for children. Likewise, each principle is clear in its implications and, with the possible exceptions of the "holiday/vacation" concept, the stop-order process, and the indications for laboratory studies, needs little or no elaboration.

Drug tolerance or fastness can occur with a diminished response to the drug on repeated intake over time. The exact nature of this phenomenon is not clear, but it may be due to an increased metabolism or excretion of the drug and its metabolites. In any case, larger doses may be required to maintain the drug's effectiveness. By allowing the child to be taken off the drug for those days out of the classroom (drug holiday) or over the longer school vacation, such drug tolerance may

Table 13.2
Principles in Prescribing Drugs *

1. No drug should be prescribed without firm indications for its use.

2. Careful control of the patient to be treated should be maintained.

3. Precautions for toxicity should be carefully determined and observed. Toxicity studies on adults cannot be applied to children, and the benefits should outweigh the risk of toxicity.

4. Clinical decisions for drug use should be based on an interdisciplinary team model including observations by teachers and parents. This team model seldom happens in actual practice (Robin and Bosco, 1976).

5. Drug potency demands respect, and prescriptions, as a rule, should be conservative:

    (a) Use of a familiar drug is preferred to a new drug, unless there is strong evidence of the new drug's superiority.

    (b) Skill in drug usage requires both knowledge of the drug's pharmacologic properties and sensitivity to the psychological implications for child and family in using medication.

    (c) Use small doses initially to avoid and rule out idiosyncratic or allergic reactions.

    (d) Do not use longer than necessary.

    (e) Use drug holiday/vacation concept when possible.

    (f) Use a stop-order process.

    (g) Use reduction of drug dosage periodically, with goal of cessation if symptoms do not return on lower dosage.

6. Undertreatment, as well as overtreatment, can result in incorrect judgments about appropriateness of drug for patient.

7. Psychotropic drugs can mask symptoms and delay diagnosis and should be viewed as *treating symptoms and not causes.*

8. Monitor drug usage by:

    (a) Laboratory studies (every 3 months when indicated).

    (b) Use of rating scale when possible.

    (c) Inclusion of careful follow-up studies while drug is being given and after it has been discontinued.

9. *Drugs are an adjunct and should not be the only treatment.* It is poor medicine to prescribe drugs when symptoms stem from correctable social, familial, biological, educational, or interpersonal disturbances, without attempting to identify, eliminate, or alter those factors causing the symptoms.

10. Family relationships or attitudes of parents toward psychotropic drugs may be such that the use of drugs without psychotherapy for treatment of hyperkinesis may add to the problem.

*Adamson, after Eisenberg, 1968.

be reduced or avoided. Prescribing a new drug may be necessary to allow a "vacation" from the first drug, should drug tolerance develop and persist on increased dosages.

Eisenberg did not include the stop-order process among his principles. Such a process improves the drug monitoring system for agencies, institutions, residential schools, and treatment centers when medications are used. Accreditation authorities, such as the Joint Commission on Accreditation of Hospitals (JCAH) and the State Offices of Mental Health, require such a procedure in dispensing medication.

The stop-order process is a medically initiated and administratively supported policy in which drugs are prescribed for a time-limited period of three to four months. After that period, all medication is stopped automatically. An interdisciplinary team, which should include the nurse, teacher or educational supervisor, residential counselor (cottage child care worker), social worker, and a qualified child psychiatrist, reviews the indications for continuing, reducing, or discontinuing the drug in current use. Within the calendar year, the stop-order process should be completed three or four times. This process guarantees staff review for the medication of all children at least three times a year.

Laboratory monitoring every three months is important for Dilantin and other anticonvulsants and for most of the tranquilizing drugs. These drugs may alter the blood-forming (hematopoietic) process, thereby inducing leucopenia (low white blood cell count) and agranulocytosis (elimination of older white blood cells). Early signs of either condition are reflected in a shift to the younger forms (lymphocytes) over the older forms (polymorphonuclear cells or neutrophils) in a differential white cell smear and in a lowered white blood cell count. This process is usually reversed by discontinuing the drug.

Another form of monitoring is the use of rating scales by parents and teachers to record observations of children's behavior, over a period of time, while on a drug and after it has been discontinued. Such scales include the Devereux Behavior Rating Scales by Spivack and Spotts (1966), which can be used by parents or cottage child care workers, the Hahnemann Elementary School Behavior Rating Scale by Spivack and Swift (1975), which is excellent for teacher observations, and scales designed by Conners, who has been very active in the field for a number of years.

In all cases, careful follow-up during medication is essential. Follow-up after the drug has been discontinued is helpful in ruling out late-developing side effects and in ascertaining the degree of sustained improvement in behavior after discontinuance of the medication. Eisenberg (1968) observed that prolonged use and careful monitoring may reveal unexpected toxicity from a new agent.

As a conclusion for this section, the theme of the entire chapter bears repeating: *drugs are an adjunct and should not be the only treatment.*

WHICH DRUGS TO PRESCRIBE

As an overview to the section on medication, Table 13.3 suggests which drugs might be given for which symptoms and indicates the range of recommended doses, the size tablets available, and the anticipated side effects of each drug. The drugs are listed under their principal activity, with the generic chemical name given first, followed by the commercial "trade" name in parenthesis. Currently, efforts are being made to encourage physicians, when possible, to order the lower-cost generic equivalent drugs rather than the brand names, thus effecting savings for the consumer.

Of the five classes of drugs useful for children to be discussed, only the first group, the psychostimulants, is used to increase attention span and decrease hyperactivity and dysinhibition. The other classes of drugs are used to treat the emotional concomitants of SLD. These five classes include the following:

    I.   Psychostimulant agents
    II. Antianxiety and antiaggression agents
   III. Antithought-process disorder or antipsychotic agents
   IV. Antidepressant agents
    V. Anticonvulsant agents

Notice

The medications and treatment regimen in this chapter have been taken from various sources, including the 1977 Physicians' Desk Reference (PDR), and do not necessarily have the specific approval of the Food and Drug Administration (FDA) for use in the situations and dosages as outlined in Table 13.3 and in the section to follow. The package insert for each drug should be consulted for indications and dosage as approved by the FDA. Because standards for usage change fairly frequently, it is advisable to keep informed of revised recommendations, especially those concerning new drugs.

Table 13.3
Overview of Available Drugs to Prescribe for Children/Adolescents

Drug	Daily Dose (mg.)	Side Effects
Psychostimulant Agents:		
Methylphenidate (Ritalin) Tabs 5, 10, 20 mg. (Not too effective on preschoolers; 12/13 years - less effective)	10-30 a.m. and noon (max. 50)	nervousness anorexia, weight loss stomach-ache, abdominal pain skin rash insomnia above 20 mg. − growth retardation occasional cardiac arrhythmia do not use under 6 years of age
Dextroamphetamine (Dexedrine) Tabs 5 mg. Spanules 5, 10, 15 mg. Elixir 5 mg. per 5 ml.	5-15 a.m. and noon	more pronounced symptoms nervousness anorexia insomnia growth retardation earlier fastness headache palpitation habituation do not use under 3 years of age
Pemoline (Cylert) Tabs 18.75, 37.5, 75 mg. (Long acting, once daily)	18.75-112.5 a.m. (max. 112.5)	rapid pulse less insomnia anorexia, weight loss liver enzymes − transaminase levels stomach-ache agitation and restlessness
Deanol (Deaner) Tabs 25, 100 mg. (Not strictly a stimulant; a precursor of acetylcholine)	50-100 (max. 400-500)	nervousness headache insomnia constipation tenseness in some muscles
Antihistamine Agent:		
Diphenhydramine (Benadryl) Elixir 12.5 mg. per 5 ml. Capsule 25 mg. Kapseal 50 mg.	25-200	few in low doses caution in seizure prone cases atropine-like action in larger doses

Table 13.3 *(Continued)*

Drug	Daily Dose (mg.)	Side Effects
Antianxiety and Antiaggression Agents:		
Thioridazine (Mellaril) Tabs 10, 15, 25, 50, 100 150, 200 mg. Concentrate 30, 100 mg. per ml.	20-100 (max. 400)	anorexia incontinence skin rash leukopenia dystonia
(Good after 12/13 years of age)		
	In Adults:	impotence retinal pigmentation (3000 mg. for 40 days)
Chlorpromazine (Thorazine) Tabs 10, 25, 50, 100 200 mg. Syrup 10 mg. per 5 ml. Concentrate 30, 100 mg. per ml. Suppositories 25, 100 mg. Spansules and injectable	25-200 (max. 500)	drowsiness apathy allergies skin sensitivity summer redness leukopenia
Diazepam (Valium) Commonly used outside USA Tabs 2, 5, 10 mg.	2-6 (max. 8-10)	strange reactions possible anticonvulsant properties
Chlordiazepoxide (Librium) Tabs 5, 10, 25 mg. Capsules 5, 10, 25 mg. Injectable	10-30 (max. 60)	nausea drowsiness ataxia leukopenia
Meprobamate (Milltown) (Equanil) Tabs 200, 400, 600 mg.	200-600	drowsiness abdominal pain, nausea skin rash leukopenia headache
Antithought-Process Disorder or Antipsychotic Agents:		
Chlorpromazine (Thorazine)	see above	
Trifluoperazine (Stelazine) Tabs 1, 2, 5, 10 mg. Concentrate 10 mg. per ml. Injectable	6-24 (max. 24)	extrapyramidal signs dyskinesia

Table 13.3 *(Continued)*

Drug	Daily Dose (mg.)	Side Effects
Haloperidal (Haldol) 　Tabs 0.5, 1, 2, 5, 10 mg. 　Concentrate 2 mg. per ml. 　Injectable	0.5-15 (max. 20)	early drowsiness dystonic reactions not yet FDA approved for 　children under 12 years muscle restlessness and spasms

Antidepressant Agents:

Drug	Daily Dose (mg.)	Side Effects
Imipramine (Tofranil) 　Tabs 10, 25, 50 mg. 　Capsules 75, 100, 125, 　　　150 mg. Widely used for enuresis: 25 mg. before h.s. to 50 mg.	10-50 (max. 100)	Not recommended for children 　under 12 years cardiotoxic over 75 mg/d leukopenia insomnia dry mouth jaundice
Desipramine (Pertofrane) 　　　　(Norpramin) 　Tabs 25, 50 mg.	25-50	FDA approved for adolescents, 　not for children
Amitriptaline (Elavil) 　Tabs 10, 25, 50, 75, 　　　100, 150 mg. 　Injectable 10 mg. per ml.	30-60	Not recommended for children 　under 12 years

Anticonvulsant Agents:

For Grand Mal and Psychomotor Seizures:

Drug	Daily Dose (mg.)	Side Effects
Diphenylhydantoin (Dilantin) 　Capsules 30, 100 mg. 　Chewable infant tablets 　Suspension, injectable	Follow PDR for guidelines in all treatment settings for this entire group of anti- convulsants	nausea, vomiting skin rash hypertrophied gums hair growth (on arms) nystagmus double vision ataxia
Mephenyotoin (Mesantoin) 　Tabs 100 mg.		drowsiness ataxia skin rash enlarged lymph glands anemia

Table 13.3 *(Continued)*

Drug	Daily Dose (mg.)	Side Effects
Phenobarbital Tabs 16, 32, 64, 100 mg.		causes excessive excitement in SLD/MBD/HKS children with neurologic involvement
Mephobarbital (Mebaral) Tabs 32, 100, 200 mg.		drowsiness skin rash
Primidone (Myoline) Tabs 50, 250 mg.		drowsiness ataxia irritability nausea, vomiting skin rash anemia

For Petit Mal Seizures:

Trimethadione (Tridione) Tabs 150 mg. Capsule 300 mg.		both are similar: drowsiness skin rash
Paramethadione (Paradione) Capsules 150, 300 mg.		sensitivity to light loss of hair (Tridione only) decrease in kidney and liver function
Ethosuximide (Zarontin) Capsule 250 mg.		drowsiness nausea skin rash occasional leukemia-like pattern
Phensuximide (Milontin) Capsules 250, 500 mg. Suspension		drowsiness nausea, vomiting dizziness skin rash ataxia
Methsaximide (Celontin) Kapseals 150, 300 mg.		drowsiness ataxia skin rash dizziness anemia redness around eye orbit psychotic-like behavior

Table 13.3 *(Continued)*

Drug	Daily Dose (mg.)	Side Effects
Sedative Agents:		
Flurazepam (Dalmane) Tabs 15, 30 mg.	15-45	not recommended for children under 15 years
(For insomnia in adolescents and EEG preparation)		
Chloralhydrate (Chloral) (Noctec) Capsules 250, 500 mg. Syrup 500 mg. per 5 ml.	250-500	wide margin of safety
Megavitamin Program - Dr. Alan Cott, New York City		
Niacinamide 500 mg. 2 tabs B.I.D. B6 Pyridoxide 100 mg. 2 tabs B.I.D. Folic Acid 1 mg. 2 tabs B.I.D. B15 50 mg. 1 tab B.I.D. Dolomite 2 tabs B.I.D. Manganese Citrate 50 mg. 1 tab B.I.D. Elemental zinc 22 mg. 1 tab daily Vitamin C 500 mg. 1 tab daily Plus B3 Niacin 500 mg. B1 Thiamine 500 mg.		no systematic observations

Psychostimulants

Indications for Use

For children up to age 11 years (or to the age of puberty) in whom the following three criteria are met, a psychostimulant can be prescribed:

(1) there is a *prolonged pattern* (months, not weeks) of motor dysinhibition and poor impulse control, at home and at school, usually associated with a short attention span, hyperdistractibility, and hyperactivity at school;

(2) the symptoms and signs are generally *manifestations of physiologic or minimal neurologic impairment* of the central nervous

system (as opposed to more severe organic brain tissue or neuronal structural damage) as discussed under the medical-psychological-educational assessments in Chapters 2, 3, 4 and 5 above; and

(3) the pattern has *persisted after* a three- to six-weeks' *trial of constructive educational and clinical interventions* (other than medication), including:

   (a) an Individualized Education Program (IEP) to establish with the child's teacher in a regular or special education classroom a well-structured learning climate consisting of clearly defined limits, partial learning tasks and goals at level of demonstrated educational competence, and well-developed behavior modification procedures to reinforce positive learning experiences and to minimize negative learning, and

   (b) an Individual Clinical Prescription (ICP), i.e., mental health in education utilizing one or more of the treatment modalities outlined in this handbook (e.g., parent counseling, Chapter 6; individual and group psychotherapy, Chapters 7 and 8; family therapy, Chapter 10; behavior modification, Chapter 11; or one of the creative art therapies, Chapter 12).

This point of view has been supported by Grinspon and Singer (1973) in their extensive survey of the research literature on the treatment of SLD children. From their review of the studies of the 1960s and 1970s, they concluded that a nonmedical model was the first approach to helping hyperactive children. They found that, while there was a possibility for a true ("organic") physiologically/neurologically based hyperkinesis which might benefit from drug treatmnt, it is difficult to distinguish such a disorder from other syndromes or disturbances which are expressed by similar behavioral patterns. Hence, with psychotropic drug use, symptoms and not underlying causes have become the focus for medical treatment. For this reason, they argue for the use of behavior modification techniques, rather than the administration of drugs simply to make children more manageable.

The conceptual framework of this handbook is focused on the Interdisciplinary Team Model which suggests that the diagnostic assessment process will seek out causes, as well as prescriptions for action, as it sifts through symptoms, signs, and educational levels. Therefore, the formula for the working Individualized Education Program (IEP) should also contain biopsychosocial and cultural data integrated with the diagnostic educational data. The resultant integration might more accurately be written as follows:

Individualized Education Program/Individual Clinical Prescription = IEP/ICP MODEL.

Choice of Drugs

METHYLPHENIDATE (RITALIN)

Unique value. Methylphenidate has been recognized in the literature as the most widely used and, perhaps, the most uniformly effective psychostimulant. It is, therefore, the treatment of choice for children over 5 years of age to the age of puberty. It does not cause cardiovascular side effects (palpitation, rapid pulse, elevated blood pressure), anorexia, or nervousness as readily as Dexedrine does. Drug tolerance or fastness seems to occur very rarely, and small amounts appear to be as effective as larger amounts. Werry and Sprague (1974) reported that results with children whose mean age was 8.9 years were as good with 0.1 mg./kg. as with 0.3 mg./kg.

Treatment regimen. It is best to start with small doses, such as 5 to 10 mg. once a day, before breakfast, for two or three days, to rule out idiosyncrasies to the drug. Stomach pain may occur and can be reduced by giving the drug after breakfast.

Increase the drug to 10 mg. twice daily for one week, and, if necessary, gradually increase in increments of 5 to 10 mg. per day per week up to 30 mg. per day, depending upon the child's size and weight. *Do not exceed* a maximum of 50 mg. per day. If improvement is not evident after one month on an appropriate drug dosage level, the drug should be discontinued.

Avoid giving the drug after 3 p.m., if possible, as it can produce insomnia and/or hyperalertness in the evening. Remember, also, that 20 mg. per day or more may induce growth retardation. A normal growth rate resumes when the drug is discontinued. The mechanism for such a decrease in growth rate was thought to be related to the disturbance in nutrition due to the loss of appetite, and possibly to the suppression of the growth hormone (Safer *et al.,* 1972). More studies are needed to clarify prolactin's relationship to growth and the cause of this growth retardation with central nervous system stimulants.

Anticipated course. Methylphenidate should begin to show its effectiveness within thirty to sixty minutes after being taken orally. No prolonged build-up of blood level seems necessary. If the drug is appropriate for the SLD/MBD/HKS child, there should be a significant improvement in the behavior pattern, with a reduction in excessive motor activity, increased ability to concentrate and center in on learning material, and an associated increase in the attention span. Some investigators use this "Ritalin response" as confirmatory evidence for the presence of the Minimal Brain Dysfunction Syndrome. Such a conclusion is open to criticism as a medical bias excluding other significant data derived from the psychological, educational, and sociocultural assessments.

The drug can be continued over several years and up to the age of puberty, if needed. In some instances, it appears to lose its effectiveness with the onset of puberty and may actually induce increased excitement and hyperactivity at that age. In a study which did not employ the double-blind method, Lerer and Lerer (1977) prescribed 20 mg. of methylphenidate twice a day for 27 adolescents: 2 girls and 25 boys with a mean age of 15.5 years and a history of hyperactivity with onset prior to 6 years of age, distractibility and short attention span for at least 4 years' duration, marked academic underachievement, and a history of clumsiness or objective documentation of poor fine-motor coordination. After a 60-day trial on the drug, 16 of the 27 adolescents showed subjective or objective evidence of improvement. Four required 60 mg. daily for optimal results. None showed mood elevation or psychological dependency, however.

As discussed earlier, the use of a holiday/vacation pattern should always be considered when prescribing this drug. If drug tolerance occurs and persists with an increased dosage, another drug may temporarily be substituted.

Side effects. These have been outlined in Table 13.3. It is important to emphasize that methylphenidate should not be used in children under 5 to 6 years of age.

Outcome. There have been many studies on the effectiveness of methylphenidate (Conners and Eisenberg, 1963; Millichap, 1968; Sykes *et al.,* 1972; Werry and Sprague, 1974; Loney and Ordona, 1975; Schain and Reynard, 1975; Schleifer *et al.,* 1975; Weiss *et al.,* 1975). Sprague *et al.* (1970) raised the question about possible differential forgetting associated with psychotropic drug use and whether or not there was interference with the memory mechanism. They also posed the question about the durability of drug-facilitated learning. Millichap (1972) observed that children with the highest levels of motor activity and the highest number of neurologic abnormalities were most likely to respond to methylphenidate, whereas those with initial lower levels of activity were sometimes made worse. He concluded that methylphenidate was indicated as an adjunct to remedial education in the short-term treatment of children with MBD. Its use in the long-term management of children with SLD/MBD/HKS must await evaluation by more controlled studies.

Sykes *et al.* (1971), Sprague *et al.* (1970), and Dykman and Ackerman (1976) supported the view that short-term studies of stimulant drug treatment demonstrate an improvement in the child's ability to concentrate on school work and in motivation and attention to tasks that normally do not engage their full interest, and secondarily dampen the pattern of restlessness. Several researchers have shown that behavior modification approaches will bring about the same general effects (Christenson, 1975; O'Leary *et al.,* 1976).

Weiss and her colleagues (1975) published one of the few long-term follow-up studies of children treated with stimulant drugs. In this study, a small group of children (24) was treated with a stimulant drug (methylphenidate), a corresponding group (22) was treated with chlorpromazine, and a third control group (20) received no drug treatment. At the end of five years, the groups could not be distinguished by relatively crude measures of social adjustment. Unfortunately, relevant data on pre- and posttreatment levels of school achievement, self-esteem, and socialization of aggressive impulses were not obtained in the study.

In a more recent study, Ackerman *et al.* (1977) completed a long-term follow-up of 116 boys, ages 8 to 10 years. Seventy-six percent of the LD subjects and 91% of the controls returned for a follow-up study as close to their fourteenth birthdays as possible. The general conclusion drawn from the follow-up was that nothing that occurred by way of educational and clinical (medication) intervention between the initial study and the follow-up study approximately four years later radically altered the course of development of the LD group, relative to the normal achievers. The authors stressed that this did not mean that the course was unalterable, but only that commonly employed intervention effects have produced no change in their ranking in the academic hierarchy. The intervention methods employed were not sufficient to "alter the growth trajectory." This conclusion is in marked contrast to the results obtained in the 24-month-old SLD/MBD child described in Case Study 1.1 in Chapter 1. Early and comprehensive interdisciplinary intervention seemed to have been the significant difference in that case.

This leads to the concluding statement for this discussion on methylphenidate. Actually, if we are faithful to the conceptual frame of reference highlighted in this handbook (i.e., that drugs are only an adjunct to the interdisciplinary Individualized Education Program/Individual Clinical Prescription model), then we should not look for or focus on the issue of long-term effectiveness of psychostimulant drugs in isolation or as a single dependent variable in the treatment of SLD/MBD/HKS children. Instead, we should view these drugs as appropriate to remediation, once the three indications for their use have been met, for the purpose of:

(1) *preparing* the child for learning,
(2) *stimulating* the automatically underaroused neurotransmitter systems necessary for information processing (Conners, 1974; Satterfield *et al.,* 1972; Wender, 1971),
(3) *improving* the child's pattern of intention (a primary autonomous ego function) sufficient to commit the perceptive and perceived information to memory or to other central nervous system processing functions (Douglas, 1972), and
(4) *facilitating* the function of the child's internal organization (ego integration) and planning skills such that memory and the complex learning processes may take place (Brown, 1976), and methylphenidate responders may be separated from nonresponders by the paired association test of visual memory developed by Swanson, Kinsbourne *et al.* (1977).

DEXTROAMPHETAMINE (DEXEDRINE)

Unique value. This was the first drug used for hyperactivity (Bradley, 1937). It has an immediate effect, within thirty to sixty minutes when taken orally. Also, it has a reasonably wide margin of safety (i.e., few life-threatening side effects at lower doses). It has special value in that it can be given to children 3 to 5 years of age and as a time-release spansule once a day. It is generally considered a second drug of choice after methylphenidate.

Treatment regimen. (a) In children 3 to 5 years of age, begin with 2.5 mg. (one half-tablet or one half-teaspoonful of the elixir) daily, on awakening, for one week. Raise in increments of 2.5 mg. per day, at weekly intervals, until the maximal effect is obtained. It is seldom necessary to go above 10 mg. per day. The elixir may be somewhat less effective than the tablets, perhaps because of the depressive effect of the alcohol in which it is compounded.

(b) In children 6 years and older, begin with 5 mg. once daily in the morning. Increase after one week to 5 mg. twice daily, in the morning and at noon. It is better to give the second dose before 1 p.m. to avoid insomnia. Increase in increments of 5 mg. per day per week, concentrating the larger dose in the morning for maximum classroom effectiveness. Use the holiday/vacation plan, unless behavioral management in the home presents a major problem. The 5-, 10-, or 15-mg. time-release spansule may be used as a suitable substitute for the total daily requirement in tablet form. Finally, should a total daily requirement of 40 mg. or more be needed, it is wise to reëvaluate the diagnosis and recommend the use of an alternative drug.

Safer and Allen (1976) suggested that there are times when these stimulant drugs are useful outside school hours: on weekends and during summer vacation. Half of the usual school dose can be given for summer camp and other social or family events which require that the child handle his/her hyperactivity and distractibility. Also, in those situations when it is difficult for parents to maintain a structured home environment during the summer months and on rainy days, half the usual school dose may be given.

Anticipated course. Teachers and parents should be well informed by the prescribing physician about the effect of psychostimulant drugs, the duration of drug activity, and the possible side effects they might anticipate from the drug. Dextroamphetamine is usually active and effective for about four hours. As a rule, the more effective the educational and clinical remedial interventions, the sooner the drug can be reduced and eventually discontinued. Responsible (and non-manipulative or punitive) parents may be instructed to monitor the dose by adding to or subtracting from the prescribed amount according to the child's social behavior, programmed activities, and ability to attend and handle his/her impulse life. In such situations, the parents must be instructed to notify the physician within 24 hours of such a change in dispensing the drug and the resulting behavior pattern. Drug tolerance with dextroamphetamine requiring an increase in medication may develop in six to eight weeks.

While many children for whom the drug is indicated may need the medication for several years, the drug should be discontinued as puberty is reached, or by ages 13 to 14 years.

Side Effects. (See Table 13.3.) The insomnia and anorexia (loss of appetite) usually disappear in two to three weeks. In addition, altering the amount and the time of administering the drug may decrease these symptoms. On the other hand, a noon dose of the Dexedrine spansule may induce insomnia.

Lasagna and Epstein (1970) found that, with a daily dose of 10 to 20 mg. of dextroamphetamine, significant appetite changes did occur, but only minor changes in blood pressure were apparent. During the first week on dextroamphetamine, and occasionally into the second week, about 15% of the children complained of headaches, stomachaches, and moodiness, with a tendency to cry (Conners *et al.,* 1972).

Growth suppression may take place with this drug in large doses but growth resumes when the drug is discontinued. Suppression of weight gain is most prominent during the initial year of treatment. When dextroamphetamine is abruptly stopped, however, there is a distinct growth rebound at the rate of two to three times the monthly rate while on medication. This has led Safer *et al.* (1975) to suggest that growth suppression in long-term use of dextroamphetamine, and with higher doses of methylphenidate, is temporary. The child's height and weight should be checked annually. A gain of 5 to 7 pounds and 2 to 2½ inches in height annually is the anticipated growth for most elementary school children.

Cole (1975) stressed that, all too frequently, not enough attention is paid to the known side effects in the long-term prescription of the psychostimulants. He also discussed the potential addictive properties of dextroamphetamine and methylphenidate. He pointed out that there was no clear support for addiction in the use of such drugs in the treatment of SLD/MBD/HKS children. The dosage and age are critical factors in addiction: abusers of stimulant drugs use up to twenty times the amount of drugs used in treating SLD children. Also, dextroamphetamine and methylphenidate are seldom prescribed after the age of 12 or 13, which suggests there is little danger that a child will automatically become an adolescent abuser.

Adequate studies have not been done on the long-term side effects of dextroamphetamine from which to draw conclusions about its accumulative effects on the body. It has been used for periods from six to twenty-eight months without close monitoring for side effects.

Cole's (1975) final point was that more attention needs to be given to the sociologic aspects of drug treatment in children. He noted that the impact of being stigmatized as a "drug taker" by a poorly informed public can have serious effects on the hyperkinetic child in terms of parental, social, and community attitudes and on the child's concept of his/her own self-worth.

Outcome. Studies on the effectiveness of dextroamphetamine extend over 30 years (Bradley, 1937; Weiss *et al.,* 1968, 1971; Lasagna and Epstein, 1970; Laufer, 1971; Steinberg, *et al.,* 1971; Winsberg *et al.,* 1972; Grinspon and Singer, 1973; Cole, 1975; Gross, 1976).

Conners *et al.* (1969) noted short-term improvement in visual-motor skills, less impulsivity, better visual and auditory discrimination, and better short-term learning skills. However, gains from prolonged use for six months seemed small (Conrad *et al.,* 1971). Aman and Sprague (1974) observed that, while attention was improved, retention of new information was not. These same investigators noted that no appreciable state-dependent learning occurred (i.e., that material initially learned under the influence of a drug was not recalled more completely with repeated use of that drug), when dextroamphetamine and methylphenidate were given in therapeutic doses to SLD/MBD/HKS children.

In general, the same conclusions apply to dextroamphetamine as were formulated with the psychostimulant methyphenidate. The choice of drug as a short-term adjunctive treatment intervention is based more on the physician's personal preference, subjective bias, and familiarity, as a general rule, than on hard evaluative data. The frequency and intensity of side effects seem to parallel one another, with a slight shading toward methylphenidate as the drug having fewer side effects, particularly less anorexia, less jitteriness, and less growth suppression. Drug tolerance also appears to be less of a problem with methyl-phenidate. However, the same criteria (indications) for prescribing dextroamphetamine would apply, and it should not be given until the educational and behavioral management programs have been under way for three to six weeks.

PEMOLINE (CYLERT)

Unique value. This is the most recent psychostimulant to be developed. It was approved by the FDA in 1974. As a mild central nervous system stimulant, it is structurally different from methylphenidate and dextroamphetamine. Although it has been only sparsely studied (Conners, 1972; Page *et al.,* 1974), it has been heavily advertised to have several advantages over other psychostimulants: a long-acting effectiveness (16 to 24 hours), with one morning dose covering the day, no insomnia, less anorexia, and no reported untoward cardiovascular symptoms.

Treatment regimen. Begin with a single dose of 18.75 mg. (one tablet) each morning for three days to rule out idiosyncratic responses. Increase to 37.5 mg. per day for three to four weeks. It is important to note that pemoline has a gradual onset and, unlike other psycho-stimulants, may take three to four weeks before its effectiveness can be observed. There is a chewable 37.5-mg. tablet for children who have difficulty swallowing a regular tablet.

The drug can be increased in increments of 18.75 mg. per week, after the third to fourth week, until the desired dosage level is obtained. Mean daily medication range is from 56.25 to 75 mg. The maximum recommended daily dose is 112.5 mg. If more than this amount appears to be necessary, one should consider an alternative drug.

Anticipated course and outcome. Clinical improvement with pemoline is very gradual. In addition, the drug is so new that few studies are available on its short-term effectiveness and on the nature of the long-term side effects which might be anticipated with its usage (Page *et al.,* 1974).

Side effects. Pemoline is not recommended for children under 6 years, since safety and efficacy have not been established for that age group. Delayed hypersensitivity reactions involving the liver have been reported in 1% to 2% of patients after several months of therapy. Although no clinical symptoms have been observed, mild to moderate increases in the serum transaminase levels (SGOT and SGPT) have occurred. These reactions appear to be completely reversible when the drug is discontinued. It is important to obtain transaminase levels at regular intervals during therapy with pemoline to detect such reactions. Other side effects may include insomnia prior to the optimum therapeutic response and occasional anorexia, with weight loss, during the first two to three weeks. This usually decreases with continuing therapy. There is a return to a normal weight curve within three to six months while on the medication.

Finally, the *Physicians' Desk Reference* (1977) indicates that other side effects include stomach-ache, skin rash, mild depression, drowsiness, hallucinations, and dyskinetic movements of the lips, face, and extremities. Occasional seizures have been reported. However, no causal relationship has been established between pemoline and these reactions.

DEANOL ACETAMIDOBENZOATE (DEANER)

Unique value. Deanol is converted into acetylcholine within the neurons and acts as a central nervous system stimulant. While, in theory, it would seem to be an ideal drug for the target symptoms of hyperactivity and short attention span, in clinical practice, it is generally considered of little, if any, value in the adjunctive treatment of children with SLD/MBD/HKS (Millichap, 1972). It does not depress appetite, suppress growth, or cause jitteriness. It also has a very low toxicity level, with a wide margin of safety.

Treatment regimen. The usual beginning dose is 100 mg. in the morning, which is increased to 300 mg. per day. No maximum dosage has been suggested, but Millichap (1972) reported dosages as high as 1,000 mg. per day for four to thirty-six weeks.

Side effects. Side effects with deanol have been minimal and infrequent. Constipation and tenseness in some muscles have been reported.

Anticipated course and outcome. This drug first became available in the 1960s, when early studies suggested it was not an effective psychostimulant for SLD/MBD/HKS children. Lewis and Lewis (1977) reviewed the literature on the use of deanol, and in two studies on hyperactive children reported no significant differences between placebo and deanol groups, although they felt that the drug merited further study for identifying the possibility of a hypocholinemic subgroup of hyperactive children. Oettinger (1977) emphasized the need for larger doses (500 to 750 mg. per day), the wide margin of safety and long duration of drug activity with deanol, and the apparent lack of response to this drug in many MBD children as an implication of the absence of noradrenalin or the presence of dopamine metabolic defects in these children.

The author has prescribed deanol for an intellectually dull-normal, 11-year-old student whose thought processes appeared to be responding in a "slow-motion" pattern due, in part, to neurologic impairment, but without fragmentation or reality distortion. There was no school history or clinical evidence of hyperactivity or short attention span. Instead, this SLD/MBD preadolescent appeared to need a neurotransmitter-facilitator to speed up the higher cortical level processing. Marked improvement was observed on 100 mg. per day (in the morning) during four months on the drug.

DIPHENHYDRAMINE (BENADRYL)

Unique value. Diphenhydramine is not a psychostimulant but an antihistaminic agent. It is the drug of choice for SLD/MBD/HKS children under 5 years of age, with a wide margin of safety, low toxicity, and easily given in the elixir form. Young children seldom have difficulty swallowing this preparation. It is quickly absorbed, has an immediate effect within twenty to forty minutes, and does not produce insomnia, except in high doses. Nor is it known to suppress either appetite or body growth.

Treatment regimen. Begin with one half- to one teaspoonful (12.5 mg. per 5 ml.) once or twice daily for infants and children up to twenty (20) pounds. For children over twenty pounds, the dose can be one to two teaspoonfuls, or one capsule (25 mg.) two or three times daily, with gradual increments up to 200 mg. per day. It is sometimes given as a sedative at night in doses of 50 to 100 mg.

Anticipated course and outcome. Children may outgrow this drug's effectiveness at around 5 to 6 years of age, and one of the more active psychostimulants may be considered.

Side effects. As shown in Table 13.3, there are few side effects with diphenhydramine in the low doses recommended. The most common one is drowsiness. One should exercise caution in prescribing this drug in seizure-prone cases. In large doses, atropine-like side effects may occur.

CAFFEINE

Outcome. Caffeine was suggested as a drug for hyperactivity in children after it was observed that black coffee seemed to help some of these children (Schnackenburg, 1973). More recent double-blind cross-over studies have shown that caffeine is no better than a placebo in its effectiveness on SLD/MBD/HKS children (Garfinkel *et al.,* 1975; Gross, 1975; Huestis *et al.,* 1975; Conners, 1975).

Gross (1975) completed a single-blind, five-week controlled study on 25 SLD/MBD/HKS children (average age 9.2 years, range 5 to 13 years) who met the diagnostic criteria of Clements and Peters (1962), comparing the effects of placebo, caffeine, methylphenidate (Ritalin), dextroamphetamine (Dexedrine), and imipramine (Tofranil, Presamine). Caffeine, at dosages roughly equivalent to a cup of coffee morning and noon (50 to 200 mg., according to age) did not help a single patient. Instead, Gross reported, it made most of the subjects worse, as rated by mothers and observations of teachers. The placebo and drugs were given on a sequential schedule, each for one week, with no time allowed for one medication to "wash out" before starting another, since previous experience had indicated this was not necessary except for imipramine, which was given last in the sequence.

Antiphobic, -Anxiety, and -Aggression Agents

Indications for Use

The antiphobic, -anxiety, and -aggression agents would be indicated in SLD/MBD/HKS children and adolescents under these circumstances:

(1) when there is a *prolonged pattern* (months, not weeks) of excessive anxiety and/or crippling phobias or socially unacceptable aggression as the predominant symptoms,

(2) when these symptoms, which are generally *manifestations of interpersonal* and/or *intrapsychic conflicts* rather than secondary to physiologic or neurologic impairment, are more pervasive than are the symptoms of motor dysinhibition and poor impulse control,

(3) when the child/adolescent and family have been *well engaged* in determining the causes for the phobic, anxiety, and/or unsocialized aggression symptoms, and one of the treatment modalities has been initiated, and

(4) when the pattern of symptoms has *persisted after a suitable period of constructive educational and clinical interventions,* or

(5) when the child reaches puberty or early adolescence and the *psychostimulant drugs no longer appear to be effective* and may, in fact, overstimulate rather than reduce hyperkinetic activity, or

(6) when the *psychostimulant drugs were never effective* with children who presented a prolonged pattern of motor dysinhibition and poor impulse control after a suitable period of constructive educational and appropriate clinical intervention.

It should be noted that studies by Werry (1968) and Sprague *et al.* (1970) have shown that, while thioridazine (Mellaril) and chlorpromazine (Thorazine) lessen anxiety and general restlessness, they do not improve the processes of attention and intention. Rather, there is evidence that they impair attention, reaction time, and motor performance. Such impairment seems related to the early onset of drowsiness. Long range studies need to be done to assay these cognitive functions when phenothiazines have been given over extended periods of time.

Choice of Drugs

THIORIDAZINE (MELLARIL)

Unique value. This is the drug of choice for SLD/MBD/HKS children with marked emotional lability, aggressive acting out, and excessive emotional problems who meet the criteria outlined above. It is not to be used for the hyperactive components but for the phobic, anxiety, and aggressive symptoms. Thioridazine is especially helpful in 12- and 13-year-olds who have been on psychostimulant drugs and are no longer responsive to those drugs.

It is a potent but less toxic tranquilizer than chlorpromazine. It has a low toxicity and a wide margin of safety, so far as life-threatening factors are concerned. Also, there is no physical or psychological dependency known to develop on this drug.

It is important, in prescribing the tranquilizing drugs, not to mask the symptoms of anxiety which are important signals of underlying problems. Hence, the list of indications for the use of the drug highlights the importance of working out and formulating the individual and family psychodynamics to some degree before prescribing the tranquilizer.

Treatment regimen. Do not use thioridazine in children under 2 years of age. For children from 3 to 10 years, begin with 0.5 mg. per kg. per day, or 10 mg. in the morning for two days, to rule out individual idiosyncrasies. Increase to 10 mg. twice or three times daily. For more disturbed or hospitalized children and children 10 years and older, 25 mg. twice or three times daily may be needed. Because it may require ten to fourteen days to reach a level of maximum effectiveness, it is important to advise parents, teachers, the child, and other interested adults of the slower action of this drug. One can increase the drug in increments of 10 to 25 mg. per day per week, after the first fourteen days, to reach the desired level of effectiveness.

The maximum daily dose for children should not exceed 400 mg. per day. It can also be given as a concentrate which comes in preparations of 30 mg. and 100 mg. per ml.

Anticipated course. There may be some drowsiness from an initial sedative effect for the first few days. As suggested, it will generally require ten to fourteen days to reach the maximum drug effectiveness. While it can be given over a period of months to years, because there are few studies on the long-term side effects, it should not be given for long periods without ample justification and periodic blood studies.

Side effects. (See Table 13.3.) Apart from the initial drowsiness, dryness of mouth, and nasal stuffiness, there are usually few side effects. There may be an increase in appetite and an associated weight gain. Skin rashes have been reported to have occurred rarely, and incontinence and sexual impotence have been reported in adults who are on higher doses. Also, on very large doses (3,000 to 4,000 mg. per day), some adults have developed pigmentary retinopathy, which appears reversible once the drug has been discontinued.

Because leucopenia, agranulocytosis, and thrombocytopenia are possible complications, a white blood count (WBC) and differential studies should be done every eight to twelve weeks. A blood platelet count should be done at the first sign of abnormal clotting function (e.g., skin bruises, petechiae, or purpuric lesions).

Extrapyramidal symptoms are rare in the doses described above for children. As with all phenothiazines, tardive dyskinesia may appear after long-term therapy or when the drug has been discontinued. It consists of rhythmical, worm-like movements of the tongue as an early sign, and involuntary protrusion of the tongue, with puffing of the cheeks, puckering of the mouth, and involuntary movements of the extremities.

Outcome. The intensity of the target symptoms of phobia, anxiety, and unsocialized aggression usually decreases. This allows the SLD/MBD/HKS child to be more amenable to some of the specific treatment modalities which should be employed to deal with the underlying psychodynamic conflicts from which the symptoms are derived.

In respect to short-term learning studies, Sprague *et al.* (1970)

found, with 12 SLD/MBD/HKS boys, that thioridazine decreased the learning performance in a population which responded more favorably to methylphenidate. Millichap (1972) reported significant improvement with 15 MBD children in the Jastak reading test, behavior conduct ratings, and finger coordination, but noted that drowsiness was sufficiently troublesome to limit the use of the drug in his practice.

There are few studies on the long-term effectiveness and side effects of thioridazine. The general conclusion has been that it is effective as an adjunct to the total education/clinical program of the SLD/MBD/HKS child whose emotional disturbance is characterized by high levels of fear, anxiety, angers, and hostile, unsocialized aggression, as distinct from the subgroup with motor dysinhibition, hyperactivity, and short attention span.

CHLORPROMAZINE (THORAZINE)

Unique value. As a stronger and more potent tranquilizer than thioridazine (Mellaril), chlorpromazine is of value when the emotional disturbances of agitation and unsocialized aggressive behavior are more intense and when there is a need for greater chemical control. It is very effective in reducing the intensity of agitation, motor activity, and hostile impulses often associated wtih unsocialized aggressive behavior.

This is a well-known and familiar drug to most physicians and, as such, has had extensive clinical trials since it was introduced in 1952.

Treatment regimen. For younger children, ¼ mg. per lb. body weight (or 10 to 25 mg. daily) may be given orally for one to two days to rule out an idiosyncratic reaction to the drug. Then increase to 10 mg. twice or three times daily for children under 6 years and 25 mg. twice or three times daily for children 6 to 10 years. For more disturbed children 6 to 10 years, and for children over 10 years, 50 mg. three times a day may be necessary. Increase in increments of 10 or 25 mg. per day per week to the desired level of effectiveness. It is important to recognize that it may require two to four weeks to achieve the desired level of effectiveness through the oral route. Since the drug effect may be cumulative, the dosage can be dropped gradually, once the maximum has been reached, to avoid overmedicating the child. In more disturbed or older children, 200 mg. daily may be necessary. The maximum daily dose should not exceed 500 mg. per day for children up to 13 years of age.

The drug is available as a syrup, 10 mg. per 5 ml.; as a concentrate, 30 mg. per ml.; as a rectal suppository in which the dose should be ½ mg. per lb. body weight every six to eight hours (in strengths of 25 mg. or 100 mg.); and as a time-release spansule, 30 mg., 75 mg., 150 mg,. and 200 mg.

This drug is also available for intramuscular injection (25 mg. per ml.) in 10 ml. vials. One should exercise caution in using the injectable form, (a) because of the conflict it may arouse in the child/adolescent about being given a needle, and (b) because of possible hypotensive side effects which sometimes occur.

Anticipated course. There is some early drowsiness which passes in a few days, and after seven to fourteen days, the drug should reach its maximum effectiveness in controlling the target emotional symptoms. The drug can be given over a long period of time with the recognition that since its effects are cumulative, periodic attempts should be made to reduce the drug level.

Side effects. Drowsiness is a common side effect, as suggested above. Skin sensitivity, including a generalized rash and summer skin redness from exposure to sunlight while on the drug, may occur with moderate frequency. These disappear when the drug is discontinued. Occasionally, there will be a lowering of the blood pressure and postural hypotension (dizziness or fainting on standing quickly from a prone or sitting position). Leucopenia, agranulocytosis, and thrombocytopenia may occur and should be monitored by white blood cell counts, differential smears, and blood platelet counts every eight to twelve weeks, or on suspicion of these side effects. Extrapyramidal symptoms and tardive dyskinesia may occur more frequently than with the less potent thioridazine (Mellaril), especially with larger doses.

The literature suggests that, in the doses recommended for children and adolescents, less than 3% will show major side effects. Most of the side effects are reversible and disappear when the drug is discontinued.

Outcome. The short-term studies show that chlorpromazine is effective for the more severe emotional problems but, because of its potency and potential side effects, it would be a second drug of choice to thioridazine (Mellaril) for the majority of phobic, anxious, or aggressive SLD/MBD/HKS children and adolescents.

Long-term studies of the drug's effectiveness and side effects from prolonged administration to children have not been systematically carried out in the SLD/MBD/HKS population. It is clear, however, that neither thioridazine (Mellaril) nor chlorpromazine (Thorazine) should be prescribed for longer than is necessary as an adjunct to the total educational/clinical program and that the stop-order process (described earlier in this chapter) should be enforced during the utilization of these medications.

DIAZEPAM (VALIUM)

This drug is reported to be used more frequently in Europe than in the United States. It is more potent than chlordiazepoxide (Librium). It is considered useful in *status epilepticus* and as a muscle relaxant, and may control acute agitation states.

The drug is given in amounts from 2 to 20 mg. per day. Drug dependence and habituation may follow from its extended usage. In addition, this clinician and others have noted occasional bizarre side effects, such as increased emotional lability, disorientation to time and place, and rare episodes of bizarre and unpredictable behavior in children who have been on the drug. Hence, there have been reservations about its use on this population.

CHLORDIAZEPOXIDE (LIBRIUM)

This drug has been used primarily with adults in reducing tension and anxiety. It is not recommended for children under 6 years of age, but has been used for older children with symptoms of hyperactivity and aggression. The dose is 10 to 50 mg. per day, depending on the size and weight of the child.

Comparative studies by Millichap and Fowler (1967) and Millichap (1968) on 237 children with hyperactivity and behavior disorders showed an average improvement of 60% in relieving anxiety, reducing aggressive tendencies, and relaxing muscular tension. The side effects were minimal in the dosage prescribed, and this drug appears to be among the safer and more effective psychotropic compounds available. It would not replace but could supplement psychostimulant drugs when these were ineffective in treating hyperactivity. Short- and long-term studies are needed to demonstrate its effectiveness vis-à-vis thioridazine (Mellaril) in treating the phobias, anxieties, and unsocialized aggressive reactions in SLD/MBD/HKS children and adolescents.

MEPROBAMATE (MILLTOWN, EQUANIL)

This is a mild tranquilizer and muscle relaxant which is a carbamate derivative and not one of the phenothiazines. It has been used with cerebral palsy children and, in anxiety states, for the reduction of tension. It was once used for agitated and unsocialized aggressive behavior in adolescents, but has not been considered as effective as thioridazine (Mellaril) for those target symptoms in SLD/MBD/HKS children.

It is not recommended for children under 6 years of age and is prescribed in amounts of 200 to 400 mg. two or three times per day. The drug has few side effects, other than allergic or idiosyncratic reactions in some children, and there have been reports of habituation and addiction with prolonged usage. It is also available as a long-acting (400-mg.) spansule (Meprospan).

Antipsychotic Agents

Indications for Use

Occasionally SLD/MBD/HKS children will present severe emotional and/or ego disturbances associated with and as an inextricable aspect of their overall functioning pattern. Psychotropic drugs may be considered as an adjunct to the total educational/clinical prescription under the following conditions:

(1) when the total educational and clinical program, other than medication and possibly including behavior modification, has been in process for *three to four months* and the *severe emotional problems persist* to the degree that the child is not available to learning and is unable to socialize within a structured classroom environment. These severe emotional problems are generally of two kinds:

   (a) major thought process disturbances in which there is fragmentation and scatter in the stream of content of thought, occasional unfixed delusions, and periods of dissociation between thought and affect, and

   (b) a persistent pattern of primitive or primary thought processes associated with motoric acting out or episodes of withdrawn and explosive outbursts, usually with minimal external provocation.

In the author's experience with a residential setting, it has been possible to develop a residential program for severely ego-disturbed children (ages 7 to 14 years) who present associated SLD/MBD/HKS without the use of medication. The key to the program's effectiveness has been the close integrative and collaborative effort between the classroom teachers and the residential counselors. Therefore, this model should be tried before instituting medication.

(2) when the SLD/MBD/HKS child or adolescent enters a program with such "force" and "disturbance" that it is precarious for the teachers, fellow students, and the disturbed child/adolescent to remain in the program without some chemical (medication) control, and

(3) when the SLD/MBD/HKS child/adolescent undergoes such severe emotional strain from external or internal conflicts as to bring about psychological regression to earlier levels of psychosocial or psychosexual development, and the individual educational/clinical program is not sufficient to alter or stabilize the degree of psychological regression.

Choice of Drugs

CHLORPROMAZINE (THORAZINE)

The properties, dosages, anticipated course, side effects, and outcome of chlorpromazine have been described above. This is the drug of choice in SLD/MBD/HKS children and adolescents who are:

(a) severely agitated,
(b) actively and potentially aggressively assaultive, and
(c) enmeshed in a regressive, psychotic-like pattern with a preponderance of primary thought processes, such as impulse-to-action behavior, as distinct from a secondary thought process disturbance characterized by fragmentation and "skidding" content of thought and hallucinatory interruption in the stream of thought.

Because of the degree of emotional disturbance, it is usually necessary to begin with 25 mg. as the trial dose to rule out allergic or idiosyncratic reactions and to prescribe 25 to 50 mg. three to four times a day. It is seldom necessary to go beyond 300 to 400 mg. per day to obtain an effective tranquilization.

Because of the increased dosage, the side effects outlined in Table 13.3 and discussed above may be more likely to occur. Also, in these higher doses, the drug may potentiate seizure patterns in children with subclinical cerebral dysrhythmic electroencephalographic patterns.

TRIFLUOPERAZINE (STELAZINE)

Although there are no studies to demonstrate the validity of such a rationale, this clinician has found this drug to be the medication of choice over chlorpromazine (Thorazine) in those instances where the secondary thought processes seem to show a preponderance of the disturbance, with less regression to the level of more primitive, primary thought process disturbance. This hypothesis needs to be verified more critically after carefully defining the differences between primary and secondary thought process disturbances in SLD/MBD/HKS children and adolescents. These studies should also include the critical evaluation of side effects in short- and long-term use of the medication.

The dosage should be adjusted to the weight of the child and the severity of the regressive symptoms. The initial dosage would be 1 mg. in the morning for the first and, perhaps, the second day, to rule out allergic or idiosyncratic reactions. The dosage may be increased to 1 mg. twice or three times per day for ten days. Gradually increase the drug by 1 mg. per day per week, until the desired level of effectiveness has been reached. It is seldom necessary to go above 15 mg. per day, although it may be necessary with disturbed adolescents. This drug is also available as a concentrate, 10 mg. per ml. Side effects include drowsiness, dryness of mouth, extrapyramidal signs, motor restlessness, muscular dystonias, and other possible reactions associated with the phenothiazine compounds.

HALOPERIDOL (HALDOL)

This drug is one of the butyrophenone series and, as such, is both a potent and toxic agent. It has not yet been approved by the FDA for children under 12 years of age and has not been extensively used for children with SLD/MBD/HKS. Werry and Aman (1975) have done one of the first reported studies on its use. However, until greater knowledge of the effectiveness and side effects have been gathered under controlled conditions and in the adolescent population, a conservative approach would suggest that this drug not be given to children.

Antidepressant Agents

Indications for Use

SLD/MBD/HKS children and adolescents may be depressed as an emotional concomitant of their underlying disability. Gualtieri (1977) has suggested that there is no clear consensus about whether depression really occurs in children under 12 years of age. It is clear that depressive reactions in children differ from the major depressions in adults.

Brumback *et al.* (1977) completed a study on 89 consecutive children referred as new patients to an educational diagnostic center for evaluation of learning and/or behavior problems noted in school. Seventeen of the children were arbitrarily eliminated because they were pubescent or 13 years and older. Of the remaining, 42 (12 females and 30 males) met the criteria for diagnosis of depression of childhood at the initial examination. The criteria for primary depression in children was determined from the work of Weinberg *et al.* (1973) and Feighner (1972). Brumback *et al.* (1977) suggested that depression in children could be characterized by "the presence of the two symptoms of dysphoric mood and self-deprecatory ideation and an additional two or more symptoms from among eight symptoms as follows: agitation, sleep disturbance, changed school performance, diminished socialization, change in attitude toward school, somatic complaints, loss of usual energy, and unusual appetite or weight gain" (p. 533). These authors observed that certain childhood behaviors were frequently associated with such depressive patterns and included hyperactivity, enuresis, temper tantrums, destructiveness, and school phobia. They also noted that the incidence of positive family history of affective disorder varied in the childhood studies reviewed in the literature from 60% to 89% but was still higher than the reported 34% positive family histories in adult depressives (Winokur and Tanna, 1969). Several other significant articles on childhood depression have appeared in the literature (Malmquist, 1971; Cytryn and McKnew, 1972; Graham, 1974; Poznanski and Zrull, 1970.) It does seem clear that depressive reactions in children may be masked by agitation and negativism, as suggested in Chapter 2 above.

Medication is seldom indicated or necessary for SLD/MBD/HKS children who show depressive reactions, inasmuch as they usually respond well to individual, group, and behavior therapies. However, in the Brumback study, 19 (56%) of 34 children who were available for follow-up study out of the total sample of 42 children were treated over a four-week period with either amitriptyline (16 children) or imipramine (3 children) in dosages ranging from 25 mg. to 125 mg. per day, according to age and body weight. The authors suggested that there was a 95% improvement of the treated depressed child over a 40% improvement of depressed children who received no medication.

Choice of Drugs

Both imipramine (Tofranil) and lithium have been given to SLD/MBD/HKS children with the rationale that they may reduce hyperactivity in children.

IMIPRAMINE (TOFRANIL)

Imipramine has been demonstrated to have cardiotoxic side effects in amounts greater than 75 mg. per day (Steel *et al.*, 1967; Winsberg *et al.*, 1975). It also appears to be a drug which is prone to the development of drug tolerance. From the data available, imipramine appears to be less effective than the psychostimulants in treating the target symptom of hyperactivity in SLD/MBD/HKS children (Huessy and Wright, 1970; Gittelman-Klein, 1974; Rapoport *et al.*, 1974; Waizer *et al.*, 1974; Quinn and Rapoport, 1975). Gualtieri (1977) concluded that imipramine ought to be reserved for those cases in which more conventional therapies have proven ineffective, and he emphasized that the use of the drug is not without risk.

AMITRIPTYLINE (ELAVIL) AND DESIPRAMINE (PERTOFRANE)

Amitriptyline (Elavil) and desipramine (Pertofrane) appear to be less cardiotoxic than imipramine (Tofranil) and appear to be the drugs of choice if an agitated depression or reactive depression persists in an SLD/MBD/HKS child/adolescent after a trial of a suitable individual educational/clinical program has been initiated. There is some evidence to show that the antidepressant agent may be helpful for children who are suffering from severe separation anxiety and its attendant reactive depression. This might include children with school refusal behavior or school phobias.

LITHIUM

Lithium has been given to SLD/MBD/HKS children who did not respond well to the psychostimulants. In studies by Whitehead and Clark (1970) and Greenhill *et al.,* (1973) unfavorable results were reported. While one would have reservations about prescribing lithium for children under 12 years of age, more studies need to be done on the use of lithium carbonate in SLD/MBD/HKS adolescents with severe agitated-depressive reaction who have not responded to other treatment modalities. The serum level of lithium sufficient for clinical effectiveness is so close to the toxic level that careful monitoring of drug levels is imperative. Side effects include drowsiness, nausea, abdominal pain, muscle weakness, twitching, tremors, slurred speech, thirst, and frequent urination.

Anticonvulsant agents

Occasionally, SLD/MBD/HKS children have a history of epilepsy, which refers to a group of convulsive disorders characterized by brief seizure episodes associated with some disturbance in or loss of consciousness. There are five forms of epilepsy which might occur in an SLD/MBD/HKS population.

Grand Mal epilepsy is the most obvious and the most distressing for the observer. It is a major convulsion with tonic and clonic phases. In the tonic phase, all the body musculature stiffens in an extension spasm occasionally associated with a short cry. This phase lasts two to three seconds and is followed by the longer clonic phase, in which there is a synchronous jerking movement of the arms and legs. This phase is usually self-limiting after thirty to sixty seconds. During both phases, the respiratory muscles are immobilized and there is a period of anoxia for the duration of the seizure. Normal respiration resumes as the seizure ends. Lethargy, confusion, disorientation, and drowsiness often follow a seizure because of the depression of the central nervous system during the period of anoxia. Loss of bladder or bowel control may accompany the seizure. Some children describe sensory sensations, referred to as auras or signals of an impending seizure in their stomachs, eyes, or ears prior to a seizure. Infrequently, the Grand Mal seizure may persist for more than a minute or two, and a second or third seizure may follow, suggesting that the child is in a *status epilepticus* pattern.

Valium should be given to interrupt the seizure pattern and oxygen administered to maintain an adequate oxygen intake in the respiratory-cardiovascular system. For infants 30 days of age up to 5 years, 0.2 mg. to 0.5 mg. can be given slowly, every two to five minutes, up to a maximum of 5 mg. Each milliliter of injectable Valium contains 5 milligrams of the drug. The intravenous route is preferred. However, if intravenous administration is impossible, the intramuscular route may be used. For children 5 years and older, 1 mg. every two to five minutes up to a maximum of 10 mg. may be given slowly by the i.v. route. Repeat in two to four hours if necessary.

Petit Mal epilepsy is more subtle and is characterized by brief moments of loss of consciousness, lasting for a few seconds, during which a pencil or fork may be dropped and there may be staring into space, blinking of the eyes, failure to answer when spoken to, or a momentary pause in speaking. Frequently, there are no observable motor components, and the child is alert and ready to continue as if nothing had interrupted consciousness. There is usually amnesia for the duration of the seizure but no subsequent disturbances of consciousness.

Psychomotor epilepsy is difficult to identify, as it is characterized by periods of confused behavior, often out of character but representing a variety of clinical behaviors in which there is momentary loss of control, confusion, and disorientation after the episode. An EEG spike and wave pattern is the most certain way to confirm this diagnosis.

Akinetic epilepsy refers to those seizures in which the child suddenly drops to the ground or falls from a seat with momentary loss of consciousness as well as loss of orientation to time, place, and person. There is no tonic-clonic episode, and seldom is there a depressed period subsequent to the seizure.

Focal Cortical epilepsy, or *Jacksonian* motor or sensory epilepsy, is the least common in children. It usually starts with a twitch on one side of the face and then "marches" down that side of the body to include the arm and leg on the same side of the body.

Table 13.3 delineates the drugs used for the different seizure patterns and lists the anticipated side effects of each drug.

DIPHENYLHYDANTOIN (DILANTIN)

There is some evidence to show that children treated with Dilantin need an increase in their folic acid and vitamin D intake which, with careful brushing and daily dental care, may reduce the hyperplasia of the gums which frequently accompanies this medication. In addition to its use in controlling Grand Mal seizures, diphenylhydantoin (Dilantin) has been used to control hyperactivity and behavior problems in SLD/MBD/HKS children (Ayd, 1967; Baldwin, 1969; Looker and Conners, 1970).

Occasionally, an SLD/MBD/HKS child will have a subclinical seizure pattern which is picked up by an EEG. Such was the situation in Case Study 1.1, where the EEG was read as quite abnormal, showing a general background dysrhythmia, with irregularity of wave forms appearing almost triangular in shape and often notched. This little boy responded in a dramatic fashion in his language development and personal-social relationships to a total remediation program including Dilantin. However, major visual-motor and fine-motor skill problems persisted for a number of years.

In an eight-week double-blind, placebo-controlled study of 47 hospitalized cultural-familial retarded children aged 9 to 14, Goldberg and Kurland (1970) reported Dilantin to be effective in improving attentional skills, self-control, and delay of immediate gratification, as well as improvement in interpersonal relationships with adults.

Wender (1971) noted that 4 MBD children who had not responded to amphetamine responded favorably to Dilantin. Millichap (1973) reported that a study of 22 children with paroxysmal dysrhythmias, learning disabilities, and behavior disorders showed significant increases in their auditory perception and discrimination skills following the use of Dilantin. Unfortunately, however, there have been few carefully controlled studies of the effects of Dilantin on SLD/MBD/HKS children. Consequently, this drug is not used as a primary choice but as a choice when other drugs are not effective or when there is indication of an underlying seizure pattern.

Orthomolecular Therapy

Orthomolecular therapy had its beginning in 1952, when Osmond and Hoffer (1964) described larger doses of niacin (vitamin B_3) and niacinamide in the treatment of schizophrenia. Hoffer *et al.* (1954) formulated the hypothesis that schizophrenia was the result of a failure of central nervous system metabolism which produced highly toxic mescaline-type compounds. Adrenochrome, a psychotoxic oxidation product of epinephrine which resulted from the increased phenolase oxidase in the serum of the schizophrenic patients, was thought to be a mescaline-like compound. The rationale was that large doses of niacin, as a strong methyl group acceptor, would compete for the methyl groups in and prevent the conversion of norepinephrine to epinephrine. The decrease in epinephrine would lower the quantities of adrenochrome in the blood plasma and extracellular tissues.

Studies by the American Psychiatric Association Task Force (1973) concluded there was no valid basis for the use of megavitamins in the treatment of mental disorders. At the same time, early double-blind studies were done in Saskatchewan and reported by Clancy *et al.* (1954) and Hoffer *et al.* (1957). Subsequently, pyridoxine (vitamin B₆), vitamin C, and vitamin E were added to the treatments. In 1968, Pauling, the Nobel Prize winner, coined the term "orthomolecular medicine."

The first application to children's populations was made by Cott (1969) in the treatment of 500 psychotic children and, subsequently, in the treatment of children with learning disabilities (Cott, 1971). The most recent publication by Cott (1977) summarizes the field from his experiences over a decade. The key issues he discusses focus on (1) the process of assessment, (2) the individualized prescription of the megavitamins, (3) the key issues related to good nutrition, and (4) the avoidance of food additives.

Critique

The Committee on Nutrition of the American Academy of Pediatrics (1976) has summarized its point of view on the use of megavitamin therapy for childhood psychosis and learning disabilities with the following observations:

(1) Most of the low molecular weight vitamins and related substances prescribed are precursors of coenzymes essential to nutrition and central nervous system metabolism.

(2) The Food and Nutrition Board of the National Academy of Sciences has defined the Recommended Dietary Allowances (RDA) sufficient to meet the known nutritional needs of healthy persons at all ages. It was the Committee's contention that normal children receiving a normal diet did not need vitamin supplementation above the RDA levels.

(3) The Committee recognized that there are a variety of clinical entities in which the daily intake of vitamins needs to be increased significantly above the RDA levels. The so-called dependency syndromes, which represent rare inborn errors in

metabolism, may involve the metabolism of the vitamin in relationship to its biologically active derivative or may affect the apoenzyme at the cofactor binding site. In these instances, the metabolic defect may be partially or completely corrected by greatly increasing vitamin or cofactor availability.

(4) The Committee recognized that a combination of timely economic and psychologic factors created a "cult" focused on the use of large doses of water-soluble vitamins to treat a wide spectrum of disease states.

(5) The Committee affirmed that there are conditions in children and adolescents where a specific vitamin deficiency can be demonstrated by biochemical tests, and increased amounts of vitamins can be shown to resolve these conditions. On the basis of current documented clinical results, however, the Committee felt that megavitamin therapy was not justified as a treatment for learning disabilities and/or psychoses in children, including autism.

Other Medical Therapies

Biofeedback

There has been a growing use of electrical and mechanical devices in the management of educational and behavioral problems in children and adolescents. This has been stimulated by rapid technical advances in instrumentation (Schwitzgebel and Schwitzgebel, 1973) and the application of learning theory to the problems of attention and cognition in SLD/MBD/HKS children.

Biofeedback is one of the more recent procedures which brings together these two emerging trends. Essentially, it is the immediate feedback of specific bioelectrical responses to the subject for the purpose of modifying those responses in vascular, neuroelectrical, and neuromuscular disorders (Blanshard and Young, 1974). Several investigators have attempted to use biofeedback training with SLD/HKS children to control the breathing pattern and thereby modify hyperactivity and increase the attention span (Simpson and Nelson, 1974; Guralnick and Mott, 1976). One of the problems has been the minimum transfer of training from the laboratory or training setting into other settings, such as the classroom. Toomin (1975) has used the galvanic skin response (GSR) feedback technique as an aid in dynamic psychotherapy in which the GSR gives an immediate feedback in response to internal (intra-psychic) and external (environmental) stimuli.

It has been suggested that alpha-wave conditioning by the biofeed-back technique might increase the attention span, reduce the hyper-activity and distractibility, and bring about an improvement in the classroom performance of SLD/MBD/HKS children. The alpha-wave on an electroencephalogram is a slow 8- to 14-cycle-per-second sine wave. Studies by Brown (1970) and Green and Green (1970) indicated that it was possible to control one's alpha-wave activity. An intensifica-tion of slow alpha-wave activity has been associated with a relaxed, yet extremely sensitive, state of mental and physical alertness recently termed the relaxation response. Such a response has been defined as an integrated hypothalamic reaction resulting in generalized decrease of sympathetic nervous system activity (Benson *et al.*, 1977).

Although it is known that many such studies are under way to ex-plore the feasibility of such a treatment program in the SLD/MBD/HKS population, few have been reported in the literature.

Antiallergic Diets

Several investigators have suggested that one of the causes of SLD in children is an allergic sensitivity of the central nervous system to specific foodstuffs (Mandell, 1974; Philpott *et al.*, 1975). Specific test techniques are described by the authors to uncover possible allergic excitants which may enter the circulatory system to be distributed to the potential shock tissue in the sensitized child's body. Up to the present, hard data have not been sufficient to establish the relationship between food allergies and SLD/HKS responses.

FOOD ADDITIVES AND PRESERVATIVES

A California allergest suggested that certain food additives and preservatives appeared to be responsible for allergic reactions which were associated with hyperkinesis and learning disabilities in children (Feingold, 1974, 1975). The possibly noxious substances have been listed in Table 13.4, and many children are being placed on diets free from such additives.

Conners *et al.* (1976) and others are attempting to verify the relevance of this hypothesis. Wender (1977) reported that studies to date of 51 children under appropriate conditions refute the general

Table 13.4
All Food Containing These Additives
Should be Avoided*

Sodium nitrite	Propylene glycol alginate
Gum arabic	Sodium benzoate
Saccharin	Disodium EDTA
Sodium acid pyrophosphate	Butylated hydroxyanisole (BHA)
FDC red No. 2	Butylated hydroxytoluene (BHT)
FDC yellow No. 5	Brominated vegetable oil
Monosodium glutamate	All artificial flavors
Heptyl paraben	All artificial colors
Sodium propionate	

*Cott, 1977.

claim that 40% or more of hyperkinetic children demonstrate global improvement in behavior and/or learning on the additive-eliminated diets.

The Conners study pointed up two significant problems: First, the psychological factors related to the major intervention of the study into the dietary habits of a family and, second, the apparent reduction of nutrient intake, especially vitamin C, in the elimination (Kaiser-Permanente) diet. It also reported on a small sample ($n=15$) of hyperkinetic children (classified as DSM II 308.0) who showed a significant reduction in hyperkinesis in teacher ratings when on the K-P diet as compared to a control diet ($p<.005$), but not in parent ratings. However, the K-P diet was significantly better than the baseline periods in both teacher and parent ratings ($p<.05$). The researchers suggested these findings be viewed with caution, due to the small size of the sample and complex factors in the design of such diet studies.

Antihypoglycemic Diets

Daily observations of children and adults suggest that there is a close correspondence between the blood sugar level and degrees of irritability and inability to tolerate stress. Cott (1971, 1977) suggested that many of the symptoms of SLD/MBD/HKS children were secondary to hypoglycemia and the syndrome of dysinsulinism. In order to establish such a relationship, a full five- to seven-hour glucose tolerance test would be essential.

Dunn (1976) reported a study of 144 children with a learning disability in which the five-hour glucose tolerance test was routinely done. Data from his laboratory indicated that 72% of this population showed some degree of abnormal carbohydrate metabolism and that one fourth of this latter group reacted with more severe flat hypoglycemic, prediabetic, or hyperinsulin curves.

In the same study, Dunn collected data on trace metals using the hair analysis technique (Strain *et al.*, 1971; Dunn, 1976). He noted that many patients with cerebral dysfunction have demonstrated a significant imbalance in the ratios of these metals. For example, any lead level in excess of 20 parts/million in hair would be significant, as would low potassium to zinc ratios, in SLD/MBD/HKS populations.

Patterning

Considerable controversy was stirred up by the claims of Doman and Delacato (1968) as to the effects of their "patterning" of simultaneous passive contralateral movements of the head, legs, and arms on the development of the neuromuscular system of children with severe brain damage (Doman *et al.*, 1960). The staff of the Institutes for the Achievement of Human Potential was one of the first to develop an active, vigorous program for severely handicapped children when most of the professions were ignoring this population. Unfortunately, an attempt was made to apply the "patterning" technique as a panacea for all children with varying degree of CNS dysfunction. Frequently, the demands of the rigid daily schedule, which required large numbers of neighborhood volunteers to work with parents, were physically and emotionally traumatic to the handicapped child. Additionally, and with no malice aforethought, the staff often instilled guilt in the concerned parents who failed to follow through with their child the method of passive manipulation, sensory "icing" of the facial musculature to encourage speech, rebreathing with a plastic face-mask to increase vital capacity and stimulate cerebral blood flow, and the restrictions imposed on listening to music and the intake of fluids, salt, and sugar.

In 1965, the American Academy of Pediatrics, the American Academy for Cerebral Palsy, and the Canadian Association for Retarded Children published statements raising critical questions as to the effectiveness of this treatment regimen. Freeman (1967) wrote a well-worded critique, at the height of the controversy, suggesting that, inasmuch as a well-controlled study of the Institute's program was impossible to design and carry out at that time, physicians and other professional persons would have to weigh carefully recommendations for such treatment.

Sensory Integrative Therapy

In his critique on acceptable and controversial approaches to treating the SLD child, Silver (1975) has placed the Ayres model (1972) of neurophysiologic retraining among the controversial therapies. Her theories were carefully reasoned, and she was cautious in going from concepts to conclusions. Vestibular, postural, and tactile stimulation were used to improve auditory discrimination processes in language-disordered SLD children. Her data suggested that immature postural reactions, poor extraocular muscle control, poor visual-spatial development, and poor auditory discrimination could be related to inadequate sensory integration in the brain stem. According to Ayres (1972), normalization of posture would organize the midbrain processes, and vestibular stimulation would improve the auditory discrimination process. These concepts must await replication and evaluative research to determine their validity.

Optometric Training

Among proposed treatment methods for SLD/MBD/HKS children, visual training/vision therapy is, perhaps, the most controversial. Silver (1975) and Sieben (1977) have been two of the more outspoken critics, along with a joint statement by the American Academy of Pediatrics, the American Academy of Ophthalmology and Otolaryngology, and the American Association of Ophthalmology (1972). The essence of the joint statement was that no known scientific evidence supports the claims for improved academic functioning in learning disabled or dyslexic children with treatment based solely on either visual training using muscle exercises, ocular pursuit, or the use of lenses, or on neurologic organizational training which employs laterality training, balance board, or perceptual training.

Getman (1964), who along with Gesell *et al.* (1949) pioneered many of the early concepts of visual development and its relationship to learning, has written a thoughtful response to these critics (1977). In it, he recognizes that the joint statement of the academies was a broad statement with which he also can agree in a general way. However, Getman makes a threefold plea for (a) a continuous unbiased search of the literature for all issues related to visual training/vision therapy, (b) a search for the creative use of multidisciplinary cooperation, and (c) a sustained search for valid replicable or refutable data gathered in the use of optometric methods in combination with other prescribed treatments.

The inclusion of Chapter 5 on visual function and visual training is an attempt toward multidisciplinary cooperation. Case 5.4 was presented to illustrate the point that no one discipline has the exclusive answer to the needs of these children, but that the concepts of visual development and visual dysfunction can contribute, in certain cases, to the total treatment and remediation of the child's special needs.

Sieben's critique (1977) covered a broad spectrum of controversial medical treatments used with these children. In the same volume, equal opportunity to respond to Sieben's presentation was given to the leading proponents of those treatments, including Ayres, Buckley, Cott, Doman and Delacato, Feingold, Getman, Powers, and Wunderlich. The result is a constructive dialogue which makes a significant contribution to the literature on controversial medical treatments.

CONCLUSION

Although this chapter has been extensive in scope, the central thesis should be underscored: *medication is not the only treatment of choice* for SLD/MBD/HKS children and adolescents. All too frequently, professional biases blind the clinician and educator alike to the necessity for a multidisciplinary treatment and remediation approach.

An effort has been made to assemble here, in usable form, the essential content of the expanding literature on medical therapies with these children, of observations from clinical practice, and of clinical impressions drawn from psychiatric consultation to the classroom and to several public and private educational systems.

Many new and significant developments related to the needs and services of the SLD/MBD/HKS population will continue to emerge in neurophysiology, neuropharmacology, neuropsychology, biogenetics, endocrinology, psycholinguistics, sociology, clinical and experimental psychology, special education, and related fields. As they appear, these developments will illluminate more fully our understanding and provide an increasingly clearer view of the optimum education/clinical intervention combinations which are indicated for each developmental phase which these children/adolescents must invariably master for their complete educational and emotional growth.

REFERENCES

Ackerman, P., Dykman, R., & Peters, J. Learning-disabled boys as adolescents: Cognitive factors and achievement. *Journal American Academy of Child Psychiatry*, 1977, *16*(2), 296–313.

Aman, M., & Sprague, R. The state-dependent effects of methylphenidate and dextroamphetamine. *Journal of Nervous and Mental Diseases*, 1974, *158*, 268–279.

American Psychiatric Association task force on vitamin therapy in psychiatry: Megavitamin and orthomolecular therapy in psychiatry. Washington, D.C.: American Psychiatric Association, 1973.

Ayd, F. New uses for an old drug. *Internal Drug Therapy Newsletter*, 1967, (2), 1–2.

Ayres, J. Improving academic scores through sensory integration. *Journal of Learning Disabilities*, 1972, *5*, 338–343.

Baldwin, R. Behavior disorders in children. *Maryland Medical Journal*, 1969, *18*, 68–71.

Bax, M. The active and the over-active school child. *Developmental Medicine and Child Neurology*, 1972, *14*, 83–86.

Benson, H., Kotch, J., Crassweller, K., & Greenwood, M. Historical and clinical considerations of the relaxation response. *American Scientist*, 1977, *65*, 441–445.

Blanshard, E. & Young, L. Clinical applications of biofeedback training: A review of evidence. *Archives of General Psychiatry*, 1974, *30*, 573–589.

Bosco, J. & Robin, S. Introduction to the hyperactive child and stimulant drugs: Definitions, diagnosis, and directions. *School Review*, 1976, *85*(1), 1–4.

Bradley, C. The behavior of children receiving Benzedrine. *American Journal of Psychiatry*, 1937, *94*, 577–585.

Brown, A. The development of memory. In H.W. Reese (Ed.), *Advances in child development and behavior*. New York: Academic Press, 1976.

Brown, B. Recognition of aspects of consciousness through association with EEG alpha activity represented by a light signal. *Psychophysiology*, 1970, *6*, 442.

Brumback, R., Dietz-Schmidt, S., & Weinberg, W. Depression in children referred to an educational diagnostic center: Diagnosis and treatment and analysis of criteria and literature review. *Diseases of the Nervous System*, 1977, *38*(7), 529–534.

Christenson, D. Effects of combining methylphenidate and classroom token system in modifying hyperactive behavior. *American Journal Mental Deficiency*, 1975, *80*(3), 266–276.

Christianson, D. & Sprague, R. Reduction of hyperactive behavior by conditioning procedures alone and combined with methylphenidate

(Ritalin). *Behavior Research and Therapy,* 1973, *11.* 331–334.

Clancy, J., Hoffer, A., Lucy, J., Osmond, H., Smythies, J., & Stefaniuk, B. Design and planning in psychiatric research as illustrated by the Weyburn chronic nucleotide project. *Menninger Clinical Bulletin,* 1954, *18,* 147–153.

Clements, S. *Minimal brain dysfunction in children: Terminology and identification.* NINDB Monograph no. 3, U.S. Public Health Service Publication no. 1415. Washington, D.C.: Government Printing Office, 1966.

Clements, S. & Peters, J. Minimal brain dysfunction in school-age child. *Archives of General Psychiatry,* 1962, *6,* 185–197.

Cohen, S. Minimal brain dysfunction and practical matters such as teaching kids to read. *Annals of New York Academy of Science,* 1973, *205,* 251–261.

Cole, S. Hyperkinetic children: The use of stimulant drugs evaluated. *American Journal of Orthopsychiatry,* 1975, *45,* 28–37.

Committee on Nutrition, American Academy of Pediatrics, *Pediatrics,* 1976, *58*(6), 910–911.

Conners, C. Behavior modification by drugs. Psychological effects of stimulant drugs in children with minimal brain dysfunction. *Pediatrics,* 1972, *49,* 702–708.

Conners, C. (Ed.) *Clinical use of stimulant drugs in children.* The Hague: Excerpta Medica, 1974.

Conners, C. A placebo-crossover study of caffeine treatment of hyperactive children. *International Journal of Mental Health,* 1975, *4,* 132–143.

Conners, C. & Eisenberg, L. The effect of methylphenidate on symptomatology and learning in disturbed children. *American Journal of Psychiatry,* 1963, *120,* 458–463.

Conners, C., Goyette, C., Southwick, D., Lees, J., & Andrulonis, P. Food additives and hyperkinesis: A controlled double blind experiment. *Pediatrics,* 1976, *58,* 154–166.

Conners, C., Rothschild, G., Eisenberg, L., Schwartz, L., & Robinson, E. Dextroamphetamine sulfate in children with learning disorders: Effects on perception, learning and achievement *Archives of General Psychiatry,* 1969, *21,* 182–190.

Conners, C., Taylor, E., Meo, G., Kurtz, M., & Fournier, M. Magnesium pemoline and dextroamphetamine: A controlled study in children with minimal brain dysfunction. *Psychopharmacologia,* 1972, *26,* 321–336.

Conrad, W., Dworkin, E., Shai, H., & Tobiessen, J. Effects of amphetamine therapy and prescriptive tutoring on the behavior and achievement of lower class hyperactive children. *Journal of Learning Disabilities,* 1971, *4,* 509–517.

Cott, A. Treating schizophrenic children. *Schizophrenia,* 1969, *1,* 44–49.

Cott, A. Orthomuscular approach to the treatment of learning disabilities. *Schizophrenia,* 1971, *3,* 95–105.

Cott, A. *The orthomolecular approach to learning disabilities.* San Rafael: Academic Therapy, 1977.

Cytryn, L. & McKnew, D. Proposed classification of childhood depression. *American Journal of Psychiatry,* 1972, *129,* 149–155.

Doman, G. & Delacato, C. Doman-Delacato philosophy. *Human Potential,* 1968, *1,* 113.

Doman, R., Spitz, E., Zeuman, E., Delacato, C., & Doman, G. Children with severe brain injuries: Neurological organization in terms of mobility. *Journal American Medical Association,* 1960, *174,* 257–262.

Douglas, V. Stop, look and listen: The problem of sustained attention and impulse control in hyperactive and normal children. *Canadian Journal of Behaviour Science,* 1972, *4,* 259–282.

Dunn, P. Orthomolecular therapy: Implications for learning disability. In G. Leisman (Ed.), *Basic visual processes and learning disability.* Springfield, Ill.: Charles C Thomas, 1976.

Dykman, R. & Ackerman, P. The MBD problem. In R. Anderson and C. Holcomb (Eds.), *Learning disability—minimal brain dysfunction.* Springfield, Ill: Charles C Thomas, 1976.

Ebaugh, F. Neuropsychiatric sequelae of acute epidemic encephalitis in children. *American Journal of Diseases of Children,* 1923, *25,* 89–97.

Eisenberg, L. Psychopharmacology in childhood: A critique. In E. Miller (Ed.), *Foundations of child psychiatry.* Oxford: Pergamon Press, 1968.

Feighner, J. Diagnostic criteria for use in psychiatric research. *Archives of General Psychiatry,* 1972, *26,* 57–63.

Feingold, B. *Why your child is hyperactive.* New York: Random House, 1974.

Feingold, B. Hyperkinesis and learning disabilities linked to artificial food flavors and colors. *American Journal of Nursing,* 1975, *75,* 797–803.

Freeman, R. Drug effects on learning in children: A selective review of the past thirty years. *Journal of Special Education,* 1966, *1,* 17–44.

Freeman, R. Controversy over "patterning" as a treatment for brain damage in children. *Journal of the American Medical Association,* 1967, *202,* 385–388.

Freeman, R. Minimal brain dysfunction, hyperactivity, and learning disorders: Epidemic or episode? *School Review, University of Chicago,* 1976, *85*(1), 5–30.

Garfinkel, B., Webster, C., & Sloman, L. Methylphenidate and caffeine in the treatment of children with minimal brain dysfunction. *American Journal of Psychiatry,* 1975, *132,* 723–728.

Gesell, A., Ilg., F., Bullis, G., Getman, G., & Ilg, V. *Vision: Its development in infant and child.* New York: Hoeber, 1949.

Getman, G. *The primary visual abilities essential to academic achievement.* Duncan, Oklahoma: Optometric Extension Program Foundation, 1964.

Getman, G. Searching for solutions or perpetuating the problems? *Academic Therapy*, 1977, *13*(2), 185–196.

Gittelman-Klein, R. Pilot clinical trial of imipramine in hyperkinetic children. In C. Connors (Ed.), *Clinical use of the stimulant drugs in children.* The Hague: Excerpta Medica, 1974.

Goldberg, J. & Kurland, A. Dilantin treatment of hospitalized cultural-familial retardates. *Journal of Nervous and Mental Disease,* 1970, *150*, 133–137.

Graham, P. Depression in prepubertal children. *Developmental Medical Child Neurology*, 1974, *16*, 340–349.

Green, A. & Green, R. Voluntary control of internal states: Psychological and physiological. *Journal of Transpersonal Psychology*, 1970, *2, 1.*

Greenhill, L., Rieder, R., Wender, P., Buchbaum, M., and Kahn, T. Lithium carbonate in the treatment of hyperactive children. *Archives of General Psychiatry,* 1973, *38, 636–640.*

Grinspon, L. & Singer, S. Amphetamines in the treatment of hyperkinetic children. *Harvard Educational Review,* 1973, *43,* 515–555.

Gross, M. Caffeine in the treatment of children with minimal brain dysfunction or hyperkinetic syndrome. *Psychosomatics,* 1975, *16,* 26–27.

Gross, M. Comparison of dextroamphetamine in treatment of hyperkinetic syndrome or minimal brain dysfunction. *Diseases of the Nervous System,* 1976, *37,* 14–16.

Gualtieri, C. Imipramine and children: A review and some speculations about the mechanism of drug action. *Diseases of the Nervous System,* 1977, *38,* 368–377.

Guralnick, M. & Mott, D. Biofeedback training with a learning disabled child. *Perceptual Motor Skills,* 1976, *42*(1), 27–30.

Hoffer, H., Osmond, H., Callbeck, M., & Kahan, I. Treatment of schizophrenia with nicotinic acid and nicotinamide. *Journal of Clinical Experimental Psychopathology,* 1957, *18,* 131–158.

Hoffer, H., Osmond, H., & Smythies, J. Schizophrenia: A new approach. II. Results of a year's research. *Journal of Mental Science,* 1954, *100,* 29–54.

Huessy, H. & Wright, A. The use of imipramine in children's behavior disorders. *Acta Paedopsychiatrica,* 1970, *37,* 194–199.

Huestis, R., Arnold, L., & Smeltzer, D. Caffeine versus methylphenidate and *d*-amphetamine in minimal brain dysfunction: A double-blind comparison. *American Journal of Psychiatry,* 1975, *132,* 868–870.

Kahn, E. & Cohen, L. Organic drivenness: A brain stem syndrome and an experience. *New England Journal of Medicine,* 1934, *210,* 748–756.

Kirk, S. & Bateman, B. Diagnosis and remediation of learning disabilities. *Exceptional Children*, 1962, *29,* 73–78.

Lasagna, L. & Epstein, L. The use of amphetamines in the treatment of hyperkinetic children. In E. Costa & S. Garattini (Eds.), *International symposium on amphetamines and related compounds.* New York: Raven, 1970.

Laufer, M. Long-term management and some follow-up findings on the use of drugs with minimal cerebral syndromes. *Journal of Learning Disabilities,* 1971, *4,* 518–522.

Laufer, M., Denhoff, E., & Solomons, G. Hyperkinetic impulse disorder in children's behavior problems. *Psychosomatic Medicine,* 1957, *19,* 38–49.

Lewis, J. & Lewis, B. Deanol in minimal brain dysfunction. *Diseases of the Nervous System,* 1977, *38*(12), 21–24.

Lerer, R. & Lerer, M. Response of adolescents with minimal brain dysfunction to methylphenidate. *Journal of Learning Disabilities,* 1977, *10,* (4), 223–228

Loney, J. & Ordona, T. Using cerebral stimulants to treat minimal brain dysfunction. *American Journal of Orthopsychiatry,* 1975, *45,* 564–572.

Looker, A. & Conners, C. Dyphenylhydantoin in children with severe temper tantrums. *Archives of General Psychiatry,* 1970, *23,* 80-89.

Malmquist, C. Depressions in childhood and adolescents, II. *New England Journal of Medicine,* 1971, *284,* 955–961.

Mandell, M. Cerebral reactions in allergic patients. *Journal of International Academy of Metabology,* 1974, *3,* 94–101.

Millichap, J. Hyperkinetic behavior and learning disorders, III. Battery of neuropsychological tests in controlled trial of methylphenidate. *American Journal of the Diseases of Children,* 1968, *116,* 235–244.

Millichap, J. Drugs in the management of minimal brain dysfunction. *International Journal of Child Psychotherapy,* 1972 *1*(3), 65–82.

Millichap, J. Drugs in the management of minimal brain dysfunction. *Annals of New York Academy of Science,* 1973, *205,* 321–334.

Millichap, J. & Fowler, G. Treatment of the minimal brain dysfunction syndromes. Selection of drugs for children with hyperactivity and learning disabilities. *Pediatric Clinic of North America,* 1967, *14,* 767–777.

Morgan, W. A case of congenital word blindness. *British Medical Journal,* November 7, 1896.

O'Connor v. Donaldson, Supreme Court Decision No. 74-8, June 26, 1975.

Oettinger, L. Pediatric psychopharmacology, a review with special reference to deanol. *Diseases of the Nervous System,* 1977, *38*(12), 25–31.

O'Leary, K., Pelham, W., Rosenbaum, A., & Price, G. Behavioral treatment of hyperkinetic children: An experimental evaluation of its usefulness. *Clinical Pediatrics,* 1976, (15), 510.

Orton, S. *Reading, writing, and speech problems in children.* New York: W.W. Norton, 1937.

Osmond, H. & Hoffer, A. Niacin therapy in psychiatry. *Acta Psychiatrica Scandinavia,* 1964, *40,* 171–189.

Page, J., Janicki, R., Bernstein, J., Curran, C., & Michelli F. Pemoline (Cylert) in the treatment of childhood hyperkinesis. *Journal of Learning Disabilities,* 1974, *7,* 42–47.

Philpott, W., Mandell, M., & von Hilsheimer, G. Allergic, toxic, and chemically defective states as causes and/or facilitating factors of emotional reactions, dyslexia, hyperkinesis, and learning problems. In A. Ansara (Ed.), *Selected papers on learning disabilities. Our challenge: The right to know.* Pittsburgh: Association for Children with Learning Disabilities, 1975.

Physicians' desk reference (31st ed.). Oradell, N.J.: Medical Economics, 1977.

Poznanski, E. & Zrull, J. Childhood depression: Clinical characteristics of overtly depressed children. *Archives of General Psychiatry,* 1970, *23,* 8–15.

Quinn, P. & Rapoport, J. One-year follow-up of hyperactive boys treated with imipramine or methylphenidate. *American Journal of Psychiatry,* 1975, *132,* 241–245.

Rapoport, J., Quinn, P., Bradbard, G., Riddle, D., & Brooks, E. Imipramine and methylphenidate treatments of hyperactive boys: A double-blind comparison. *Archives of General Psychiatry,* 1974, *30,* 789–793.

Robin, S. & Bosco, J. The social context of stimulant drug treatment for hyperkinetic children. *School Review,* 1976, *85*(1), 141–154.

Rutter, M., Graham, P., & Yule, W. *A neuropsychiatric study in childhood.* Philadelphia: J.P. Lippincott, 1970. (a)

Rutter, M., Tizard, J., & Whitmore, K. *Education, health and behaviour.* London: Longman Group, 1970. (b)

Safer, D. & Allen, R. *Hyperactive children.* Baltimore: University Park Press, 1976.

Safer, D., Allen, R., & Barr, E. Depression of growth in hyperactive children on stimulant drugs. *New England Journal of Medicine,* 1972, *287,* 217–220.

Safer, D., Allen, R., & Barr, E. Growth rebound after termination of stimulant drugs. *Journal of Pediatrics,* 1975, *86,* 113–116.

Satterfield, J., Cantwell, D., & Satterfield, B. Pathophysiology of the hyperactive child syndrome. *Archives of General Psychiatry,* 1972, *128,* 1418–1424.

Schain, R. & Reynard, C. Observations on effects of a central stimulant drug (methylphenidate) in children with hyperactive behavior. *Pediatrics,* 1975, *55,* 709–716.

Schleifer, M., Weiss, G., Cohen, N., Elman, M., Cvejic, H., & Kruger, E.

Hyperactivity in preschoolers and the effect of methylphenidate. *American Journal of Orthopsychiatry*, 1975, *45*, 38–50.

Schrag, P. & Divoky, D. *The myth of the hyperactive child: And other means of child control.* New York: Pantheon Books, 1975.

Schnackenburg, R. Caffeine as a substitute for Schedule II stimulants in hyperkinetic children. *American Journal of Psychiatry*, 1973, *130*, 796–798.

Schwitzgebel, R. & Schwitzgebel, R. (Eds.), *Psychotechnology: Electronic control of mind and behavior.* New York: Holt, Rinehart and Winston, 1973.

Sieben, R. Controversial medical treatments of learning disabilities. *Academic Therapy*, 1977, *13*(2), 133–148.

Silver, L. Acceptable and controversial approaches to treating the child with learning disabilities. *Pediatrics*, 1975, *55*, 406–415.

Silver, L. Drug therapy with children and adolescents. In M. Cohen (Ed.), *Drugs and the special child.* New York: Gardner Press, in press.

Simpson, D. & Nelson, A. Attention training through breathing control to modify hyperactivity. *Journal of Learning Disabilities*, 1974, *7*, 274–283.

Spivack, G. & Spotts, J. *Devereux child behavior rating scale.* Devon, Pa.: The Devereux Foundation, 1966.

Spivack, G. & Swift, M. *Hahnemann elementary school behavior rating scale* (HESB). Philadelphia: Hahnemann Medical College and Hospital, 1975.

Sprague, R. Minimal brain dysfunction from a behavioral viewpoint. *Annals of the New York Academy of Sciences*, 1973, *205*, 349–361.

Sprague, R., Barnes, K, & Werry, J. Methylphenidate and thioridazine: Learning reaction time, activity and classroom behavior in disturbed children. *American Journal of Orthopsychiatry*, 1970, *40*, 615–628.

Steel, C., O'Duffy, J., & Brown, S. Clinical effects and treatment of imipramine and amitriptyline poisoning in children. *British Medical Journal*, 1967, *3*, 663–667.

Steinberg, G., Troshinsky, C., & Steinberg, H. Dextroamphetamine responsive behavior disorder in school children. *American Journal of Psychiatry*, 1971, *128*, 174–179.

Strain, W., Pories, W, Flynn, A., & Hill, O. Trace element nutriture and metabolism through head hair analysis. In W. Strain (Ed.), *Trace substances in environmental health.* Columbia: University of Missouri Press, 1971.

Strauss, A. & Lehtinen, L. *Psychopathology and education of the brain-injured child* (Vol. 1). New York: Grune & Stratton, 1947.

Swanson, J., Kinsbourne, M., Roberts, W., & Zucker, A. *A time response analysis of the effect of stimulant medication on the learning of children referred for hyperactivity.* Manuscript submitted for publication, 1977.

Sykes, D., Douglas, V., & Morgenstern, G. The effect of methylphenidate on sustained attention in hyperactive children. *Psychopharmacologia,* 1972, *25,* 262–274.

Sykes, D., Douglas, V., Weiss, G., & Minde, K. Attention in hyperactive children and the effect of methylphenidate. *Journal of Child Psychology and Psychiatry* 1971, *12,* 129–137.

Toomin, M. G.S.R. biofeedback psychotherapy: Some clinical observations. *Psychotherapy: Theory, Research and Practice,* 1975, *12*(1), 33–38.

Waizer, J., Hoffman, S., Polizos, P., & Engelhardt, D. Outpatient treatment of hyperactive school children with imipramine. *American Journal of Psychiatry,* 1974, *131,* 587–591.

Weinberg, W., Rutman, J., Sullivan, L., Penick, E., & Dietz, S. Depression in children referred to an educational diagnostic center: Diagnosis and treatment. Preliminary report. *Journal of Pediatrics,* 1973, *83,* 1065–1072.

Weiss, G., Kruger, E., Danielson, U., & Elman, M. Effect of long-term treatment of hyperactive children with methylphenidate. *Canadian Medical Association Journal,* 1975, *112,* 159–165.

Weiss, G., Minde, K., Werry, J., Douglas, V., & Nemeth, E. Studies on the hyperactive child. VIII. Five-year follow-up. *Archives of General Psychiatry,* 1971, *24,* 409–414.

Weiss, G., Werry, J., Minde, K., Douglas, V., & Sykes, D. Studies on the hyperactive child. V. The effects of dextroamphetamine and chlorpromazine on behavior and intellectual functioning. *Journal of Child Psychology and Psychiatry,* 1968, *9,* 145–156.

Wender, E. Food additives and hyperkinesis. *American Journal of Diseases of Children,* 1977, *131,* 1204–1208.

Wender, P. *Minimal brain dysfunction in children.* New York: Wiley–Interscience, 1971.

Werry, J. Studies on the hyperactive child. IV. An empirical analysis of the minimal brain dysfunction syndrome. *Archives of General Psychiatry,* 1968, *19,* 9–16.

Werry, J. & Aman, M. Methylphenidate and haloperidol in children. *Archives of General Psychiatry,* 1975, *32,* 790–795.

Werry, J. & Sprague, R. Methylphenidate in children—effect of dosage. *Australia and New Zealand Journal of Psychiatry,* 1974, *8,* 9–19.

Whitehead, P. & Clark, L. Effect of lithium carbonate, placebo, and thioridazine on hyperactive children. *American Journal of Psychiatry,* 1970, *127,* 824–825.

Winokur, G. & Tanna, V. Possible role of X-linked dominant factor in manic-depressive disease. *Diseases of the Nervous System,* 1969, *30,* 89–93.

Winsberg, B., Bialer, I., Kupietz, S., & Tobias, J. Effects of imipramine and dextroamphetamine on behavior of neuropsychiatrically impaired children. *American Journal of Psychiatry,* 1972, *128,* 1425–1431.

Winsberg, B., Goldstein, S., Yepes, L., & Perel, J. Imipramine and electrocardiographic abnormalities in hyperactive children. *American Journal of Psychiatry,* 1975, *132,* 542–545.

PART IV

THE CENTRAL SPAN: PLANNING EDUCATIONAL REMEDIATION

A top priority of congressional action for the promotion of programs for handicapped children is termed child find. The child find concept is based on at least two major conclusions about children who are disabled. First, many handicapped children are not detected until their late primary years in the second or third grade. Second, when the children are found and diagnosis is completed, much of the information is not directly related to daily instructional plans of remediation.

Larry A. Magliocca, Robert T. Rinaldi, John L. Crew, and Harold P. Kunzelmann, *Exceptional Children.*

CHAPTER 14

INTERVENTION IN EARLY CHILDHOOD EDUCATION

LOUISE SANDLER, Ph.D.

AGNES BORNEMANN, B.A.

The school is seen as responsible for fostering the child's psychological development in a broad sense, as encompassing affective and social as well as cognitive development . . . the growth of cognitive functions . . . acquiring and ordering information, judging, reasoning, problem solving, using systems of symbols—cannot be separated from the growth of personal and interpersonal processes—the development of self-esteem and a sense of identity, internalization of impulse control, capacity for autonomous response, (and) relatedness to other people.

—Edna Shapiro and Barbara Biber, *The Education of Young Children: A Developmental-Interaction Approach*

INTRODUCTION

This chapter will focus specifically upon a method of utilizing preschool, kindergarten, and early grade classrooms as effective identification and intervention settings for the promotion of healthy development.

When thousands of young children enter Day Care and Kindergarten settings with low motivation for achievement, low self-esteem, and high susceptibility to problems in emotional and behavioral areas, it is unrealistic to expect teachers alone to fulfill the educational mandate to teach each child so that development progresses toward increased autonomy and competency in learning. A system of interdisciplinary participation which brings together the available knowledge and resources in the fields of education and child and family mental health is needed.

Faced with a class of 20 to 30 young children, the teacher cannot adequately determine what a child requires in order to overcome cognitive and behavioral deficiencies without extensive knowledge of the child's accumulated experiences and their possible impact on his/her present abilities. In the day-to-day classroom experience of the teacher, there is an acute awareness that individual children are unhappy, unable to learn or to live in peace with themselves or their world. Teachers are frustrated in their efforts to reach these children or even to obtain the often complex data required to meet their needs. Asking the teacher to act as a counter-force in helping a child develop the abilities he/she needs to succeed in life assumes that teachers combine the training and skills of psychiatrist, psychologist, social worker, therapist, *and* parent.

In general, only young children who present the greatest difficulty in classroom management or in learning are referred to the school psychologist for evaluation. It is not uncommon for preschool and kindergarten classes to "drop" children for reasons such as "immaturity" or "disruptive behavior."

In order to learn effectively, a child must want to listen, look, and imitate, be able to trust and accept an adult's demands, be able to delay direct expressions of impulses, and feel gratification in mastery. Such ego strengths are developmentally dependent upon the quality of cumulative experiences of infancy and the toddler period. Unfortunately, there are growing numbers of children within all social, racial, and economic family groups whose early life situations have damaged their abilities to work and love.

RATIONALE FOR EARLY INTERVENTION IN EDUCATION

During the preschool and early primary school years, the home and the school most directly share the responsibilities for the socialization of the child whose world is largely defined by experience within the family and the classroom. The school, as a social institution, is charged with the responsibility of supporting and communicating the treasured values and concepts of society as children prepare for participation in the adult world. Since World War II, an increase in the number of working mothers and single-parent families, a decrease in home stability, and a dispersion of the extended family have placed on the school a larger burden of responsibility for "raising" the children.

For large numbers of children entering schools at 3, 4, or 5 years of age, the "crisis of continuity" can be a severe and crippling episode rather than an appropriate coping experience which serves the course of healthy development. Most children are born into families who have the energy and "know-how" to love a child. However, there are vast numbers of young children who suffer from lifelong neglect of their needs. Such children have damaged self systems. They have been denied the emotional experiences essential for successful school learning.

The beginning of school is a critical period when these children can be helped without stigmatizing them with "labels" or jeopardizing their future chances for becoming accepted members of the larger society. Although we may not know the specific ways in which the schools exert influence on the development of young children, there is no doubt that the educational climate affects them significantly (Minuchin *et al.,* 1969).

Until recent years, the traditional philosophy of the nursery and kindergarten movement placed emphasis on a child's social-emotional development, since the majority of the children who attended early childhood classrooms came from middle-class families in which intellectual development was emphasized. With the advent of contemporary early childhood programs like Project Head Start, however, concern for raising the intelligence of disadvantaged children caused the emphasis to shift to cognitive development as measured by IQ gains.

A controversy in educational theory and practice between the "education model" vs. the "mental health model" in early childhood programs produced an artificial and unproductive division between cognition and affect (White, 1965). Such divisiveness between the "pedagogical" and "psychodynamic" approach in education has evolved largely from the pressures exerted by a "society that is never totally sure of what it wants from its educators. It wants first of all, the inculcation of custom, tradition, and all that socializes the child into the good citizen. . . . Secondly, however, society wants the child to absorb new learning which will benefit that society and enhance the individual's prospects of success (Eiseley, 1962, p. 38). Certainly, the investigations throughout the 1960s and 1970s support the view that all "learning is of apiece" (Piaget and Inhelder, 1969). Thus, learning is never isolated from feelings; behavior in a situation is never either purely intellectual or emotional (White and Fishbein, 1971; Moriarity, 1961; Hertzig *et al.,* 1968).

Currently, there is a growing acceptance of the view that the practices in early childhood education must be responsive to the child as a changing individual interacting with changing environments. This concept calls for the interchange of knowledge in the fields of cognition and personality development. There is no rational basis for dichotomies in the early childhood curriculum.

A most explicit formulation of the union between psychological theory and educational practice is the "developmental-interaction" approach. Shapiro and Biber (1973) describe the "distinctive features" of this approach in preschool education as practiced at Bank Street College of Education:

> Developmental refers to the emphasis on identifiable patterns of growth and modes of perceiving and responding which are characterized by increasing differentiation and progressive integration as a function of chronological age. Interaction refers, first, to the emphasis on the child's interaction with environment, adults, other children, and the material world, and second, to the interaction between cognitive and affective spheres of development. The developmental-interaction formulation stresses the nature of the environment as much as it does the patterns of the responding child. (p. 688)

These authors point out that a basic tenet of the developmental-interaction approach is the total interdependence of developmental processes for cognition and personal-social functioning. Accordingly, the goals in education "are conceived in terms of developmental processes, not as concrete achievements along the route to a specified accomplishment" (Shapiro and Biber, 1973, p. 689). To promote increasing autonomy and self-esteem, the developmental-interaction approach, stated by Shapiro and Biber (1973), views the central responsibility of the school as "that of fostering the development of ego strength, the individual's ability to deal effectively with his environment" (p. 689). Fundamental to this approach is the assumption that normal growth and development happen when the child has experienced caretaking that binds him/her to one or more adults in ways that are associated with productive growth. Bronfenbrenner stresses that, "In order to develop physiologically, mentally, emotionally, motivationally, socially and morally, a child requires the enduring, *irrational involvement* of one or more adults in joint care and joint activity with him. This means that somebody has got to be crazy about the kid!" (Bronfenbrenner, 1977, p. 13).

When young children enter preschool and kindergarten from homes in which this "requirement" has not been met, they are handicapped in their abilities to regulate their actions and relate to the world in increasingly satisfying ways. The view that preschool and early primary classes are concerned with the socialization of children in preparation for the next school stage encourages the fullest practical utilization of these settings for both enriching the healthy child's experiences and for detecting and helping the developmentally disordered child (Poulton and James, 1975; Cook, 1966; Fenichel, 1966).

All good nursery and kindergarten classrooms are therapeutic. An educational environment is a therapeutic environment when teachers are: (1) aware of children's feelings, strengths, and needs, in addition to understanding the nature of their development, and (2) capable of fostering emotional growth and competency. As Cox (1974) points out:

> The field of early childhood education, "borrowing" freely from both psychoanalysis and academic child psychology, has historically reached a more profound understanding than any other branch of psychology of how body, intellect, emotion, and social interaction meet and fuse with environmental opportunity to produce successive levels of maturity. In their close association with young children developing at a very rapid pace, nursery school teachers long ago saw that growth must be understood as a holistic phenomenon, indivisible into its separate compartments. (p. 215)

To the extent that a teacher is concerned with healthy personality development, he/she appreciates the present and potential dangers of both learning and emotional disorders in a child. The teacher may share this concern with the parents and encourage them to secure professional help from a pediatrician, psychologist, psychiatrist, or social worker, recognizing that the most effective help for the child depends largely on understanding the nature of the problem(s). Unfortunately, for large numbers of children, particularly those in families of low economic status, the community mental health agencies may be the only source of help. These agencies are generally understaffed and overburdened by large case loads.

The lack of available services for children in the United States was sharply documented in a survey of 206 community mental health centers. Only three centers reported operating a therapeutic nursery, and only three reported offering consultation services to nursery or preschool programs (Glasscote *et al.,* 1972). In addition, the most prevalent treatment modality was crisis intervention. Although this survey was carried out in 1972, the intervening years have not produced noteable improvement in the availability and quality of services to young children and their families (Berlin, 1975). While it is generally asserted that the young child "cannot wait," the systems and agencies designated to intervene and deliver services are shamefully limited in resources for helping young children. Each social and health agency determines its own services to be provided for or withheld from children or their families (Polier, 1975). The difficulties in linking up and coordinating the wide spectrum of needed services have bewildered teachers and families. The end result is, too often, files of fragmented findings from a variety of disciplines, observations, examinations, interviews, and recommendations without an appropriate remedial plan.

Effective early detection/intervention programs in education require the removal of barriers created by separating the mental health, educational, and social agencies into self-contained systems. As Hobbs (1975) states, "schools should play a coordinating and advocacy role to assure that these early intervention services and all necessary treatment are provided to all who need and want them" (p. 250). He conceives the schools as the single agency responsible for making these the services responsive to particular children. The potential of the schools for early identification of mental disorder and learning failure must be captured through interagency cooperation and interdisciplinary teamwork.

THE CENTER FOR PRESCHOOL SERVICES*

Specific Need for Service

Seven years ago, the Center for Preschool Services was designed to help young children whose case workers and teachers recognized that they were in trouble. The idea for the Center evolved out of experiences with large numbers of preschool children in an outpatient pediatric setting operated by Hahnemann Medical College and Hospital, Philadelphia, Pennsylvania. Most of these children were brought in by their mothers or other family members. Others were brought by case workers from welfare agencies or by foster parents.

Long periods of waiting, typical of a busy clinic setting, provided the therapist an opportunity to discuss the children's adjustment with parents or caretakers, to play with the children, and to observe their

---

*As of June 1978, The Center for Early Childhood Services, Inc.

interactions with the parents. Within a 15- or 20-minute interaction, these experiences yielded an impression of a child's ability to relate, think, play, speak, and understand. At the time, the Philadelphia School District administered a large, city-wide system of federally funded Get Set day care centers designed for children between 3 and 5 years of age whose families were recipients of welfare. Many of the children seen in the pediatric setting either attended these day care programs or were eligible for attendance. Since large numbers of these children demonstrated apparent deficiencies in speech, play, thinking, and relating, it appeared logical that they could receive the greatest help if the skills of mental health were brought into the school classrooms—a "captured population."

Funding**

Funding by a local foundation in the first pilot year provided the basis for submission of a proposal to the Bureau of Education for the Handicapped (Office of Education) requesting support for the development of a comprehensive, multidisciplinary, early intervention program in education that would serve as a prototype at the national level for replication by departments of education and mental health. This was granted in 1971. At that time, Pennsylvania law only provided for education of handicapped children over the age of 7 years. Although this age limit was lowered to 4.7 years in 1975, younger children in the state must still be professionally diagnosed as "handicapped" under special classifications in order for their school districts to receive the necessary additional funds for therapeutic education.

Because these "referral" classrooms are viewed as "day-treatment" settings (the descriptive term employed under Mental Health rules for partial hospitalization services, Title XIX, Medicaid), the Pennsylvania State Office of Mental Health approved the Center's application for partial hospitalization status in 1973, permitting the costs of mental health services to be supported by reimbursements, through Medical Assistance, or fee for service to children and their families. This unprecedented action established support of the mental health services in the Center model. Simply stated, school districts support the costs of the educational staff, and mental health systems support the costs of the mental health staff.

**For a more detailed discussion of the initial setting up and funding of a multidisciplinary early intervention program, please contact the senior author. *Ed.*

At that time, very few behaviorally disordered preschool children were referred to psychiatric clinics for evaluation and treatment. Those referred were showing the dramatic signs of autism and psychosis. In addition, few people perceived cognitive and social lags in development as unusual among a very disadvantaged population. The prevalent point of view assumed that such children could not be expected to draw a human figure or reproduce a circle or a square on a piece of paper, as their middle-class peers could, an assumption which denied children the help they needed. On the contrary, previous investigation using a developmental screening test with over 300 Day Care children in Philadelphia showed that the only significant lag in comparison to a middle class white population was in the area of word definition! (Sandler, 1972). Professional experience with inner-city poor children strongly supported the impression that there was an epidemic of serious developmental disabilities within the larger population of economically deprived preschool children. They needed help immediately. Such disabilities not only would prevent their learning, but also would block their progress in knowing how to respond to and adapt in social situations. Although a very strong impression indicated that the major origin of problem for many of these children was disorganized, inconsistent, or inadequate nurturing, there was much to be explored concerning the nature and correction of the problems.

Setting

From the start, it was believed strongly that the day care, kindergarten, and early primary grades should be the settings for a comprehensive service program aimed at preventing serious cognitive failures and social-emotional disorders. It was also felt that these services should be integrated into the system of basic or regular education, as distinguished from special education.

The selection of a setting for the Center required that it be both administered and housed in "neutral territory," i.e., a nonmedical, noneducational, and nonsocial agency. In 1970, the Franklin Institute Research Laboratories, located within the Hahnemann Hospital patient service area, offered to administer and house the Center program, which was to serve as an ongoing model for a network of similar "referral" classrooms based in other preschool and school settings throughout the city. Since 1973, two such programs have been initiated with teachers trained in the Center program and health teams staffed through the "neighborhood" Mental Health Base Service Unit. Each neighborhood "host" school or preschool setting provides an office area for needed space and basic office equipment to carry out social work interviews and evaluations, including psychological testing and psychiatric examinations.

Overall Program Description

The Center program is concerned about children who enter preschool, kindergarten, first, and second grades at risk for school failure and mental health problems. Such children often behave like toddlers in one or more areas of functioning. In descriptive terms, they may appear dull and unconnected with classmates and play activities, or they may be disruptive and defiant. On standardized tests, they can test within the Superior through Mentally Deficient ranges of intelligence. In classrooms, their symptoms are manifold and teachers describe them as: hyperactive, passive and withdrawn, bizarre, uncommunicative, laughing too much, fearful, exhibitionistic, continuously thumb-sucking or masturbating, listless, and so on. In general, these children do not present obvious physical handicaps. Regardless of the origins of developmental disabilities, they are inadequately equipped to cope with the challenges of life.

The Center's concern is with the "first step" towards early prevention and correction. A child and his/her parents, foster parent, or guardian are first seen by the team psychiatrist and social worker. Past medical records are requested and appointments made for pediatric, neurologic, or other medical evaluations as needed. The classroom teachers meet with the psychiatrist and social worker to discuss the child and family and arrange for additional evaluations as needed, such as speech and language examinations. The psychologist assesses the child with both standardized intelligence tests and selected projective techniques. A functional rather than categorical assessment of each child is carried out to determine the strengths and deficits in child and family functioning. Intervention plans are formulated to meet the specified service needs of each child and family, whether these needs are for therapeutic classroom settings, legal aid, individual child or family therapy, medical services, or protective services. In many cases, remediation planning requires the integration of numerous intervention strategies, the operational link-up serving as the essential foundation for delivery of effective services. Responsibility is carried by the classroom team for insuring that the child and family receive the services prescribed.

As a resource model for service and training, the Center has two nursery classrooms and a number of interview and examination offices which are equipped with one-way window viewing. Great emphasis is placed upon the training of mental health specialists in educational intervention, as well as the training of preschool, kindergarten, and primary grade teachers in the understanding and employment of skills considered essential for leading diagnostic/therapeutic classrooms. The training program for teachers consists of a three-month full-time practicum at the Center. Training objectives include preparing teachers to lead diagnostic/intervention classrooms for a growing network of classroom-based services.

The Center classrooms can serve 40 preschool and kindergarten children at a time. These children are referred from day care and kindergarten classrooms within the Hahnemann Medical College and Hospital patient service area. Thus, the Center is viewed as the "neighborhood" classroom for this health service area.

Based in public (host) schools or preschool facilities, each replica of these diagnostic/therapeutic classrooms employs a basic core teaching staff of one teacher and two assistants for the preschool or Day Care (3- to 5-year-olds) and one teacher with one assistant for the kindergarten to second-grade classroom. To provide appropriate diagnostic, remedial, and referral services as needed, the staff also includes a full-time social worker, part-time psychiatrist, and clinical child psychologist who work with the teachers in close team partnership. Each classroom receives children referred by their regular classroom teachers for a half-day, five-day-per-week, intensive diagnostic/intervention program. The children remain in their regular classroom setting for the balance of each day. Since the "referral" classroom is considered part of and not the total corrective experience for the child's school day, it is important that the child maintain contact with the teacher and his/her peers in the regular classroom. Through maintaining direct communication with the regular day care or school teachers, the therapeutic classroom team builds a supportive life for each child.

Differentiation of Children for Early Intervention Program

The differential diagnosis of children appropriate for early intervention classrooms as distinguished from those requiring special education settings is not always easy. Concerning such assessments, the Center approach states:

(1) It is not always possible to know the nature of a young child's behavior or learning disabilities in the absence of intervention.

(2) Procedures for determining a category or label are very inadequate and do not describe the condition of the child.

(3) There must be a range of professional resources available within the system of education to provide assessment and intervention in an effort to prevent further failure and emotional disturbance.

Thus, the Center stands as a vital advocate for a new system of prevention and early intervention, urging local and state administrators to change school codes and regulations in order that children in age range 3 to 7 may benefit from combined educational and clinical practices. However, without change in laws and regulations governing what we do to help the "hurt," "troubled," "bruised," "disabled" young child, vast numbers of children will join the ranks of the retarded, illiterate, delinquent, and mentally disturbed.

Two brief case vignettes will highlight the dilemmas presented by existing regulations:

> A little boy in kindergarten is disruptive, attacking other children, and unable to sit still and involve himself in play. Seen by the school psychologist, he is untestable because he does not attend or adapt to tasks. Medical history and current evaluations show no evidence of neurologic or sensory handicaps. Is he emotionally disturbed? If he is to be "diagnosed" as an emotionally disturbed child, at least 35% of the preschool and kindergarten population would receive similar classifications.

In the Center program, this child required two months within the referral classroom before a highly experienced staff (trained in early childhood clinical skills) could state, with confidence, that his primary problem was a panic reaction to a psychotic grandparent living in his home who was literally tormenting the boy with frightening threats to mutilate him. Only in the everyday situation of a diagnostic/intervention classroom in which a team of trained teachers, psychiatrists, psychologists, and social workers work together to unravel a complicated family picture could the child's behavior be understood and explained. Although this "incorrigible" little boy did not require any special education setting in the traditional sense, help for him required a most sophisticated collaborative "link-up" among all agencies bearing responsibility for child and family health.

A second child, age 4, in a day care setting, appears to be a "slow child." His cognitive skills and speech development are similar to a 2-year-old. He has a history of lead encephalopathy and suffered extreme neglect in his first year of life. His present foster parents appear supportive and interested in the child. Is he mentally retarded? What is this child's primary diagnosis? If he is to be "diagnosed" as a retarded child, at least 25% of the children with similar functioning levels and histories would fall into this classifiication.

This case of possible mental retardation required five months in the Center diagnostic/intervention classroom before the evaluation staff could, with some certainty, explain the behavior on the basis of a severe organic language problem. This child had good learning potential. He was not pathologically retarded but had specific learning disability, which none of the clinical and teaching staff could have detected from initial tests and evaluations. The classrooms permitted extended evaluation to go along simultaneously with corrective and intensive educational therapy. The child began to learn, to show joy and interest in mastery. Fundamental education—the development of a self system—permitted the child to "learn to learn." The regular primary grades can now educate the child with specific help provided to compensate for his communication problems.

If the two children presented had been placed in classrooms for the emotionally disturbed and mentally retarded respectively, they would probably have lived up to their specific "diagnostic" labels and the placements, although in error, would have seemed appropriate. Thus, provisions must be made to support the needs of these young, developmentally disabled children through early diagnostic/intervention classrooms that link the expertise for a "global" approach to the needs of children.

The Classroom Intervention Model

The classrooms in the Center for Preschool Children provide two major services to children and families. One is the assessment of a child's development and current functioning in all areas. The second is a recommendation for and active involvement in effecting an appropriate treatment program for the child and his/her family which may or may not involve actual enrollment in the diagnostic/intervention classroom.

Referrals of children are made primarily through teachers of the children attending day care programs within the Hahnemann service area. However, it is not unusual for the classroom secretary to receive a call from a pediatrician, an agency social worker, or a nurse about a child for whom there is concern. In these cases, the staff social worker inquires whether the child could be eligible for enrollment in a preschool day care program. If this is possible, cooperative steps are taken by the staff social worker and the Day Care social service staff to place the child in a "neighborhood" setting, thereby fulfilling eligibility requirements for the referral diagnostic/intervention classroom.

Eligibility for Classroom

1. Child shall be 36 months to 72 months of age.
2. Child shall be enrolled in or eligible for enrollment in a day care or kindergarten program.
3. Child is seen by teacher, parent, physician, etc., as not developing well in some way: i.e., speech and language, behavior problems, withdrawal, etc.
4. Parent(s) or legal guardian agree to child's participation.

The guidelines to teachers and other school personnel for referral of a child are in the form of behavioral descriptors. It is considered absolutely essential that the diagnostic/intervention classroom be recognized as the locus for prophylactic intervention. Whenever possible, teachers and parents should consider the benefits of a "check-up" *before* gross learning failure or emotional problems are evident.

Guidelines for Referral

I. General Behavior Characteristics
1. The child appears physically neglected (e.g., seems hungry, unwashed, in unclean clothes), appears abused, either mentally or physically (e.g., unexplained irregular attendance, unexplained bruises on body).
2. The child demands his/her own way in most situations, cannot tolerate limits or prohibitions.
3. The child cannot defend himself/herself in most situations, is very passive allowing others to do as they wish, cannot stand up for his/her own rights.
4. The child has absence of contact with either peers or adults and,

in addition, seems to avoid such contacts (or withdraws from them).

5. The child is overly friendly and dependent with adults, appears to be ready to walk away with a stranger, is a clinging type of child.
6. The child acts like a grown-up and will not accept the help or guidance of an adult (unrealistic independence).
7. The child cannot acept any delay of gratification of needs, will "act out" feelings regardless of adults' attempts to control.
8. The child is listless, lacks energy, and appears to enjoy little or nothing, seems to need nothing and feel nothing.
9. The child responds to any stress with temper tantrums.
10. The child responds to any stress by withdrawing (e.g., excessive thumb sucking, rocking, nail biting, masturbation, pulling out own hair).

II. Cognitive and Skill Characteristics
1. Child is awkward or clumsy in comparison to children of similar age.
2. Speech for communication is not developed in line with expectancies for age.
3. Understanding of ideas or instructions is not developed in line with expectancies for age.
4. Poor development of initiative, curiosity, interest, and motivation for exploring and mastering new experiences.

When a child characteristically shows one or a combination of behaviors described above, referral for diagnostic/intervention is indicated.

Equally crucial is the early intervention for children who may appear to be functioning well but are known to come from families who are presently dysfunctioning. Such families include the following situations and/or characteristics:

1. One or both parents with serious physical or mental disabilities.
2. Death of a parent without adequate parent substitutes.
3. Recurrent involvement with law agencies, truancy, alcoholism, drug addiction.
4. Parents who exhibit markedly overprotective, overdemanding, overperfectionistic, overpermissive, seductive, neglectful, or rejecting attitudes.
5. Severe neglect of children by families.

The assessment of a young child's development is seen as a comprehensive process involving the classroom, psychiatric, social work, psychological, and educational staffs. Medical and other needed assessments are carried out at the cooperating medical units.

Process

1. Information on the child is recorded by social worker or secretary on Intake Form (Face Sheet).
2. Appointment is set by social worker for parent(s) and child to meet with the psychiatrist and social worker.
   After this meeting, the psychiatrist and the social worker make a tentative decision regarding the procedures to be followed for the child.
   All referrals will be recorded and reported at the next staff meeting for staff review.
3. If there is an opening, the child is brought immediately into the classroom for an evaluation period of approximately one month, during which time he/she will be observed by staff, given appropriate psychological assessment, and scheduled for pediatric, neurological, and audiological evaluations at the cooperating base service unit.
4. If there is no immediate opening in the classroom, the child is placed on the waiting list and is scheduled for psychological testing and necessary medical evaluations, with appropriate contacts with Center Social Services.
   In some cases, it may be possible at this point (upon completion of all of the above evaluations) to make a professional judgment regarding the child's development and problems and to recommend a treatment program for the child and family such as:
   (a) enrollment in the Preschool Center Classroom.
   (b) referral to a school for special education, public or private, if an appropriate classroom is available.
   (c) referral to child psychiatry clinic for individual, conjoint, or family therapy.
   (d) continuation in regular classroom with special support for child and teacher.
5. In other cases, a period for observation and therapy in the classroom is essential in order to determine the primary sources of problems and the appropriate intervention, and the child will be brought into the classroom at the earliest opportunity. This

classroom observation is so important that it should be included as part of the diagnostic process whenever possible.

6. If at any time referral and intake systems are overloaded, it may be necessary to refer a child and family to a neighborhood child clinic to avoid a long waiting period. In that case, the Preschool Center staff makes every effort to insure that the family contacts the clinic and the child actually receives the necessary services.

THE CLASSROOMS

Each classroom serves 10 children in the morning and 10 children in the afternoon. Blending the best knowledge about how children grow and learn from the fields of education, medicine, and psychology, they provide a continuous, consistent educational experience for each child.

Beginning with an assessment of the developmental level(s) on which the child is functioning (based on teacher observations and psychiatric, psychological, and medical preliminary evaluations), the classroom staff works to establish a relationship of trust with the child, to meet him/her at the present level(s) and to help him/her progress. It has become increasingly apparent that, regardless of the "primary diagnosis" eventually determined, most of the children referred have one thing in common—a nurturing experience that has seriously interfered with healthy ego development. On the basis that all development is interrelated and interdependent and that a good mother-child nurturing experience is necessary for all healthy development, such a trust relationship is the essential starting point. When the child begins to trust and is willing to risk, then he/she begins to learn, as does the much younger child who experienced an early positive nurturing relationship.

Regardless of the specific diagnosis of the child's problem—whether it is one of a neurologically impaired child with a language disability or an intact youngster with situationally based behavior disorder—the classroom program for all children is based upon the assumption that experiences which contribute to the child's positive feelings about himself/herself and the surrounding world are a necessary condition for successful academic, social, and emotional learning.

There are several *essential aspects* of this work with young delayed and disabled children:

1. Total acceptance of the child, regardless of what he/she does or says, as a person to be respected and loved. Although he/she

may curse, kick, run away, or tell the teacher to leave him/her alone, the teacher will not desert the child. The teacher will say this and prove it many times, if necessary in actions, thus showing himself/herself to be a person also worthy of trust and love.

2. Demonstration of the concern for and ability to protect the child in every situation, even from him/herself. If he/she withdraws excessively into his/her own inner world, the teacher will intrude, sensitive and alert to his/her feelings but demonstrating a caring for the child, knowing the need for human relationships.

3. Recognition of the child, who was born with a desire and the potential to grow, to learn, to be happy, to be loved, and who, regardless of problems of any nature, deserves every opportunity to experience childhood.

4. Recognition of the delayed emotional and cognitive developmental levels at which the child is actually functioning, in spite of the frequently contradictory evidence of a 3- to 7-year-old body. The teacher must present living/learning experiences at actual developmental levels in order to meet the needs and to provide the child with knowledge of his/her own goodness and competence. If a 4-year-old is functioning at a 2-year-old level, the teacher must know how a 2-year-old thinks, feels, and learns, and must provide experiences that meet his/her 2-year-old needs. At the same time, this child, who is really 4 years old chronologically, cannot be permitted to remain like a 2-year-old. This delicate balance must be established between teacher and child—accept and stretch, give and expect.

5. Concurrent recognition that the developmental level is not totally the "true" level. This seeming 2-year-old has lived for three, four, or five years, and has not lived in a vacuum. He/she has learned things that can be his/her strengths and the teacher's cues, as well as things that must be "unlearned" because they worked well only in his/her first environment which produced them.

Such highly sensitive and knowledgeable responses are necessary to establish a relationship of trust, which is essential to any forward movement in these children. Work with children who have been severely "burned" requires a willingness to prove again and again that we are, indeed, trustworthy, that we care enough to set and enforce appropriate limits, to protect, to love, to teach. Nothing very significant can happen in the way a child views himself/herself and others, especially adults, unless there has been a binding emotional experience in which the child wishes to respond, to give of self, to change for love of the other. The child uses the relationship to grow and learn to believe in other human beings. It cannot happen quickly.

TEACHER QUALIFICATIONS

The teacher who can respond to children in these sensitive and responsive ways must, above all, be a mature, sensitive, warm, and intelligent adult human being who can allow himself/herself to give unselfishly to a negative, manipulative child with no expectation of immediate return and without falling prey to his/her games, or to a sad and needy waif, without losing the realistic objectivity that is required to love for the sake of the child and not to satisfy the needs of the adult.

The teacher must also have sufficient knowledge of and experience with human development, problems in development, therapeutic techniques, dynamic, holistic early childhood education ,'and classroom management, to be able to assess the children's developmental levels and plan classroom experiences that encourage exploration and mastery on the individual level and for the group. At the same time, just as the parent must consistently provide protection and comfort, set limits, and help the young child internalize controls, this is what the teachers in the therapeutic classroom must do for many children deprived of adequate parenting.

While accepting and reflecting the children's feelings in an effort to interpret and show them healthy ways to deal with these feelings, the teacher must be able to give the children a clear message of what is expected of them. The teacher must let them know that he/she thinks they are capable of doing everything that any child can do and that he/she will help them do it. For this, the teacher must make careful assessment of their abilities and interests in order to provide the experiences and supports that will insure success for them.

TEACHER GOALS

Since this is a classroom in an educational setting, the teacher's primary purpose within the holistic, interactional-developmental early childhood education framework is to help children to learn. The teacher's goals are realistic and must deal primarily with the "now," while understanding and appreciating what has gone before. This is an approach that says, "I know how angry you are right now, but I won't let you hit me." This outer control from the adult is provided over and over again, consistently, firmly, with love. Such an approach creates opportunity later, when the child is in control, not only to demonstrate and talk about other ways he/she can control anger and express it appropriately, but also to let him/her know that more will be expected the next time, with the teacher's help.

Through the strength of binding children and teachers together in their relationships of trust and love, delayed and disordered children become capable of loving, moving, and learning. Staff accepts them at the earlier stages at which their development has been stopped and helps them begin to make emotional attachments appropriate for those earlier stages, begin to explore and play in ways that are appropriate for the earlier stages, begin to laugh, cry, and get angry, begin to speak, perhaps to use the toilet, to draw and paint, to become children. Then, without shielding from the world these children with problems (and thus denying them many of the basic experiences of childhood), teachers in the Center classrooms, with every support necessary, make it possible for them to begin to learn how to cope with the world.

EVALUATION

The effectiveness of the intervention program for each child is constantly evaluated by the interdisciplinary staff and changed to meet his/her changing needs and growth. This assessment is accomplished by means of case study and progress reports, regularly scheduled evaluations and observations, and semimonthly staff conferences.

FAMILY INVOLVEMENT

Even a coordinated treatment program is of little value unless the family is able or willing to take the necessary steps. Therefore, aggressive parental follow-up and involvement in the recommended program are an integral part of this work. Acting on the basis of the interdisciplinary assessment, each classroom team acts as a catalyst to bring to the child and his/her family necessary services (educational, medical, mental health, legal, and financial aid, etc.) which, in many cases, already exist in the community but which, for a variety of reasons, some of the most needy families have been unable to utilize. The full-time social worker approaches the parent(s) on an individual basis, seeking to assess and meet the parent's needs, whatever they are, so that the lives of both parent(s) and child can be more satisfying and productive.

No family is excluded from services; no child is ever "dropped" because his/her parent(s) is unable or unwilling to cooperate with the classroom. Although most parents want to help their children, many are unable to do so because of their own overwhelming problems. Knowing this, the trained staff makes intensive, personal efforts to meet the parents' human needs. Experience shows that, when parents begin to see hope for themselves and their children, they can begin to respond to their children in a more positive way.

The Center's Children and Their Families

The Center serves children in an inner-city area which is ranked first among Philadelphia's seven State-designated Poverty Areas. The area contains a predominantly black and Puerto Rican population most of whose children are categorized as "disadvantaged" and are enrolled in or eligible for a federally funded day care program. Thus, this prototype program runs the risk of being perceived as needed for poor minority group children living in large inner-city neighborhoods. It is well recognized that development is affected by socioeconomic status and race (Deutch *et al.,* 1967; Golden and Berns, 1968; Hertzig *et al.,* 1968; Pavenstedt, 1967), and there is ample documentation of the higher rates of family breakdown, unemployment, marital conflict, and father absence in the subculture of poverty (Chelman, 1966). Certainly, children of poverty are most vulnerable or "at risk" for disturbances in development. Nevertheless, psychologically pathogenic conditions predisposing a child to developmental disabilities are not confined to the poor or the uneducated, and preventive intervention in early childhood education is needed throughout all regional areas and socioeconomic levels. The philosophy and structure of the Center program is applicable in all school systems where resources in mental health and medical services can be made available for children. One of the heuristic findings from studies of deprivation is that, for optimal cognitive functioning, we need healthy, well-functioning children. There is more than sufficient evidence that "hurting" young children are to be found in classrooms throughout the country.

The vast majority of the children referred to the Center have suffered from continuous and devastating deprivation. Their potential for healthy growth and development has been crippled by the omissions and commissions of acts that leave them susceptible to severe problems in learning and behaving (Riese, 1962; Roberts, 1974). The Center receives these children in mid-childhood, knowing that chances may be meager for full reversibility of the effects of earlier emotional deprivation, rejection, and abuse. These children are seriously developmentally delayed, giving the appearance of profound retardation and severe ego disturbance. Yet, for numbers of them, regardless of whether or not stress in their homes is greatly relieved, the classroom intervention proves effective.

Case Study 14.1: Jean

Reason for Referral

When Jean first came with her brother to the Center, when she was 4 and he was 2, the two children were like sturdy little Raggedy Ann and Andy dolls, with tow hair and cherubic smiles. Jean's smile disappeared quickly as the gentle young psychiatrist suggested separating from her mother and brother to play with him, and, even with her mother in the room, she could do nothing but cry. Her mother was very angry with Jean. Observers and the psychiatrist in the room felt the tension as mother exhorted Jean to stop crying and do what the man said. Jean was stubborn and refused to do anything at all. (Observers felt that Jean would certainly "get it" as soon as they were out of sight.)

In a small classroom area with Jean, her little brother began to play in the sandbox. While his sister had been crying and negative, he had been engaging every adult (except his mother) with his endearing smile and bright toddler curiosity. At the sandbox, he repeated this kind of performance. Mother turned a stony face to both children. Jean hung her head over the sandbox, hiding her face in her ragged, too-long hair. An adult played a finger game, "walking" her fingers up to Jean's hand and tickling it slightly. Two bright eyes peered out from the tangle of hair; there was a tentative smile and a silent invitation to do it again.

It was not possible to evaluate Jean using standard psychological testing procedures. She entered the Center classroom as soon as possible after the initial meetings.

History

Jean's mother described her daughter as a "fresh-mouthed retard," with something physically wrong. Developmental milestones were remembered as being essentially normal, with no serious illness or problems in the first eighteen months.

The mother was a very depressed, unhappy woman for whom nothing had gone right in recent years. Now in the process of getting a divorce, she and her husband had separated when Jean was 2, shortly after the second child was born. Her mother, with whom mother and Jean were very close, had died suddenly at about that same time, also. Jean refused to accept her father's leaving and insisted that he was "upstairs," while looking and crying for him constantly. She had interacted, since before the age of 2, with a seriously depressed mother whose husband had left her, had experienced the death of a loved grandmother, the loss of her father, and the birth of a baby brother. In recent months, she had turned away from her mother, telling her to go away and leave her alone when she took her to the day care center (from which she was referred to the Center). Teachers there saw her as "somewhat young" but were more concerned about her attitude toward her mother and the fact that she did not listen to them.

The Center staff saw her as severely developmentally delayed, about two years behind in all areas. Even her body retained many characteristics of a 2-year-old (a "pot belly" and 2-year-old gait), and her language, play, and representational abilities were also observed to be at that level.

Most characteristic, however, was her "elusive" quality. She seemed almost not to be there. If someone, especially an adult, entered the area in which Jean had chosen to play, she immediately disappeared. Without protest, without any communication, she simply managed to remove herself to another more isolated area. Later, she was able to remain in a selected area but kept herself isolated from anyone nearby.

Her first technique was to avoid any activity or involvement that she did not initiate. These were narrowly limited to the housekeeping corner, where she daily put on a "dress up" prop, such as wedding or other fancy dress, and completely engrossed in herself in the presence of other children and adults, proceeded to put on play makeup, jewelry, perfume, etc., observing herself very closely in the mirrors with obvious enjoyment.

When pressed to explore other areas of the room (such as the arts, water play, music, science, books, etc.) she became obdurate, refusing to look, touch, or listen. Jean was locked into a lonely, meagre, joyless world that gave back no reflection of her real selfhood and worth, but only the "make believe" reflection of her impoverished fantasy life.

Of course, teachers could not leave her locked up inside. Patiently they played and talked with her, sang to her, and read to her in the small group and on the one-to-one occasions during the bus rides, snack times, and class activities. They responded to her with love, warmth, and the expectation that she could, with help, do what other children do. They would not take "no" for an answer; they would not go away and leave her alone. They helped her try something new before she went into the housekeeping corner. In that area, one-to-one with an adult, and with props changing to suggest new play ideas, she slowly tried new things. As the days passed, she experienced again and again with the adults the reflection of herself as a beautiful, pleasing, increasingly competent child. She began to seek out the adults who responded to her in these ways and looked and asked for their approval.

Individual therapy sessions began in her second year at the Center. Obviously feeling very safe, she openly expressed terrible, angry thoughts, which she directed at her therapist in vivid word images no one could have imagined were in this little Raggedy Ann's thinking. The therapist was to provide one special person for Jean who could accept her totally, with the one restriction that she could not harm herself or the therapist. She was able to use the therapist to express anger she felt and had not dared to express. She asked her therapist, "Can I say all the bad words I want?" Perhaps as a result of having been able to express extremes of anger without being destroyed, together with the safe, consistent environment of the classroom, a whole new range of emotions was clearly evident. She became capable of reaching out, first to adults and, more slowly, to children, expressing her anger verbally, and feeling comfortable with the stamp of her foot or occasional throwing of an object for emphasis. On one occasion, she burst into tears of disappointment because she would not have enough time left at school to do one more special thing she had in mind. Her face sparkled with excitement as she initiated a conversation about a class experience. She frequently joined other children in small-group activities and took pride in her accomplishments in various arts and crafts experiences, alone and with other children. She was able to share a delightful sense of humor frequently. Her language skills moved significantly, keeping up with her movement in other areas, and no problems are anticipated in language development.

As Jean became interested in pleasing adults and herself and in doing things because she saw other children's accomplishments, Center Staff saw indications of specific difficulties in fine and gross motor activities. For example, she showed clumsiness in using scissors, brushes, paste, etc., and was awkward and uncertain when she ran, climbed, walked, attempted to skip or hop. There was, however, still a question of whether the observed "clumsiness" in this child was a part of her total impoverishment. Pediatric and neurological evaluations failed to support suspicions of central nervous system impairment. In such cases, the emphasis in planning must be upon maintaining an optimally supportive educational experience for the child, rather than allowing a possibly incorrect label of Specific Learning Disability to determine her future school placement. In Jean's case, there was an additional danger in a special class placement because of her mother's perception of her as a defective child.

For Jean's immediate educational placement within the school system, she was fortunate that, in her neighborhood school, there is a rare classroom, a "transitional" kindergarten-first grade, with a skilled teacher, knowledgeable about development, assessment, and the intervention possibilities of the classroom. Here it was hoped Jean would receive essential basic educational and emotional support which must be maintained if she is to continue her total developmental progress which the Center staff saw.

Staff had strongly recommended that Jean continue in a one-to-one therapeutic relationship. However, her school, like most in the area, does not have on its staff psychologists and psychiatrists to work individually with children. This meant that Jean's mother was expected to take the responsibility for Jean's psychotherapy outside of school hours and in another resource. As this mother had not been able to seek help of any kind for herself or to accept the outreach services provided by the Center, we hold little hope for her taking this responsibility for Jean. It required many hours of work by the Center social worker, in the face of repeated rejections, to help the mother take the most elementary step of recognizing that Jean was not retarded but, rather, a child with problems who can learn.

When Jean left the Center classroom, there were no longer social services available to maintain close contact with the home, to see that the child received routine medical treatment (a service we had to provide at times during our relationship), or to continue to help the mother understand the nature of Jean's problems and her normal potential, with support. Therefore, this child is totally dependent upon the school to nurture her. Sadly, the burden falls entirely on an outstanding teacher of a nearly standard-size class working with few supports.

After eighteen months in the Center program, Jean still had many problems. She was reluctant to give to any person to whom she was not attached and became verbally negative and openly abusive and defiant if she felt pushed or threatened. It was obvious that these characteristics could have a serious effect on her ability to learn. This was demonstrated in her psychological reevaluation eighteen months after entry into the program (Wechsler Preschool and Primary). In contrast to the initial attempts in the previous fall, she came for this session only somewhat reluctantly, was able to tolerate the test situation, and was somewhat cooperative. Nevertheless, the examiner felt that in much of the session she was resistant, negative, and acutely aware of her deficiencies. She refused even to try many test items, thus depressing her score further.

Also, despite the significant progress made, especially in social and emotional growth, Jean was not developmentaliy a 5-years, 6-months-old child. When she left, she was more closely a three- to four-year-old in all developmental areas.

The significance of this evaluation/intervention was that Jean needed a continuing opportunity to grow, to be nurtured like the 3- to 4-year-old she was mentally, socially, and emotionally, while her forward movement was continually encouraged towards the sound and educational goals we know she has the potential to reach.

Case Study 14.2: Mike

Reason for Referral

Mike was referred to the Center by his day care center because of "incorrigible behavior."

History

Everyone in the neighborhood knew Mike: the owners of the candy shop, the barber, the entire day care center. He was "bad," "mean," "the Devil possessed him," and "his great-grandmother spoiled him." No one could control him. He hit adults and children, kicked, screamed, and bit when he did not get his way. The day care center was threatening to dismiss him. This "terrible" child, who sounded like a monster, was 3 years old—a baby.

Mike's mother had been ready to enter college when she became pregnant with him. Her parents sent her away to have her baby, and after his birth, she did not return but went to live with her grandmother. He was a healthy baby, had all the immunizations, and developmental milestones were normal. When Mike was referred to the Center at just past 3, his mother was only 21 and was struggling to reclaim her life. Attractive, intelligent, and ambitious, she was trying to work, attend evening college classes, and enjoy a social life. She saw little of her baby, leaving him to her grandmother night and day. It was reported that great-grandmother alternated between thinking that Mike could do no wrong and beating him because she could not control him. As Mike grew into a demanding, willful toddler, his mother wanted to see even less of him. Nevertheless, she dressed him beautifully and saw that he had good physical care. Recently, because he was so "bad," she had been threatening to send him away to her parents. She was bitter, feeling guilty and depressed, and desperately in need of help for herself and her child.

Mike's family history is a classic story of rejection and inconsistent nurturing, of which his behavior was symptomatic. With mixed feelings of guilt and anger toward him, his mother took excellent physical care of Mike while rejecting him, threatening to send him away, and leaving him in the care of his great-grandmother. Great-grandmother, on her part, provided the child with bewildering, inconsistent nurturing, sometimes allowing him to do anything he wished, sometimes beating him because he was out of control and "bad." This little boy was calling for help!

The Classroom

Teachers in the Center classroom found that the referral description was accurate. In the beginning, Mike was in constant trouble with children and adults. He ran around the classroom, gathering up every toy he could carry, only to hold them tightly in his arms, refusing to put them down, play with them, or give them back. He wanted all of the cookies and juice, every turn on the tricycles: there could never be enough to satisfy him. Adult intervention was met with screams, kicking, hitting, and biting. Frequently, his cry was a plaintive, "Mommy!" It was like a baby's cry, forlorn and helpless. He literally could not play with anything or anyone. He had no skills. He was socially primitive and severely delayed developmentally.

His most obvious characteristic was his negativism. No matter what was suggested, requested, or required, Mike's answer was "No!" He could not be enticed into an activity like an actual 2-year-old. For a while, nothing seemed to matter to him, making it extremely difficult to deal with him.

Several other characteristics, however, became evident to classroom staff. He was observant, curious, and verbal. On the initial psychological testing, for example, he was virtually untestable and scored in the defective range. Yet, when he was asked to build a tower of blocks, he built, instead, four deliberately different variations of the required tower, indicating his superior abilities as well as his negativism.

Despite the problems he constantly created, staff admired his stubborn courage and his refusal to let the adult world crush him. Mike was a challenge which the staff accepted, knowing that just beneath the swagger and defiance was a very small, frightened boy who needed love, protection, and realistic limit-setting from adults who were capable of taking an appropriate nurturing role with a child. The "bad" little boy knew no values in accomodating his desires to the demands of the classroom. Mike had obviously missed the essential nurturing mother-child relationship which provides the foundation for growth in impulse control and appropriate social behavior.

The staff set and enforced consistent limits for Mike, with consequences for rules broken and rewards for appropriate behavior. It was important for him to know that, as the adults would protect other children's rights, so they would, and did, protect his. Even more important was their unswerving caring for him, regardless of what he did or said. This had to be reiterated again and again, just as, again and again, limits had to be enforced and consequences endured. It was not easy for him or the staff, but he did come to love and to trust. "The Franklin Institoot" became his haven as he began to grow.

At all times in the course of this "battle," the classroom activities went on, and Mike was expected to be part of them. With a tremendous investment of time and energy on the part of the staff with this little boy, he first came to love books and records and could attend for long periods of time. Very slowly, almost in spite of himself and still resisting adult direction most of the way, he became interested in other areas of the room, such as paints, crafts projects, blocks, trucks, role play, puzzles, and prereading activities. However, it was always necessary to have an adult available to help him if he was becoming frustrated or threatening to destroy his work.

As long as he attended the Center, it was difficult for him to participate in group activities with the other members of the class, but it became possible for him to play parallel with other children, occasionally sharing an idea or a toy. Outdoors, using his superior gross motor skills, he became a leader in climbing, riding a tricycle, racing. Before the end of his second year at the Center, it was also possible for him to tolerate another child's annoying display of affection for him and sometimes even to respond.

Parents

Mike's mother had initially been very resistant to the efforts of the Center social worker to help her understand either Mike's or her own problems and need for help. However, the man with whom she was very deeply involved was interested not only in her, but also, fortunately, in Mike. He not only influenced her to come to individual and group counseling sessions, but began to come with her. When they drifted apart in the spring, she abruptly became unavailable for several months, refusing to continue any contact with the Center and complaining that the Center had not "cured" Mike. During this period, the day care center began to complain anew about Mike's behavior, threatening once again to dismiss him if his mother did not become more cooperative.

One day in early fall, his mother appeared unexpectedly at the

Center to see the Director, pouring out her personal problems and those related to Mike. It became clear that this young woman could no longer deny the sense of inadequacy and guilt she felt about herself and her little son. She was asking and ready for help.

She revealed that she had not spoken to Mike or had any contact with him for several weeks (although they lived together in the grandmother's small apartment), because she knew that, if she did, she would physically hurt him. He was "so bad" that she could not stand it any longer. She had "given" him to her grandmother and was again considering sending him away. The Director helped her make a realistic appraisal of her feelings toward her child and suggested a plan of action for her to reestablish her relationship with him. She agreed to enter an intensive program of psychotherapy.

Things did improve at home, and Mike reflected this in the classroom and in day care. He came in happier and less ready to overreact to every situation, making it easier for him to respond to and enjoy the classroom experience.

Psychiatric Reevaluation

The original diagnosis was of an ego-disturbed child with marked aggressiveness and low frustration tolerance who seemed to respond to reasonable limit setting.

After eighteen months, the psychiatrist wrote, "There is no question that we are dealing with a child who is still not in control of his impulses and who requires a classroom which will provide a lot of structure and warm, understanding teachers who can set the limits for this child, who has not internalized the need for controls.

"He has shown how tenuous are the gains and how rapidly he can regress when he is subjected to an environment and personalities which are threatening and threatened by this child. This child cannot make it without special classes in an appropriate setting."

Psychological Reevaluation

Psychological reevaluation (Wechsler Preschool and Primary) at the Center at the end of his eighteen months' stay showed him to be more able to tolerate the formal testing situation, to be more interested in pleasing the examiner, and willing to try most test items, although he did refuse difficult items and tried to arrange others on his terms.

His score was within the average range, with indications of greater potential.

Concerns

This child illustrates the need for a long-term corrective classroom experience. Although Mike profited significantly from the day-to-day opportunities to grow in a consistent and nonpunitive climate, this did not mean that he was ready for the large kindergarten classrooms in the neighborhood public schools. At 5 years, his emotional needs required teachers who had available time and energy to help him handle frustration effectively. Mike was not "cured" of his feelings of rage and helplessness. He had learned to trust adults a little and to begin to find emotional gratification in learning.

Follow-Up

Follow-up psychological evaluations (WISC-R) for two years after he left the Center indicate that he had maintained the cognitive gains but still had problems with behavior. As a result of Center advocacy for appropriate treatment for this child and the private school's concern, individual psychotherapy was arranged for Mike during the school year. His mother recently contacted the Center to arrange for his current reevaluation and expressed pleasure in Mike's progress.

The Center staff is hopeful that Mike will grow more able to put his excellent endowments to positive use. However, the human relationships in the home and school situation will remain a crucial factor in determining his future development.

Case Study 14.3: Peter

Reason for Referral

Peter was referred by the Children and Youth Services of Hahnemann Hospital because of delayed speech.

History

Peter, age 4, was a "wet noodle," in the words of an observer, after he had been in the Center classroom for about two weeks. His body was limp and slow-moving, his face without expression. He did not speak at all. Only his eyes moved, watching everything; staff could only guess what they saw.

Peter had a speech and language evaluation at one of the city hospitals at 30 months because his mother was worried about his "slowness." After twenty speech therapy sessions, therapy was discontinued because Peter had not added one word to his vocabulary (then about 5 words). At 4 years of age, the Hahnemann child neurologist felt that the combined diagnostic/intervention experience at the Center was necessary in order to determine what was wrong.

Psychological evaluation (Merrill-Palmer Scale of Mental Tests) at the time of his referral to the Center indicated that Peter attained a score placing him in the average range of intelligence, although there were no verbal responses. Speech evaluation at entry placed him at a 12-month level, which increased to the 24- to 29-month range by spring. The psychiatrist saw "bland affect, psychomotor retardation and total disinterest in his environment . . . marked passivity and withdrawal as possible defenses against people. His mistrust was due not so much to previous bad experiences, as to a previous void in emotionally pleasing experiences with adults. It is possible that the trauma surrounding the tracheotomy and acute epiglottitis when he was two years old is related to his marked speech retardation . . . "

Medical records showed that Peter had been hospitalized at about age 2 for acute epiglottitis, which had required a tracheotomy, a frightening ordeal for a 2-year-old child. Just previous to his hospitalization, he had been sent to his grandparents' home for several weeks because of the birth of a baby brother. His records also showed a sickle cell anemia trait.

The Family

Peter's parents were young, in their early 20s, and emotionally even younger. His father also had had a speech problem as a child and was, therefore, not concerned about Peter. He expected Peter to "grow out of it," as he had. Father appeared to be of low intellectual ability, held a marginal job, was suspicious and afraid of authority, and scarcely ever spoke. (His wife later complained that he never spoke to her or the children, except when he was intoxicated and abusive, which happened frequently).

Peter's mother, with three children to rear virtually alone, was like a little girl. For months, when she came to visit the Center, she was afraid to take off her hat and coat or to talk to or look at anyone except her social worker. In the classroom, on her early visits, she wanted to play with the toys herself and sat in the rocking chair fingering the one- to two-year level Pat the Bunny Book, rocking and mouthing the words. The Center social worker was able to gain her trust and became, in many ways, a mother to Peter's mother.

She had had a difficult, unhappy childhood as an unloved twin and ran away at 15 to find a life better than the misery she had experienced at home. Although she had finished high school on her own initiative, she was barely literate and knew nothing about child care and little about cooking, shopping, or housekeeping. She had not wanted a boy, having suffered with her father and her husband, but had borne Peter first, and then his brother, before the wanted little girl.

The three children took care of each other, not expecting and not receiving anything from their mother except child-like teasing, irritation, petulance, and anger. She was lonely, unhappy, and worried about Peter's not speaking. She told the social worker that she had tried to teach Peter words, but when he did not speak, she became angry and slapped him in the mouth. This seemed to be the only way she knew to handle most situations.

The Center social worker began to help her to cope with the immediate, everyday problems, such as how to get food stamps to supplement the family's inadequate diet, how to cook simple, nutritious meals, and how to shop for the children's shoes. The mother responded well to this, coming regularly to their meetings, following the recommendations, and bringing more problems to the social worker, including her own personal frustrations, thoughts, and hopes. Through this growing bond from which she received care for her own needs, the mother began to give, in turn, to her children Energy was released which, in the past, was unavailable for mothering.

The Classroom

When Peter entered the classroom, he was exactly as the psychologist, psychiatrist, and former speech therapist has seen him: limp, expressionless, and totally silent. He stood motionless, his mouth hanging open, only staring, unless someone took him by the hand to lead him, and then it was as if he were a robot moving. He did not reach out in any way to child or adult, and there was only the slow, compliant body movement in response to their reaching out. He did not even drink his juice until someone assured him that it was all right. Always, his eyes watched everything.

After only a few days, however, staff began to observe small changes. He did not initiate sitting on an adult's lap to read a book, but when he was gently lifted up, he moved just enough to lean back against her body, and, scarcely discernibly, hung his arm over hers. On the playground, he rode a tricycle and began to tag along after a gentle child who had befriended him. His friend talked to him as though Peter were chattering back, when, actually, Peter remained silent. It was his friend who elicited Peter's first smile and something approaching abandon as they rode their bikes together, seeing how fast they could go and how daringly they could turn the corners.

In the classroom, Peter began, very slowly and cautiously, to move toward a calm, patient, gentle woman on the staff. She was willing to allow him to take his time and was able to support every tiny gesture, smiling and talking to him, playing infant games with him, reflecting back her approval of him and her joy at his every accomplishment. Observers watched, fascinated, as the child began to look to her for direction and corroboration, for approval and pleasure. He began to smile at her and even to tease her. He began to explore materials in the classroom with her, and, with her, gradually came to enjoy group experiences. He also began to speak, an event greeted by his special adult with a joy very much like a parent with her toddler's first words.

At first, playing with onomatopoetic sounds (i.e., bang, swish, splash), he moved quickly into one- and two-word phrases that expressed basic needs. The Center language therapist worked with him, and also with classroom staff, so that therapy goals could be continued in natural play situations. By spring, Peter's mother was able to become involved in the therapy also, bringing him regularly and eventually working with Peter at home.

Peter came alive. He tolerated leaving his first special adult who had provided the gentle bridge for him, moved into a new responsiveness with an unusually warm and gifted adult, and then settled into a steady pattern of continuing growth in almost all areas of his capabilities.

Concerns

Verbal communication continued to be an area of great concern to Center staff. It became increasingly evident that Peter had a serious language disability that would require many years of intensive therapy. In addition, however, there was the disturbing realization of his lack of motivation to use speech to communicate and his tendency to withdraw, even in a small group.

Sensitive, knowledgeable teachers, working closely with the speech therapist, were needed to keep Peter involved in classroom small-group activities and using his developing verbal abilities. This would not be an easy "prescription" to fill for his future educational placement, as it requires an understanding and implementation of ego development as the basis of motivation, self-esteem and mastery. Just as, at 30 months, speech therapy alone did not help Peter to speak, so at 5 years, speech and language therapy alone would not help this child to continue his growth and learning.

By the end of his twenty months at the Center, Peter's development had not "caught up" with his chronological age. He had, however, made remarkable advances in social-emotional development and significant gains in language and representational abilities in the classroom, with a continuation of change that indicated that his potential had not been realized.

While standardized tests given after twenty months at the Center indicated that Peter was functioning in the retarded range of inelligence, Center staff felt that the profound speech and language problem, together with severe emotional deprivation, prohibited a true diagnosis of mental capacity at that time. A continuation of the emotionally supportive classroom of the Center for 5- to 7-year-old children, with intensive speech and language therapy, was necessary. However, because area school-age classrooms did not combine preventive resources, referral was made to a private school for learning disabilities as the best alternative.

Follow-Up

Follow-up evaluation of Peter one year after he left the Center was discouraging. The school which he attends has not been able to provide a total program of speech and language therapy, and the classroom has been far from emotionally supportive.

We have learned from Peter's mother, also, that the school has made no attempt to include her in the education of her child, thus wasting the potential of help for Peter and the opportunity to continue to help his mother grow.

CONCLUSION

It is clear that PL 94-142, providing for assistance to all educationally handicapped children, will be the stimulus for an increasing emphasis on the need for obstetricians, pediatricians, nurses, developmental specialists, occupational therapists, speech pathologists/therapists, physical therapists, preschool and day care teachers, and all educators and clinicians working with newborn and preschool children to develop high levels of suspicion about the existence of SLD/MBD/HKS in these children. Along with this, there is a need to develop the remedial expertise to influence to the maximum degree possible, given our current state of scientific knowledge and the biological maturation, cognitive development, and psychosociocultural parameters of personality development.

As this and other chapters in this handbook have emphasized, effective early detection/intervention programs in education, for all ages of children and adolescents, require the removal of barriers created by separating the mental health, educational, and social agencies into self-contained systems. The staff of the Center for Preschool Services has developed and presented both a model and a method for early intervention in early childhood education as a first step in helping young children grow and learn. As the cases show, the need for early intervention is great and requires a total integration of the institutions and agencies serving such children and their families.

REFERENCES

Berlin, I.N. *Advocacy for child mental health.* New York: Bruner/Mazel, 1975.

Bronfenbrenner, U. Doing your own thing—our undoing. *MD,* 1977, *21,* 13.

Chelman, C. *Growing up poor.* U.S. Department of Health, Education, and Welfare, Welfare Administration Division of Research, Washington, D.C., 1966.

Cook, M. Therapeutic preschool. In J. Hellmuth (Ed.), *Educational therapy.* Seattle: Special Child Publications, 1966.

Cox, R.D. The concept of psychological maturity. In S. Arieti (Ed.), *American handbook of psychiatry* (2nd ed., Vol. 1). New York: Basic Books, 1974.

Deutsch, M., Jansen & Katz. *The disadvantaged child: Studies of the social environmental and learning process.* New York: Basic Books, 1967.

Eiseley, L. *The mind as nature.* New York: Harper & Row, 1962.

Fenichel, C. Psycho-educational approaches for seriously disturbed children in the classroom. In J. Hellmuth (Ed.), *Educational therapy.* Seattle: Special Child Publications, 1966.

Glasscote, R.M., Fishman, M.E., & Sonis, M. *Children and mental health centers: Program, problems, prospects.* Joint Information Center of the A.P.A. & N.I.M.H., Washington, D.C., 1972.

Golden, M. & Berns, B. Social class and cognitive development in infancy. *Merrill-Palmer Quarterly of Behavior and Development.* 1968, *14*(2), 139–149.

Hertzig, M.E., Birch, H.G., Thomas, A., & Mendez, O.A. Class and ethnic differences in the responsiveness of preschool children to cognitive demands. *Monographs of the Society for Research in Child Development,* 1968, *33*(1, Serial No. 117).

Hobbs, N. *The futures of children: Categories, labels, and their consequences.* Center for the Study of Families and Children, Vanderbilt Institute for Public Policy Studies. Vanderbilt University, Nashville, Tenn., June 1975.

Magliocca, L.A., Rinaldi, R.T., Crew, J.L. & Kunzelmann, H.P. Early identification of handicapped children through a frequency sampling technique. *Exceptional Children,* 1977, *43*(7), 414–420.

Minuchin, P., Biber, B., Shapiro, E., & Zimiles, H. *The psychological impact of school experience.* New York: Basic Books, 1969.

Moriarity, A. Coping patterns of pre-school children in response to intelligence test demands. *Genetic Psychology Monographs,* 1961, *64,* 3–127.

Pavenstedt, E. *The drifters.* Boston: Little, Brown & Co., 1967.

Piaget, J. & Inhelder, B. *The psychology of the child.* New York: Basic Books, 1969.

Polier, J.W. Professional abuse of children: Responsibility for the delivery of services. *American Journal of Orthopsychiatry,* 1975, *45*(3).

Poulton, G.A. & James, T. *Preschool learning in the community, strategies for change.* London and Boston: Routledge and Kegan Paul, 1975.

Riese, H. *Heal the hurt child.* Urbana: University of Chicago Press, 1962.

Roberts, A. *Childhood deprivation.* Springfield, Ill.: Charles C Thomas, 1974.

Sandler, L. Developmental test performance of disadvantaged children. *Exceptional Children.* 1972, *39*(3).

Shapiro, E. & Biber, B. The education of young children: A developmental-interaction approach. In S. Sapir & A. Nitzburg (Eds.), *Children with learning problems.* New York: Brunner/Mazel, 1973.

White, M.A. The mental health movement and the schools. In R.J. Ofemann (Ed.), *The school and the community treatment facility in preventive psychiatry.* Iowa City, Iowa: University of Iowa, 1965.

White, S.H. & Fishbein, H.D. Children's learning. In N. Talbot, J. Kagan, & L. Eisenberg (Eds.), *Behavioral science in pediatrics.* Philadelphia: Saunders, 1971.

CHAPTER 15

EDUCATIONAL REMEDIATION: FROM PLANNING TO IMPLEMENTATION

BENJAMIN W. CHAMPION, Ed.D.

The goal of clinical teaching is to tailor learning experiences to the unique needs of a particular child. Using all the information gained in the diagnosis and through the hypothesis of the child's learning disabilities, a specific teaching program is designed ... It requires flexibility and continuous probing by the teacher, but does not require any one particular system of educational services, setting, form, or style of teaching.

—Janet W. Lerner, *Children with Learning Disabilities*

When considering educational remediation, the establishment of one's own philosophy becomes the foundation on which thoughts, feelings, and actions are based. Some contend that the less information one has about a student before working with him/her, the better. This writer adopts the opposite position: the more known about the student, the better. It is on this position that an interdisciplinary philosophy and approach to educational remediation is based. Information provided by the social worker, psychologist, psychiatrist, learning disability/reading specialist, etc., is considered in an attempt to understand "the whole child." From a comprehensive interdisciplinary approach to assessment and diagnosis, a team approach to remediation is derived. Coordinated efforts then become necessary for optimal benefit from the various team members involved in the therapies.

While a variety of educational approaches is available for academic therapy, the most important factor seems to be the systematic application of the one(s) chosen, with opportunities for adequate repetition and reinforcement provided for the students. Approaches available include the psycholinguistic, psychomotor, behaviorist, and various others. For a complete description of these and other approaches for academic therapy, consult the references listed at the end of this chapter. The most comprehensive book on all aspects of learning disabilities appears to be the one by Lerner (1976). An equally significant contribution by Haring and Bateman (1977) focuses on a one-system approach, the Direct Instructional System for Teaching Arithmetic and Reading (DISTAR).

ESTABLISHING THE NEED FOR CORRECTIVE OR REMEDIAL INSTRUCTION

The need for educational remediation is established when a significant discrepancy is noted between the level at which a student is functioning and the level at which he/she should be functioning chronologically (grade level) or intellectually. A 10-year-old student with an IQ of 100 based on a mental age (MA) of 10.0 is generally considered to be intellectually capable of fifth-grade work. If the 10-year-old student has an IQ of 120 based on a mental age of 12.0, he/she could be expected to function on a seventh/grade level. Likewise, a 10-year-old student with an IQ of 80 based on a mental age of 8.0 could be expected to function on a third-grade level intellectually or a fifth-grade level chronologically. The student's learning capacity or mental age, rather than grade placement or chronological age, can be one criterion for academic achievement to which assessed achievement levels are compared (Otto *et al*, 1973). Otto *et al.* (1973) further suggest degrees of discrepancy between achievement and capacity which can be used flexibly to determine which students need the intensive diagnosis and tutoring of remedial instruction:

Grade 2	six months or more
Grades 3-4	one year or more
Grades 5-8	two years or more
Grades 9-12	three years or more

Students at these grade levels whose achievement-capacity discrepancy is not as great as the above criteria should be provided with individualized corrective instruction within the classroom.

INDIVIDUALIZED EDUCATION PROGRAM PLANS

The Individualized Education Program (IEP) required by Public Law 94-142 is to be based on accurate assessment and diagnosis. Before remediation is initiated, the IEP providing the blueprint for instruction is written. All the short-term objectives which will guide instruction within a school year cannot be easily written for an IEP; the result could be voluminous. Therefore, certain high priority objectives can be selected for this document. As these objectives are achieved, the record of instruction should document this, and new objectives are then to be established.

In order to illustrate the recording of objectives for an IEP, two instructional areas related to Case Study 4.1, in Chapter 4 above will be represented next. Tables 15.1, 15.2, 15.3, and 15.4 deal with the reading and language arts instructional area; Table 15.5 is concerned with mathematics.

The goals and objectives for reading and language arts represent one type of organization which offers more detail than the form for mathematics; there are other objectives which could be written in the reading and language arts area, but space and time limitations must be considered. The form of organization for the mathematics area is shorter but refers to all of the 77 short-term objectives within the Addison-Wesley Book 1 program and follows a diagnostic/prescriptive

Table 15.1
Instructional Area: Reading and Language Arts
Annual Goal: Jimmy will increase his sight vocabulary

Short-Term Objective	Instructional Methods Media/ Material Title(s) (Optional)	Evaluation of Instructional Objectives	
		Tests, Materials Evaluation Procedures To Be Used	Criteria of Successful Performance
1. Jimmy will pronounce pre-primer and primer level words.	1. Use a language-experience approach and a basal approach with the READ series implemented through directed reading activities.	1. Given 20 words randomly selected from preprimer and primer levels, Jimmy will pronounce them as they are presented tachistoscopically to him.	1. 90% accuracy on each task.

Table 15.2
Instructional Area: Reading and Language Arts
Annual Goal: Jimmy will be able to spell the words he is learning to read.

| | | Evaluation of Instructional Objectives | |
Short-Term Objective	Instructional Methods Media/ Material Title(s) (Optional)	Tests, Materials Evaluation Procedures To Be Used	Criteria of Successful Performance
1. Jimmy will spell preprimer and primer level words.	1. Provide a pretest, instruction and post-test format. Instruction can provide opportunities for writing the words to be learned and using them in context.	1. Given weekly tests of words dictated, Jimmy will write them.	1. 80% accuracy on monthly tests involving at least 20 words.

format. The limitation to this approach is that it is restricted to the objectives and strategies provided by the Addison-Wesley Book 1 program.

That which is planned and recorded for instruction should be viewed as one's *means* rather than one's *master*. The program plan and objectives are to be used flexibly and should be changed when assessment or evaluation data suggest revision.

When assessment, diagnosis, and prescriptive planning have been completed, the time has arrived for academic remediation or therapy. A question to be answered at this point could be, "On what basic concepts or principles should instruction be based?"

A variety of basic concepts or principles of remedial instruction have been enumerated by various writers (Wallace and Kauffman, 1973; Otto *et al.*, 1973). Cruickshank (1977) rejects the terms remedial and rehabilitation, suggesting *habilitation* as the term of preference to represent a developmental program. Wallace and Kauffman (1973) have operationalized their principles of academic remediation or academic therapy by stating them as specific teaching competencies. Teacher-training programs and certification requirements are changing in many places to competency-based criteria.

Table 15.3
Instructional Area: Reading and Language Arts
Annual Goal: Jimmy will increase his word attack skills.

Short-Term Objective	Instructional Methods Media/ Material Title(s) (Optional)	Evaluation of Instructional Objectives	
		Tests, Materials Evaluation Procedures To Be Used	Criteria of Successful Performance
1. Jimmy will pronounce long and short vowel sounds in isolation and in words not in his sight vocabulary.		1. The short-term objective is the evaluation task. Five words for each vowel sound are to be used.	1. 80% accuracy on each task.

The competencies which this writer considers to be important for those engaged in academic instruction/therapy for learning disabled students involve the abilities to:

(1) follow a systematic instructional model like the one noted in Chapter 4 above (Educational Assessment, Diagnosis and Evaluation),

(2) involve students in diagnosing and evaluating their own learning problems and progress,

(3) present learning tasks at an instructional level,

(4) manage students' behavioral interferences to instruction,

(5) articulate the goals, objectives, strategies, and results of the instructional program, and

(6) document the mastery of objectives and the methods and materials used.

This list of competencies or those by other authors can be criteria used in the initial selection and hiring of teachers. Then the listing of competencies can be included in the job description for teachers. When performance evaluations are conducted with teachers, the competencies can be referred to as criteria of satisfactory performance.

Table 15.4
Instructional Area: Reading and Language Arts
Annual Goal: Jimmy will increase his listening comprehension.

Short-Term Objective	Instructional Methods Media/ Material Title(s) (Optional)	Evaluation of Instructional Objectives	
		Tests, Materials Evaluation Procedures To Be Used	Criteria of Successful Performance
1. Jimmy will correctly answer comprehension questions related to a selection read to him.		1. Ten questions on factual, inferential and vocabulary information will be asked Jimmy after reading to him.	1. 80% accuracy on each task.

Follow a Systematic Instructional Model

The ability to proceed through the steps of a systematic instructional model with demonstrated competency in each phase is one of the most basic or foundational requirements for effective teaching. Within a diagnostic-prescriptive model, too often there is a distance between psychoeducational assessment and instructional planning (Heiss, 1977). One of the reasons given is that, frequently, the diagnostician is not the same person who implements the instructional plans. The teacher should be involved in assessment, clinical or diagnostic teaching, and evaluation of whether instructional objectives are being mastered. Unless the teacher is involved in these areas, the diagnostic/prescriptive model lacks the ongoing benefit of the dynamic relationship between analyzing students' performance and decisons concerning instructional objectives and strategies. *This is the heart of clinical teaching.*

Involve Students in Diagnosis and Evaluation

One of the most common faults of diagnosticians and teachers is to exclude students from having significant input into the formation of the diagnosis of their learning problems and to withhold feedback from students concerning how well they have done on evaluations or what

Table 15.5
Instructional Area: Mathematics
Annual Goal: Jimmy will master mathematics skills at the first grade level.

Short-Term Objective	Instructional Methods Media/ Material Title(s) (Optional)	Evaluation of Instructional Objectives	
		Tests, Materials Evaluation Procedures To Be Used	Criteria of Successful Performance
1. Jimmy will master the 77 performance objectives at 1st grade level.	1. Addison-Wesley *Investigating School Mathematics* Book 1.	1. Begin administering pretest 10 and proceed prescriptively with instruction of non-mastered objectives. Administer posttest 10 following instruction.	1. 80% accuracy.

has been written about them in progress reports. Students are much more cooperative and interested when they are included in these areas than when they feel that assessment and evaluation are secretive processes being done *to* them. The opinions and insights of students often make significant contributions to their assessment by helping the examiner to understand the students' perspectives on their learning problems. Likewise, most students are interested in receiving feedback regarding their performance on tests and the examiner's analysis of how well they did and why they did not do better.

Present Learning Tasks at an Instructional Level

The developmental readiness of the student needs to be considered when planning and implementing an educational program. Furthermore, the concept of readiness has application at all levels of instruction, not just at a beginning level. Ausubel (1959) has stated that readiness is "the adequacy of the existing capacity in relation to the demands of a given learning task" (p. 246). There seems to be general agreement that both hereditary and environmental factors are involved in one's capacity to learn. The interplay between these factors results in a student's attained capacity. The student's capacity at a given time is tested by the demands of a learning task. The teacher's responsibility is to be able to assess the student's capacity or ability in relation to the demands of the task. It is also important to recognize that the demands of the task may differ in the method used by the teacher and in the proficiency with which the teacher executes the method.

When analyzing why a student is having difficulty in learning, the teacher's choice of methods and his/her competency in using the methods require as much scrutiny as does the determination of the student's capacity or ability to handle the task. Durkin (1976), commenting on this issue, first asked the question, "Is the child ready to succeed *with this particular kind and quality of instruction?* Such questioning recognizes the equal significance of the child's abilities and of the instruction that will be available" (p. 83).

Before receiving remedial instruction, students often experience difficulty and frustration because of being expected to handle tasks which require more skill than they are capable of at that time. The concept of presenting tasks at an appropriate level of difficulty has been discussed in relation to Informal Reading Inventories (Johnson and Kress, 1965). Performance percentages have been established for presenting reading material at an instructional level requiring the student to be able to handle word recognition in context with 95% accuracy while comprehending with 75% accuracy. The principle on which this is based has application to all areas of instruction: "The child, in order to profit from instruction, should encounter no more difficulty than can reasonably be expected to be overcome through good instruction" (Johnson and Krees, 1965, p. 9).

When a student is presented with an instructional task which is too difficult for him/her to handle, it represents a frustration level which obviously should be avoided. The remedial program is to be presented at an instructional level whose goal is to guide the student to experience success and to feel successful.

Manage Students' Behavioral Interferences to Instruction

Perhaps taken for granted but too important to be assumed is the observation that a basic initial step in educational therapy is the establishment of a good relationship between teacher and student (Lerner, 1976). When a student feels rapport with his/her teacher and feels supported, encouraged, and cared about by the teacher, he/she is usually more accessible to instruction and more willing to risk failure. A teacher who can perform the technical skills of clinical teaching but falls short in establishing and/or maintaining an affirming, supportive relationship with students may find it difficult to motivate students and may find them resorting to passive aggression or acting out when confronted with the teaching activity. "I like my teacher," as a student's appraisal, strongly suggests that rapport has been established.

Without the student's involvement and cooperation, remedial teaching will be fruitless. Much has been written on this topic, and it is one of the vital areas in which some teachers or prospective teachers fall down. The issue of a student's accessibility to instruction involves the student's willingness and the teacher's attitude and skill. It is unfortunate when a teacher's attitude and/or lack of skill in behavioral management contributes strongly to the student's not wanting or not being willing to learn. The teacher's role in this area is broad and all-encompassing. Programming for students with appropriate expectations and tasks affects behavioral management, as does setting realistic limits and communicating concern, warmth, and support.

Articulate the Goals, Objectives, Strategies, and Results of the Instructional Program

One's understanding of what he/she is doing is demonstrated by competency to enumerate and explain the various aspects of the instructional program. Clear and concise oral reporting and discussion is necessary when sharing information with an interdisciplinary team and when meeting with parents. Narrative writing for progress reports likewise affords the opportunity to describe in detail information about the instructional program and the student's response to it. Oral and written reporting should reveal organized thinking which involves the analysis and synthesis of the various parts of the assessment/instruction/evaluation process. An important component of reporting follows.

Document the Mastery of Objectives and the Methods and Materials Used

While a few people have phenomenal memories for detail, the wiser and more believable course is to provide written documentation of the plans for and the results of instruction. Many publishers are offering management systems which include such devices as cards with places to punch when objectives are mastered. A system which this writer prefers involves providing space for teachers to write the date when instruction is initiated in relation to a specific objective and, later, the date when, through evaluation, it is determined that the objective has been mastered.

As a student is moved from one classroom to another, the new teacher can use information about which methods and materials have been used with the student. These can be organized by instructional areas, so that recording methods and materials used will be cumulative, e.g., all information about reading recorded on one page and math data on a different page. The combination of data on methods and materials which have been used and objectives that are mastered, along with testing data of instructional levels and grade equivalent scores, provide the reader with a comprehensive view of a student's instructional program and rate of progress.

CLINICAL TEACHING

Clinical or diagnostic teaching combines the functions of diagnosis and teaching. Therefore, clinical teaching is useful in assessment and instruction. In Chapter 4, on educational assessment, the model for clinical teaching and its application for assessment were discussed. Clinical teaching as an instructional approach will now be considered.

Systematic and directed instruction are basic to clinical teaching. Proceeding systematically within clinical teaching involves planning and implementation based on student performance analysis and task analysis. Tasks are presented to the student, performance observed, and feedback provided about what was done correctly and what was done incorrectly. Errors are then analyzed in terms of the student's response and the appropriateness or adequacy of the task presentation. The student's inaccurate performance is evaluated from the standpoint of the modality abilities and the learning skills he/she does and does not exhibit. The task is analyzed as to the modality strengths and the skill levels necessary for correct completion. Lerner (1976) advanced the belief that clinical teachers should display competency in analyzing tasks both from a modality-processing viewpoint and from that of the sequence of skills, which requires a thorough understanding of the curriculum's scope and sequence. The abilities and skills displayed by the student and the demands of the tasks should be matched to effect an optimally productive clinical teaching activity.

SETTING FOR THE DELIVERY OF SERVICES

The appropriate setting for the delivery of services is of great concern for the learning-disabled student. The concept of placing students in the least restrictive environment, considering their academic and emotional problems and needs, has been recently introduced. If a student with learning disabilities or a specific learning disability can be programmed for and properly managed in regular classes, then keeping him/her completely in the mainstream is appropriate. His/her needs may be of a kind and/or degree that would be scheduled for remediation in a resource room for some time while attending other regular classes.

When a student does not deal well with changing classrooms and/or the generality of the learning disabilities and/or behavioral problems presents too much of a challenge in regular classes, the self-contained classroom can be prescribed. Lerner (1976) noted that the goal of self-contained special classes is to help children organize themselves for increased independent learning so that they will eventually be able to return to regular classes.

In some states, there are county or intermediate unit classes and services which are available within or outside of the local school district. If the classes and services are outside of the regular school, the student has to deal with his/her feelings and the reactions of others regarding why he/she is receiving this special treatment.

Special private day schools for learning-disabled students are available in some geographical areas. The services provided by these schools vary from those which have only educational programs to others which provide supportive clinical and medical services. Once again, the needs of the student should be matched with the services available in the special private day schools. Wallace and McLoughlin (1975) feel that, with LD programs available in many public schools, a minority of learning-disabled children need this type of special placement.

Special residential schools provide services for students who do not have day schools to meet their needs in their geographical area and for students who require a full-time placement away from home. Fewer students than those who need special day schools are in need of residential placement. The same variations in the availability of supportive clinical and medical services for day schools apply among residential programs. For optimal habilitative benefit, educational, residential, clinical, and medical services should be complementary and coordinated through regular and systematic planning together.

COORDINATION OF INPUT AND EFFORTS FOR REMEDIATION

Lerner (1976) recommends that the learning disability specialist assume the crucial role of building a cooperative interdisciplinary team that works together, rather than allowing team members to follow a splintered and isolated approach which can work at cross-purposes with each other. Team meetings chaired by the learning disability specialist afford opportunities to review the information available on the student and to plan a continuing, coordinated program for the student. The areas discussed and the recommendations made should be recorded and filed with other program data about that student.

SUMMARY

Planning the instruction for SLD/MBD/HKS students involves analyzing the assessment, diagnostic, and evaluation data, establishing the prescriptive instructional objectives, and using strategies that take into consideration task analysis, appropriate instructional levels, and the strengths and weaknesses of the student's modality-processing abilities.

The quality of ongoing educational planning and implementation is largely dependent upon the teacher's competency. Some important areas of teacher competency were discussed. The competent special education teacher is skilled in clinical teaching which, among other things, involves task analysis.

Finally, the various settings for the delivery of services were reviewed. The one offering the appropriate services and the least restrictive environment for that particular student is preferred. Over a period of time, moving a student toward complete mainstreaming, or as near to it as is realistically appropriate, is the overall goal.

Implementation of instructional programs for SLD/MBD/HKS students should evolve from diagnostic/prescriptive planning. Excellent reports and recommendations remain unfulfilled without quality implementation by teachers possessing the necessary competencies. The total process and total habilitative team need to be integrated and coordinated in order to offer these students the services, the opportunities, and the encouragement they need and deserve.

REFERENCES

Ausubel, D.P. Viewpoints from related disciplines: Human growth and development. *Teachers College Record,* 1959, *60,* 245–254.

Cruickshank, W.M. *Learning disabilities in home, school, and community.* Syracuse: Syracuse University Press, 1977.

Durkin, D. *Teaching young children to read* (2nd ed.). Boston: Allyn and Bacon, 1976.

Haring, N. & Bateman, B. *Teaching the learning disabled child.* Englewood Cliffs: Prentice-Hall, 1977.

Eicholz, R.E., O'Daffer, P.G. & Fleenor, C.R. *Investigating school mathematics.* Reading, Mass.: Addison-Wesley, 1976.

Heiss, W. Relating educational assessment to instructional planning. *Focus on Exceptional Children,* 1977, *9*(1), 1–11.

Johnson, M.S., and Kress, R.A. *Informal reading inventories.* Newark, Del.: International Reading Assn, 1965.

Lerner, J.W. *Children with learning disabilities* (2nd ed.). Boston: Houghton Mifflin, 1976.

Myers, P.I. & Hammill, D.D. *Methods for learning disorders* (2nd ed.). New York: Wiley, 1976.

Otton, W., McMenemy. R.A. & Smith, R.J. *Corrective and remedial teaching* (2nd ed.). Boston: Houghton Mifflin, 1973

Wallace, G. & Kauffman, J.M. *Teaching children with learning problems.* Columbus, Ohio: C.E Merrill, 1973.

Wallace, G. & McLoughlin, J.A. *Learning disabilities: Concepts and characteristics.* Columbus, Ohio: C.E. Merrill, 1975.

EPILOGUE
THE COMPLETED BRIDGE

Teachers, parents, clinicians, children, and adolescents caught up in the complexities of the SLD/MBD/HKS syndromes seemed to be asking for a hand in bridging the gaps among the variety of theoretical positions taken about this population and some of the basic principles, operational suggestions, and therapeutic interventions which might enhance their growth and development. This handbook has been an attempt to bridge those gaps at a time when the enactment of PL 94-142 dredged the channel of fiscal, familial, educational, and clinical accountability for all handicapped children.

This handbook has attempted to put into focus some of the questions, definitions, and historical perspectives which cut across medicine, education, sociology, and psychology. It has defined the cornerstones for bridging the gap as a psychoeducational evaluation complemented by a psychosocial, medical, neurological, and visual assessment process.

Many columns of support for this population through interpretation, prescription, and intervention have been described. The construction of these columns has come out of the daily experiences of the authors. Their presentations attempt to answer questions raised by parents and teachers who have become increasingly concerned about the social, emotional, and educational growth and development of SLD/MBD/HKS children and adolescents.

Finally, with a bridge completed for these students in our local school systems and supporting community resources, it becomes possible for SLD/MBD/HKS children and teenagers to walk from the side of self-doubt and inadequacy to the side of self-assurance and self-sufficiency. No child or teenager walks the bridge alone. Each needs and must have the caring, loving, supporting hands of parents to walk with him/her. In addition, the builders of the bridge must also walk with these children; special education teachers, school administrators, parents, parental surrogates, and the clinical support personnel can walk and join hands with each boy and girl as he or she crosses the educational/clinical bridge so carefully and conscientiously constructed.

SUBJECT INDEX

aggression, 214–218, 224–226, 288
amblyopia, 150
amitriptyline (Elavil), 426
anticonvulsant drugs, 427–429;
  diphenylhydantoin (Dilantin),
  428, 429
antidepressant drugs, 425–427;
  amitriptyline (Elavil), 426;
  imipramine (Tofranil), 426;
  lithium, 427
antiphobic, -anxiety, and -aggression
  drugs, 416–422;
  chlordiazepoxide (Librium), 421;
  chlorpromazine (Thorazine),
  419–421;
  diazepam (Valium), 421;
  indications for, 416;
  side effects with, 418–420;
  tardive dyskinesia with, 418;
  thioridazine (Mellaril), 417–419
antipsychotic drugs, 422–424;
  chlorpromazine (Thorazine),
  423, 424;
  haloperidol (Haldol), 424;
  indications for, 422, 423
art therapy:
  application to SLD, 364, 367, 368,
  370–376;
  definition, 362;
  goals with SLD, 362, 374
associative word finding problem, 97

Bannatyne analysis, 80, 86
behavior modification, 298,
  301, 302;
  use of drugs with, 390, 405, 408
behavior therapy:
  classroom, 334–349;
  ethics of, 354, 355;
  extinction, 334–336
  group consequences, 341–344;
  home, 349–355;
  overcorrection, 346–349;
  parent training programs, 355;
  parents as change agents, 349–354;
  procedure for, 334;
  punishment, 344, 345;
  reinforcement in, 337–339, 344;
  response cost, 345, 346;
  strategy for parent training, 353;
  token economies, 339–341
behavioral management, in
  classroom, 494, 495
Benadryl
  (see: diphenhydramine)
Bender Visual-Motor Gestalt Test,
  48, 55, 56, 76, 81, 88
binocular fusion, 148–150
biofeedback, 431–432
body image, 158, 370

caffeine, 415, 416
chlordiazepoxide (Librium), 421

chlorpromazine (Thorazine), 419–421, 423, 424
clang associations, 98
classroom intervention, 460–464, 467, 481
clinical teaching, 496;
cycle, 110
conceptual difficulties, 97
conditioned response-learning, 302
counseling process, with parents:
as opposed to therapy, 242;
collaboration in, 242;
contract in, 243;
coping with the child, 249–252;
educational focus in, 245;
goals of, 241, 246;
parents/child communication in, 246;
phases in, 243–252
criterion-referenced test, 112
Cylert
(*see*: pemoline)

dance/movement therapy:
application to SLD, 365, 366, 379-383;
definition, 363,
goals with SLD, 382
Deaner
(*see*: deanol)
deanol (Deaner), 414
defense mechanisms:
(*see*: ego defense mechanisms)
depression, 214, 215, 273
developmental assessment, 463–465
developmental-interaction approach, 451, 453, 464–466
developmental vision, 147
Dexidrine
(*see*: dextroamphetamine)
dextroamphetamine (Dexidrine), 409–412
diagnostic evaluation:
differential diagnosis, 101, 102, 458–460, 464;

educational, 141, 492–494;
gestational history, 41;
indices of suspicion, 26;
labeling, 28, 29, 246, 390, 451;
over time, 5, 8, 9, 241;
parental permission, 35;
parents' role in, 244;
preliminary case study information, 37–40
Diagnostic Statistical Manual II, 11, 12
Diagnostic Statistical Manual III, 12, 14, 15
diazepam (Valium), 421
difference, psychology of, 262–265
Dilantin
(*see*: diphenylhydantoin)
diphenhydramine (Benadryl), 415
diphenylhydantoin (Dilantin), 428, 429
disinhibition, 91
Draw-a-Person Test, 48, 208, 364
dreams, 225–227, 234
drugs
(*see*: use of drugs)

Education for All Handicapped Children Act, 10, 238
educational assessment:
important areas of information, 112;
informal measures, 112, 113;
purposes, 108, 141;
systematic approach, 109;
task analysis, 110, 111.
educational diagnosis, 141, 492–494
educational remediation, 487–496
ego coping mechanisms, 44, 45, 260, 304
ego defense mechanisms, 230, 264, 314, 315, 373, 374
Elavil
(*see*: amitriptyline)
emotional concomitants of SLD/MBD/HKS, 43, 44
eye movements, 152, 153

family involvement, 467, 476, 477, 480
(*see also*: Chapter 10)
family scapegoat, 213, 320
family therapy, 326–331
fear:
of body injury, 198, 207–209, 211, 213;
of sexual impulses, 227, 228
Feingold diet, 432, 433
fine motor manipulation skills, 53, 55
food additives, 432, 433
funding, program, 455

gender identity, 228
gratification, immedate, 218, 219, 260
Gray's Oral Reading Paragraph Test, 49
group psychotherapy:
coed leadership in, 279, 280, 284;
group suggestion method, 268, 269;
in public school special classes, 269;
interpretive method, 267, 268;
with adolescents, 276, 278–284;
with late latency, early adolescents, 270–278, 284;
with preschool, early latency cases, 257–270, 284.

Haldol
(*see*: haloperidol)
haloperidol (Haldol), 424
hyperactivity, 90
hyperdistractibility, 91
hyperkinetic reaction:
classification, 12
definition, 11
hypoglycemia, 433, 434

imipramine (Tofranil), 426
Imitation of Gestures Test, 48
impulse control, 218, 220, 221, 261, 304

impulsivity, 92
inadequate impulse control, 90
individual psychotherapy, 322;
beginning phase, 199–206, 229, 230;
contextual framework, 196, 205;
criteria for termination, 232;
ending phase, 229–234;
lexicon of feelings, 203–205;
middle phase, 206–231;
parents' role in, 248, 249;
preparation for, 198
resistance in, 202, 203
Individual Clinical Prescription (ICP), 31, 249, 405
Individualized Education Program (IEP), 41, 108, 110, 113, 238, 239, 247, 249, 405, 406, 489–492;
components of, 24, 25;
due process notice, 36;
organization, 30
Informal Reading Inventories, 112, 143
intertest and intratest variability, 85, 86

Key Math Diagnostic Arithmetic Test, 112, 142
Keystone Telebinocular Vision Screening, 142

lability of affect, 94
language developmental milestones, 52–55
Librium
(*see*: chlordiazepoxide)
Life Space Interview:
critique of, 305–307;
goals, 303, 304
guidelines for, 308–310;
procedure, 310;
process, 302–308;
lithium, 427

megavitamin therapy, 429–431
Mellaril
   (see: thioridazine)
methylphenidate (Ritalin), 406–409
minimal brain dysfunction (MBD):
   classification, 12, 14;
   definition, 13
motor dysfunction, 94
movement therapy
   (see: dance/movement therapy)
music therapy:
   application to SLD, 366–369,
      377–379;
   definition, 363;
   goals with SLD, 379

narcissistic hypersensitivity,
      99, 100, 215, 216, 261
Neonatal Behavioral Assessment
   Scale (Brazelton), 56
neurological evaluation:
   newborns, 51–56;
   school age children, 57
neurological soft signs,
   14, 27, 28, 51, 57
neurometric study, 50
norm-referenced test, 111

optometric training (therapy),
      435, 436;
   (see also: Chapter 5)
optometric vision therapy,
   161, 167, 178–180
organic brain syndrome
   classification, 12
Orthomolecular therapy, 429–431

parents:
   counseling with, 467, 476, 477,
      480,
   (see also: Chapter 7);
   groups, 239, 322
passive-resistance, 216–218
Pathway School, The, 195

patterning, 434
Peabody Picture Vocabulary Test,
      47, 76, 81, 93
pemoline (Cylert), 412, 413
perceptual difficulties, 154:
   figure-ground relationships,
      96, 155;
   gross and fine visual-motor
      functioning, 96;
   memory, 97;
   sequencing skills, 96;
   skip-counting, 97;
   spatial relationships, 95;
   visual imagery, 96
perseveration, 93
Photo Articulation Test, 142
Physician's Handbook:
   Screening for MBD, 34
primary autonomous ego function,
      13
psychiatric assessment, 56–58
psychoeducational evaluation:
   fine screening methods, 49
   gross screening methods, 46–48
   guidelines, 27
   normal personality development,
      31–33
psychological assessment:
   developmental process approach,
      64, 65;
   methods of testing limits, 75, 76;
   preparing the child, 69;
   role of examiner, 70–72;
   selection of assessment battery,
      68, 69;
   use of structure, 72–74
psychosocial adaptation, 190
psychosocial assessment, 33
psychostimulant drugs, 404–416;
   addiction with, 411;
   caffeine, 415, 416;
   choice of drugs, 406;
   deanol (Deaner), 414;
   dextroamphetamine (Dexidrine),
      409–412;

diphenhydramine (Benadryl),
415;
follow-up studies, 408;
growth suppression with,
406, 408, 411;
indications for, 404;
methylphenidate (Ritalin),
406–409;
outcome with, 407, 412, 413;
pemoline (Cylert), 412, 413;
side-effects from, 400, 407,
411–413, 415
psychotherapy:
concurrent with parents and child,
323–326;
group, (*see* group psychotherapy)
individual,
(*see* individual psychotherapy)
Public Law, 94–142, 10, 23–26,
107, 108, 211, 238, 392, 393,
483, 501

referral, guidelines for, 461–463
Ritalin
(*see*: methylphenidate)
Roswell-Chall Auditory Blending
Test, 142
Roswell-Chall Diagnostic Reading
Test of Word Analysis Test, 142
Rutgers Drawing Test, 48, 55
self-concept, 209–213, 315
defective, 99, 100

self-esteem, 263, 264, 270,
274–276
sensory integrative therapy, 435
Slosson Drawing Coordination
Test, 48
socialization process, 220, 221
special education:
parents' role in, 247, 248
specific developmental disorders:
classification, 12
specific learning disabilities (SLD),
263;

acceptance of, 316, 317;
art therapy in, 364, 365, 367, 368;
basic assumptions, 240;
classification, 11;
clowning behavior in, 373–376;
clusters of symptoms, 65, 66;
dance/movement therapy in,
365, 366, 379–383;
definition of, 10, 13;
ego development in, 195;
family dynamics in, 318–322;
impact on family, 315–318;
interventive strategies for,
322, 323;
music therapy in, 366–369;
operational requirements, 11;
therapy for, 204
strabismus, 150
structure:
life relationship, 220
systematic instructional model, 492

tangential associations, 98
task analysis:
modality-processing approach, 111;
skills-sequence approach, 111
teachers:
competencies, 491, 496;
qualifications, 466
therapy:
art (*see*: art therapy);
behavior (*see*: behavior therapy);
dance/movement
(*see*: dance/movement
therapy);
educational (*see*: educational
remediation)
family (*see*: family therapy)
movement (*see*: dance/movement
therapy);
music (*see*: music therapy);
psychological
(*see*: psychotherapy);
vision (*see*: visual training)
thioridazine (Mellaril), 417–419

Thorazine
(*see*: chlorpromazine)
Time Out process:
concept of, 294;
effect of duration, 344;
freedom room, misuse of,
288, 289;
indications for, 294–296;
method of, 296–300, 344
precautions in use of, 300–302;
seclusion, 298;
seclusion room, 298–300, 302
Tofranil
(*see*: imipramine)

use of drugs:
behavior control with, 391;
behavior modification and,
390, 405, 408;
central issues, 394;
drug metabolism, 395, 396;
follow-up studies in, 391, 398;
indications for, 390;
learning facilitation by, 390;
principles in prescribing, 396–399
Utah Test of Language
Development, 142

Valium
(*see*: diazepam)
visual accommodation, 150, 151
visual directionality, 157.
visual fixation, 152
visual form perception, 158
visual imagery, 159
visual-motor coordination, 48, 96,
158
visual training, 179
visual-verbal match, 154

Wechsler Intelligence Scale for
Children, 68, 79, 84
Wechsler Intelligence Scale for
Children, Revised, 68
Wechsler Primary and Preschool
Scale of Intelligence, 68
Wepman Auditory Discrimination
Test, 49, 142
Wide Range Achievement Test, 142

AUTHOR INDEX

A

Abercrombie, M., 152, 157
Abrams, J., 44, 45, 316, 318, 322
Ackerman, N., 320, 326
Adams, R., 57
Allen, F., 193, 225, 231, 234
Allen, K., 335, 337
Amatruda, C., 65
Anderson, J., 256, 276
Anderson, N., 256, 269
Ayllon, T., 340, 354
Ayres, A., 145
Azrin, N., 348

B

Bandura, A., 334, 336, 344
Bannatyne, A., 86
Bateman, B., 10, 392, 393, 488
Becker, R., 361
Bender, L., 16, 194
Benton, C., 149, 150
Bernstein, M., 305, 308
Birch, H., 57, 154
Bitcon, D., 377, 378
Black, F., 208
Blanck, G. & Blanck, R., 228–230
Bowen, M., 323, 326
Brazelton, T., 56
Brumback, R., 425, 426
Burchard, J., 345, 348

C

Campbell, D., 369
Cantwell, D., 13
Carlson, C., 335, 336, 341
Clements, S., 16, 34, 393, 415
Cohen, F., 383, 385
Cohen, S., 29, 30, 393
Cole, S., 411, 412
Conners, C., 398, 407, 409, 411,
    412, 429, 432, 433
Coopersmith, S., 211, 213
Cott, A., 404, 430, 433
Cruickshank, W., 154, 158, 367, 490

D

Dawley, A., 206
DiLeo, J., 364

E

Ebersole, M., 158
Eisenberg, L., 155, 396–399
Erikson, E., 32, 33, 270, 291, 293

F

Feingold, B., 393, 432
Flavell, J., 159, 178

Flax, N., 153, 155
Forrest, E., 146
Foxx, R., 346, 347
Freeman, R., 238, 389, 390, 394, 434
Freud, A., 58, 231, 270, 314
Freud, S., 32, 33, 291, 293
Friedman, R., 328
Frostig, M., 145
Furth, H., 159, 160

G

Gardner, J., 355
Gardner, R., 258, 259, 261–263, 265, 266
Gesell, A., 52, 65, 146, 152, 157, 435
Getman, G., 145, 435, 436
Ghiselin, B., 361
Gibran, K., 287, 313, 314
Gold, A., 50–53
Green, D., 350
Grinspon, L., 405

H

Haring, N., 488
Harris, I., 320
Hartman, H., 13, 194, 206
Hebb, D., 157
Hersh, A., 31
Hobbs, N., 29, 454

I

Illovsky, J., 256, 268

J

Jastak, J., 47
John, E., 50

Johnson, M., 112, 202, 494
Jones, S., 334

K

Kanfer, F., 336
Kaufman, K., 345
Kazdin, A., 333, 339, 341, 347, 348
Kellogg, R., 364
Kephart, N., 52, 152, 157, 158, 160, 161
Kestenberg, J., 366
Kinsbourne, M., 409
Kirk, S., 10, 16, 52, 107, 392, 393
Klopfer, B., 228
Koppitz, E., 88, 208, 364
Kovitz, K., 355
Kraft, I., 276, 277
Kramer, E., 364
Kress, R., 112

L

Laban, R., 379, 380
Langeveld, M., 211
Laufer, M., 393
Lehtinen, L., 16, 154, 194, 393
Lerner, J., 67, 110, 111, 487, 488, 494, 496–498
Lewis, M., 57, 58
Lindgren, H., 308, 309
Loeb, R., 322
Long, N., 307
Lovaas, O., 355

M

Machover, K., 208, 364
MacLennan, B., 255, 256, 277
Mahler, M., 32, 33, 288, 290, 291, 293
Marrone, J., 256, 269

McCormick, D., 57
Metzler, R., 377
Miller, W., 352
Millichap, J., 408, 414, 419, 421, 429
Morse, W., 308, 309
Murphy, L., 63
Marrone, J., 256, 269

N

Nagy, I., 327
Naumburg, M., 364
Nelson, K., 52, 53
North, M., 365

O

O'Leary, K., 333, 339, 351
Olshansky, L., 244
Orton, S., 393
Ostwald, P., 366, 367

P

Parsons, T., 291
Pearson, G., 16, 45, 194, 231, 232, 315
Peiser, I., 146, 151
Phipps, M., 368
Piaget, J., 32, 33, 153, 265, 273, 291, 293, 451
Popham, W., 143
Premack, D., 338

Q

Quinn, P., 49

R

Rank, O., 234, 263, 291, 293

Rappaport, S., 23, 41, 43, 73, 89, 90, 194, 249
Redl, F., 302–308
Richmond, J., 189, 190
Rome, H., 256
Ross, A., 11, 14
Rutherford, D., 53
Rutter, M., 390

S

Safer, D., 406, 410, 411
Salzinger, K., 352, 355
Satir, V., 326
Satterfield, J., 13, 34, 409
Sattler, J., 66
Schain, R., 57
Schrag, P., 287, 389
Sears, W., 369
Shafto, F., 337
Shapiro, E., 452
Sherman, A., 149–151, 153, 158
Silver, A., 155, 158
Silver, L., 321, 435
Skeffington, A., 145
Skinner, B., 291, 293
Slavson, S., 255
Small, L., 67, 71
Smith, R., 109
Solan, H., 145, 146, 179
Spivack, G., 398
Sprague, R., 407, 417, 418
Strauss, A., 15, 52, 154, 194, 393
Sugar, M., 256, 259, 267, 268

T

Tams, V., 352
Taylor, E., 151
Tyler, R., 302
Tyler, R.H., 147

Author Index

V

Vurpillot, E., 145

W

Wäelder, R., 206
Wahler, R., 349–351
Walder, L., 349, 352
Wallace, G., 113
Weiss, G., 391, 408

Welsbacher, B., 368
Wender, P., 14, 16, 409, 429, 432
Werry, J., 13, 406, 417, 424
White, G., 344
Williams, D., 350
Wolf, M., 344
Woolf, D., 151, 153, 157

Y

Yalom, I., 256